Remapping Gender in the New Global Order

T0320286

This book analyses changes in gender relations, as a result of globalization, in countries on the semi-periphery of power. Semi-periphery refers to those nations which are not drivers of change globally, but have enough economic and political security to have some power in determining their own responses to global forces. Individual countries obviously face challenges that are to some extent unique, although the prescriptions for economic and social restructuring are based on a common competitive logic.

Remapping Gender in the New Global Order draws on examples from four countries on the semi-periphery of power but still located in the top category of the UNDP's Human Development Index. At one end is Norway, one of the world's richest and most developed welfare-states, and, at the other, is Mexico, a country that is considerably poorer and more susceptible to the power of the United States and international agencies. Australia and Canada, the other two semi-peripheral countries examined, are in the middle. Also included are comparisons with the epicentre of the 'core' base of power – the United States.

The individual chapters focus on the effect on specific groups of people, including males and indigenous groups, the mechanisms people use to both cope with dramatic social changes, and the strategies and alliances that are used to affect the course of changes. It covers topics that range from implications of labour migration on care regimes to globalism's effect on masculinity and the 'male breadwinner' model.

Marjorie Griffin Cohen is an economist who is a professor of Political Science and Women's Studies at Simon Fraser University in British Columbia, Canada.

Janine Brodie is a professor of Political Science and Canada Research Chair at the University of Alberta in Edmonton, Canada.

Routledge Frontiers of Political Economy

Remapping Gender in the New Global Order

Edited by Marjorie Griffin Cohen
and Janine Brodie

Routledge
Taylor & Francis Group

LONDON AND NEW YORK

First published 2007 by Routledge
2 Park Square, Milton Park, Abingdon, OX14 4RN

Simultaneously published in the USA and Canada
by Routledge
270 Madison Ave, New York NY 10016

Routledge is an imprint of the Taylor & Francis Group, an informa business

Transferred to Digital Printing 2009

Typeset in Baskerville by Bookcraft Ltd, Stroud, Gloucestershire

British Library Cataloguing in Publication Data
A catalogue record for this book is available from the British Library

Library of Congress Cataloging in Publication Data
Remapping gender in the new global order / edited [by] Marjorie Griffin
Cohen and Janine Brodie.

  p. cm.

  Includes bibliographical references and index.

1. Man-woman relationships–Cross-cultural studies. 2. Sex role–Cross-
cultural studies. 3. Globalization Social aspects–Cross-cultural studies.
I. Cohen, Marjorie Griffin, 1944– II. Brodie, M. Janine.
HQ801.R346 2007
305.409–dc22   2006032648

ISBN10: 0-415-76997-3 (hbk)
ISBN10: 0-415-54784-9 (pbk)
ISBN10: 0-203-09994-X (ebk)

ISBN13: 978-0-415-76997-6 (hbk)
ISBN13: 978-0-415-54784-0 (pbk)
ISBN13: 978-0-203-09994-0 (ebk)

Contents

PART II
Remapping gendered spaces

PART II
Remapping gendered spaces   **109**

PART III
Surviving and resistance: strategies and action   **185**

Illustrations

Tables

Figures

Appendices

Contributors

Janine Brodie is a professor in the Department of Political Science at the University of Alberta in Canada. She is a Fellow of the Royal Society of Canada and was appointed as a Canada Research Chair (Tier 1) in Social Governance and Political Economy in 2004. Dr Brodie's publication and research foci are Canadian political economy and politics, gender and politics, social theory and policy, and governance in an era of globalization.

Ray Broomhill is an adjunct associate professor of labour studies within the School of Social Sciences at Adelaide University, South Australia. His academic research has spanned the areas of Australian political economy with a special focus on gender, labour and public policy issues. His current research work is focused on the impact of neoliberal globalism on the Australian political economy.

Marjorie Griffin Cohen is an economist who is a professor in the Departments of Political Science and Women's Studies at Simon Fraser University in British Columbia, Canada. She has written extensively in the areas of public policy and economics with special emphasis on issues concerning women, international trade agreements, the Canadian economy, electricity deregulation, and labour.

Jennifer Cooper coordinates the programme for Gender Studies and Feminist Economics in the Economics Faculty of the National Autonomous University of Mexico UNAM. She has participated in training programmes with Mexican women unionists on labour market issues and in the formulation of working women's agenda within Mexico. She worked as a consultant for the Mexican Women's Institute (el Instituto de las mujeres) during 2003–5 as a gender budget advisor and trainer of government functionaries on gender responsive budgets.

Edmé Domínguez Reyes (born in Mexico, resident of Sweden) is an associate professor (docent) in the area of peace and development studies at the University of Göteborg. She is a senior lecturer and researcher at the Institute of Iberoamerican Studies, University of Göteborg, and associate professor and lecturer in international politics in the Department of Political Science and Economics at the University of Linköping in Sweden. Since the beginning of the 1990s, she has been working on the social implications of NAFTA for Mexico and on gender issues regarding academics, citizenship, international relations and regional integration.

Randi Drevland is a doctoral candidate in the Department of Political Science at Simon Fraser University in British Columbia, Canada, where she worked as a research assistant for the Globalism project for three years. Currently, she is working full time in the nonprofit sector within community healthcare services while also volunteering on a crisis line.

James Goodman is a professor who teaches social inquiry at the University of Technology in Sydney, Australia, where he co-convenes the Research Initiative on International Activism. He has edited and co-edited a number of books on globalism and social movements.

Satoshi Ikeda is a professor who teaches sociology of globalization in the Department of Sociology at the University of Alberta in Canada. With a background in economics and sociology (world-system studies) he explores a political sociology critique of neoliberal globalization and possible alternative futures that are sustainable, non-discriminatory and participatory. His other research interests include political economy of Japan and East Asia, environmental sociology, and the method of Polanyi-Hopkins historical sociology.

Lise Widding Isaksen is a professor in the Department of Sociology at the University of Bergen in Norway. She works with feminist studies related to the sociology of welfare states and in particular fields related to gender, bodies and carework.

Isabel Altamirano Jiménez holds a joint appointment as an assistant professor in the Department of Political Science and the Faculty of Native Studies at the University of Alberta in Canada. She has done extensive research and presented numerous papers comparing indigenous politics in Canada and Mexico.

Elaine Levine, a native of Atlanta, Georgia who has lived and worked in Mexico City since 1968, is currently a researcher and professor at the UNAM's Centre for Research on North America (CISAN) in Mexico. Her research is focused on the US economy and, in particular, topics related to income distribution, the labour market and the socioeconomic status of Latinos in the US.

Rhonda Sharp is a professor of economics at the Hawke Research Institute for Sustainable Societies, University of South Australia. She researches in the areas of gender and economics and women and public policy. She has been a researcher and advisor to governments on gender budget initiatives and the restructuring of women's paid and unpaid work. She is a former president and journal advisory board member of the International Association for Feminist Economics.

1 Remapping gender in the new global order

Marjorie Griffin Cohen and Janine Brodie

Globalization appears unstoppable, according to *The Economist*, despite the collapse of the Doha round of the World Trade Organization's (WTO) trade liberalization negotiations in 2006. After five years of serious and difficult negotiations, the inability to reach an agreement among the world's wealthiest countries was severely criticized by the champions of globalization, not least because it slows the march toward their vision of a fully integrated global economy. What is worse, according to globalization's supporters, it is unlikely that new global trade talks will begin any time soon. But despite this pessimism, almost no one considers the failures at Doha as a substantial deviation from either accelerating global trade or the neoliberal policies that structure it. According to *The Economist*, 'the seas of world trade are calm', and trade continues to grow faster than world GDP (29 July 2006: 11). Trade liberalization certainly is not the only marker of globalization's success, but it is a touchstone for a global adherence to its philosophical underpinnings. Economic globalization shows no sign of abating in the restructuring of either domestic or international institutions.

Although globalization is most commonly associated with the creation of global production process and markets, as the chapters in this book demonstrate, this epochal shift in the international political economy is far more complex, multidimensional and multilayered, profoundly affecting governmental policies, political activism and the daily lives of women and men across the globe. In the process, the terrains of all manner of political and social relations, as the title of this book suggests, are being 'remapped' – new networks and connections are being established, albeit often in contradictory and unequal ways. To better grasp the extent of this remapping, it is useful to draw on Beck's distinction between globality and globalism because this conceptual distinction recognizes the dramatic social changes that define this globalizing era while leaving open to analysis and activism the pressing question of how these changes are and should be governed (2000).

In brief, globality refers to contemporary transformations in social, political and economic organization that have fundamentally altered our shared experience of time and space as well as self and community. Globality focuses our attention on, among other things, the global movement of people, goods and services, the reshaping of local communities and households by global forces, the increasing porousness of national boundaries, the critical importance of transnational social problems and political movements, and the emergence of the planet as a relevant space for political action. As Beck explains, the concept of globality underlines the increasingly inescapable conclusion that, in the contemporary era, 'all interventions, victories and catastrophes affect the whole world' (ibid.: 11, 15). Local, regional and national terrains, in other words, are being remapped by the many and varied forces of globality.

Globalism, in contrast, refers to the ascendancy of a common transnational worldview and philosophy of governance. In the contemporary era, the term globalism is often used as a shorthand for neoliberal globalism, since there is not a unified worldview that stands in opposition to it. Sometimes also called the 'Washington Consensus', neoliberal globalism is an experiment in transnational governance that prioritizes economic growth and the creation of markets over all other goals and institutions of government. Through the dictates of international financial institutions, trade agreements, structural adjustment and poverty reduction strategies, and the actions of national governments themselves, neoliberal globalism enforces privatization, deregulation, trade liberalization, commodification, individualization and the erosion of collective provision, especially in the social policy field (Brodie 2003). Globalism thus remaps social and political relations in different ways, shifting axes of power away from citizens, governments and democratic decision-making to corporate actors, market mechanisms and the logic of supply and demand. This remapping, contrary to the smug assurances of neoclassical economists, is not gender-neutral. As the chapters in this book underline, neoliberal globalism has reconfigured processes of both production and social reproduction, and, in the process, has profoundly changed the ways in which women and men sustain themselves and their families, form alliances and political strategies and are represented in public policies.

This shift to neoliberal approaches to economic and social policy also has enormous significance for equality-seeking groups. Many of the successes of the North American and European feminist movements in the second half of the twentieth century were premised on the idea of a strong welfare state. The welfare state's foundational commitment to the idea of universal citizenship equality provided individual women and a nascent women's movement with the political space to pronounce themselves as more than dependents, wives and mothers. Women made claims to citizenship equality and demanded that the state intervene to reduce gender-based discrimination in markets, erase bastions of male privilege, and expand the basis of entitlement for women to economic, social and political programmes (Sainsbury 1999). As a result of decades of sustained feminist activism, most industrialized countries now have formal legal language about gender and racial equality, particularly with regard to anti-discrimination in labour markets and in public policy. But the formal language of equality has not prevented the deterioration of gender equality in the contemporary reconstruction of economic institutions and public policy. And, it has not eliminated growing inequalities among women located along such other lines of social differentiation as race, class and ethnicity. With the ascendancy of neoliberalism, many of the ideals and programmes of equality-seeking groups have been undermined by privatization, government cut-backs of social programmes, the introduction of market principles in the management and delivery of social services, and a general ethos that prefers individual to collective solutions to social issues.

The past ten years have occasioned continual debate about globalization, usually focusing on its definition, its causes, its dimensions and whether it is truly a distinct phase in world relations that is different from previous eras (Bonoli *et al.* 2000). These debates are significant for a clear sense of the nature of change that is affecting virtually every section of the globe. This book engages in these debates, focusing in particular on the remapping of gender inequalities and gender orders in the contemporary era. But this book is distinct from others on globalization in that it deals with issues that are not normally at the centre of discussion. The chapters focus on the ways that the forces of globality and globalism are embedded in daily lives and in gender relations in varying circumstances. Individual countries obviously face challenges that are to some extent unique, but the prescriptions for economic and social restructuring are largely based on a common competitive logic. This means that the ways that people deal with their everyday problems of feeding and reproducing themselves not only change, but are substantially affected by forces outside the nation. The responses within nations are sometimes political and associated with national goals and ideals, but they are also personal, as people devise strategies to confront or adjust to change.

This book also focuses on changes in gender relations in countries on the semi-periphery of power. The concept of the semi-periphery as a site for examination will be fully explained in the next chapter (see Cohen Chapter 2). Semi-periphery refers to those nations which are not drivers of change globally, but have enough economic and political security to have some power in determining their own responses to global forces. This book takes examples from four countries on the semi-periphery of power, but still located in the top category of the United Nations Development Programme's (UNDP) Human Development Index, to examine the ways that gender relations change in this globalizing era. At one end is Norway, one of the world's richest and most developed welfare-states, and, at the other, is Mexico, a country that is considerably poorer and more susceptible to the power of the United States and international agencies such as the World Bank (WB), the International Monetary Fund (IMF), the World Trade Organization (WTO), and the North American Free Trade Agreement (NAFTA).[1] Australia and Canada, the other two semi-peripheral countries examined, are in the middle. Comparisons will also be made with the United States (US), since this is the epicentre of the 'core' base of power. As the following chapters demonstrate, the impact of globalization on gender relations in these countries is often quite similar but the responses vary considerably.

Remapping gender on a global order

Feminist critiques of globalization have met with stiff opposition from the supporters of neoliberal globalization who tend to see what they perceive as a natural and inevitable process as unfairly characterized by inflamed rhetoric, muddled thinking, insufficient understanding of economic processes, and just plain wrong-headedness. Jagdish Bhagwati is probably the best example of a well-known economist who meets feminists head on. His claim is that 'globalization is on balance socially benign' while being responsible for enormous economic progress worldwide (2004: 30). He attempts to prove that the economics of globalization does have a human face specifically by showing that it has beneficial effects on women's rights, poverty, child labour, employment standards and wages, democracy and the environment (ibid.: Part II).

Bhagwati's argument that women (and other disadvantaged groups) are beneficiaries of globalization ultimately rests on the notion that discrimination of any type will be eliminated when competition is intense and global. This is based on the classical economic theory that asserts that when competition is 'perfect' any act of discrimination on the part of an employer will ultimately cost the employer money. As employers compete with each other for workers, the employers who discriminate against women will either have to pay more for male workers or ultimately be forced to hire women on the same basis as men. In theory, this is correct.[2] Classical economic theory is founded on models where all markets are perfect. There is no unemployment, no entity can control any prices, no monopolies exist, and correct prices ensure that all resources, including labour, will be paid the price that is appropriate for its contribution to the production process.[3] It assumes that all labour will be paid a wage that reflects its level of productivity. Bhagwati's argument is that in a competitive system, discrimination becomes impossible because 'faced with increased competition, firms that were happy to indulge their prejudice will now find that ... the price paid for prejudice will become unaffordable' (ibid.: 76). Under these circumstances the only explanation for different wages for males and females would be differences in productivity.

It is important to understand the theory behind this claim that women and other marginalized social groups will inevitably benefit from globalization because this theory is the basis for the entire structure of the institutions that have been erected to ensure the global dominance of neoliberal economic thinking and structures. The point that feminists have made is that there is a fundamental contradiction between this idea of the ultimate positive outcomes of neoliberal globalism with the methods that are essential to pursue it and the policies and institutions that have been developed to improve women's economic, social and political circumstances in northern and western countries.[4] The problem, of course, is that while 'perfect competition' is a useful concept in theory, there are few examples of perfect competition in practice and especially in the current configuration of global markets. International trade is now dominated by relatively few mega-players in each industry, and tremendous unemployment and poverty, especially in the South, forces workers to accept low wages and deplorable working conditions or, indeed, to migrate to other countries to find any form of waged work. The claim that markets, by themselves and without strong government controls, will eliminate poverty and inequality defies intuition. But more importantly, it is an idea that runs counter to experience of the vast majority of women across the globe, as the chapters in this volume demonstrate.

Bhagwati specifically discounts the work of feminist critics of globalization who focus on the conditions and institutions that expand global care chains, the exploitative nature of export processing zones, and the constraints placed on poor countries through the directives of international financial institutions such as the IMF. The issue of global care chains involves women migrants from poor countries, who must leave their children in the care of others, to care for households in wealthy countries (Hocshchild 2001, Arat-Koc 1989). Usually these migrant workers are not accorded full citizenship rights in the host countries and often are subjected to oppressive work-related conditions. At the very least, they must be considered disadvantaged when they must sacrifice normal family ties in order to make a living in distant places. Bhagwati discounts the information gained from interviewing women in these circumstances as not convincing proof of a problem, but even if proper samples were taken, 'as long as the choice to migrate had been made voluntarily', according to Bhagwati, the psychic and economic gains outweigh the costs. 'The idea of a global care chain as a chain that binds rather than liberates', he insists, 'is almost certainly a wrongheaded one' (ibid.: 77–8). What is happening as care chains expand, according to Bhagwati, is a validation of care work. As women have gone into the workplace, the demand for childcare and the price of childcare has risen. This means the social value of childcare becomes more manifest and visible. This last point is not entirely untrue in a market economy, but not so the notion that 'the migrant female worker is better off in the new world of attachments and autonomy; the migrants' children are happy being looked after by their grandmothers, who are also happy to be looking after the children; and the employer mother, when they find good nannies, are also happy' (ibid.: 78).

As will be seen in Chapter 3 of this volume, which examines migration for care work in Norway, the politics of care work is considerably more complex than the chain of happy women that Bhagwati depicts. Migration may be a partial solution to growing and severe care shortages throughout the advanced capitalist world. However, in Norway such migration has also brought a disturbing increase in inequalities in a society that is known for its commitment to social equality. As Lise Widding Isaksen shows, the solution to a care problem displaces the need to increase the wages of care workers in hospitals and old age homes. Rather than wages and conditions improving and work being evenly shared between men and women, according to their preferences, as in Bhagwati's theoretical world, importing care workers from poor countries allows for the perpetuation of these poor working conditions and the gendered (and raced) segregation of care work.

The feminist critique of export processing zones and the exploitation of women that occurs in these zones comes under Bhagwati's criticism for unrealistic expectations. He is particularly critical of the US-based feminist organization the National Organization for Women (NOW) for its condemnation of Mexico's export processing zones (EPZ), the maquiladores, for their poor conditions of work, sexual harassment, physical abuse, mandatory pregnancy testing, and long hours. The danger to women in the maquiladores has been most horrifically and dramatically highlighted by the murder of over 200 women in recent years in Ciudad Juarez. Most were young workers who had migrated from the countryside and many were killed during their journeys to work. For Bhagwati, the fact that these types of murder are not a generalized phenomenon in EPZs throughout the world should place the blame on the Mexican government for failing to provide security to workers, rather than on the shoulders of an entire process or foreign firms. His main point, however, which is one that cannot be dismissed casually, is that EPZs often provide much better wages and conditions of work than outside the EPZs and that EPZs diminish in importance over time as their outward-oriented strategy becomes more generalized and the advantages offered by EPZs become available nationwide.

As the chapters of our book show, the argument about whether globalization improves or worsens conditions of work for women needs to take into consideration a wide range of factors, not simply those associated with specific institutions such as EPZs. It is rarely one specific aspect of neoliberalism that can be understood outside the context of the general shift in the economic conditioning frameworks of neoliberal forces and EPZs have different impacts in different economic and cultural settings. It is the entire framework of neoliberalism that conditions the 'choices' that workers make. Both Elaine Levine, in Chapter 4, and Isabel Altamirano Jiménez, in Chapter 7, show how the complexities of the structural changes that occurred in Mexico as a result of free trade, and the conditions imposed by the international economic institutions on that country, have had cascading effects that do not follow the neat progressive path that Bhagwati traces.[5] As Elaine Levine demonstrates, the export-led growth pattern imposed on Mexico by international institutions has not led to a better integrated industrial sector or to a more diversified economy. Rather, the entire country has experienced deteriorating wages and working conditions. This is primarily because of a general decrease in non-maquiladora manufacturing employment and the inability of maquiladora employment to offset the job losses that have taken place in the agricultural sectors. The maquiladores, which once had a predominately female workforce, now increasingly employ more male than female workers. The neoliberal prescriptions for Mexico accentuate the historical problems in the country and have certainly shifted gendered spaces for different groups of women and men as a result. Isabel Altamirano Jiménez also shows the ways that international forces have undermined the resources that were integral to the lives of indigenous people. There is nothing subtle about the changes that force these people into global market-oriented networks. Families are wrenched apart through urban and US migration and gendered roles take on new dimensions as 'certainty politics' for resource exploitation displace traditional ways to make a livelihood on the land.

The stabilization programmes of the IMF and the WB that impose conditionality on countries like Mexico long have concerned feminists. This conditionality usually involves drastic austerity programmes, shifting to an export-led model of growth, increased foreign borrowing, free trade, and programmes to encourage foreign ownership and investment. To economists like Bhagwati, these conditionalities only arise when there is a stabilization crisis and, if they were not imposed, the economies would suffer even more (ibid.: 88). Bhagwati recognizes some feminist concerns such as, for example, the disproportionate job losses that women experience when government programmes are cut and the problem of women acting as 'shock absorbers' when social policies and public services are eroded. These are problems, but feminists' concerns are wider and deeper than this. As the authors in this book demonstrate, the effects of prescribed stabilization programmes are even more serious than these two problems because they often involve regime changes that last well beyond the period of the crisis. The changes that Levine and Altamirano Jiménez discuss are life-changing and show few signs of bringing about positive conditions for the future.

The conditionalities imposed on poor or indebted countries such as Mexico are blunt and binding, but they are not limited to countries that are financially weak or insecure.[6] In countries like Canada and Australia, wealthy countries at the upper level of the Human Development Index, the pronouncements of international institutions like the Organization for Economic Cooperation and Development (OECD), while less immediate and coercive, have a substantial effect in supporting neoliberal forces within each country. In Canada, for example, the OECD's frequent warnings about the country's level of taxation and debt, its alleged inability to attract foreign investment, and its ideas about how labour should be treated are regularly front-page news in national newspapers (McBride and Williams 2001). These pronouncements then become benchmarks for the country and the success of specific policy issues is measured in the public eye and by governments according to the grading of international institutions. Even more fundamentally, however, feminists have criticized neoclassical economists such as Bhagwati for failing to adequately account for the ways in which the shift in governing paradigms from post-World War II social liberalism to neoliberal globalism has affected the complex and multiple processes of social reproduction, gender orders, and relations between governments, social movements and citizens. Neoclassical economic theory and neoliberal public policies are largely silent on the questions of gender roles, the sexual division of unpaid domestic labour, and gender inequalities. Indeed, this governing paradigm is largely silent with respect to all structurally embedded social inequalities. This silence, however, should not be taken to mean that neoliberal policies are gender neutral in their impacts. The contrary is increasingly evident in, among other things, the feminization of poverty, persistent wage, income and wealth gaps, and the double-burden of work experienced by a growing proportion of women who attempt to balance participation in the paid labour force with domestic caring responsibilities.

Feminists have long emphasized the integral relationship between the ways economies are organized and governed, the social reproduction of individuals, families and communities, and particular models of gender relations or gender orders (Bakker 2003). Gender orders, as Broomhill and Sharp explain in Chapter 5, are comprised of power relations between men and women and are embedded in formal and informal institutions, and cultural norms and practices that contribute to reproduction of social formations. Broomhill and Sharp explain that, in the past century, the economic order as well as the politics and policies of the welfare state in Australia, and across advanced liberal democracies, were premised on the male breadwinner model of gender relations. Both public policy and cultural norms were premised on the assumption that the ideal and 'natural' unit for social reproduction was the nuclear family comprised of a male breadwinner, who earned the family wage, and a dependent wife and children. Women's paid labour, according to this particular construction of gender order, was considered unnecessary, or failing that, secondary to that of her husband. Instead, women were expected to provide the unpaid domestic work of cooking, cleaning, and caring – the three Cs upon which the male breadwinner model depended.

Although dominant, the post-war male breadwinner model was neither universal nor uncontested. Women in working poor and racially marginalized families as well as unmarried women often had to engage in paid labour to support themselves or their families. Similarly, as already noted, the post-war women's movement struggled against the second-class citizenship that this model assigned to women. And, in the face of insistent and sustained feminist political activism, western governments were forced to enact policies that broke down barriers to gender equality in all walks of life. These pressures also were felt internationally, especially after the UN Decade of Women when all national governments were pressured to advance gender equity policies and establish national machinery to achieve this goal.

As the chapters that follow variously describe, the post-war model of gender relations (and traditional indigenous forms) as well as governmental gender equity policies have gradually but surely broken down, leading to a different configuration of gender relations and different forms of gender inequalities. In Chapter 6, for example, Satoshi Ikeda argues that the decline of the male breadwinner model, and the full employment policies that underwrote it, have contributed to a crisis in masculinity that has many different manifestations around the world. The globalization of production, which has seen once secure manufacturing jobs move from the North to the South, as well as the unprecedented entry of women into the paid labour force has created a large population of men who are downwardly mobile and unable to fulfil the gendered expectations of the male breadwinner model. At the same time, globalization has created a new set of winners and losers and a new construction of masculinity. According to Ikeda, this emerging cultural form – transnational business masculinity – is characterized by egocentrism, conditional loyalties and a declining sense of responsibility for others. Transnational business masculinity, Ikeda argues, subjects women to the 'discipline' of the market and justifies and perpetuates gender inequalities and exploitation through the neutral language of supply and demand.

The chapters in this collection point to the many and diverse terrains upon which gender and gender relations are being remapped in the semi-periphery. However, several themes appear to be consistent across the countries. These are:

1   the growing crisis in care and processes of social reproduction more generally;
2   the erosion of welfare-state capacity and governmental will to address gender-based inequalities; and

3   the necessity for feminists to devise new strategies and alliances in light of the challenges and constraints of the new global order and especially of neoliberal globalism.

As Marjorie Griffin Cohen documents in Chapter 2, the relative commitment to gender equality and the extent of the development of the welfare state have considerable significance for the nature of change in each country. But the overall commitment to neoliberal structures negatively affects even the most progressive countries. Some gross indicators of change in all countries are positive. These include improvements in female labour force participation, reductions in pay differentials between males and females, improved literacy and education, and increased life expectancy. But the initial redesign of social programmes that occurred during periods of economic constraint has persisted and has fundamentally changed the understanding of the nature of the welfare state and its commitment to social equality. In all the countries the idea that inequality is a necessary feature of the new regime in increasingly accepted. This inequality affects individuals and families in very different ways, but for those most marginalized in wealthy countries it means more work under worse conditions. In the poorer countries, as Levine and Altamirano point out, women have migrated to find paid labour in order to support their families and local communities. Whatever the motivation, the effect, as Esping-Anderson notes, is that most countries are in the 'midst of a revolution in demographic and family behaviour' (2000: 2).

This analysis of semi-peripheral countries shows that governmental responses to this revolution have been slow and inadequate, especially with respect to alleviating or redistributing the burden of unpaid care work. As Cohen notes, among the four countries studied here, Norway has the best system of support for childcare. Yet, many families still turn to migrant workers to perform domestic and caring work which, in turn, puts downward pressure on wages in a sector that is disproportionately populated by women workers. In Australia, Sharp and Broomhill report that women's entry into the labour force has been less pronounced than elsewhere and that the male-breadwinner model, while diminished, has withstood the pressures of insecure and competitive labour markets and shrinking public services. Women in working class families, however, are increasingly accepting part-time work to help maintain their households. These women, in effect, work a double-shift because there is little evidence that men have accepted greater caring responsibilities within the home. Moreover, the costs of childcare often consume any marginal gains in family income provided by its one-and-a-half or dual income status. This dual burden on women workers only promises to intensify as neoliberal policies download or 'refamilialize' an ever broader range of caring responsibilities on individuals and families, including care of the elderly, disabled and ill.

Randi Drevland in Chapter 8 explores the ways in which the non-profit sector and local organizations in Canada are increasingly taking responsibility for providing services and supports for vulnerable populations that were previously provided by the state before it embraced neoliberal-inspired cutbacks and offloading in the social sector. Although the women's movement has always been active at the grassroots level, she notes that they are increasingly playing a substitute role for the social state but they do so under considerable constraint. Nonprofit groups that respond to the growing crisis in care often do so in partnership with governments and under strict guidelines that limit, if not silence, their capacity as advocates for marginalized groups.

This observation draws us to a theme that flows through the chapters in this book – notably the capacity and will of governments and other authority structures to recognize and respond to gender equity, and indeed all equality-seeking groups. As Janine Brodie shows in Chapter 9, the ascendancy of neoliberal goals within nations delegitimizes feminist voices and with the dismantling of governments' public capacity, issues of gender equality disappear from the public policy agenda. She argues that at the same time as Canada was signing on to international agreements, such as the Beijing Platform for Action, the federal government was systematically disengaging both from the goal of gender equality and the Canadian women's movement. Brodie describes how this process unfolded in three stages, involving, first, the delegitimization of women's claims-making as the voices of 'specific interests', next, dismantling and disempowering gender units within the federal bureaucracy, and, finally, elevating children as the primary focus of social policy making. Somewhat paradoxically, the federal government's partial and half-hearted implementation of Gender Based Analysis (GBA) has not strengthened the capacity of governments to track and be held accountable for the gendered impacts of its policies. Instead, the implementation of GBA strengthened the case for dismantling gender-based policy units, leaving gender concerns 'everywhere and nowhere' inside the federal government's policy machinery.

Many of the chapters in this book underline the complexities and contradictions that confront women's activism and resistance in the new global order. Isabel Altamirano (Chapter 7), for instance, discusses how indigenous resistance and treaty making in Canada and Mexico have, in effect, reinscribed patriarchal relations in these communities both by reinforcing old gender-based power inequalities and inscribing new ones. In a somewhat different vein, Edmé Domínguez in Chapter 12 discusses how the regional economic integration, induced by NAFTA, has opened up possibilities for transnational solidarity and resistance movements that span the North American continent. Such transnational movements have the potential to link gendered resistance to neoliberal policies at the grassroots level to a more powerful and fully resourced transnational advocacy network. However, Domínguez cautions that this promising political strategy also carries its own politics and risks. While transnational networking does bring new resources to local movements, national asymmetries tend to reproduce themselves within the transnational networks themselves.

As James Goodman concludes in Chapter 10 globalization, and especially the neoliberal conditioning framework that underpins it, has reordered gender relations, redefined many aspects of patriarchy, and redefined the terrain of feminist activism and struggle. The question of where feminists should focus their political activism and through what channels, has been complicated both because national states have been hollowed out and because of the ascendancy of economistic discourses and practices. In the face of these new constraints, Cooper and Sharp suggest in Chapter 11 that one way that feminists can highlight gender inequalities and hold governments accountable to women is to focus on the budgetary process. Neoliberal budgetary practices that withdraw services, privatize public assets, and cut back on social spending are not gender neutral, and have disproportionately hurt poor and vulnerable women. Cooper and Sharp, drawing on the examples of Australia, the Beijing Platform, and, most recently, Mexico, argue that, although limited, gender responsive budget initiatives can place gender back on the public agenda and open new spaces for feminist activism. Although debt repayment schemes in countries such as Mexico may limit the amount of money that governments can direct to new initiatives, gender responsive budgets raise awareness of the gendered impacts of budgetary decisions not only among citizens and grassroots activists but also importantly among the international donor and development communities.

Neoliberal globalism has placed significant brakes on the feminist activitism that grew ever wider in scope and influence in the twentieth century. The tactics honed by generations of feminists to transform individual relationships, the family, the policies of the state, and the gender-based inequalities of the market have been substantially undermined both by the shift in sites of power from the national state to global institutions and by the ascendancy of neoliberal globalism. However, as James Goodman notes, although women's movements have been reconfigured by globalism, their ongoing struggles demonstrate the resilience and political force of the idea of gender equality. Women have been able to engage with globalism in a myriad of ways, but a critical and shared agenda has been to put gender back onto the governing agendas of both national governments and international financial organizations – in effect to re-embed women's experiences in the discourses of globalism. As the following chapters will show, the experiences of women and men drawn from Mexico, Australia, Canada and Norway differ in ways that sometimes suggest distinct gender regimes are emerging. The ways that this will ultimately unfold is, to a significant degree, dependent on the activism of women and men at all scales of contemporary governance – from the local to the transnational. Globalization has remapped many familiar sites of politics but it has also opened spaces for new feminist solidarities and renewed political activism.

Notes

1   Mexico is included in the UN's Human Development Index's 'high human development' section, but at the bottom end of this section, whereas Norway is ranked first. See Chapter 2 for further discussion on this.
2   Bhagwati bases his analysis on Gary Becker's work on discrimination (Becker 1978).
3   A perfectly competitive market has specific characteristics that do not allow any individual or group of producers or buyers to control the price of anything. The main characteristic is that there are a large number of buyers and sellers in the market and that they are freely and easily able to enter and leave the market.

4   This has been the approach of feminist organizations such as the International Gender and Trade Network (IGTN) and other individual feminist analysts that will be discussed throughout this book.

5   To be fair to Bhagwati, it is important to note that he does not see globalization as having no downsides. He understands that modern afflictions that can attend 'normal, empire-unrelated globalization' and require both national and international attention. He is referring specifically to abuse of female workers abroad (he specifically cites their conditions under Islamic laws), tourism-induced prostitution, and trafficking across borders. But other than feminists' focus on these issues, he finds that 'the broader criticisms that many women's groups have voiced about the negative effects of globalization on women are not convincing' (Bhagwati 2004: 90–1).

6   In the case of Mexico the inability to repay loans to foreign banks was the motivation for the drastic conditions that radically affected the wage rates and standard of living in the country.

References

Arat-Koc, Sedef (1989) 'In the Privacy of our own Home: Foreign Domestic Workers as Solution to the Crisis in the Domestic Sphere in Canada', *Studies in Political Economy*, 29, Spring: 33–58.

Bakker, Isabella (2003) 'Neo-liberal Governance and the Reprivatization of Social Reproduction: Social Provisioning and Shifting Gender Orders', in Isabella Bakker and Stephen Gill (eds) *Power, Production, and Social Reproduction*, London: Palgrave, pp. 66–82.

Beck, Ulrich (2000) *What is Globalization?*, translated by Patrick Camiller, London: Polity Press.

Becker, Gary (1978) *The Economic Approach to Human Behavior*, Chicago: University of Chicago Press.

Bhagwati, Jagdish (2004) *In Defense of Globalization*, New York: Oxford University Press.

Bonoli, Guiliano George, Vic and Taylor-Gooby, Peter (2000) *European Welfare Futures: Towards a Theory of Retrenchment*, Cambridge: Polity Press.

Brodie, Janine (2003) 'Globalization, In/Security, and the Paradoxes of the Social', in Isabella Bakker and Stephen Gill (eds) *Power, Production, and Social Reproduction*, London: Palgrave, pp. 47–65.

The Economist, 'The Future of Globalisation', July 29, 2006: 11.

Esping-Anderson, Gösta (2000) *Why We Need a New Welfare State*, London: Oxford University Press.

Hochschild, Arlie Russell (2001) 'Global Care Chains and Emotional Surplus Value', in Will Hutton and Anthony Giddens (eds) *On the Edge: Living with Global Capitalism*, London: Vintage, pp. 130–46.

McBride, Stephen and Williams, Russell (2001) 'Globalization, the Restructuring of Labour Markets and Policy Convergence: The OECD "Jobs Strategy"', *Global Social Policy*, 1, 3: 281–309.

Sainsbury, Diane (ed.) (1999) *Gender and Welfare State Regimes*, Oxford: Oxford University Press.

Part I

Changing gender landscapes of globalization

2 The shifts in gender norms through globalization

Gender on the semi-periphery of power

Marjorie Griffin Cohen

Gender and globalization are increasingly a focus for analysis with a clear understanding that gender relations are as much a part of global restructuring as are changes in other power relations (Marchand and Runyan 2000). However, there is a great deal that is still at a relatively elementary stage of understanding. Uncertainty exists, especially with respect to the question of whether the many changes that have occurred typify 'regime' changes in gender relations, or are simply variations on fairly familiar constructions of gender within national contexts.

Several themes are common in the discussion of gender and globalization. One is that the gendered implications of structural changes have been insufficiently considered in the construction of international agreements and institutions that further economic globalization (such as the World Bank, World Trade Organization, the International Monetary Fund, and the North American Free Trade Agreement). In addition, gender is generally ignored within nations when restructuring to further or accommodate globalization occurs (Waylen 2004, Freeman 2001).[1] A second frequent theme is that the restructuring associated with globalization has been more disadvantageous to both men and women in developing countries than it is to people in wealthy countries and, in general, is more disadvantageous to women than to men in both the developed and developing countries (Hawthorne 2004, Peterson 2003). However, since the earliest discussions of gender and globalization, which generally focused on the horrors for women of Structural Adjustment Programmes (SAP) aimed at developing countries, the notions of victimization or disadvantage have become more nuanced. Analysts now point to a multiplicity of effects associated with gender changes, effects that do not allow for neat categorizations by gender or by country location (Tzannatos 1999, Koggel 2003).

A third major theme in the work on gender and globalization is that, as gender norms change, the personal and political strategies of women, men, and households that were developed under specific national conditions are less effective in a world conditioned by global restructuring. The implication is that there may be a strengthening of patriarchal hegemony in the new configuration of gender relations in both the domestic and international arena and that new methods of political activism are required to deal with the shift in the sites of oppression from the domestic to the global (Moghadam 1995, Cohen 2004).

These analyses of gender and globalization have taken place in the context of an ongoing argument about the changing power of states in the new global economic configuration. The initial critique of globalization assumed that the strengthening of international institutions to support economic liberalization would impinge significantly on state powers and would constrain the ability of states to assert the specific interests of their citizens – both domestically and in the international arena. This idea was quickly contested by both those who supported globalization and those who felt that, while globalization did constrain democratic will, it was not because states themselves were powerless. Some analysts felt that the constraints that international institutions imposed on states were greatly exaggerated and that states could determine the extent and pace that they pursued the economic liberalization project (Weiss 1997). Others pointed to the complicity of states in the construction of international regimes that restricted certain types of state powers, most notably those dealing with progressive social policy (Panitch 2003). But whatever the critique of the changes in state power, the boundaries of the state have remained the primary focus for analysis in understanding the implications of changes on people and in analyzing the effect of globalization on gender relationships.

What happens within states is crucial to changes in gendered power relationships. The context in which changes occur and the starting point and pace of the race to neoliberal social constructions will shift hierarchies in ways that look substantially different in different places. While neoliberal economic policies are designed to ultimately bring convergence in economic systems, there are large social variations that are possible within the neoliberal framework. Any understanding of possible variations in effects, then, needs to recognize at least two things. One is how states respond to the pressures of globalization as well as different kinds of domestic pressures. The other relates to responses at a more micro-level. These involve changes that occur through the adaptations or conflicts that people have, as individuals and in communities, as they experience new conditions in daily life. Because of the historical and institutional settings for change, examining whether gender relations deteriorate, improve, or are substantially reconfigured must necessarily be understood on a case-by-case basis in a slow building of categories through time. This is one of the objectives of this book – an examination of a specific type of country, situated neither at the heart of international power, nor on the periphery, but on the semi-periphery, and how gender relations have been affected though restructuring. As will be seen in the next section, the semi-periphery can be understood in the traditional context of economic hierarchies, or as a way of conceptualizing the discrepancies in political power in the global context. It is the latter that shapes the use of the term in this book.

While change within nations has and will continue to be an important point of departure, the focus on national location can be conceptually limiting. With globalization the construction of an international society has begun and we need to construct analyses of global social spaces. That is, within nations there are very different types of experiences that can be linked to those of people in different locations in the global context. These are experiences that relate to the various kinds of hierarchies that globalization exploits, including those based on the usual categories of gender, race and class, but also may relate to other categories of human stratification (Peterson 2003).

One objective of this chapter is to examine the concept of the semi-periphery of power both in the context of national power and of global social spaces. The first two parts of this chapter discuss this dual concept of the semi-periphery: how the semi-periphery is perceived as a national location and how the concepts of core, periphery and semi-periphery play out with regard to gendered issues as the 'social' in the global is reconfigured. The third part examines the relative hierarchy of states and their social programmes and the implications of these hierarchies for changes in gender configurations. The focus here will be on some of the major indicators of changes for women and men in countries representing different points in the global semi-periphery. While each of the subsequent chapters of this book will show the complexities of gender relations and restructuring, this chapter points to some of the crucial comparisons between the countries on gender issues.

Nations as the semi-periphery of power

The concept of the semi-periphery of power in this analysis is used in a way that is distinct from the usual connotations associated with the term. The traditional notions of the semi-periphery deal with economic locations of countries that are neither 'core' nor 'periphery' in economic strength (Wallerstein 1985, Ikeda 2004). Most generally it is understood that core countries are rich and powerful while countries on the periphery are poor, have little political power and are usually dependent on the core. However, there is a substantial literature that further distinguishes the core and periphery based on the distinctions in economic characteristics that were originally related to the divide between industrial production in the core and resource extraction in the periphery (Chase-Dunn 1990). But this distinction no longer characterizes the core from the periphery as more industrial production shifts to countries that have historically been considered on the periphery.

While the specific economic characteristics of the periphery have changed over time, the main analytical contribution of the notions of core and periphery is in understanding power dynamics in changing international regimes. This understanding in recent times strikes at the heart of economic neoliberalism because it relates to the ways that the economic and political power of the rich and powerful nations affect poor ones. Core nations have a high degree of power relative to other nations in the world. In some cases, as with the US, this means they can be effective in asserting their own objectives in both international arenas and domestically. Countries on the periphery have virtually no power in an international setting and are usually so dependent on core countries that their domestic power is also curtailed. This means they are highly subject to the directives of international agencies that have uniform patterned responses to economic problems. Each country has little room to pursue economic and social policies that would best meet its needs and objectives. The very success of the wealthy countries is essentially a coercive power that stifles progress for the periphery, such that the successes of the core cannot be duplicated in areas where the conditions are radically different. These core countries, through a variety of strategies including physical coercion, market power and the design of global institutions, lock the poor and powerless in their roles (Laxer 2004).

Semi-peripheral countries, in the traditional definition, were neither rich nor poor, but had some characteristics of being economically secure, albeit dependent nations. In some respects this still defines a semi-peripheral country, but in the use of the term in this book, the country need not be in the middle of the hierarchy of economic wealth to be considered on the semi-periphery. Rather, here the term refers to power relations and to those countries that are neither drivers of international change, nor powerless in their responses to global economic liberalism, regardless of their place in the hierarchy of wealth.

The countries on the semi-periphery are distinct because politicians and the people in them are usually acutely aware of their relationship, if not actual subordination, to the centre, or core, of power. This is quite unlike the people in countries at the core, who attribute their international influence to their general superior ability, their superior ideology and their commitment to freedom and democracy. They do not associate their dominance with their assertion of raw power, but to an inherent superiority. Within the core countries the relative international hierarchies appear natural and the collective understanding within these nations lacks the consciousness that anything could or should be different. It should be noted, however, that politicians in many semi-peripheral countries are often ambivalent about the relationship to the centre. This ambivalence often takes the form of engaging in international matters as the 'junior partner' for the leading team. In this sense, the countries on the semi-periphery are both implicated in and benefit from an international system that produces winners at the expense of the periphery.

The other distinguishing feature that makes the semi-periphery an identifiable group is that these countries share a political strength that allows them, at least potentially, to resist certain forms of domination from the core (while benefiting from and participating in other forms). Countries on the periphery lack the means to resist what is happening, or risk too much if they actually do assert a position distinct from the core.

So, in sum, semi-peripheral countries have a consciousness of the power of imperialism lacking in the core, as well as the potential and resources to exert their own power that is all but absent in countries truly on the periphery of power. This makes the categories of change within these countries distinct: some countries may actively embrace all of the social implications of neoliberal globalization, while others may resist those aspects that place people in a subordinate position to the competition objectives of market fundamentalism. This focus on power in the semi-periphery is especially important because solutions to social problems rely on the capacity and will of states to protect their citizens from the growing power of international institutions of capital (Brodie 2004).

Table 2.1 Relative distinction in state power

	Core	Periphery	Semi-Periphery
International Power	Effective	Ineffective	Marginal
Domestic Power	Effective	Ineffective	Variable

Source: Author

Each of the governments of these countries is making critical choices in economic and social policy at a crucial time and much that is being decided now will shape or limit choices in the future.

The four countries represented by case studies on gender issues in this book fit the category of semi-peripheral countries very well. Each country is highly dependent in its relationship to the global economic order. But their position, while largely subordinate ones within the global order, have relatively more political autonomy than truly powerless countries. Canada and Mexico are extraordinarily dependent on the US for exports and for each the US is its major trading partner. As a result, each has bowed to US designs for economic liberalism in significant ways and acquiesces to US superior power on important, future-shaping issues in the international sphere. But they do resist on enough issues to truly irritate the U.S, especially with respect to domestic issues and cultural politics. Canada, for example, was the first nation in the Americas to institute same-sex marriage; some provinces provide safe injection sites for drug users, despite strenuous US objections; Canada continues to maintain a universal public health system, and Canada still has no taste for instituting the death penalty. Similarly, one of the major irritants for the US from Mexico is its steadfast insistence that resources remain in the public sector.

All of these countries support the kinds of economic policies that are conditioned by market neoliberalism much as Americans do, but generally they are not as unilateralist on international issues and in many instances are not as conservative on social issues. This, in some respects, explains the contradictions between the way people clearly feel about specific social issues (according to polls) and their willingness to elect neoliberal leaders and governments, as has been the case in all of these countries. (The contradiction here, of course, is that these neoliberal leaders identify with the kind of economic programmes that habitually undermine strong social programmes.)

In both Canada and Mexico, however, there is strong public will to be distinct from the US, a persistent sentiment that national politicians ignore at their own peril. Both Mexico and Canada refused to join the American's 'coalition of the willing' to engage in a war with Iraq because there was strong public opinion opposed to US unilateralism and the leaders at the time, Vincenté Fox and Jean Chrétien, knew this refusal to join the US would appeal to their national electorates. This decision enraged the Bush administration and US commentators began referring to Canada as 'Canuckistan' in order to make it clear that this time the country had gone too far.

Both Norway and Australia are more independent of the core than Canada and Mexico. Norway has defied European convention by not joining the European Union (EU) and Australia is so physically distinct that, until recently, this has provided some degree of insulation from political domination by the core. But each in its own way bows to the core's neoliberal trajectory. Norway is officially out of the EU and the public has repeatedly voted in referendums to stay out, mainly because it does not want to further neoliberal trends. However, Norway is part of the European Economic Area (EEA) and as such, its policies tend to be similar to other EU member states. Participating in the EEA has the effect of breaking down the distinctions between foreign and domestic policy in ways that allow neoliberalism to have a large effect in the design of social and economic policies (Claes and Fossum 2004).[2]

Australia's government under John Howard has become the 'deputy sheriff' to US imperial designs.[3] It readily supported the US in the Iraq war and as a result has won the strong approval of the US. But on economic issues, there are few distinctions between the approaches of Australia and Canada. Both have chosen the path of economic neoliberalism and both fully support the US in any international initiatives that advance free trade, lower taxes, the privatization of public assets and the restriction of social provisioning by government (Bryan 2004, Clarkson 2002). While Mexico has an economic position on the semi-periphery distinct from Canada and Australia, it too has wholeheartedly embraced neoliberal structural change. This was dictated by the International Monetary Fund (IMF) and the World Bank in the 1980s, but was further cemented by Mexico joining Canada and the US in the North American Free Trade Agreement (NAFTA) in 1994 (Alvarez 2004, Gutiérrez-Haces 2004). Mexico is an 'emerging economy' that has major significance on the semi-periphery, mainly because of its strategic importance for the US.[4] Its reform policies, like Canada's, have two major objectives: one is to increasingly integrate the economy with that of the US and the other is to dismantle the historically precarious institutions of the welfare state (Alvarez 2004).

None of these four countries can claim to drive global change, but each has responded to change in different ways that have significant implications for social and gender relations. These countries are, however, dramatically different with regard to the nature of their economies and the size and configuration of their social systems, and each have distinct gender configurations. The third section will specifically look at the distinctions between the countries on the major indicators for gendered experiences, but before this, a second reading of the semi-periphery needs to be considered.

Gendered social spaces and the semi-periphery

What constitutes the core, periphery and semi-periphery when it comes to discussions of gender and global power? So far, the distinctions have been categorized by nation – or broad groupings of nations. But this geographical concept of national power does not capture many significant aspects of political subordination, agency and control that could be considered through a focus on hierarchies in a global society. Normally the global is associated with the actions of states and corporations. But with the increasing globalization of economic and social issues that impinge on societies within nations, and with the increasing institutionalization of many governance functions at the global level, the concept of a global society that has a collective stake in globalization's institutional configurations is emerging. This idea of a global society is a concept of the global which extends the definition of social actors beyond those of nations and corporations.

Within all nations there exists a social core and social peripheries. The social actors who make up the core are the people not only with wealth, but with the power to determine the shape and objectives of the nation to meet their own needs. They also get to negotiate the nation's objectives in the global context. Those on the periphery have the least power and those on the semi-periphery can exert some agency sometimes. Where individuals and groups fit within nations will often correspond to their placement in the global social regime, but there is a significant difference in that in the global configuration, the placement at the core, periphery or semi-periphery is not confined by geographical space. The commonalities of experiences and interests across nations are beginning to have a global dynamic that is specific to this era of global integration, a dynamic that is beginning to change the politics of the global (Ayres 2003, Yeates 2005).

Pressures on gender relations and changes are usually understood in a national perspective, but the concept of core, periphery and semi-periphery can also be applied to the global construction of gender as the 'social' is being reconfigured and globalized. This idea of the gendered nature of changes in the global context has received attention in relation to gendered migration issues and changes in the gendered nature of the global division of labour (Ehrenreich and Hochschild 2002, Willis and Yeoh 2000, Standing 1999). But it can also be applied to gendered relationships in global power structures. Figure 2.I is a schematic approximation of a continuum of relative global social power with the extremes of unpaid individuals and workers in the informal sectors as typifying the periphery and people at the head of large international corporations and global institutions as the core. At the core are multiple spaces of power including those institutions that enforce neoliberal regimes, and the large transnational business elite. Straddling the core and the semi-periphery are the domestic owners and managers, who can, at times, exert tremendous power in the design of global structures. The semi-periphery constitutes the economically secure, but less powerful positions globally. These sites of activity are usually more responsive to changes initiated internationally, but are not always powerless in carving out unique solutions that can be more responsive to local needs than the wholesale shift to marketization would imply.

Cutting through the quadrants are the separate continuums for males and females, with the female experience confined primarily to the periphery and semi-periphery of the global society. While the core is disproportionately reflective of the male experience, most males, like females, experience periphery or semi-peripheral status.

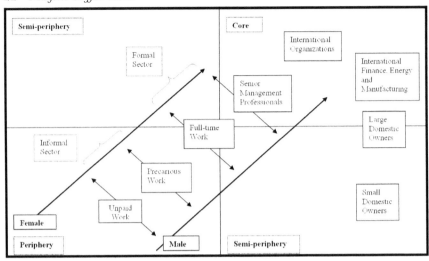

Figure 2.1 Global spaces of social power

As an international society and its social institutions are constructed, so too is its gendered nature. It matters who is in charge of international institutions that shape the decisions made by nations and while it would be simplistic to say that gender itself can be of great significance in affecting the approach of these institutions, the relative disproportion of males in certain types of position can give some indication of the gendered power imbalances. As Table 2.2 shows, the gender disparity is great in key positions in powerful international organizations.

It is no exaggeration to say that the more powerful the organization, the fewer women are present in senior positions. These findings confirm the old adage that where power is, women are not. Women are most prominently represented in UNICEF, a UN agency that deals with children, a representation that follows stereotypical notions of women's interests. Their lowest representation is the WTO and NATO, institutions that deal with such stereotypically male issues as trade and defence. Of the 100 largest companies in the world, only one has a female CEO – Meg Whitman, CEO of Ebay.[5]

This under-representation in powerful international institutions does not mean that women have been inactive in the debates and actions on globalization. Through a variety of national and transnational organizations women have struggled to have their voices heard (Macdonald 2002, Barton 2004).[6] This is not a uniform voice because some groups definitely 'want in' and want their issues to be incorporated in the new economic, political and social structures that are emerging at the global level (Peebles and Kartini International 2005, O'Regan-Tardu 1999). Often this position is representative of either government or non-government organizations (NGOs) who work specifically with international organizations of power, like the IMF and the World Bank, to incorporate more gender awareness in their programmes. Others find the entire neoliberal reconstruction of international

Table 2.2 Gender makeup of key positions in international organizations and institutions

Organization	Positions	% female
WTO	Director General, Deputy Directors (5 positions)	0
World Bank	President, Managing Director, Senior Vice-President	0
	Network Head, Controller, Chief Economist, CFO,	0
	Vice-Presidents (29 positions, 3 female v-p)	10.3
OECD	Secretary General, Deputy Secretary General, Directors (28 positions, 1 deputy, 2 directors female)	10.7
NATO	Permanent Representatives (26 positions, 1 female)	3.8
	Secretary General, Assistant Secretary General, Chiefs of Staff Military Representatives (no women ever in positions)	0
IMF	Managing Directors, Deputy Managing Directors, Counsellors (32 positions, 3 female)	9
	Executive Directors appointed (5 positions, 1 female)	20
49446	Executive Directors Elected (28 positions, 1 female)	4
EU	Commissioners (25 positions, 7 female)	28
	Elected (731 elected, 222 women)	30
UN**	Executive Directors/Programs (27 positions, 3 female)	11
	UNCTAD Secretariat (12 positions, 4 female)	33
	UNICEF, Pres, V-Ps (5 positions, 2 female	40
	WHO Executive (positions 33, female 3)	10
	ILO Executive positions, directors, regional coordinators (15 positions, 1 female)	7
OAS	Secretariat, Permanent Council and Subsidiary Organs (17 positions, 8 female)	47
NAFTA	Dispute Resolution Panels	
	Canada	17
	US	15
	Mexico	4

Source: Calculated from 'Guide to Women Leaders' (2006), available online, www.guidetowomenleaders.com>

** The UN has had only one female president, Mrs. Vijaya Lakshimi Pandit, since it began.

society a problem that cannot be rectified by more female representation. From this perspective gender equality within the hierarchies of neoliberal globalization holds little promise for people on the periphery of social and economic power (Kabeer 2004). In this book, Chapter 12 by Edmé Domínguez, and Chapter 10 by James Goodman provide an analysis of the kinds of activities and alliances that have occurred among women across and within countries on global changes.

Relative gender and welfare-state hierarchies

Neoliberal economic fundamentalism has set the restructuring agendas in all four countries but their experiences reflect what policy analysts refer to as path dependency, that is, the starting point for each state greatly affects the nature and consequences of restructuring. Among the most significant factors in the shaping of gender relations and the relative status of women in each country have been both the welfare-state hierarchy among the countries and the level of economic success in each country. Highly developed welfare states like Norway have distinct advantages, even when neoliberal economic directions and marketization of social programmes become more pronounced. The strength of a welfare state in itself seems to indicate each country's success in subduing the effects of a variety of social differences and changes (including class and gender) that occur through the restructuring associated with globalization. It also affects the way that gendered issues are treated in the restructuring process.

The assumption behind this focus on the relative strength of welfare states is that a strong public sector that provides universal public support for all people is crucial for the improvement of the conditions of women and other equality-seeking groups: public services are significant for realizing the collective economic rights of people. Access to public infrastructures, such as clean water, sewage disposal, electricity, transportation and other services like education, healthcare, social assistance, childcare, maternity leave and disability service, keep many people from becoming poor and provide those who are poor or the victims of discrimination some access to facilities that might enable them to escape poverty or other disadvantages.

Relative country ranking in gender and social provisioning

In this selection of nations on the semi-periphery of power, there is a sharp ranking from the women-friendly welfare state of Norway, to the least developed welfare regime of Mexico, where provision of services for women is slight. All of these countries are listed in the 'high human development' section of the Human Development Index (HDI). Mexico is at the bottom of this ranking of countries having 'high human development', while Norway, Australia and Canada consistently have among the highest ratings in the word, with Norway at the top (Table 2.3).[7] The HDI is a composite index to measure the relative differences between basic human provisioning in various countries. Its three components are average life expectancy, education levels (adult literacy rates and school attendance) and gross national product.

Table 2.3 Gender Development Index (GDI) and Human Development Index (HDI) 2003

GDI Rank	Country	Score	HDI Ranking	Score	Gini Index
1	Norway	0.960	1	0.963	25.8
3	Australia	0.954	3	0.955	35.2
5	Canada	0.946	5	0.949	33.1
8	US	0.942	10	0.944	40.8
46	Mexico	0.804	53	0.814	54.6

Source: United Nations (2005) *Human Development Report: International Cooperation at a Crossroads; Aid, Trade and Security in an Unequal World*, New York: United Nations Development Programme, Tables 1 and 25, pp. 219, 299. Available online, http://hdr.undp.org/reports/global/2005/pdf/HDR05_complete.pdf>

The HDI gives the median value for the entire national population, but does not reflect inequalities across different social groups or between men and women. The Gini coefficient for each country gives some indication of the general level of inequality in each country (Table 2.3). A value of zero represents perfect equality and a value of 100 perfect inequality.

In the early years of the twenty-first century the relative levels of class inequality in Norway, Australia and the US have remained fairly stable while in both Canada and Mexico's inequality has increased. From 2001 to 2005, inequality increased by 1.6 points on the Gini Index in Canada and by 2.7 points in Mexico. This increase in inequality may well indicate a trend in these two countries as they increasingly follow US neoliberal economic and social strategies. But among the four semi-periphery countries examined in this book, only Norway has had a consistently low level of class inequality.

Two other measures, the Gender Development Index (GDI) and the Gender Empowerment Measure (GEM) try to capture some of the issues that do not receive a gendered weight in the HDI. The GDI is calculated on the basis of life expectancy, adult literary, school attendance and earned income by gender. As can be seen in Table 2.3, this index puts the four semi-periphery countries and the US in the same order as in the HDI, although both Mexico and the US are ranked higher in this index than in the HDI index. This index is highly correlated with the strength of the welfare state and gendered sensitivity in the provision of social programmes.

The GEM is a separate measure that tries to evaluate whether women are able to participate actively in economic and political activities and take part in decision-making within nations (Table 2.4). The weighted elements of the index include the ratio of income earned by women workers, the ratio of female professional and technical workers to the total working population, the ratio of the seats held by women in the national legislature and the proportion of female senior officials in government.

Table 2.4 Gender Empowerment Measure (GEM)*

Country	Rank	Value	% Females in National legislature	Female/male Income	% Senior government officials female
Norway	1	0.928	38.2	0.75	30
Australia	7	0.826	28.3	0.72	36
Canada	10	0.807	24.7**	0.64	35
US	12	0.793	14.8	0.62	46
Mexico	38	0.583	23.7	0.38	25

Source: United Nations (2005) *Human Development Report: International Cooperation at a Crossroads; Aid, Trade and Security in an Unequal World*, New York: United Nations Development Programme, Table 26, p. 303. Available online, http://hdr.undp.org/reports/global/2005/pdf/HDR05_complete.pdf>.

* Data from *Human Development Report* 2005 includes the most recent years available at that date.
** In the 2006 elections this proportion decreased to 20.7 per cent in the House of Commons.

In this measurement, the rankings of the four semi-peripheral countries and the US are in the same order as in the HDI, but with lower rankings for Australia, Canada and the US and a substantially higher ranking for Mexico than in the HDI. The improvement in the relative position for Mexico relates to several things, including the fairly dramatic increase in numbers of women in the national government. This was a result of a change in 1994 when one political party, the PRD (Party of the Democratic Revolution) placed a 30 per cent quota on women in its nominations. This, in itself, may not have had a substantial impact had not a party list system of proportional representation been in place in national elections. In 1995 only 7.3 per cent of Mexico's elected members were female: this increased to almost 22 per cent in 2005, which means that a greater proportion of women serve in the Mexican national legislature than in many countries that have a more educated and wealthier female workforce, such as the U.S and Canada.[8]

After this significant decision by the PRD to include women the two other major parties also began to work on improving female representation. The Institutional Revolutionary Party (PRI) moved to a quota system in 1997, and the National Action Party (PAN), while not adopting a quota, also increased its nominations of women (Bruhn 2003). The improved relative standing for Mexico in the GEM was also a result of substantial improvements for Mexico in the relative significance of women's earnings, even though women earn only 38 per cent of the earnings of males, on average (see Appendix 2.1). This figure includes all non-agricultural wage workers and all types of work, not just full-time, full-year work, which is the configuration of workers normally used for comparisons. Also, the proportion of women who worked in the labour force increased substantially in a fairly short period, from 34 per cent in 1990 to about 40 per cent in 2003. The Mexican example shows that the GEM index is highly correlated with direct political action to increase women's political participation and can change fairly rapidly when there is a political will to include women. It also reflects the pace of women's access to paid jobs.

Altogether these measurements on gender capture gross differences in experiences between countries there is a great deal that cannot be understood from these data including the gender inequality in level of economic activity in the household, the distribution of total wealth by gender and class, access to government programmes by gender, and availability of specific programmes to lessen inequalities. Some of this information can be accessed through general country-specific data and a comparison of gender access to social programmes. But as everyone who tried to compare social programmes understands, the comparisons are always rough ones because it is difficult to find reliable and valid indicators for gendered aspects of social policy design (Korpi 2000: 144). Also, there are great variations in what is covered in each programme, something that complicates neat comparisons. And, while the availability of social programmes, their nature and the changes are significant, so too are the general conditions in which they exist. This reflects a country's capabilities, to a large extent, and the problems that need solving. The following table reflects major indicators of population changes within

Table 2.5 Issues affecting gender changes, total population growth

	Population(millions)			Fertility*		Urban population (% of population)		
	1975	2003	growth % per year	1975	2004	1974	2004	growth % per year
Norway	4.0	4.6	0.5	2.2	1.8	68.2	78.6	10.6
Australia	13.6	19.7	1.3	2.5	1.7	85.9	91.9	6.0
Canada	23.1	31.6	1.3	2.0	1.5	75.6	80.4	4.8
US	220.2	292.6	1.0	2.0	2.0	73.7	80.1	6.4
Mexico	59.3	104.3	2.0	6.6	2.4	62.8	75.5	12.7

Sources: United Nations (2005) *Human Development Report: International Cooperation at a Crossroads; Aid, Trade and Security in an Unequal World*, New York: United Nations Development Programme, Table 5, p. 232. Available online, <http://hdr.undp.org/reports/global/2005/pdf/HDR05_complete.pdf>, and OECD (2005) *Society at a Glance, OECD Social Indicators*, Paris: Organisation for Economic Co-operation and Development.

*births per woman

these countries. These relate to population growth, fertility rates and the population shift from rural to urban areas.

Both low and high fertility rates have significant effects on public policy, particularly with regard to policies to encourage labour force participation and public spending on childcare. While social policy analysts tend to focus on the economic and social implications of fertility rates in less developed countries, the implications for wealthy countries are attracting more attention. In Canada, for example, low fertility rates in the province of Quebec have affected both the province's support of childcare and the province's distinct view on the provision of childcare at the national level. As will be seen in Lise Isaksen's chapter in this volume, the fertility rates in Norway, a country that has supported childcare with public programmes and has a high labour force participation rate for women, creates labour shortages that are solved in ways that reflect the increasing global nature of care services.

In all of the four countries the majority of people live in urban areas (Table 2.5). The biggest changes have occurred in Mexico, a country that has not been able to support this change sufficiently with urban infrastructure to replace to kinds of community structures that dealt with child and elder-care issues. The pressures on a large proportion of the population in urban centres have also occurred in Norway. But they are dealt with in very different ways – largely because of the small numbers of people involved in the shift and the wealth of the country itself.

Some general indicators of gender changes

The correlation between gender and the effects of restructuring associated with globalization and the rise in neoliberal social policy is varied. Some indicators show that there have been some positive improvements for women in the four semi-peripheral countries over the past 20 years, despite the neoliberal restructuring of economic and welfare state policy. Among the improvements are those in labour force participation, pay differentials between males and females, educational participation, literacy and life expectancy (See Appendix 2.1 for tables related to the discussion of these indicators).

All countries have improved the expected age of death for both males and females since 1980. Mexico's changes have been greatest: women's life expectancy increased from 70 years in 1980 to over 77 years in 2003. This is not too different from the female life expectancy in the US (79.8 years). Norway, Australia and Canada have very similar lengths of lives for both men (around 77 years) and women (around 82 years) and the figures for both have improved over this period. In all of these countries females outlive males by about five years.

The female proportion of the labour force has increased for all four countries since 1980. Mexico's participation rate for women is considerably lower than in the other countries, at 33 per cent, but it is growing fairly rapidly. Australia's participation rate is lower than that of Norway and Canada, which reflects historical trends in each of these countries. The female share of earned income has increased substantially from 1995 to 2003 in all countries except Mexico. This positive income change reflects both the increase in the average of female to male earnings and the increase in the female proportion of the labour force. Since females in Mexico have not increased their proportion of total earned income, but have increased their proportion of the labour force, it is clear that something else significant is happening to women's hours of work and wages. The wage gap between males and females for all work is the lowest in Norway, with women earning 75 per cent of the total income of males, and the largest in Mexico, where women's average income is 38 per cent of that of males. But Canada's wage gap is fairly large as well, with women earning on average 64 per cent of men's wages.

These broad indications of improvements in women's conditions in all four countries mask some trends that are less positive. One of these is related to women's work. While there have been improvements in labour market participation and wages, these factors do not indicate either the intensity of women's employment or other factors related to the gendered ways work patterns differ over time (Orloff 2002).

One marked change is the shift from full-time employment as the norm to more precarious forms of labour in some industrialized countries (Vosko 2004). There

Table 2.6 Full-time employment (permanent and temporary), percentage of labour force

Year	Canada	Australia	US
1980	86	84	83
1990	83	79	83
1995	81	75	81
2002	81	71	83

Source: Vosko, Leah (2004) Confronting the Norm: Gender and the International Regulation of Precarious Work, unpublished paper, July: Figure 1.

Table 2.7 Employment variations

Year 2000	Canada %	Australia %	US %
Permanent Full-time	63	47	72
Permanent Part-time	11	8	14
Temporary Full-time	7	8	1
Temporary Part-time	4	16	2
Self Employment Full-time	12	15	8
Self Employment Part-time	3	5	3

Source: Vosko, Leah (2004) Confronting the Norm: Gender and the International Regulation of Precarious Work, unpublished paper, July: Figures 2A–2C.

appear to be clear economic and social pressures on women to scale back their paid economic activities through part-time and temporary work. This is particularly significant in Australia and Canada where all work is increasingly diverging from 'standard' work (permanent, full-time jobs), but which also increasingly typifies women's work.

The biggest decline in full-time work is in Australia where this type of work typifies only 71 per cent of the labour force. The trend is similar in Canada, although less dramatic. Since 1980 there has been no decline in full-time work in the US. While there are problems with the decline in full-time work, the existence of permanent, full-time work, which used to be the norm, is even more dismal, especially in Australia.

More than half the employment in Australia and over one-third of the employment in Canada differs from what used to be considered the employment norm. In Canada permanent part-time and self-employment are dominant forms of non-standard work, whereas in Australia temporary part-time and self-employment are dominant as the non-standard types of employment. In both countries, self-employment generally means self-employment as the only worker in the business and it is the kind of work that is dominated by females. Forty-six per cent of the females in the labour force in Australia work part-time. The dominance of part-time work for women reflects historical patterns in Australia, where women have consistently had low levels of participation in full-time employment. According to one analyst, it has remained relatively constant since the 1930s: in 1933 only 25.2 per cent of women were in full-time employment and in 1994 the figure was 27.1

Table 2.8 Part-time work percentage of total work by gender

	Female	Male	Both
Australia	46%	14%	28%
Canada	28	11	19
US	26	11	18

Source: Vosko, Leah (2004) Confronting the Norm: Gender and the International Regulation of Precarious Work, unpublished paper, July: Figure 3.

per cent (Vosko 2004). Some analysts attribute the relatively high level of gender inequality in the Australian labour force to a long tradition of family wage principles and to immigration as the solution to labour shortages (Korpi 2000: 170).

As will be seen in Elaine Levine's Chapter 4, labour conditions in Mexico are increasingly precarious. NAFTA clearly did not shift production from the US to Mexico, as was anticipated by many.[9] Rather, the labour market became more mobile and flexible. The changes in the labour market are highly correlated with the neoliberal economic policy changes that began in the 1980s and accelerated through NAFTA (Cortez 2001). The problems of wage inequality and casualization of work has resulted in high migration, increasingly of females, to the US. So, despite increasing education levels (discussed below), the employment prospects are not increasing in commensurate ways.

This shift in working patterns in countries where employment is increasingly precarious has a dramatic impact on the kinds of social programmes that women can access. As governments increasingly assume that women are not dependent on men, and design access to social programmes accordingly, the shift to non-standard employment reduces women eligibility for many work-based benefits. This shift in many states' construction of social policy from a 'male breadwinner' model to a 'dual earner model' is now fairly well recognized (Orloff 2002, Walby 2001, Korpi 2000). And while the assumption of the 'male breadwinner' model disadvantaged women in specific contexts, so too can building social programmes premised on the ability to find full-time, permanent work – especially when the trend is away from this type of work as the norm.

In Canada and Australia there has been an increased selectivity in targeting state benefits, specifically those that are employment related. In Canada the effect this has on women is most obvious with Employment Insurance (EI). This programme has been redesigned to eliminate government contributions as well as to tighten eligibility and to reduce the payouts in the programme. This means that full benefits are accorded to those for whom full-time, permanent employment is the norm. The result is that currently only one-third of females are likely to receive benefits when unemployed. Related to this are the reductions in labour market protections through labour standards reductions, which have been considerable as each province tries to become more 'business friendly'. This has involved a lengthening of the standard work week, reductions in minimum wages for some workers, loss of benefits for part-time workers, and the exclusion of trade union members and agricultural workers from employment standards protection.[10] The level of state provided pension benefits are also related to work patterns and are affected by the shift to more precarious work forms.

In Mexico benefits are also related to attachment to the labour force. But since the 'informal sector' constitutes approximately 58 per cent of the labour force, few receive these benefits. The term 'informal sector' refers to those who are in employment where employers do not pay into the social security system because they are not 'regular' workers. Only 29 per cent of the labour force is covered by the IMSS (social security system) and another 13 per cent by ISST (the social security system for government workers) (Levine, Chapter 4).

When governments redesign programmes to target benefits and reduce labour market protections, the most vulnerable workers experience a decrease in economic security. The policies themselves encourage more precarious work forms as people are pushed into whatever types of work they can get (Standing 1999). Probably the most significant policy design that forces women into precarious work forms relates specifically to childcare burdens. In order to deal with childcare and elder-care issues, women adjust their employment patterns more frequently than do men. Even in Nordic countries, where women have the highest levels of formal participation and where the public and market services are well developed, many women who remain in the labour force are on parental leave. This is in contrast to male patterns, where even with good state support relatively few men take leave to care for babies (Jensen 1997).

Welfare state provisions

Examining the relative ranking of the four countries in their social welfare programmes and expenditures gives some insight into the relationship between women-friendly state policy on gender differences and the impact this can have as restructuring occurs. In addition to total social spending there are two parts to this examination of welfare provisions. One deals with the general and universal social policies and their changes over time and the other deals with policies that specifically focus on improving conditions for women.

Norway spends a larger proportion of its national income on social programmes than any other country. This is also larger than OECD average. Australia and Canada spend less than the OECD average (See Appendix 2.2 and 2.3 for tables). It is significant how this money is spent and what are the priorities of the state. Mexico has clearly made education a priority and this has had a large impart on literacy rates and female access to education (Table 2.9). The Mexican government spends almost one-quarter of its budget on education and has increased the proportion of this spending considerably since 1990. In contrast, Australia and Canada have reduced the proportion they spend on education, although this does not appear to have had significant implications for educational access for women. Women constitute a greater proportion of tertiary enrolment than do men in both countries.

Table 2.9 Gender in education: enrolment by level – ratio of female to male 2003

	Primary	*Secondary*	*Tertiary*
Norway	1.00	1.01	1.55
Australia	1.01	1.02	1.23
Canada	1.00	1.00	1.34
Mexico	1.01	1.04	0.97
U.S.	1.01	1.01	1.37

Source: United Nations (2005) *Human Development Report: International Cooperation at a Crossroads; Aid, Trade and Security in an Unequal World*, New York: United Nations Development Programme, Table 27, p. 307. Available online, <http://hdr.undp.org/reports/global/2005/pdf/HDR05_complete.pdf>

Mexico's commitment to education has meant that almost the entire population is literate. All children attend primary school and 64 per cent of females attend secondary school, a proportion that is greater than that of males who attend secondary school. Twenty-two per cent of females obtain post-secondary education, a smaller proportion than males..

Healthcare and education are the two most costly programmes provided by governments. The privatization of healthcare is increasingly an issue in Australia and Canada. Australia has 32 per cent of the total spending in the private sector and Canada has 30 per cent private.[11] Norway has the smallest proportion of healthcare in the private sector and the US the largest and, as a result of this, the US pays the most per person. Mexico still has a larger proportion of healthcare in the private sector than in the public sector. Considering the similarities in the life expectancy rates of Mexico and the US the contrast in the levels of spending on healthcare is remarkable (See Appendix 2.2).

Differences in women-friendly social programmes

The differences in the four countries in providing programmes that promote women's social and economic security are strong. Among the three wealthier countries, these differences reflect the different political responses to the restructuring associated with globalization as well as the country's historical approaches to both collective responsibility for social issues and their commitment to women's equality. Since these are indicators that are not collected in comparable ways at the international level, these comparisons are rough.

Appendix 2.4 shows the way each of these countries deal with a range of programmes that are essential for the economic security of its population. Other than the basic commitment that a country has to women's access to education and healthcare, the commitment to maternity/parental leave and childcare gives an indication of the need to recognize the distinct needs of working women.

Maternity/paternity leave

Government maternity and parental pay and leave provisions are best in Norway and virtually non-existent in Mexico and Australia. Norway allows new parents to choose between 52 weeks of paid maternity leave at 80 per cent of assessed earnings, or 100 per cent of assessed earnings for 42 weeks. To be eligible a woman is required to have had six months of employment or self-employment during the previous ten months. If the mother returns to work, the father may care for the child at the same rate. Four weeks of the total maternity cash benefit period are reserved for the father as the 'father quota'. A mother may also return to work at a reduced work level and still receive partial maternity benefit (Social Security Online 1999).

In Canada maternity and parental benefits are provided under the EI system. To receive maternity benefits a mother must qualify for EI, that is, she must have worked at least 600 insured hours in the 52 weeks before the claim – the equivalent of 20 weeks of work at 30 hours a week. Two of the 52 weeks are unpaid, but of the remaining, 15 weeks of paid benefits are specifically for new mothers and either parent may take the remaining 35 weeks. The basic benefit rate is 55 per cent of average insured earnings up to a maximum amount of $413 per week. EI payments are taxable income.

Australia has no public paid leave provision. One year unpaid leave is possible and it is estimated that less than 40 per cent have access to seven weeks paid leave through their workplaces. Mexico has maternity leave at 100 per cent of pay for those who have contributed to IMSS for 30 weeks in the year preceding the leave. But this is an extremely small proportion of the female working population.

Childcare

It is especially difficult to compare government-supported childcare because it varies considerably depending on the composition of the family and its income. None of our countries has a public child or daycare programme, but Norway, Canada and Australia have varying cash benefits and tax credits related to raising children. Norway's support for children is best, and Australia's is better than Canada's. The form of funding is varied in nature but normally comes in the form of one or more of the following:

- universal child benefits, or family allowances, which are paid regardless of the family income;
- income-related child benefits where levels vary by income and are usually targeted at low-income families;
- tax deduction or allowance which is subtracted from the taxable base income and is of greater value to taxpayers with higher incomes
- tax credits, which reduces tax liability after assessing tax obligation.

Norway provides a universal non-taxable child benefit of about $1,830 US for each child, and children aged between one and three receive an additional benefit for a total of $3,034 per year. Lone parents receive an extra supplement for each child. Norway also provides a tax deduction for childcare for children under 12 up to about $4,000 US for one child. It is estimated that about 45 per cent of childcare is publicly funded (OECD 2002).

Canada has long promised that it would institute a national childcare programme for children of working parents. This has not happened, despite repeated promises by successive governments. Instead, in 2006 it instituted a taxable Universal Childcare Benefit of $100 per month for each child under six or $1200 a year. According to the government, this benefit is 'designed to assist Canadian families, as they seek to balance work and family life, by supporting their childcare choices' (Canada Revenue Agency 2006). This wording reflects the political tension in Canada between those who support a childcare programme for working parents and those who want to reward the family with stay-at-home parents. In addition to the federal programme there are various programmes to support children of working parents in the province. The best is in Quebec where public funding for daycare costs for parents is extremely low at $7 Cdn ($6.20 US) per day. The problem, however, is that there is not enough supply of spaces to meet demand. It is estimated that about 45 per cent of daycare in the country is publicly funded. Canada also has federal childcare tax deductions based on family income.

Australia provides a childcare benefit for parents who are both working or studying and for a single parent. This benefit is means tested and benefits decline until they are eliminated at A$83,184 (US 74,865).[12] The benefit is not taxable. The maximum per week for a 50 hour week for a non-school child is A$133 or about A$6,600 per year.

Conclusion

The early stages of neoliberal restructuring associated with global change brought about economic crises in Mexico, Canada and Australia. This was evidenced through large government deficits, high unemployment rates, and a redesign of social and economic policy that in many cases profoundly shifted the nature of state responsibility for social issues (See Brodie in this volume, Broomhill and Sharp in this volume). When this initially occurred many social analysts within these countries understood that the logic of global economic competition, coupled with new international institutions that limited states' control over corporate activity, dramatically shaped the conditions for changes in employment and wage levels and with ways of coping with the increased insecurity of people through social programmes. As neoliberal ideas dominated activities in the economic sphere, the demand by the corporate sector for their needs to be supported in public social policy was taken up by governments. This took the form of increased privatization of social supports that were formerly provided by the state, considerable downsizing of the public sector, increased marketization of the remaining social supports and reductions in taxes.

Since these early problems there has been some turnaround in the economic fortunes of all of the countries. But the consequences of the redesign of social programmes to meet the crisis in neoliberal economic policies have remained and programmes characteristic of the welfare state are not being restored. The changes that have occurred in each country have changed the gender relationships within the countries. As the subsequent chapters will show, these changes have been very dramatic for some segments of society in each country, particularly for those who are the most vulnerable. These changes are complex and not neatly characterized solely by a country's economic circumstances, but are related to the general commitment to equality and fairness, and the political climate within the countries.

The extent to which the neoliberal idea that the economic should dominate social life is challenged greatly affects the direction of changes in gender relationships. As was shown in this chapter, some of the changes regarding equity between males and females are positive, although they may have been changes that would have occurred simply by virtue of the decline in fertility rates, the growth in the tertiary sectors of society, and the sheer power of economic growth itself. These are most marked in the areas of the labour market and in the provision of healthcare and educational services. But other changes are occurring that might represent gender regime changes. As always, when looking at changes as they are occurring, it is not easy to distinguish between short-term changes that relate to temporary circumstances, and long-term changes. However, the comparative data in this chapter shows several things: whether or not the changes are permanent, there is considerable variation in the spaces for negotiating new gender regimes, and the economic limits and constraints of globalization themselves need not be the over-riding consideration for a society as it chooses between more or less equity in its social relationships.

The aggregate statistics presented in this chapter can give only an impression of the extent and nature of change in gender relations as women and men live their lives under new conditions. The chapters that follow provide detailed examina-tions of how changes affect people as they are differently positioned in the semi-peripheries. What will be most clear is that it does matter how governments posi-tion themselves in their public policies. However, the chapters also show that social activism is critical in ensuring that governments genuinely pursue the public's interests. The changes in gender relations and perhaps even gender regimes appear to have been generated by the vast economic and political changes that we think of as globalization. But whether these changes close spaces for equal gender relations, as most analysts seem to think, or open other avenues for new possibili-ties, as many would hope, is a story that is unfolding. In the new international society that is beginning to be developed, new alliances across national landscapes may become strong enough to make a difference in the nature of the formation of international institutions.

Appendices

Appendix 2.1 Changes in gender indicators

Life Expectancy	Male		Female	
	1980	2003	1980	2003
Norway	73	76.4	79	81.5
Australia	71	77.4	78	82.6
Canada	71	71.4	78	82.2
México	64	72.1	70	77.1

Labour force participation (female % of total labour force)		
	1980	2000
Norway	41	46
Australia	37	44
Canada	40	46
México	27	33

continued on next page

Appendix 2.1 Changes in gender indicators (cont.)

Female participation rate (% of total female working age population)*

	2003
Norway	72.9
Australia	62.2
Canada	67.7
México	39.4

Female share of earned income (%)

	1995	2003
Norway	37.8	43
Australia	36.0	47
Canada	29.3	39
México	27.4	27

Ratio of female to male earnings

	2003
Norway	0.75
Australia	0.72
Canada	0.64
México	0.38

Employment structure % of male and female paid labour forces	Male		Female	
	1990	2003	1990	2003
Norway				
Agriculture	9	6	4	2
Industry	36	30	11	10
Services	55	64	85	87
Australia				
Agriculture	7	6	4	3
Industry	34	30	13	10
Services	59	64	84	87
Canada				
Agriculture	6	4	3	2
Industry	34	33	12	11
Services	60	64	85	87
Mexico				
Agriculture	39	24	3	6
Industry	30	22	21	28
Services	31	48	67	72

Sources: World Bank Group (2002) GenderStats: Database of Gender Statistics, United Nations (2005) *Human Development Report: International Cooperation at a Crossroads; Aid, Trade and Security in an Unequal World*, New York: United Nations Development Programme, OECD (2005) *Society at a Glance: OECD Social Indicators*, Paris: Organisation for Economic Co-operation and Development.

Appendix 2.2 Country comparisons of social spending

	% of Total	Pensions	Healthcare (2002)		
	GDP 2001	2001	Total	% public	% private
Norway	23.9	4.8	8.7	7.4	1.3
Australia	18.0	4.3	9.1	6.2	2.9
Canada	17.8	5.3	9.6	6.7	2.9
US	14.8	6.1	14.7	6.6	8.1
Mexico	na	na	6.2	2.8	3.4
OECD Average	20.9	8.0	8.4	6.0	2.4

Source: OECD (2005) *Society at a Glance: OECD Social Indicators*, Paris: Organisation for Economic Co-operation and Development.

Appendix 2.3 Changes in education spending

	% of Government spending	
	1990	2002
Norway	14.6	16.2
Australia	14.8	13.3
Canada	14.2	12.7
Mexico	12.8	24.3
US	12.3	17.1

Source: United Nations (2005) Human Development Report: International Cooperation at a Crossroads; Aid, Trade and Security in an Unequal World, New York: United Nations Development Programme.

Appendix 2.4 Differences in welfare state programmes

	Canada-benefits and incentives; 'market-oriented'*	Norway-individualist, 'dual earner'*	Australia-means tested, individualist, 'market oriented'*	Mexico-social spending 8.8% of GDP (2000), has increased in the last ten years, but is still below the OECD average
Maternity Leave	17 weeks maternity, 35 weeks parental; 55% of pay from EI; work for at least 600 hours prior to claim; not extended to self-employment	52 weeks, 80% of yearly salary, Social Security pays	1 year personal, unpaid; 39% of women have access to paid mat leave (7 weeks)	12 weeks maternity (6 before birth, 6 after), 100% of pay; must contribute to IMSS (social security) for 30 weeks in the 12 months prior to taking leave
Education and Training	6.1% of GDP (2004); 99.6% primary enrolment (2000)	6.4% of GDP (2004); 99.9% in primary enrolment (2001)	6.0% of GDP (2004); primary enrolment-96.% (2001)	83% of basic education is covered (ages 5-14) (2000); 5.9% of GDP (2004); 99.4% enroled in primary (2001)
Childcare $	Nationwide child allowance $100/month/child under 6 years	Based on income, tax deduction; 45% is publicly funded	Fee assistance for approved care; childcare benefit (income-tested)	Access is scarce, but national programme exists
Social Assistance $	Stringent eligibility criteria, administered by provinces and territories; needs tested	Complementary to other subsistence programmes, of last resort; municipalities are responsible; means-tested benefit	Conditional and only as a last resort; means-tested against any income with a 100% reduction rate (2002)	Regressive income transfer (southern states); new private pension system (1997) is mandatory
Disability **&	0.8% of GDP; Workers' Comp is provincial, and covers 75% of workers; Temp benefits vary from 75%–90% of gross earnings (prov) CPP based on contributions of the last four years	3.9% of GDP; Earnings Related-3 years earnings above base amount; minimum 50% of projected old-age benefit	2.2% of GDP; 43.5% with private insurance (2003); benefits are means-tested unless blind	35% of earnings in the last 500 weeks of contribution

continued on next page

Appendix 2.4 Differences in welfare state programmes (cont.)

	Canada-benefits and incentives; 'market-oriented'*	Norway-individualist, 'dual earner'*	Australia-means tested, individualist, 'market oriented'*	Mexico-social spending 8.8% of GDP (2000), has increased in the last ten years, but is still below the OECD average
Healthcare	9.6% of GDP (2002); 70% is public (2004); 6.7% public (2002); 2.9% private (2002) visits to public sector Drs are free at point of delivery	8.7% of GDP (2002); 85% publicly funded (2004);7.4% public (2002); 2.9% private (2002); insured is required to pay co-payments	9.1% of GDP (2002); 68% publicly funded (2001);6.2% public (2002); 2.9% private (2002); insured is required to pay co-payments	6.2% of GDP(2002); 45% is publicly funded (2004); 2.8% public (2002); 3.4% private (2002); unequal services and benefits; half the population have no health insurance; varies in quality
Employment Insurance	Those with insured employment are eligible after 52 weeks; 1.4% of GDP (1999)	Unemployment insurance based on time worked and income level; 1.6 % of GDP (1999); recipient must have worked 1.25 the basic amount in the preceding year	Means-tested/ activity tested; employers supply 9% of employee's salary (2002)	Entire social security costs, approx. 2% of GDP; accessible to 70% of population; employers must pay 3 months pay plus 20 days pay for each year of service; 79.2% financed by employer-17.3% by employee-3.5% by government (2001)
Pension Expenditure	5.3% of GDP 2001; 33% of workers covered by RPP (2002)Statscan; 9.9% contributions split between employer and employee	4.8% of GDP 2001; universal is independent of previous income; and other portion is earnings related; one-third are covered by the private sector; no mandatory personal pension plans; based on earnings and years worked	4.3% of GDP 2001; means-tested unless blind can get lump-sum; mandatory, fully-funded individual account scheme	7.6% of GDP 2001; age 65 and 1250 weeks of contributions

* Korpi's (2000) typology of gendered welfare
** OECD 2004 statistics
*** Human Development Indicators
Sources: Social Security Online (1999) *Social Security Programs through the World*, U.S. Social Security Administration; OECD (2001), *Insurance and Private Pensions Compendium*; OECD (2002) 'Benefits and Wages', *Society at a Glance: OECD Social Indicators*, OECD (2004), Health Data, 1st ed.; OECD (2004), *Social Expenditure Database (SOCX), 1980–2001*, Paris: Organisation for Economic Co-operation and Development.

Notes

1 The related assumption is that if the gendered implications of changes were sufficiently understood, either things would be done differently or sufficient objections would occur to force governments to act responsibly.

2 But in other ways Norway is able to confront neoliberalism directly. One interesting example is its unprecedented directive to all corporate boards demanding that women comprise 40 per cent of the board's directors (Nergaard 2006).

3 This is the term John Howard used to describe his role in support of the Iraq war.

4 Mexico is important for the US for energy, people who migrate to the US, and for trade.

5 Fifty-five per cent of the 100 companies have the US as their country of origin. The next most significant country origin is the U.K., with 11 per cent of the 100 largest companies in the world (Internet information calculated from Forbes, available online, www.forbes.com/2006/03/29>.

6 The Monthly Bulletin of the International Gender and Trade Network (IGTN) offers on-going critiques of international trade issues and IGTN itself helps to coordinate gendered work in this area.

7 The US is included in these tables for comparison purposes.

8 In 2005 women were 15 per cent of the House of Representatives and 14 per cent of the Senate (United Nations Human Development Report 2005, 'Women's Political Participation', Table 30: 316).

9 Ross Perot referred to NAFTA as 'A giant sucking sound of US jobs going to Mexico' (Perot 1993: p. 41–2 and 47) and Bill Clinton explained that 'if you have more jobs on both sides of the border and incomes go up in Mexico, that will dramatically reduce the pressure felt by Mexican working people to come here for jobs' (Clinton 1993).

10 Labour standards are under provincial jurisdiction in Canada, so vary from province to province. For an example of these changes to employment standards, which are under provincial jurisdiction in Canada, see David Fairey (2005).

11 The privatization of healthcare takes a variety of forms, including private hospitals, contracting out of various services, such as home care, the contracting out of patient care and support services within hospitals, private insurance, and private drug schemes.

12 These benefit figures are based on 2002 data.

References

Alvarez, Alejandro (2004) 'Mexico: Relocating the State within a New Global Regime', in Marjorie Griffin Cohen and Stephen Clarkson (eds) *Governing under Stress:* Middle Powers and the Challenge of Globalization, London: Zed Books, pp. 90–9.

Ayres, Jeffrey (2003) 'Contesting Neoliberalism: The Political Economy of Transnational Protest', in Marjorie Griffin Cohen and Stephen McBride (eds) *Global Turbulence: Social Activists' and State Responses to Globalization*, Aldershot, England: Ashgate, pp. 89–104.

Barton, Carol (2004) 'Global Women's Movements at a Crossroads: Seeking Definition, New Alliances and Greater Impact', *Socialism & Democracy*, 18, 1, Winter–Spring: 151–85.

Brodie, Janine (2004) 'Globalization and the Social Question', in Marjorie Griffin Cohen and Stephen Clarkson (eds) *Governing under Stress: Middle Powers and the Challenge of Globalization*, London: Zed Books, pp. 12–30.

Bruhn, Kathleen (2003) 'Whores and Lesbians: Political Activism, Party Strategies, and Gender Quotas in Mexico', *Electoral Studies*, 22: 101–19.

Bryan, Dick (2004) 'Australia: Asian Outpost or Big-time Financial Dealer?', in Marjorie Griffin Cohen and Stephen Clarkson (eds) *Governing under Stress: Middle Powers and the Challenge of Globalization*, London: Zed Books, pp.110–31.

Canada Revenue Agency (2006) Universal Childcare Benefit (UCCB), Canada Revenue Agency. Available online, www.cra-arc.gc.ca/benefits/uccb/menu-e.html.

Chase-Dunn, Christopher (1990) 'Resistance to Imperialism: Semiperipheral Actors', *Review*, 13, 1, Winter: 1–31.

Claes, Dag Harald and Fossum, John Erik (2004) 'Norway, the EEA, and Neo-liberal Globalism', in Marjorie Griffin Cohen and Stephen Clarkson (eds) *Governing under Stress: Middle Powers and the Challenge of Globalization*, London: Zed Books, pp. 52–69.

Clarkson, Stephen (2002) *Uncle Sam and US: Globalization, Neoconservatism, and the Canadian State*, Toronto: University of Toronto Press.

Clinton, Bill (1993) Remarks by The President during 'A California Town Hall Meeting', KCRA-TV, Sacramento, California, 3 October 1993. Available online, www.clintonfoundation.org/legacy/100493-remarks-by-president-at-california-town-hall-meeting.htm.

Cohen, Marjorie Griffin (2004) 'Globalization's Challenge to Feminist Political Economy and the Law: A Socialist Perspective', in Robert Albritton (ed.) *New Socialisms: Futures beyond Globalization*, London: Routledge, pp. 33–49.

Cortez, Willy W. (2001) 'What is Behind Increasing Wage Inequality in Mexico?' *World Development*, 39, 11: 1905–22.

Ehrenreich, Barbara and Hochschild, Arlie Russell (eds) (2003) *Global Woman: Nannies, Maids and Sex Workers in the New Economy*, London: Granta Books.

Fairey, David (2005) *Eroding Worker Protections: BC's New 'Flexible' Employment Standards*, Vancouver, BC: Canadian Centre for Policy Alternatives, November.

Freeman, Carla (2001) 'Is Local: Global as Feminine: Masculine? Rethinking the Gender of Globalization', *SIGNS: Journal of Women in Culture & Society*, 26, 4, Summer: 1007–38.

Gutiérrez-Haces, Teresa (2004) 'The Rise and Fall of an "Organized Fantasy": The Negotiation of Status as Periphery and Semi-periphery by Mexico and Latin America', in Marjorie Griffin Cohen and Stephen Clarkson (eds) *Governing under Stress: Middle Powers and the Challenge of Globalization*, London: Zed Books, pp.70–89.

Hawthorne, Susan (2004) 'Wild Politics: Beyond Globalization', *Women's Studies International Forum*, 27: 243–59.

Ikeda, Satoshi (2004) 'Zonal Structure and the Trajectories of Canada, Mexico, Australia, and Norway under Neo-liberal Globalization', in Marjorie Griffin Cohen and Stephen Clarkson (eds) *Governing under Siege: Middle Powers and the Challenge of Globalization*, London: Zed Books, pp. 263–90.

Jensen, Jane (1997) 'Who Cares? Gender and Welfare Regimes', *Social Politics*, 4: 182–87.

Kabeer, Naila (2004) 'Globalization, Labour Standards, and Women's Rights: Dilemmas of Collective (In)Action in an Interdependent World', *Feminist Economics*, 10, 1: 3–35.

Koggel, Christine M. (2003) 'Globalization and Women's Paid Work: Expanding Freedom?', *Feminist Economics*, 9, 2–3, July–November: 163–84.

Korpi, Walter (2000) 'Faces of Inequality: Gender, Class and Patterns of Inequalities in Different Types of Welfare States', *Social Politics*, Summer: 127–91.

Laxer, Gordon (2004) 'Preface', in Marjorie Griffin Cohen and Stephen Clarkson (eds) *Governing under Stress: Middle Powers and the Challenge of Globalization*, London: Zed Books, Preface pp. x–xx.

Macdonald, Laura (2002) 'Globalization and Social Movements: Comparing Women's Movements' Responses to NAFTA in Mexico, the USA and Canada', *International Feminist Journal of Politics*, 4, 2: 151–72.

Marchand, Marianne H. and Runyan, Anne Sisson (eds) (2000) *Gender and Global Restructuring: Sightings, Sites and Resistances*, London and New York: Routledge.

Moghadam, Valentine M. (1995) 'Gender Dynamics of Restructuring in the Semiperiphery', in Rae Lesser Blumberg, Cathy A. Rakowski, Irene Tinker, and Michael Monteon (eds) *EnGendering Wealth and Well-Being*, Boulder: Westview Press, pp. 17–37.

Nergaard, Kristine (2006) 'Rules on Minimum Gender Representation on Company Boards Come into Force', Norway: European Industrial Relations Observatory. Available online, www.eiro.eurofound.eu.int/2006/02/feature/no0602102f.html.

OECD (2005) *Society at a Glance: OECD Social Indicators*, Paris: Organisation for Economic Co-operation and Development.

—— (2004) *Health Data*, 1st edn, Paris: Organisation for Economic Co-operation and Development.

—— (2004) *Social Expenditure Database (SOCX), 1980–2001*. Available online, www.oecd.org/els/social/expenditure.

—— (2002) 'Benefits and Wages', *Society at a Glance: OECD Social Indicators*, Paris: Organisation for Economic Co-operation and Development. Available online, www.oecd.org/dataoecd/3/26/34005067.pdf.

—— (2001) *Insurance and Private Pensions Compendium*, Paris: Organisation for Economic Co-operation and Development. Available online, www.oecd.org/dataoecd/62/6/1816289.doc.

O'Regan-Tardu, Louise (1999) *Gender Mainstreaming in Trade and Industry*, London: Commonwealth Secretariat.

Orloff, Ann Shola (2002) 'Women's Employment and Welfare Regimes: Globalization, Export Orientation and Social Policy in Europe and North America', Programme Paper Number 12, New York: United Nations Research Institute for Social Development, June.

Panitch, Leo (2003) 'Globalization Begins (and Ends) at Home: Bringing the State Back In', in Marjorie Griffin Cohen and Stephen McBride (eds) *Global Turbulence: Social Activists' and State Responses to Globalization*, Aldershot: Ashgate, pp. 13–25.

Peebles, Danada and Kartini International (2005) *Increasing Gender Inputs into Canadian International Trade Policy Positions at the WTO*, Ottawa: Status of Women Canada.

Perot, Ross (1993) *Save Your Job, Save Our Country; Why NAFTA Must Be Stopped—Now!*, New York, NY: Hyperion Books.

Peterson, V. Spike (2003) *A Critical Rewriting of Global Political Economy: Integrating Reproductive, Productive and Virtual Economies*, London and New York: Routledge.

Social Security Online (1999) *Social Security Programmes through the World*, US Social Security Administration. Available online, www.ssa.gov/policy/docs/progdesc/ssptw/index.html.

Standing, Guy (1999) 'Global Feminization through Flexible Labour: A Theme Revisited', *World Development*, 27, 3: 583–602.

Tzannatos, Zafiris (1999) 'Women and Labour Market Changes in the Global Economy: Growth Helps, Inequalities Hurt and Public Policy Matters', The World Bank Social Protection Series, *World Development*, 27, 3, March: 551–69.

United Nations (2005) *Human Development Report: International Cooperation at a Crossroads; Aid, Trade and Security in an Unequal World*, New York: United Nations Development Programme. Available online, http://hdr.undp.org/reports/global/2005/pdf/HDR05_complete.pdf.

Vosko, Leah (2004) Confronting the Norm: Gender and the International Regulation of Precarious Work, unpublished paper, July.

Walby, Sylvia (2001) From Gendered Welfare States to Gendered Regimes: National Differences, Convergence or Restructuring?, unpublished paper. Available online, www.sociology.su.se/cgs/Walbypaper.doc.

Wallerstein, Immanuel (1985) 'The Relevance of the Concept of Semi-periphery to Southern Europe', in G. Arrighi (ed.) *Semiperipheral Development*, Beverley Hills: Sage, pp. 31–9.

Waylen, Georgina (2004) 'Putting Governance into the Gendered Political Economy of Globalization,' *International Feminist Journal of Politics*, 6, 4 December, pp. 557–78.

Weiss, Linda (1997) 'Globalization and the Myth of the Powerless State', *New Left Review*, 1, 225, September–October: 1–18.

Willis, Katie and Yeoh, Brenda (eds) (2000) *Gender and Immigration*, London: Edward Elgar.

World Bank Group (2002) GenderStats: Database of Gender Statistics. Available online, http://72.14.203.104/search?q=cache:QZyVNK2MJjsJ:genderstats.worldbank.org/+World+Bank+Group+GenderStats:+Database+of+Gender+Statistics,&hl=en&gl=ca&ct=clnk&cd=1.

Yeates, Nicola (2005) 'Globalization and Social Policy in a Development Context: Regional Responses', Social Policy and Development (2000–2005), Programme Paper No. 18, New York: United Nations Research Institute for Social Development, April.

3 Gender, care work and globalization

Local problems and transnational solutions in the Norwegian welfare state

Lise Widding Isaksen

Introduction

In this chapter I will analyze the ways a traditional gender-specific division of housework and care in the family, recruitment problems in the welfare state and changes in the production of public health and welfare services opens the doors for the commercialization of services and increased immigration of health and care workers. My question is: will the labour of immigrant women from poorer countries be the primary solution for care problems in the Norwegian welfare state?

At present, the welfare state in Norway is still the main supplier of the kind of care services that are needed to maintain a certain level of harmony in the everyday life of Norwegian families. But recruitment problems, and changes both in women's participation in the labour market and in the demographic profile of the population, may lead to new and private ways of solving the problems of care for children and the elderly. During the first years of the new millennium, our conservative government and its neoliberal politics changed the culture of public provision of services as it was institutionalized in the social democratic welfare state. This cultural change has led to an increased acceptance of individual and private welfare solutions that seem to create new patterns of social inequalities related to the way immigrant labour is employed.

After May 2004 when the European Union (EU) included ten new member states from former communist Eastern Europe, new migration patterns emerged. Thousands of Polish men and women have found work in Norway. Skilled and unskilled people from the Baltic countries provide for their families by participating in the Norwegian labour market. This immigration changes the composition of the population in Norway and challenges the rights and duties connected to the use of welfare state services and the production of such services as well.

It is reasonable to question how changes in established cultures of care appear to affect a restructuring of gender relations. The main point of this paper is to show that new forms of marketization and commercialization of housekeeping services seem to initiate increased social differentiation, but, at the same time, do not necessarily affect the traditional gender-based division of labour in a more positive direction.

The Norwegian welfare state, as it was constructed and realized in the 1960s and 1970s, could rely on a stable supply of a female reserve army willing to work both part and full time. This reserve care pool no longer exists for a number of complex reasons and Norway is facing a gap between the demand for and supply of care services. This gap seems to constitute a social and economic space to encourage neoliberal ways to provide care services.

Norway, like other 'greying' European countries, has experienced a change in the demographic composition of the population. Improved living conditions and increased life expectancy have led to a situation where increased numbers of children have the pleasure of growing up while both grandparents and great-grandparents are still alive. The number of people aged over 80 is increasing and those over 85 years constitute the fastest-growing age group. On the other hand, the fertility pattern among Norwegian women has changed. Young women are better educated than earlier generations and many women in their forties are still mothers to small and dependent children. Women in their fifties may be working full time in professional careers during a period when their parents are retired and developing increased need for help. Since many of the youngest generation of grandmothers gave birth to children early in their twenties, they may have grandchildren in need of care at the same time as they have parents with increasing need of daily help and support. In many family networks the youngest grandmother generation can be said to live in a sandwich position as they are attractive as care givers for the youngest as well as the oldest family members. The concept of double burdens as a description of professional female workers taking care of their own households in addition to full-time participation in the labour market has to be extended to include the new situation of having double care burdens on their shoulders as a result of the recent development of new demographic profiles.

Given the gender based division of labour, women, rather than men, are picking up the added task of caring for family members. This is so, not only in Norway, but in most European countries (Stark and Regner 2001). Today, the average western woman can plan on spending 17 years of her life on childcare and 18 years assisting aged relatives (Dahle and Isaksen 2002).

Gender and the welfare state

In the 1970s, when the Norwegian parliament (Stortinget) was debating the implementation of new state-subsidised and public-organized home support services, middle-aged women were described as 'freed hands' that could be employed as part-time care workers (Isaksen 1984). Among the parliament's members (most of them male) there existed a common perception of women between 40 and 65 years old as an available care reservoir that could be used as a common resource to solve care problems in society. It was assumed that this group had grown-up children and, since people did not live as long as they do today, most had already lost their parents. This group of female carers represented an important resource for the provision of public welfare state services as well as for the private informal provision of social care. Even today, when most women in these age groups are employed in the labour market, the majority of help that the frail and elderly receive comes from the informal sector.[1] It seems that this pattern of informal predominance is likely to continue (Stark and Regner 2001). But given the increased gap between the supply and demand of care, normative changes and neoliberal privatization ideas, the social care systems of today are challenged by new global realities. The care reservoir is no longer available and help previously provided by dutiful middle-aged daughters has now been reformulated as demand for public care. If this care cannot be provided by an increasingly cost–benefit oriented welfare state, social care services must be bought from commercial agencies. Since the fall of the iron curtain and inclusion of new EU member states, families have new solutions for care through the ability to employ immigrant maids and/or nannies from poorer countries.

Central social institutions like the family, the commercial market and the welfare state are facing changed normative and economic realities where unpaid middle-aged women no longer represent a classic free good. The paradox however, is that informal care still has the normative priority over that of formal care. There is not only a numerical gap between supply and demand of care: there exists, in addition, a cultural gap shaped by modern ideas of gender equality and traditional ideas of women as the 'best' care providers. For women this is a serious problem because the world's population is ageing fast and care services for the elderly must be expanded quickly to cope with increasing needs.

The absence of men

Even if Norway is a modern welfare state, it has not succeeded in solving the problems of gender equality in the division of labour in either the public or private spheres. In the informal sphere it is still women who bear the main responsibility for housework and care. And Norway still has one of the most sex-segregated labour markets in Europe. But since Norway has a desire to be seen as a generous and innovative nation state, it is eagerly constructing a picture of itself as a women-friendly country supporting and protecting mothers in their struggle to find a harmonic work–family balance.

In public policy debates related to equality problems, 'absent fathers' are a problem when it comes to childcare. But in debates about unpaid female-dominated carework for home living elderly, 'absent sons' are still not constructed a 'problem' worth putting on the political agenda. Care for the elderly is deeply gendered both in the terms of the care that ageing women and men receive and regarding those who perform care work. While today's fathers of babies talk publicly about changing nappies and giving their children baths, we have still not arrived at a situation where middle aged masculine men and sons of old mothers talk with pride about their experiences with the changing of their parents' nappies and helping them to take a bath.

The lack of skilled healthcare workers such as doctors and nurses (particularly in rural areas and in public elder care services) has led to negative changes in the working conditions for all care workers. Publicly organized care services for home living elderly have become more 'industrial' and 'fordist' (Vabø 2003). The labour scarcity means that more people have to share fewer resources and receive less help. This labour care shortage also means that the moral and practical pressure on the family (elder) care systems is increasing. More and more families are left to care for the elderly with almost no outside support.

Budget cuts have increased the stress in the system. Public elder care has today a negative reputation and there is an extremely low social prestige attached to it. Students in nursing do not generally want to work with seriously ill and dying patients after their training. And jobs in the public elder care sector on the municipal level are at the bottom of their preference list of future jobs.

Local and global solutions

Some nursing homes have solved their problems by importing nurses from former communist states like Latvia and Poland. Other municipalities have started to build nursing homes abroad where care services can be bought for 'better prices'. This solution in effect exports elderly patients to Mediterranean countries. Eleven municipalities in Norway have built apartments for elderly people in Spain. Twenty-two other Norwegian municipalities purchase nursing home places in Spain. It is expected that this approach might be increasingly used by other regions in Norway. Currently this solution to care giving problems is chosen by municipalities where the neoliberalist political party (The Progress Party) holds a strong position. It remains to be seen if this global solution continues in popularity when other political parties come into power.

The mayor (Jacinto Mulet) of the region in Spain where the elderly are housed, was pleased with this development and saw the region's future as a 'Mediterranean Florida' and a 'Paradise for Senior Citizens' as a positive one. The municipality is short on industry and the global solution to local Norwegian care deficits creates jobs and income for Spanish men and women (*Spaniaposten* 2003).

Reports from elderly people who go to Norwegian nursing homes in Spain indicate that these homes are provided primarily for middle-class people who are used to foreign travel and know how to benefit from the climate and the tourism culture on the Spanish Costa del Sol. Patients there are treated more like 'guests': they are not 'in a home' and the care workers are portrayed and treated as 'tenants' and 'service providers'. This is different from Norwegian nursing homes where people are 'patients'; they are made to feel that they are 'in a home' and the staff has influence and power as members of a medical profession (Hillestad 2000).

Another model used to solve the local care deficit is to import qualified staff from other countries. The Norwegian Employment Agency (A etat) started a branch for health service recruitment abroad in the late 1990s (Savides 2005). Its job was to recruit skilled healthcare workers like doctors, dentists and nurses from Nordic and European countries. Norway traditionally has not looked to east and south

European countries when looking for medical personnel. Usually other Nordic countries have had a surplus that Norway used. But today, Sweden, Finland and Denmark need their trained health personnel themselves. Also, Norway has not been allowed to recruit labour actively in other European Community countries.

The gap between supply and demand for care services has become a problem for many countries, and the competition for health workers has increased not only in Europe, but on the global level as well. Despite the shortage of nurses in Norway, those students who go abroad to train as nurses run the risk of not meeting the rigid set of regulations that govern the authorization of the work permits they need to work as public registered nurses in medical institutions. Foreign nurses who come to Norway from ex-communist countries often risk ending up in subordinate positions as nurses' assistants or nurses 'on licence' than do individuals from Western Europe (ibid).

Globalization of domestic work

The care deficit in both public and private sectors, and lack of sufficient childcare for under-fives at a time when families have serious difficulty finding an acceptable balance between family and work, seems to be opening up a new cultural acceptance of commercial and market-organized childcare services. For middle-class families who have not succeeded in achieving a more equal division of labour at home, the gendered-based conflicts and negative atmosphere that come from conflicts can be resolved by outsourcing. To avoid daily disputes on how to divide household responsibilities like cleaning, the problems are being solved with the help of firms like the City Maid that sell housekeeping services to private and public institutions.

To directly employ a maid is another solution. In Sweden the use of housemaids from the Philippines has become an accepted solution and the 'early bird' buses from downtown Stockholm to the suburbs are called 'The Philippine Express'. However, in Norway the employment of maids is still not socially and culturally accepted as a good solution to childcare problems. Normally most families prefer public kindergartens, sometimes in combination with paid help from local neighbourhood mothers known as 'day mothers'. But the number of families that find private and individualized market solutions like the employment of foreign live-in care givers (mostly au pair girls) from poor ex-communist countries and the Philippines is increasing (Hovdan 2005). Labour force deregulation and demand for more labour flexibility create the need for more flexible childcare services as well. After-school arrangements and kindergartens usually end at five o'clock. At the same time the numbers of parents with dependent children who work longer and late hours are growing.

Until recently Norway was in the position of sending their young girls to other countries to work as au pairs (mainly to the USA and Great Britain). Today statistics from the Norwegian Immigration Authorities (UDI) indicate a dramatic increase in the numbers of foreign girls finding jobs as au pairs with Norwegian families. In 2000 there were 277 au pairs in Norway. Four years later the number was 1021 (Hovdan 2005). In the new millennium the number of Au Pair Agencies has sky rocketed in nearly all European countries. According to the agencies the supply is in fact higher than the demand (Griffith and Legg 2001).

On the surface hiring a live-in care worker could be a good solution to a family's problem. But from the worker's point of view the reality of the work situation is more likely to be dominated by long hours and low pay. And ultimately, live-in care arrangements do not challenge established gender cultures in families. It is the women in the families who pay and interact most with the au pairs. Aside from the gender inequality these solutions support, analyses of host mothers of au pair girls indicate that there exists an ethnic ranking list based on cultural stereotypes as well. Hovdan (2005) finds that Scandinavian girls are considered to be lazy and immature, while Baltic girls are understood to be more willing to work hard and accept low pay. Usually au pairs earn about 2500–3000 Norwegian Kroner per month (350–450 US dollars).

While au pairs are legal (temporary) immigrants who are allowed to stay in Norway for a maximum of two years, rumours abound about the increase in illegal immigrants from ex- Soviet states like the Baltic countries and from Ukraine and Russia. These immigrant women clean houses illegally in Norway on tourist visas. In their home countries they often have sisters or mothers taking care of their own children. When they return after three months, their sisters or other younger female family members sometimes take over and clean the same houses for the same customers.

It is not only just private families who are coming up with private solutions to narrow the gap between the supply and demand for housekeeping services. Employers are increasingly offering their employees household services as fringe benefits. These involve, for example, flexible work schedules for parents of small children and paid help with cleaning, ironing, folding clothes etc. Female professionals (not male) may get help to manage the work–family balance, and even if the intention is to improve the women's quality of life in general, the gender ideology clearly does not promote a change in established power and gender cultures. Since there is also a shortage of flexible public care services for the elderly, commercial firms have begun selling what they define as 'surrogate child services', such as assistance to go to the dentist or a doctor. One firm, for instance, is called 'Human Care Assistance'. According to the owner, the market for services like this is growing fast and the services are based on 'security, care, professional health services and practical help' (Isaksen 2001). Another firm, an insurance company called Gjensidige NOR offers a service called 'Help 24' which includes help with housework, gardening, cleaning, preparing meals and changing car tyres. Through membership of the Academic Researchers Trade Union one can get a discount when buying (handyman) services ranging from wallpapering, to building a patio or plumbing.

Self-realization as a cultural 'must'

Few young Norwegian women today envisage their lives including long periods at home. Most of them see themselves combining children and family life with stable full-time careers. Care work at home has always carried low status, but now the status of public paid care work is falling as well. In a recently published book called *Matricide* (Bakken 2001) the author claims that one of the reasons that so few people want to become nurses is that it is not perceived to be particularly attractive to be identified with the 'caring mother figure'. The emergence of this shift in the culture of care at a time when welfare states need an increase in the production of healthcare professionals may have dramatic consequences. In a consumer oriented culture the norms of self-realization have become 'a must', and being other-oriented and caring seems to be normatively judged as a loser project. However, one must be aware of the fact that this is only one of many contradictory and multifarious signals about the value of care work. The head of the Norwegian Nurses Association claims that nurses do actually want to work as nurses. The reason for the flight from the profession is that younger people find other jobs because of nurses' poor wages, disgraceful working conditions and extra shifts that are tiring them out. It is likely that nurses would return to the profession if wages and working conditions were better.

Another relevant aspect affecting the decline in paid care work is that childcare services are too expensive, particularly if one compares the prices to the wages for care work where so many young mothers find their jobs. Many nurses prefer to stay home because when childcare and transportation costs are included in the family budget, they are left with a pittance.

New market regulations and recently established commercial agencies that employ healthcare staff and rent them out to hospitals or other medical institutions have become a way for individual nurses to increase their earnings. Since 2001 local agencies have been organized for temporary healthcare workers, and if one is hired on temporary basis, one can earn up to $10,000 US dollars more a year than through long-term employment. But then a lot of benefits associated with long-term employment are lost. It may be an attractive solution in the short run, but in the long run the loss of crucial benefits might become more problematic.

Normative changes

Changed perceptions of care work are taking place in both the public and the family-based cultures of care. This takes place not only because of local social changes, but also because it is a part of a larger picture dominated by processes of increased individualization, greater market orientation and globalization of the economy. Care work is linked to the idea of covering other people's needs for help, recognition, and social and emotional support. The work should be done in a way that does not humiliate the receiving person. The work ethic in carework is based on values like other-orientation and support of individual independence. In the decades after the Second World War when the modern welfare state was constructed in Norway, professional care workers were seen as 'modern' according to the ideas of femininity that dominated that particular historical period. Today women see participation in the labour market as something to be taken for granted and they want to have professional careers, live a meaningful life, and realize their personal potentialities. New generations want to base their life on life-long learning and stimulating challenges. Female university students in contemporary Norway study subjects like law, the arts, medicine, popular cultures and social sciences. Social work and other care related fields are not 'hot'.

The normative foundation of care work can go hand in hand with a 'meaningful life' if one finds contributing to helping people rewarding and interesting. But if a person is looking for what a meaningful life is to themselves then they are looking at an inverse care motive. 'The careful mother' or 'Mother Earth type' are figures that young professional women today seem old-fashioned ways of constructing one's womanhood (Bakken 2001). It may be an image that is increasingly attached to 'the other (unskilled) women' or to 'immigrant women'.

In contrast to the Norwegian perceived inferiority of the culture of care as a life's work is the care culture associated with immigrants. The need to sacrifice one's own life projects for the benefit of the family is a response third world women formulate when asked why they leave their families to find work as maids and nannies and take care of other women's families in rich western countries (Parrenas 2001, 2003). This culture of sacrifice is closely related to extended poverty and unemployment problems. Many of the women finding care work abroad are themselves educated and trained as professional women, but global neoliberal politics and structural changes force them to look for better paid jobs abroad.

Masculinity and care work

The lack of male participation in care work, the increase in full-time working grandmothers, and a more cost effective welfare state are the cause of local care crisis problems that fuel the search for global solutions to local problems. But why do men not participate more in the cultures of care? A survey among unemployed young men in several European countries found that the majority of them preferred continued poverty and unemployment to a job in the care sector (*The Economist* 1996). This was particularly true when it was related to public care for the elderly.

Today family care in different forms plays a major role in providing care for the oldest people. Not only in Norway, but in most countries there is a lack of male participants in family-based elder care (Stark and Regner 2001). Studies show that for men who have chosen care jobs, such as nursing, not many stay for long in ground level work. They frequently end up in specialized medical units such as intensive care and surgery, that is, in departments which carry high status because they use advanced technological equipment and which are in harmony with masculine ideals (Vigdal 1995, Dahle and Isaksen 2003).

Men working in female professions are often regarded as 'weak' and unsuited to 'real work'. Researchers who evaluated a project aimed at getting boys to make untraditional choices concluded that cultural stereotypes and prejudices were the greatest hindrance to attempts to get more boys to make untraditional choices (Buland and Havn 2001). Male nurses sometimes face ridicule from other men who regard care work as 'washing bums and carrying bedpans'. It was not only other men who had problems with seeing men carrying bedpans: patients who needed help with their elimination functions openly asked for female nurses because they think dealing with bedpans is not appropriate work for men (Kjaergård 2004). Some male nurses found intimate care problematic because of its association with homosexuality and because patients themselves prefer female nurses to perform physically intimate work (Vigdal 1995).

An early Norwegian study on men in nursing reported that many men were afraid of being associated with 'low caste' symbols if they performed care for bedridden patients (Eitunggjerde 1988). But recent studies indicate that it is a common stigma among male and female nurses who work 'on the floor' in hospitals, and who are taking care of basic body functions (Boge 2001). It must, however, be said that this gender equality between male and female nurses is related to the fact that female nurses increasingly prefer to work in 'male' areas in medical cultures because of the higher social status that comes with modern surgery and advanced use of new technology (ibid.). They leave the lower status spaces open to newly qualified young nurses and/or unskilled persons (Dahle and Isaksen 2002).

Male immigrant nurses who come from Eastern European countries to work in Norwegian health services have the same career pattern. As soon as they master the language they find administrative jobs in high status units in urban university hospitals. Female nurses from former communist regimes seem to find jobs in the lower area of the local status ladders (Savides 2005).

Social and ethnic stratification in local cultures of care

The individualization and globalization of the cultures of care create several scenarios for the future of the welfare state. Sharing the burdens of housework may be more possible for upper-middle-class couples since they can more often afford to hire a maid or an au pair. The hired hands take care of the most boring and tiresome duties and leave the pleasant work and easy tasks to family members. This initiates new social stratifications and is likely to give rise to a cultural and political backlash to the political struggle to share housework more equally between mothers and fathers in all parts of society. From studies of other care services for children and other dependent family members we know that mothers, wives and daughters are the ones who use their income to pay for hired services (Isaksen 1996). But outsourcing of work that might give rise to domestic gendered conflicts may also imply some negative consequences for the children involved. Having a maid or an au pair living in the family makes it possible for parents to work longer hours during the week and sometimes also permits parents to work during the weekends. In sum, children growing up in these families might spend less time with their parents than children in other families.

In Norway the introduction of a state-subsidized cash allowance to parents with small children created more demand for private care solutions to childcare. Commercial agencies supplying care services to families with dependent children actively refer to this state support in their Internet advertisements promoting their services. The cash allowance also permits parents to hire an au pair, instead of sending their children to a public kindergarten. Altogether the cash allowance makes various private solutions more attractive than earlier, and the tradition of preferring public welfare solutions is undermined.

Several differentiated public and private cultures of care may emerge as a result of changes in the culture of care and changes in public policy. As the picture is now (in 2005) it seems to be possible that the welfare state will take the form of an hour-glass in which fewer people stay in the middle section, with more people become upwardly socially mobile and downward social mobility will be the destiny of the servicing groups. The upwardly mobile will have better earnings and experience a changed culture where private hired hands doing domestic work will be more accepted. Even if modern fathers are more involved in the care of smaller children, most of the other parts of housework (cleaning, shopping, etc.) are still done by the mothers. Of course, the stress that comes with the combination of full-time work, family life and developing an individual career, can be dealt with by a growing number of expensive professional massage clinics. If we can use the metaphor of a 'bath' to describe this, it could be said that the contrasts are between those occu-pying the upper levels, who take 'luxury baths' in well-being centres with access to aroma baths, colour therapy, massage services and all sorts of offers contributing to relaxation and wellbeing after a strenuous working day, and those at the bottom on the other hand – the elderly who are bathed by community nurses and care workers for hygienic reasons every other week. These baths are often combined with what are called 'evacuation days' (or 'emptying days'): days on which the care patrol arrives in the morning and administers an enema, returning later to 'empty the user' after lifting him/her on to a commode. Then the elderly person is wheeled or carried to the shower and washed in a rather industrial manner. Care-workers who wash the elderly often wear knee length plastic stockings and dispos-able gloves. What little bodily contact the elderly experience is the feeling of warmth from a hand protected by plastic.

In Norway, as in other countries, care work for home bound elderly people increasingly becomes entry level jobs for immigrants. The cultural and political legitimation for this development is the stereotypical attitude that people from poorer countries have more respect for the elderly than ethnic Norwegians usually have. That is why they are more suited to the work. Contemporary changes in the cultures of care subordinate values associated with old-fashioned motherliness and attach such images to a culture of sacrifice that is attributed to immigrant women. Cultures of individual self-realization among younger mothers and middle-aged family women stand in opposition to full-time home based care giving.

Nurses from Latvia, Poland and former communist Germany have started to come to Norway and fill jobs in areas domestic nurses avoid. In rural areas and in local hospitals in smaller cities nursing homes wholeheartedly welcome profes-sional immigrant women. People over 85 years old and with extended loss of control over basic bodily functions dominate patient groups in public nursing homes. Lack of professional staff, low budgets and mental and physical burn-out among the employed healthcare workers give this sector a bad reputation among local health workers. But for professionals from other countries the wages are good compared to their own local wages, and they are willing to work longer hours for less pay than local staff.

The following is an example of how Norwegian nursing homes are experienced by immigrant nurses.[2] Nadia comes from Latvia. Back home she worked in an institution for children with orthopaedic problems. In Oslo she works in a nursing home for elderly:

> On Friday afternoons all of us come together to have a cup of coffee and share a cake. Last Friday I suddenly realized why my Norwegian still is so limited. Taking a look around the table I saw women from Poland, Ukraine, Bosnia and Africa. Only two ethnic Norwegians work in my unit. Even if I am a trained nurse I have to work as a nurse's aide until I can speak Norwegian more fluently.

> Interviewer: Have you become personally close to any of your patients? (The question goes to the Ukrainian nurse Zofia. She works in a small nursing home in a rural district.)

> No, most of our patients are senile. They do not remember us from one moment to the next. They are totally dependent on around-the-clock care from us. They cannot eat, drink, go to the toilet or do anything without help … .Once the daughter of an old woman that lives here approached me and said that her mother wanted to give me a nice present … .I was very surprised … .when I came home I realized that I was very, very happy …
>
> (Isaksen 2005).

Care work surely has normative rewards in addition to the human burdens it entails, for immigrants as well as for local workers. But the creative, playful and positive rewards are often under-communicated since they are not understood as 'professional' and seen as a result of the use of expert knowledge. Perhaps the lack of understanding of care as a complex work is a part of the increased buying and selling of care services?

Commercialization of care

What kind of cultures of care are immigrant nurses bringing to Norway? And how will these cultures affect and challenge existing cultures? Hiring nurses from other countries is not a simple and unproblematic solution to local care deficits. One aspect is the moral issue related to our helping to empty poor countries of healthcare personnel that they, in fact, need themselves. Another less debated aspect is linked to the lack of solutions both to gender equality within private homes and the public sector and the issue of global labour inequalities and low wages in general.

From a Norwegian point of view the hiring of women from poorer countries can look like a win–win situation. But women coming to Norway might have their own work–family projects to solve. Besides, who is taking care of their children and their elderly family members? What happens to the families left behind? Do Norwegian solutions create new problems for them? Do we develop 'two-mother'families and export 'absent mother families' to less well-off countries? Norwegian families choosing to hire a maid, nanny or an au pair from a poor country to keep the peace at home, contribute to a global gender-based wage inequality gap. It is a solution to care issues that certainly does not challenge existing structures of masculine dominance and traditional gender ideology.

Care as a service is complex since it is related to our most human emotional and physical needs. The buying and selling of care work in the international market does not treat care as different from other services exchanged in the marketplace. But the importing of care workers is related to new ways of meeting local people's needs. This requires more than technical and professional competence alone. Public and private care work is related to values and norms associated with dignity, shame, pain and suffering. The work is not only gender specific; it is also culture specific. In Denmark for instance, the appointment of African male nurses in the community healthcare services gave rise to a heated debate on whether it was right to expect an 85-year-old women to be washed and personally attended to by African men (Sjørup 2001).

Conclusion: Transnational care workers and the future of the welfare state

Like other western countries, Norway has experienced a change in the demographic structure of the population. Healthcare advantages and declining mortality foster a vertical expansion of more and more families into three, four and even five generations. Although needs for care have grown, the supply of it has declined: as the proportion of dependent citizens increases, the ranks of their potential carers dwindle. The result is a widespread deficit of care that social institutions such as the family and the welfare state adjust to in different ways. For families with dependent children new public policy reforms have made it possible for fathers of newly born babies to stay at home and share the care. This is called 'the father's quota' programme and has proved to be a successful reform. Most fathers today spend some time at home to take care of their babies. Still, when it comes to childcare for children older than three years, the lack of public spaces is a problem. The traditional gender pattern of childcare is difficult to change. However, official public policy has succeeded in triggering the start of an important change even if the speed of it still is very slow. When it comes to the care of elderly people, the picture is more traditional and elder care as well in families as in public services are heavily female dominated.

It seems that at least four different approaches are emerging to deal with care solutions. Each has implications for gender relations and social stratification.

One is to increase the importation of transnational care workers from other and poorer nations. However this solution creates problems aside from the problem of pilfering care work from these countries. It is likely to contribute to maintenance of traditional gender divisions of labour both in the public and private sectors, and it seems to stratify and lower the status of care work (Hovdan 2005, Savides 2005). Two-career families with small children, for example, when employing an au pair to share the care with them, may experience this solution as a convenient one. But it does not demand more involvement in housework from the men and does not challenge established gender ideologies.

The second approach is to increase the buying of commercial services from the market. This can help relatively well-paid women solve domestic intragenerational care problems. And women in the labour force may also be helped through the services of commercial cleaning services that are provided by their employers. Since it is these services that are increasingly employing immigrant men and proportionately fewer women, it is possible, then, for paid domestic cleaning to become more male dominated. This is something that certainly has the potential to change gender roles. But new stratifications among women may emerge since more working-class women than middle-class women reduce their labour market involvement to take care of ageing parents (Stark and Regner 2001).

The export of senior citizens to Mediterranean areas where care services can be bought at better prices does not solve the problems Norway as a nation state has with it's 'absent sons' culture in informal elder care. People on the lower social strata have less ability to pay for care assistance or reduce labour market participation to better take care of old relatives. They have to rely on help from public welfare-state services. On the other hand, recent research indicates that there are changes occurring that affect some cultures of masculinity. Sons and men with more than average education and income do participate more in informal elder care than other men.

A third approach to the problems of care may be based on a more extended use of technological solutions in the care sector. More video cameras installed in private homes and more technological centralization of public services might be related to new efforts to rationalize public healthcare. It is an approach that can give more security to older people. But from a human point of view it must be said that the warmth from a helping hand may be better than technological surveillance.

A fourth approach is also possible. As an oil-rich nation Norway has the ability to experiment with different welfare state models. It might be possible to introduce a six-hour working day for all. This could make it possible for everyone, men and women, fathers as well as mothers, to take better care of each other, their children and other dependent family members and participate more in the civil sector of society where all can benefit from the work done. Different forms of wages for informal care and housework and citizen's basic income programmes could be organized to solve care deficit problems in a collective way and as such challenge the tendency to privatize, commercialize and individualize all kinds of health and care services.

Norway can benefit from the fact that many of our immigrant healthcare workers come from ex-communist countries and have been socialized to think in terms of collective solutions to citizens' welfare problems. Immigrants from ex-communist countries share our ideals of a fairer share of domestic work between men and women. New manifestations of middle-class female gender roles, like the expanded use of commercial housekeeping services and employment of domestic workers, may, on the surface, bring changed social and cultural configurations of gender relations and ideologies. These changes can be a reflection of a lack of flexibility in public arrangements and a scarcity in the provision of public care services.

Fortunately, underlying most public policy is the Scandinavian culture that is very strong and in this culture public care is widely seen as better than commercial care. Even if social democratic values are challenged by conservative neoliberal policies and an increased supply of cheap labour has emerged as a result of changes in the European Union, Norway's status as a wealthy semi-peripheral country outside the European Union makes it possible to choose alternative political and ecological solutions. This would allow the expansion of ideas to include policies to promote a family friendly and well functioning welfare state which also includes immigrants and a new multicultural reality.

Notes

1 The informal sector refers to care work that is done primarily by unpaid family members with some support from local state-subsidized home care services.
2 The following are from interviews taken for a study of global nursing in Norway (Isaksen, 2005).

References

Bakken, Runar (2001) *Modermordet (Matricide)*, Oslo, Norway: Universitetsforlaget.
Boge, Jeanne (2001) 'Menn og sjukepleie' ('Men in Nursing'), *Tidsskrift for kvinneforskning (Journal for Women's Research)*, 4, Kilden, Oslo, Norway: 33–43.
Buland, Trond and Havn, Vidar (2001) 'Beviste utdanningsvalg' ('How to Choose Education'), SINTEF, Norway: University of Trondheim.
Dagbladet (Daily News) (2000) Available online, HTTP://online edition, 1 October 2000.
Dahle, Rannveig and Isaksen, Lise Widding (2002) 'Sjukvård som maskulinitetsprosjekt' ('Nursing as a Masculine Project'), *Kvinnovetenskapelig tidsskrift (Journal for Research on Women)*, University of Gothenburg, Sweden: 71–5.
The Economist, 'Youth Unemployment in Europe', The Economist Group, USA, 28 September–4 October 1996: 12–14.
Eitunggjerde, Åge (1988) 'Menn i sjukepleien – "brødre berre i skinnet"' ('Men in Nursing – "Brothers in disguise"?'), *Nursing*, 19: 20–5.
Griffith, Susan and Legg, Sharon (2001) *The Au Pair's and Nanny's Guide to Working Abroad*, London: Oxford Press.
Hillestad, Adelheid Hummelvold (2000) *'Tiden går så altfor fort' En komparativ studie av to sykehjem – Oslo og Spania ('Time is passing too quickly': A Comparative Study of Nursing Homes in Oslo and Spain)*, Department of Social Anthropology, University of Oslo, Norway.
Hovdan, Marianne (2005) Au Pair in Norway, Master thesis, Department of Sociology, University of Bergen, Norway.
Isaksen, Lise Widding (1984) Omsorg i grenseland (Care in the Social Space between Public and Private) Master thesis, Department for Social Sciences, University of Tomsoe, Norway.

—— (1996) Den tabubelagte kroppen (The Body Tabooed), Ph.D. thesis, Department of Sociology, University of Bergen, Norway.

—— (2001) 'Kommer din praktikant også fra Lithauen?', *Kvinneforskning* (*Journal for Women's Research*), 2, Kilden, Oslo: 63–71.

—— (2005) 'Globalization' in M. Elmgren and I. Dragset (eds) *The Welfare Show*, Germany: Walter Konig Publication, p. G1.

Kjaergård, Peter (2004) 'Portraits of Male Scientists in Danish Media', BIOZOOM, 2, Denmark: Department of History of Ideas, University of Århus.

Parrenas, Rachel Salzar (2001) *The Global Servant: Migrant Filipina Domestic Workers in Rome and Los Angeles*, Palo Alto, CA, US: Stanford University Press.

—— (2003) 'The Care Crisis in the Philippines: Children and Transnational Families in the New Global Economy', in Barbara Ehrenreich and Arlie Russell Hochschild (eds) *Global Women: Nannies, Maids and Sex Workers in the New Economy*, New York: Henry Holt and Company, Metropolitan Books, pp. 39–54.

Savides, S.J. (2005) Omsorg fra Øst til Helse i Vest (Care from East to Healthcare in West), Master thesis, Department of Sociology, University of Bergen, Norway.

Sjørup, Karen (2001) 'Nye dimensjoner i omsorgen', *Sygeplejen* (*Nursing*), 9: 42–45.

Spaniaposten (2003) 'Vennskapavtale mellom Bærum og Altea' ('Cultural and Medical Exchange between Bærum and Altea'), *Spaniaposten* (Norwegian newspaper), 3: 1, 3.

Stark, Agneta (2005) 'Warm Hands in Cold Age – On the New World Order of Care', *Feminist Economics*, 11, 2: 7–36.

Stark, Agneta and Regner, Åsa (2001) *'I vems hender?' Om arbete, genus, åldrande och omsorg i tre EU land* (*'Whose Hands?' Work, Gender, Ageing and Care in Three EU Countries*), Tema Genus, Rapport 1, Sweden: Linköpings Universitet.

Vabø, Mia (2003) 'Forbrukermakt i omsorgtjenesten – til hjelp for de svakeste?' in L. W. Isaksen, *Omsorgens pris. Kjønn, makt og marked i velferdsstaten* (*The Price of Care. Gender, Power and Markets in the Welfare State*), Gyldendal: Oslo, Norway, pp. 102–27.

Vigdal, Roar (1995) Om menn i sykepleien (Men in Nursing), Master thesis, Department of Sociology, University of Bergen, Norway.

4 Northward-bound Mexican labour migration with a gender perspective

Elaine Levine[1]

Saskia Sassen maintains that there is a systemic relationship between globalization and 'the incorporation of Third World women into wage employment on a scale that can be seen as representing a new phase in the history of women' (Sassen 1998: 111). Immigration is one of the prime mechanisms for this incorporation, as evidenced by the Mexican case. Many Mexican women participate in paid labour for the first time upon migrating to the United States (hereafter the US), where they accept wages and working conditions that are usually unacceptable to other sectors of the US labour force.

Female migration from Mexico to the US is not a new phenomenon. Of the approximately 891,000 Mexicans that Manuel Gamio estimated were residing in the US at the end of 1926, 335,000 or 37.6 per cent were women (Gamio 1969: 2). In the 1920 US census out of a total of 486,400 Mexicans residing in the US, 209,900 were women – an even higher percentage (43 per cent) than in 1926. However, the deportations of Mexicans during the years of the Great Depression curtailed the migratory flows until the Second World War when the Bracero programme was implemented to bring in single males temporarily for work in agriculture and the railroads. In the early postwar decades it was generally assumed that most women migrants to the US went to join husbands who had found steady work north of the border. The Immigration Reform and Control Act (IRCA) of 1986 subsequently allowed many Mexican women and children to enter the US under family reunification provisions. The Mexican Consejo Nacional de Población CONAPO (National Population Council) now maintains that women may have been migrating to the US primarily for work motives for the past 50 years or so (Avila, Fuentes and Tuiran: 151).

Nevertheless, both male and female migrations to the US have increased significantly over the last three decades. The once circulatory patterns, of going and coming between the US and Mexico on a regular basis, have given way to more permanent settlement for many. The Current Population Survey for 2004 estimates that the 10.6 million Mexican-born people residing in the US represents more than a 13-fold increase over the 1970 census figure (Passel 2005: 37). Immigration has increased from 122,000 migrants per year in the 1970s to 450,000 per year since 2000. The female component has consistently been between 41 and 47 per cent of these averages by decade and women are currently estimated to be approximately 45 per cent of the total Mexican-born population in the US (US Census Bureau 2004). These women are among the lowest paid and most highly exploited workers in the US labour force.

Economic changes in both countries that are attributable to restructuring related to globalization are mainly responsible for the large increases in migration. Indiscriminate trade liberalization and the privatization of most state enterprises, along with other neoliberal economic policies implemented in Mexico from the early 1980s onwards, eroded the basis of subsistence agriculture without significantly increasing opportunities for industrial employment. At the same time, industrial restructuring in the US created a large number of low skilled, low paying jobs that quickly became labour market niches for newly arrived unskilled immigrants form Mexico. These economic pressures in Mexico have increased the flow of undocumented migration, which continues in the post-IRCA period at unprecedented levels. According to Pew Hispanic Center calculations, approximately half of all Mexicans in the US and from 80 to 85 per cent of the more recently arrived are unauthorized (Passel 2005: 36). This situation enhances the vulnerability of almost all Mexican workers in the US.

One of the main arguments invoked, on both sides of the (US–Mexico) border, when promoting NAFTA was that it would help stem Mexican migration to the United States. This, along with other false expectations that were generated to sell the idea of a trilateral trade agreement, is belied by the realities of the past 12 years. Contrary to those a priori expectations, deteriorating employment conditions in Mexico have coincided with a continuing demand for cheap Latino labour in the US, thus bolstering the migratory process. On the Mexican side of the border there seemed to be some sort of subliminal dissemination of the idea – even though there were no official statements or declarations to that effect – that Mexico would somehow benefit from a trade agreement with its more prosperous partners in the same way that Spain, Greece and Portugal have benefited from membership in the European Union.

On the US side, however, it was constantly and explicitly reiterated that NAFTA was conceived as a trade liberalizing agreement and nothing more. Nevertheless the idea that eliminating existing barriers would increase trade among all three partners, and thus increase the demand for each others' exports, which would in turn create new export related jobs in each country, was actively espoused by promoters of the agreement. While some sectors expressed concerns about the possibilities of job losses, such preoccupations were played down in official rhetoric and discourse. Indeed, a major selling point in the US was not only that new jobs would result but also that there would no longer be so many Mexican immigrants competing for jobs north of the border. An often repeated slogan was that Mexico would be able to export 'goods instead of people'.

This chapter focuses on what I consider to be a certain degree of *de facto* labour market integration, further accentuated by NAFTA, under conditions that are mostly disadvantageous for Mexican migrant workers. I briefly analyze labour market conditions in Mexico – characterized by declining real wages, insufficient job creation to absorb the increasing labour supply, and marked expansion of the informal labour market – to explain why low wage jobs in the US are so attractive for both male and female Mexican migrants. I then proceed to examine, by gender, the labour market outcomes for Mexican workers in the US, in terms of occupations and earnings. I will analyze the socioeconomic status of Mexican-origin Latinos over the past decade or more to underline the increasing earnings differentials that emerge between Latinos and others, and those that persist between Latino men and women. Given the increasing segmentation and stratification of the US labour market it is likely that upward mobility will prove to be more difficult for most recently arriving Mexican immigrants and their children than it was for previous cohorts of Mexicans and other groups of immigrants throughout most of the twentieth century. This chapter also shows that Mexican women migrants who join the US labour force experience the double negative impact of both gender and ethnic discrimination.

Changing conditions in Mexico

The economic context

Most of Mexico's current economic ills cannot be attributed solely to NAFTA, or to globalization, in and of itself. The country has experienced a long history of pervasive corruption at all levels and self serving economic policies implemented by the dominant élites. However, the neoliberal economic policies initiated from the early 1980s onwards have exacerbated existing inequalities. Since Mexico's economic woes began to intensify in the early 1970s, successive governments have been trying to find easy solutions to problems that require more radical changes, which would affect vested interests and alter the status quo in many respects. It was hoped that NAFTA would help Mexico find new trading partners and interested investors from other regions through the country's enhanced relationship with the US market. Instead it seems to have merely intensified Mexico's connections with and growing subordination to the US economy.

Mexico's highly protective import substitution model, which provided 30 years of generally favourable macroeconomic performance, began to falter in the 1970s. President Lopez Portillo's hopes that oil resources would provide a quick fix were dashed by mismanagement, corruption and adverse external conditions. The oil boom in the second half of the 1970s postponed the impending crisis for a few years but rapidly led the country into unsustainable indebtedness. When oil prices fell to more normal levels at the beginning of the 1980s, reducing the flows of foreign exchange, Mexico was on the verge of defaulting on its international loans. Both renegotiated payment schedules and economic adjustment programmes initiated an abrupt change of course in economic policy. The country abandoned its import substitution/interventionist state model in favour of market liberalization and privatization policies aimed at achieving export oriented industrialization. This economic approach has proven, thus far, to be an elusive mirage.

For Mexico, as was the case for many other Latin American countries, the 1980s proved to be a lost decade in terms of economic growth and the wellbeing of most of the country's inhabitants. Between 1980 and 1988 GDP growth averaged only 1.1 per cent per year (Salas 2003: 39) which means that GDP per capita declined significantly. The subsequent improvement registered during the Salinas administration rested on very weak foundations – including volatile flows of foreign capital attracted by high interest rates and manipulation of the exchange rate – as was abruptly evidenced by the peso crisis at the end of 1994. Since his own credibility was at stake along with Mexico's and NAFTA's, President Clinton responded immediately and used discretionary funds to help bail out the newly affiliated, and now discredited, trading partner.

After a severe drop in GDP growth in 1995 (–6.2 per cent), the Mexican economy grew at an average rate of just under 5.5 per cent for the next five years. In 2001 real GDP was stagnant (registering a 0.0 per cent growth rate) and since then growth has edged upward from 0.7 per cent to 3.8 per cent in 2002 (Presidencia de la Republica 2004: 177). However, only the top 10 per cent of all households saw any rise in their share of national income, as a result of those favourable GDP growth rates, while the remaining 90 per cent either suffered a loss of income share or experienced no change (Polaski 2004: 17). Furthermore, the improvement registered in the second half of the 1990s and the subsequent slump as of 2001 seem to indicate that Mexico's macroeconomic performance now depends increasingly on the US business cycle. The recession in the US immediately showed up as a decline in Mexico's merchandise exports and imports, foreign investment levels, employment levels, and GDP growth rates.

One of the arguments invoked against NAFTA, especially during the debates before signing the deal, was that Mexico would become even more dependent on trade with its number one trading partner. The American supporters of NAFTA, however, had insisted that inclusion in a North American trading block would make Mexico a more desirable trading partner for countries outside of the region as well. Mexico now imports more merchandise from Asia than before (approximately 18 per cent of total imports) while the US currently purchases almost 90 per cent of Mexico's exports. Exports have grown from 16 per cent of GDP in 1990 to 28 per cent in 2004 and imports have increased from 16 per cent to 29 per cent. Thus while foreign trade has increased considerably in the post-NAFTA years, the Mexican economy is now all the more vulnerable to macroeconomic fluctuations in the US.

Rather than moving towards a more diversified and better integrated industrial sector with greater forward and backward linkages, Mexican industry has become even less integrated domestically and more dependent on imported inputs and technology. The maquiladora sector, which has grown significantly, typically imports 97 per cent of the value of its final output and only 3 per cent of the final value of these goods, which are subsequently exported, is produced in Mexico. A most disturbing fact is that the non-maquiladora export sector is increasingly behaving in a similar fashion. As Sandra Polaski points out,

> The intra-firm production carried out by multinational firms operating in Mexico in sectors such as the auto and electronics industries depends heavily

on imported inputs. It seems probable that Mexican manufacturers that previ-ously supplied inputs to large manufacturing firms have lost a significant share of input production to foreign suppliers...

(Polaski 2004: 7–8).

Employment changes

Maquiladora output and employment increased significantly between 1994 and 2001 and has fallen off somewhat since then. Meanwhile employment in non-maquiladora manufacturing was just beginning to recuperate from the peso crisis decline in the mid-1990s, when the 2001 recession provoked new job losses. Thus non-maquiladora manufacturing employment was lower in 2004 than in 1994, with a net loss of about 160,000 jobs. In spite of the fact that over 200,000 maquiladora jobs were lost between 2001 and 2003, current employment is considerably higher, by approximately 529,000, than it was in 1994. Because of the substantial increase in maquiladora employment which now represents close to half of total manufacturing employment (maquiladora plus non-maquiladora manufacturing), as compared to less than 30 per cent before NAFTA, the sector as a whole showed a net gain in employment over the past decade, of approximately 387,000 jobs between 1994 and 2004 (Romero and Puyana 2004: 97–102, Polaski 2004: 4–11).

However this most modest job growth in manufacturing was not nearly enough to offset the decline that took place, over the same period, in agricultural and agri-culture related employment. According to Romero and Puyana the net job loss in agriculture was approximately 0.7 million – from 6.9 million prior to NAFTA to 6.2 million in 2001 (2004: 97). Polaski maintains that 'agricultural employment in Mexico actually increased somewhat in the late 1980s and early 1990s, employing 8.1 million Mexicans at the end of 1993 just before NAFTA came into force. Employment in the sector then began a downward trend, with 6.8 million employed at the end of 2002, a loss of 1.3 million jobs' (Polaski 2004: 9). Even given their more modest estimations of job losses, Romero and Puyana conclude that growth in the production of agricultural export crops was by no means sufficient to absorb those displaced from non-export agriculture who were thus forced to seek employment elsewhere. Limited growth in manufacturing employment indicates that not many of people were able to find jobs there either. Most were eventually employed in low-paying service and construction jobs offering no legal benefits and protections or worked in the informal economy, and the rest migrated to the US (2004: 98–100).

Calculations based on data from the Cuarto Informe de Gobierno (President's Fourth Annual Report) (Presidencia de la Republica 2004) show that the economi-cally active population grew from 33.7 million in 1993 to 43.4 million in 2004, an increase of 9.7 million. At the same time only 2.7 million new jobs were created in the formal economy. Thus the ranks of the unemployed, underemployed or infor-mally employed have grown by at least 7.0 million since NAFTA began. If we consider the fact that a significant number of those in the working age population (all persons aged 12 and older) counted as economically inactive (which rose by 7.4 million over the same period) would be looking for a job if they had expectations of finding one, the employment deficit accumulated over just the past ten years is even larger, similar to the million a year deficit that Polaski mentions (Polaski 2004: 3, Presidencia de la Republica 2004).[2]

The official 'open unemployment' rate of 3.7 per cent for 2004, which is about 1.6 million persons, grossly understates Mexico's job deficit in a blatant attempt to cover up the fact that half or more of those who are counted as employed actually work in the informal economy.[3] According to Polaski, informal employment rose throughout most of the 1990s approaching 50 per cent of the total in 1995 and 1996 'following the peso crisis and the subsequent economic contraction. After economic growth resumed in the late 1990s the informal sector shrank somewhat, but still accounts for about 46 per cent of Mexican jobs' (2004: 12). An International Labour Organization (ILO) report released in 2004 maintains that informal sector employment in Mexico has increased from 55 to 62 per cent of total employment over the past few years (Martinez 2004: 3). In recent declarations President Fox[4] celebrated the fact that jobs registered by the IMSS in February 2005 reached a historical high for that time of the year of 12.6 million (Fernandez-Vega 2005: 28). However, that figure represents only 29 per cent of Mexico's economically active population (EAP).

Women currently make up approximately 35 per cent of the Mexican labour force. In rural and semi-rural areas throughout Mexico, as well as among the urban poor and lower income groups, women still spend most of their waking hours engaged in unpaid labour to satisfy their families' various needs, generally without the aid of modern labour saving domestic appliances and gadgets. In rural areas this usually involves the additional tasks of transporting water to the dwelling, caring for any livestock that the family may own and gathering wood for cooking fuel (which in some contexts may be more of a male task). Nevertheless the overall labour force participation rate for women rose from 31.5 per cent in 1991 to 37.5 per cent in 2004, while at the same time the male participation rate declined slightly, from 77.7 per cent to 75.5 per cent (INEGI). Furthermore women who do participate in the labour force are subject to wage discrimination and occupational segregation, which is often self-imposed because of cultural norms.[5] Also women are frequently employed in extremely small family businesses and receive no wages. While it is difficult to determine statistically, it is safe to assume that women's participation in the informal economy is significant.

Aside from the problems of underemployment and disguised unemployment the Mexican labour force experiences the additional hardship of declining real wages, which has been eroding individual and family incomes for over 20 years. Price control policies were implemented after the 1982 crisis and their main objective has been to keep wages down. According to official data the nominal minimum wage increased 150.5 per cent between 1982 and 2002 while at the same time prices rose 618 per cent. As a result purchasing power declined by 75 per cent (Ortiz Rivera 2003: 4–5). The federally mandated minimum wage in the US is currently more or less 10 times greater than Mexico's minimum wage of $46.80

Table 4.1 Wages in Mexico 2004 (for some selected types of workers)

	Average daily wage (in pesos)	Percentage of Mexican minimum wage
Workers covered by Mexican Social Security System	177.51	380%
Average contractual wage	86.91	190%
Retail sales employees	179.95	380%
Wholesale sales employees	246.25	530%
Construction workers	149.76	320%
Maquiladora manufacturing	243.42	520%
non-maquiladora manufacturing	364.92	780%
US federal minimum wage	432.60 to 453.20	920% to 970%

Source: Author's calculations based on data from the Cuarto Informe de Gobierno 2004, Anexo Estadístico p. 223–4

pesos per day – which fluctuates between approximately $4.06 dollars and $4.25 dollars per day depending on the exchange rate. As Table 4.1 and Figure 4.1 indicate, the overwhelming majority (86.7 per cent) of the population earns up to only five times the Mexican minimum wage. This amounts to approximately half of the US minimum wage or $20.60 per day.[6] Official data, for various sectors and sub-sectors of the Mexican economy in 2004, also indicates that even the most highly paid wage earners, those employed in non-maquiladora manufacturing, earn significantly less than the US federal minimum wage (see Table 4.1).

Given the highly unfavourable conditions that prevail in the Mexican labour market – lack of employment opportunities, growing underemployment and disguised unemployment, growth of the informal economy, declining real wages

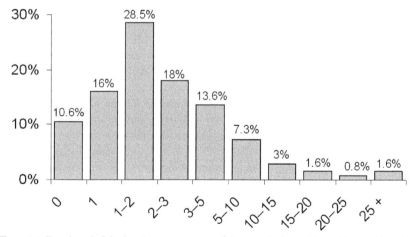

Figure 4.1 Earnings in Mexico, by percentages of the population with multiples of Mexican minimum wage

Source: INEGI cited by journalist Alicia Ortiz Rivera, *El Independiente*, August 15, 2003.

and incomes for most workers, and greater inequality of incomes with persistently high rates of poverty and extreme poverty – migration to the US appears to be a reasonable option for many of the country's unemployed, underemployed, and underpaid workers. Migration to the US rose significantly in the mid-1980s and has continued to grow since then, while at the same time becoming more diverse in terms of the sending regions as well as with respect to destinations.[7] Many factors are involved in this process: among others, the generally adverse economic conditions, changes in agricultural policies and land tenure regulations, the fact that many potential migrants have family members, relatives or acquaintances who reside in the US, and the employment opportunities offered there.

Woo argues that women's decisions to migrate are determined by a rather complex set of interacting factors of an economic and non-economic nature and that other family members are often involved in such decisions (Woo 2001). There is also testimonial evidence that many women migrate to escape from oppressive and often abusive family relationships. In a number of cases women have preceded their husbands in migrating because of the relative ease with which they can find live-in domestic work in the US. Jobs for young women in the maquiladora plants in the border region are another factor, since they make crossing the border, for much better-paying jobs, all the more feasible. For many Mexican women their first paid work has been in the maquiladora plants far from their homes or even further away in the US. Women who do migrate have a much higher labour force participation rate (54 per cent) than those who remain in Mexico (38 per cent).

As general economic and labour market conditions deteriorated in Mexico, migration to the US provided an important escape valve for the excess labour supply. Clearly the Mexican government has no interest in limiting this growing out-migration. Their main concern is how to make sure that those who have gone will continue to send money back to family members remaining in Mexico. The Central Bank (Banco de México) recognized that as of 2003, remittances from workers in the US have become the country's second source of foreign exchange after oil exports. About one out of every ten households receives remittances from the US and these flows were essential in bolstering consumer spending in an otherwise stagnant economy, from 2001 to 2003. Up until fairly recently the Mexican government was generally accused of ignoring the vicissitudes of the country's migrants. Recent administrations have made active attempts to maintain and strengthen migrants' ties to Mexico – by approving dual citizenship, supporting and promoting hometown associations, issuing identification cards to those soliciting them at any Mexican consulate in the US, and considering the possibility of absentee voting in Mexico's next presidential elections. All of these actions help assure the continued flow of remittances, which have become a vital source of income for many families. Nevertheless, in spite of all the increased pressures on the Mexican side, emigration would not have increased nearly as much as it has if migrants were not able to find jobs in the US with relative ease.

Mexican migrants in the United States

Just as remittances from emigrants have become vital for the Mexican economy, immigrant labour is becoming more and more important for the US economy. The US 'experienced the greatest wave of new foreign immigration in its history, with nearly 14 million net new immigrants arriving on its shores between 1990 and 2000' (Sum *et al.* 2002: 2). According to Andrew Sum and his co-authors, this record new wave of immigrants played a crucial role in filling the new and old jobs in what had been referred to, before the 2001 recession, as the 'New American Economy'. While many, including George W. Bush and Alan Greenspan, have recognized that immigrant labour played an important role in the unprecedented economic expansion that occurred between 1991 and 2001, others argue that their presence is detrimental to native workers particularly during what has been to some extent a 'jobless recovery' from 2002 through 2004 (Camarota 2004).

In spite of the increasing difficulties Mexican migrants have had to confront since 2001, it seems that they are still finding better employment perspectives north of the border than at home. Since their main motivation for migration is work, it is not surprising that the Mexican-origin population in the US, as a whole, has a higher labour force participation rate (68.9 per cent in 2004) than any other group in the US. The men's rate (82.2 per cent in 2004) is significantly higher than all others, although the women's rate is somewhat lower (54.1 per cent) (see Figure 4.2). For the past three decades unemployment rates for Mexican-origin Latinos, and in fact for Latinos in general, have been consistently higher than the rates for whites and lower than those for African Americans (US Department of Labor 2005: 202–3). Mexican-origin women are currently the only group that has an unemployment rate higher than that of their male counterparts (see Figure 4.3).

Recently arrived unskilled immigrants almost always end up in the least desirable and lowest paying jobs in the US where they, nevertheless, earn considerably

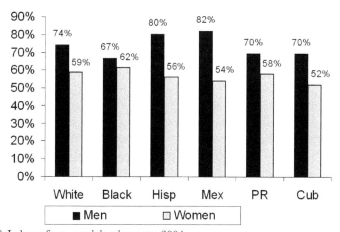

Figure 4.2 Labour force participation rates 2004

Source: U.S. Department of Labor (2005) *Employment and Earnings*, Washington, D. C.: Bureau of Labor Statistics, January, pp. 202–3.

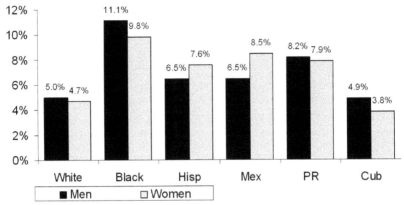

Figure 4.3 Unemployment rates 2004

Source: U.S. Department of Labor (2005) *Employment and Earnings*, Washington, D. C.: Bureau of Labor Statistics, January, pp. 202–3.

more than they could in their countries of origin. This has certainly been the experience of most Mexican migrants given their low educational attainment and limited English proficiency. It is often reported that Mexicans who emigrate have more years of schooling than the national average in Mexico which is approximately seven years. Unfortunately this is much lower than the minimum of at least a high school diploma which is required for almost all types of employment in the US. According to Edward Lazear of the Hoover Institution, the typical non-Mexican immigrant has a high school diploma whereas the typical Mexican immigrant has less than an eighth-grade education, and about two-and-a-half fewer years of schooling than other Hispanic immigrants. He also maintains that 80 per cent of non-Mexican immigrants are fluent in English compared with 62 per cent of non-Mexican Hispanic immigrants and only 49 per cent of Mexican immigrants (Lazear 2004). These same disadvantages seem to persist for subsequent generations in the US and, no doubt have an impact on labour market outcomes for Mexican-origin Latinos.

US Labor Department data for the Mexican-origin labour force as a whole shows that it is more or less evenly distributed among four of the five major occupational category classifications: service occupations 24.4 per cent, sales and office occupations 19.7 per cent, natural resources, construction, and maintenance occupations 21.0 per cent and production, transportation and material moving occupations 20.7 per cent.[8] Participation in management, professional and related occupations (14.1 per cent) is considerably lower than for any other racial or ethnic group (see Table 4.2). Only 3.2 per cent of the Mexican-origin labour force is employed in farming, fishing and forestry occupations but that far exceeds any other group's participation in those activities. Significant numbers of Mexican-origin workers are employed in production and construction occupations (11.7 and 13.9 per cent, respectively) where there are some high paying jobs for highly skilled and experienced workers, along with many lower paying jobs for the less skilled. Eleven percent is employed in

Table 4.2 Occupational distribution 2004

Occupations	Total %	White %	Black %	Mexican %	P-Rican %	Cuban %
Management, professional, and related occupations	**34.9**	**35.6**	**26.5**	**14.1**	**23.8**	**30.1**
Management, business, and financial operations	**14.5**	**15.3**	**9.4**	**6.0**	**8.8**	**14.7**
Management	10.5	11.2	5.8	4.3	6.3	11.3
Business and financial operations	4.1	4.1	3.6	1.7	2.5	3.4
Professional and related	**20.3**	**20.3**	**17.0**	**8.2**	**14.9**	**15.4**
Computer and mathematical	2.3	2.1	1.6	0.7	1.6	1.1
Architecture and engineering	2.0	2.0	0.9	0.7	1.1	1.2
Life, physical, and social science	1.0	1.0	0.5	0.3	0.7	0.8
Community and social services	1.6	1.4	2.8	1.0	2.0	1.0
Legal	1.1	1.2	0.7	0.3	0.5	1.5
Education, training, and library	5.7	5.8	5.0	2.7	5.1	3.8
Arts, design, entertainment, sports, and media	1.9	2.0	1.1	1.0	1.1	1.9
Healthcare practitioner and technical	4.8	4.7	4.5	1.5	3.0	4.1
Service	**16.3**	**15.2**	**23.8**	**24.4**	**22.6**	**15.2**
Healthcare support	2.1	1.7	5.1	1.8	3.8	2.2
Protective service	2.0	1.9	3.4	1.6	3.4	2.3
Food preparation and serving related	5.2	5.1	5.6	8.5	5.5	3.3
Building and grounds cleaning and maintenance	3.7	3.6	5.2	9.5	5.5	5.7
Personal care and service	3.2	3.0	4.5	2.9	4.3	1.9
Sales and office	**25.5**	**25.5**	**26.3**	**19.7**	**28.9**	**27.6**
Sales and related	11.5	11.8	9.6	8.7	10.7	11.7
Office and administrative support	14.0	13.7	16.7	11.0	18.2	15.9
Natural resources, construction, and maintenance	**10.5**	**11.2**	**6.8**	**21.0**	**9.6**	**13.6**
Farming, fishing, and forestry	0.7	0.8	0.4	3.2	0.5	0.1
Construction and extraction	6.1	6.6	3.8	13.9	4.5	6.5
Installation, maintenance, and repair	3.6	3.8	2.6	4.0	4.6	6.9
Production, transportation, and material moving	**12.9**	**12.4**	**16.7**	**20.7**	**15.1**	**13.3**
Production	6.8	6.6	7.5	11.7	7.4	6.0
Transportation and material moving	6.1	5.9	9.1	9.1	7.7	7.3

Source: U.S. Department of Labor (2005) *Employment and Earnings*, Washington, D. C.: Bureau of Labor Statistics, January, p. 216–17.

office and administrative support jobs. These tend to be female dominated occupations with moderately low earnings levels. This is also the case for many of the sales-related occupations that employ 8.7 per cent of the Mexican-origin labour force. An additional 8.5 per cent and 9.5 per cent, respectively, work in food preparation and serving occupations and building and grounds cleaning and maintenance occupations. Wages tend to be extremely low in these last two categories (US Department of Labor 2005: 210–17, 250–4).

Another way of analyzing labour market outcomes for Mexican workers is to see how concentrated they are in specific occupational categories and to look at median earnings in categories that have particularly high percentages of Mexicans. The US Labor Department's detailed occupation tables only provide information for the entire Latino population; it is not disaggregated by national origin (US Department of Labor 2004: 209–13, 249–53). However, since Mexican-origin Latinos usually constitute about two-thirds of all Latinos in the US, and Mexicans were 64 per cent of the Latino labour force in 2003, the degree of Latino participation in each occupational category is probably a satisfactory proxy for the degree of Mexican participation in most cases. In all of the cases where the concentration of Latinos was high or very high (that is two or three times higher than the percentage they represent in the total labour force which was 12.6 per cent in 2003) median weekly earnings were significantly lower than the overall median of $620.00 dollars. Among these, only skilled construction workers – three out of the thirty occupations where 25.6 per cent or more of the workers are Latinos – registered median earnings anywhere close to the general median. Latinos showed varying degrees of concentration (in other words they made up 12.6 per cent or more of the labour force employed) in 102 of the US Labor Department's 302 detailed occupational categories. However, median earnings were above the overall median in only 10 of these 102 occupations. On the other hand, out of the remaining 200 occupations where Latinos were under-represented (where they were less than 12.6 per cent of those employed) two-thirds of these showed median earnings above the overall median. Thus even at this highly aggregated national level it is quite clear that Latino workers, both male and female, are extremely concentrated in low wage or otherwise undesirable or dangerous jobs.

Mexican women in the US

Even though women now make up almost half of the US labour force (46.5 per cent in 2004) they still confront high degrees of *de facto* occupational segregation and wage discrimination, in spite of legislation prohibiting such practices. Latina and African American women experience labour market discrimination derived from the combined effects of both gender and race or ethnicity (Brown 1999). Mexican-origin Latinas, who tend to be among the lowest paid workers throughout the US, are further limited by their low levels of educational attainment. In general there are more women employed, both relatively (as a percentage of all women employed) and absolutely (as a percentage of all workers) in what are often referred to as white collar and pink collar occupations, which include professional and related occupations and sales and office occupations respectively, and in service occupations; while blue collar occupations and agricultural-related activities are, on the whole, dominated by men. This trend also holds for Mexican-origin men and women in the labour force.

Among and within each of these broad general categories women, and especially Latina women, tend to be concentrated in the more subordinate and/or lower paying sub-categories. For example, men dominate managerial posts, and most office and administrative support occupations are female dominated. There are more men teaching at the post-secondary level, and more women teaching at all lower levels. There are about twice as many male as female lawyers, whereas most of the paralegals, legal assistants and other legal professionals are women. There are more male than female supervisors of both retail and non-retail sales workers but 76 per cent of all cashiers are women. While most production occupations are male dominated, there are a few areas where the majority of the workers are women, such as electrical and electronics assemblers, packaging and filling machine operators, and textile and garment industry workers. In each of these areas median weekly earnings are below the overall median for production occupations ($526 in 2004), which is in turn much lower than the overall median ($638). Even within the same specific occupational categories women tend to have lower median weekly earnings than men (US Department of Labor 2005: 210–15, 250–4).

There are some female-dominated occupations where the concentration of Latina workers is also relatively high or at least higher than the Latino component of the labour force which was 12.6 per cent in 2003. In all of the 32 specific occupations where both of these conditions hold, median earnings were well below the overall median ($620 in 2003) and in only two cases was it higher than the median for all full-time female workers, which was $552 (see Table 4.3). In those categories where Latina concentration is highest (over 37 per cent which is approximately three times greater than Latinos' representation in the labour force as a whole) median weekly earnings are extremely low. This situation holds for the following occupations: pressers, textile, garment and related materials ($323); graders and sorters of agricultural products ($387); hand packagers and packers ($348); maids and housekeeping cleaners ($323); sewing machine operators ($344); packaging and filling machine operators ($390) (US Department of Labor 2004). There has been some significant growth, over the past decade, in Latino concentration by industry, as well, which generally coincides with the occupations data (see Table 4.4).

There are also several female dominated industries (that is, where women constitute 50 per cent or more of those employed therein) particularly in the areas of retail trade, educational and health services, accommodation and food services, and some areas of professional and business services, and other services. However, Latina presence is only highly significant[9] in a few of these, such as sugar and confectionary products; retail bakeries; textiles, apparel and leather; soaps, cleaning compounds and cosmetics; and traveller accommodation. Latina presence is extremely significant (over 30 per cent) in cut and sew apparel; services to buildings and dwellings; dry cleaning and laundry services; and private household services (US Department of Labor 2005: 226–30). All of these are generally considered to be low wage industries. For live-in domestic service actual wages may be extremely low since part of the compensation is provided through room and board. Private household service is particularly important as a form of first entry into the

Table 4.3 Female dominated occupations 2003 (ordered by percentage of Latinos)

Occupations 2003	Total employed (thou.)	Percentage of total:		Median weekly earnings:		
		% Women	% Latinos	All full- time $	Men $	Women $
Total, 16 years and over	137736	46.8	12.6	620	695	552
Pressers, textile, garment, and related materials	81	74.9	46.4	323	*	*
Graders and sorters, agricultural products	73	68.0	43.8	387	*	*
Packers and packagers, hand	419	61.1	39.8	348	345	350
Maids and housekeeping cleaners	1370	88.4	38.7	323	371	317
Sewing machine operators	341	78.6	38.5	344	389	326
Miscellaneous media and communication workers	79	68.8	37.6			
Packaging and filling machine operators and tenders	294	56.5	37.3	390	430	362
Laundry and dry-cleaning workers	193	59.6	29.9	348	*	328
Food preparation workers	612	57.3	28.3	320	334	310
Tailors, dressmakers, and sewers	118	71.0	21.4	472	*	*
Food preparation and serving related occupations	7254	56.6	19.9			
Credit authorizers, checkers, and clerks	52	77.2	19.6			
Electricial, electronics, and electromechanical assemblers	240	59.6	19.4	440	510	404
Service occupations	22086	57.2	18.9	403	463	366
Food servers, nonrestaurant	180	66.3	18.8	382	*	368
Hotel, motel, and resort desk clerks	113	70.9	17.8	397	*	392
Child care workers	1284	95.1	17.2	330	*	326
Eligibility interviews, government programs	78	76.2	17.0	581	*	571
Telemarketers	187	63.2	16.0	375	*	346
Human resources assistants, except payroll and timekeeping	71	85.0	16.0	580	*	585
Teacher assistants	932	91.6	15.2	351	422	344
Models, demonstrators, and product promoters	73	87.2	15.1			
Cashiers	2903	76.4	15.0	319	339	315
Telephone operators	57	85.8	15.0			
Order clerks	108	72.1	14.9	517	*	485
Reservation and transportation ticket agents and travel clerks	179	67.8	14.9	542	*	502
Personal and home care aides	512	88.4	14.8	351	*	342
Dental assistants	251	95.0	14.7	492	*	490
Medical, dental, and ophthalmic laboratory technicians	100	49.4	14.3	527	*	*
Medical records and health information technicians	107	92.6	14.1	505	*	502

continued on next page

Table 4.3 Female dominated occupations 2003 (ordered by percentage of Latinos) (cont.)

Occupations 2003	Total employed (thou.)	Percentage of total:		Median weekly earnings:		
		% Women	% Latinos	All full-time $	Men $	Women $
Counter attendants, cafeteria, food concession, and coffee shop	349	66.7	14.1	276	*	271
Bill and account collectors	225	69.8	14.0	498	518	491
Gaming services workers	85	50.7	13.8	446	*	*
First-line supervisors/managers of food preparation and serving workers	667	56.3	13.4	413	485	391

Source: U.S. Department of Labor (2005) *Employment and Earnings*, Washington, D. C.: Bureau of Labor Statistics, January, pp. 210–15 and 250–4.

Table 4.4 Industries with very high concentrations of Latino workers in 2003

Industries 2003	% Latino 1994	% Latino 2003	number of Latinos 2003	% of all Latinos
Total, 16 years and over	8.8	12.6	17,354,736	100
Animal slaughtering and processing	25.0	43.4	204,848	1.2
Support activities for agriculture and forestry	24.0	41.1	75,213	0.4
Carpet and rug mills	6.3	37.8	29,862	0.2
Landscaping services	25.2	36.8	397,808	2.3
Cut and sew apparel	23.1	35.5	146,260	0.8
Fruit and vegetable preserving and speciality foods	24.9	33.1	46,009	0.3
Private households	25.4	31.8	242,952	1.4
Sugar and confectionery products	16.1	31.7	31,383	0.2
Services to buildings and dwellings	20.3	31.0	360,220	2.1
Dry-cleaning and laundry services	15.7	30.9	111,549	0.6
Food manufacturing	18.3	29.1	469,965	2.7
Bakeries, except retail	13.0	29.0	68,730	0.4
Crop production	25.4	28.3	251,304	1.4
Speciality food stores	13.1	27.4	85,488	0.5
Car washes	22.5	26.3	48,129	0.3
Textiles, apparel, and leather	21.4	26.2	270,122	1.6
Warehousing and storage	16.8	25.7	57,825	0.3
Traveller accommodation	17.8	25.2	359,100	2.1

Source: Author's calculations based on data from U.S. Department of Labor (1995 and 2004) *Employment and Earnings*, Washington, D. C.: Bureau of Labor Statistics, January.

US labour force for many Latina women. According to Labour Department statistics it employs about 3.4 per cent of all Latina workers. However, there is a high degree of informality in private household service work thus official figures may, in fact, understate its significance.

Location, unemployment and poverty

Since 75 per cent of all Latinos reside in just seven states, labour market segmentation and stratification for them is, in fact, probably even more pronounced than these national figures indicate. Occupational concentration and geographical concentration appear to be closely linked. However, Latinos are often recruited for, or encouraged to settle in, non-traditional destinations in the Southeast and Midwest to work in agriculture, poultry processing, meat packing plants, or carpet mills, for example, to fill jobs that local residents disdain. These and other 'immigrant jobs' or 'immigrant labour market niches' as they are frequently called, usually offer working conditions or salaries that most US born workers will not accept. The demand for workers to perform such tasks for low wages increased dramatically towards the end of the twentieth century as did the new wave of immigrant workers, particularly those from Mexico and other Latin American countries, who were willing to fill those jobs (Sum *et al.* 2002). The non-Hispanic labour force is projected to grow only 9 per cent between 2000 and 2010. Over the same period the Latino labour force will probably increase by 77 per cent due to the combination of newly arriving immigrants and the number of young US Latinos who will reach working age. Thus by 2010 Latinos are projected to constitute about 17.4 per cent of the EAP (Vernez and Mizell 2001, Suro and Passel 2003).

Although Latinos are a significant and growing share of the US labour force, 'working Latinos have had persistently high rates of poverty and unemployment, as well as low incomes' (Thomas-Breitfeld 2003: 1). As was mentioned earlier, for the past several decades unemployment rates for Latinos have been consistently slightly lower than African Americans' unemployment figures and higher than those for non-Hispanic whites. Their relative earnings, however, have deteriorated (Levine 2001: 81–116). Since the early 1980s, in the case of female workers, and from the early 1990s to the present for men, Latino workers have had lower median earnings than any other population group: median earnings for Latino men is slightly lower than the median for African American men and much lower than the median for non-Hispanic white men. In the case of men who work full time year round, Latinos have consistently had a lower median than African Americans since the mid-1980s and the gap is growing as it also has between Latino men and non-Hispanic whites (see Figures 4.4 and 4.5). The median of earnings for Latina women is much lower than for African American women or non-Hispanic white women. In the case of women who work full time year round, Latinas have had lower median earnings than African Americans and non-Hispanic whites since the early 1970s when such statistics were first recorded, and the gaps have been growing consistently (see Figures 4.6 and 4.7) (US Census

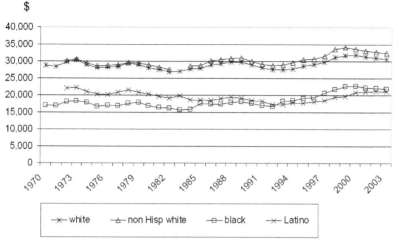

Figure 4.4 Median earnings all men 1970-2003

Source: U.S. Census Bureau (2005) Current Population Survey, Historical Income Tables, Table P-2.

Bureau 2004). Mexican-origin men and women tend to have lower median earnings than other groups of Latinos in the US (Levine 2001).

The differences in Latinos' and African Americans' median family and household incomes with respect to non-Hispanic whites' is growing; nevertheless, Latinos have slightly higher medians (for families[10] and households) than African Americans. This latter difference is not derived from higher individual earnings – we have just seen above that both Latino men and women tend to have lower earnings – but from the fact that there are usually more workers per Latino family or

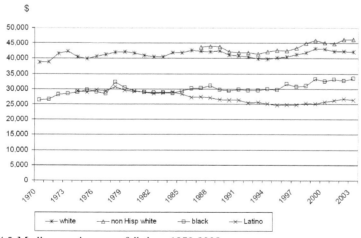

Figure 4.5 Median earnings men full-time. 1970-2003

Source: U.S. Census Bureau (2005) Current Population Survey, Historical Income Tables-Persons, Table P-2.

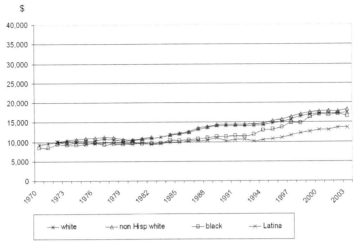

Figure 4.6 Median earnings all women 1970-2003

Source: U.S. Census Bureau (2005) Current Population Survey, Historical Income Tables-Persons, Table P-2.

household. Adolescents often drop out of high school before graduating in order to contribute to the family income or even, as is sometimes the case for females, to take care of younger siblings so that the mother can work outside of the home. Many Latino households include extended family members – aunts, uncles, nieces, nephews, grandparents – and often non-family members who may be from the same home town. The net effect is that slightly higher median family and household incomes are divided among a greater number of individuals so that from 1988 on Latinos' per capita income has been somewhat lower than African Americans' and much lower than non-Hispanic whites'. The per capita income figures were

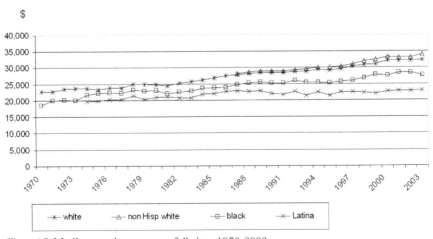

Figure 4.7 Median earnings women full-time 1970-2003

Source: U.S. Census Bureau (2005) Current Population Survey, Historical Income Tables-Persons, Table 2.

$13,492, $15,583, and $26,774 per year, respectively, in 2003 (US Census Bureau 2004).

Increasing labour market segmentation in the US has a negative impact on Latinos' incomes. Lisa Catanzarite analyzed data for 38 different metropolitan areas and found that wages were lower in what she has called 'brown collar occupations' where significant numbers of Latinos are employed. These wage differentials have a larger impact on racial and ethnic minorities than for non-Hispanic whites and mainly affect earlier Latino immigrants, since they are the ones most likely to be employed in these sectors. She cites 'devaluation of the work performed by low status groups; the poor market position of labour intensive occupations; the limited political power of low status workers; and the willingness of low status workers to accept poor wages' as the underlying causes of the observed differentials (2003: 3). A recent National Council of La Raza (NCLR) document on the Latino workforce points to low levels of educational attainment as a fundamental reason why Latinos tend to be concentrated in low skilled, low paying occupations and industries with little access to fringe benefits. However, the author also mentions other contributing factors such as discrimination, immigration status, and (lack of) union participation (Thomas-Breitfeld 2003).

Given the low wage rates for Latino workers it is no surprise that in 2001 they were slightly more likely to be poor than African American workers (11.2 per cent versus 10.4 per cent) and much more so than white non-Hispanic workers (4.0 per cent) (ibid). As Figure 4.8 shows, the second half of the twentieth century brought a very significant decline in the poverty rate for African Americans, in general. Meanwhile, the Latino poverty rate rose from the beginning of the 1980s through the early 1990s then dropped to its earlier levels during the economic expansion of the 1990s. Even so, the Latino poverty rate was higher than the African American rate from 1994 to 1997. Furthermore, while African Americans now constitute a

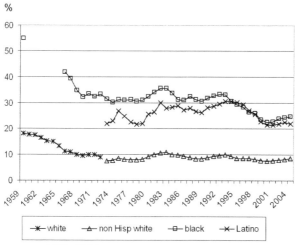

Figure 4.8 Poverty rate 1959–2004

Source: U.S. Census Bureau (2005). Current Population Survey, Historical Poverty Tables, Table 2.

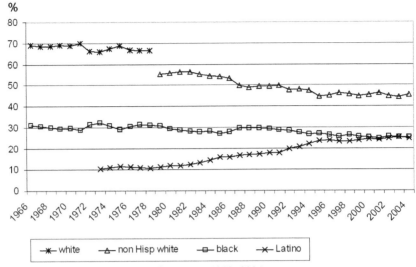

Figure 4.9 Distribution of persons in poverty 1959–2004

Source: U.S. Census Bureau (2005) Current Population Survey, Historical Poverty Tables, Tables 3 and 14.

smaller percentage of those living in poverty than they did before, Latinos constitute a much larger percentage (see Figure 4.9) (US Census Bureau 2005).

Wage differentials for Latino immigrants and subsequent generations can be largely explained by differences in educational attainment (Lowell 2004). Unfortunately Mexican-born workers seem to have not only lower educational attainment but also lower returns to education than all other groups. There are more Mexicans than other Latinos with less than a high school education and fewer with

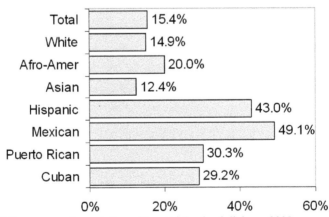

Figure 4.10 Percentage of population without high school diploma 2003

Source: U.S. Census Bureau (2005) Statistical Abstract of the United States 2004-2005, Washington, D.C.: USGPO, p. 141.

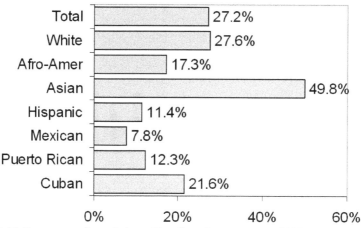

Figure 4.11 Percentage of population with college degree or more 2003

Source: U.S. Census Bureau (2005) Statistical Abstract of the United States 2004-2005, Washington, D.C.: USGPO, p. 141.

college degrees (see Figures 4.10 and 4.11) (US Census Bureau 2005: 141). Furthermore, in spite of the fact that in some Mexican families schooling for boys is still given more importance than that for girls, the educational attainment profile for Mexican-origin females in the US is slightly more favourable, or a bit less unfavourable, than that of males (see Figure 4.12) (US Census Bureau 2005). Thus gender discrimination also contributes significantly to Mexican-origin women's lower incomes.

Lindsay Lowell found that from 1994 to 2002 Mexican-born workers who were high school graduates had slightly higher weekly earnings than others

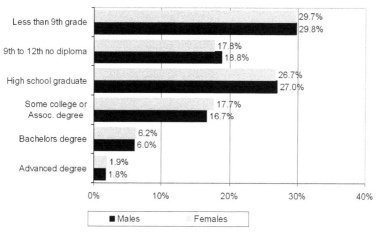

Figure 4.12 Educational attainment Mexicans in U.S. 2004

Source: U.S. Census Bureau (2004) Current Population Survey, Annual Social and Economic Supplement, 2004, Ethnicity and Ancestry Statistics Branch, Population Division, March, Table 6.2, p. 141.

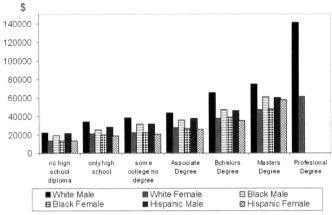

Figure 4.13 Mean earnings by highest degree earned, 2002

Source: U.S. Census Bureau (2005) *Statistical Abstract of the United States 2004-2005*, Washington, D.C.: USGPO, p. 142.

without a high school diploma; nevertheless these are the lowest paid members of the labour force. For high school graduates and holders of Bachelor's degrees or advanced degrees Mexican-born workers had lower wages than all other groups. Thus Mexicans earn less not only because of lower educational attainment, but also because they tend to get lower returns to education from high school graduation onwards. Furthermore these differentials continue, although to a lesser degree, for second and third generations and up (Lowell 2004). For many Mexicans, henceforth, educational attainment and incomes or socioeconomic status appear to be not only highly correlated but also mutually determined and reinforcing across generations.

Unfortunately, women at all levels of educational attainment have lower average earnings than their male counterparts (see Figure 4.13). The differences are greatest for white women with respect to white men and tend to rise as educational attainment increases. The differences are lowest for African American women with respect to African American men, except for the very small difference in mean earnings for Latinos with Master's degrees, who are in turn a very small percentage (3.1 per cent) of the Latino population (US Census Bureau 2005: 142). These somewhat less pronounced differentials for African American and Latina women with respect to their male counterparts are not, however, the result of a more favourable labour market position. They reflect the much less favourable labour market outcomes that all groups, including white women, have with respect to white men at the same educational levels. Among Latinos, Mexicans have the lowest levels of educational attainment; and Latinos overall, because of the high Mexican component, have lower levels of educational attainment than non-Hispanic whites or African Americans.

Conclusion

Globalization and economic restructuring at the international level, combined with internal factors such as the high levels of corruption and elite-focused economic policies, have had devastating effects for most of the Mexican population. As a result, migratory pressures have increased over the past two or three decades. While significant female migration – in addition to the traditional flow of male migrants – is not a new phenomenon, it has increased rapidly since the 1980s. For many Mexican women jobs in the US provide their first experiences as members of the paid labour force.

At the same time immigrant labor is becoming more and more important for the US economy and the occupational profile of Mexican migrants is changing rapidly. Only a very small percentage of the Mexican origin population is currently employed in agriculture. Over the past few decades more and more recent Mexican immigrants have found work in low skilled manufacturing and service sector jobs. The demand for workers to perform such tasks, for low wages, increased dramatically towards the end of the twentieth century. By 2010 Latinos are projected to constitute about 17.4 per cent of the US labour force. Certain occupations and industrial subsectors – a few of which are female dominated – have rapidly become "immigrant niches" within the US labour market.

Employment opportunities for men quite often involve tasks that alter traditional gender roles – such as building or house cleaning services and food preparation jobs. Male socioeconomic stature would certainly not be enhanced by many of the types of jobs that immigrants are obliged to perform were it not for the monetary gains involved. Hence, I believe, their need to return to Mexico periodically to exhibit their "success". Women, on the other hand, may increase their socioeconomic status simply by becoming wage earners. This of course does not generally free them from traditional household tasks, which means they have a double workday – that is lightened somewhat, in the US context, because of access to labour-saving devices and appliances like washing machines, vacuum cleaners, and so on. However, female labour force participation may provide the basis for a greater role in family decision-making processes and more personal autonomy.

In spite of their growing importance as part of the labour supply, many Latinos who live and work in the US have persistently high rates of poverty and unemployment, as well as very low incomes by US standards. Mexican origin women in the US labour force clearly suffer from the combined effects of both gender and ethnic discrimination in terms of occupations and earnings. While educational attainment is not the only factor that determines low wages for Latinos, it can easily be used to justify and disguise other discriminatory practices. Unfortunately, in the US today, women from all racial and ethnic groups still earn considerably less than their male counterparts with similar levels of educational attainment.

Because of the increasing segmentation and stratification now prevailing in the US labour market upward mobility will most likely prove to be more difficult for most recently arriving Mexican immigrants and their children than it was for previous cohorts of Mexicans and other groups of immigrants throughout most of the twentieth century. Nevertheless, it can probably be safely assumed that in the long run these ethnically determined socioeconomic differences will eventually tend to disappear, although getting to that point may prove to be a very painful and socially disruptive process. On the US side this means accepting the fact that those so welcomed and sought after as low wage workers will at the same time become community residents and neighbors.

In Mexico tastes and customs acquired in the US may clash with the more communal traditions and habits still prevailing in small towns. It is often the case that indigenous women, who have spent time living alone in the US, are no longer accepted in their communities of origin upon returning to Mexico. On the other hand, women who do reestablish themselves in small Mexican villages or towns frequently become agents of change and role models for others. They dress differently, wear their hair differently and may think differently about birth control. Many of them have learned how to drive. It is quite likely that they have grown accustomed to earning, and managing, their own money.

Because of the hazards involved in entering the US as undocumented migrants, women in that situation tend to go and come less frequently than men. Furthermore, once they have become settled and adapted, they tend to be more reluctant than men to return to Mexico to live. Children born in Mexico but raised in the US rarely contemplate going to Mexico, except for brief visits. After years of working and saving, some migrants return to Mexico to set up successful business in their home towns, while many who have spent years planning to retire there find it too difficult to readjust and end up going back to the US.

Independently of these individual decisions and choices, a mechanism has been set in motion – through the migratory process – that inevitably transforms life on both sides of the border. Remote Mexican villages sprout Internet cafes and ATMs to facilitate communication with and remittances from family members who have gone "north" to live and work. Some neighborhoods in the US have become "barrios" replete with taco stands, street vendors and signs in Spanish. In the midst of the transnational social spaces formed by establishing a continuum between "here" and "there" women migrants have been perceived as playing a pivotal role in transmitting ancestral traditions and conserving the mother tongue. It may turn out, however, that they are playing an even more definitive role as agents of adaptation, transformation and change.

Notes

1   The author wishes to thank the UNAM's Programa de Apoyo a Proyectos de Investigación e Innovación Tecnológica (PAPIIT) (Programme to Support Research and Technological Innovation Projects) for supporting the research for this article.
2   Jobs registered by the Instituto Mexicano del Seguro Social IMSS rose by 1.8 million and those registered in the Instituto de Seguridad Social al Servicio de los Trabajadores del Estado ISSSTE rose by 0.3 million, the net increase registered in maquiladora employment was 0.6 million (Presidencia de la Republica 2004).
3   I have defined as informal employment all jobs not registered in either of Mexico's social security systems (one for workers in general and the other for government workers) which basically

coincides with those who have no binding contractual agreement with their employers, that would guarantee the benefits and protections provided by Mexican labour laws, and whose incomes are probably not subject to regular withholding procedures for tax purposes.

4 President of Mexico from December 1, 2000 to November 30, 2006.

5 For a detailed description of women's participation in the labour force in Mexico, see Teresa Rendón (2003).

6 Calculations based on applying the current minimum wage rate to wage distribution data from the Instituto Nacional de Estadística, Geografía e Informática, INEGI's labour census for the year 2000.

7 For a more comprehensive vision of recent changes in migration trends and characteristics, see Jorge Durand and Douglas S. Massey (2003).

8 Author's calculations based on US Department of Labour (2005) pp. 216–17. As of 2004, that is with the data for 2003, the Labor Department modified the way the occupational categories list is organized, by regrouping various occupations and somewhat modifying the major headings. For example, farming forestry and fishing is no longer listed as a separate major category and has been included as a sub-heading under natural resources, construction and maintenance occupations.

9 I have considered Latina presence as highly significant when it is at least 1.5 times higher than the Latino presence in the labour force which is 12.9 per cent for 2004, in other words a figure of 19.4 per cent or more.

10 This is generally true in the case of families; however from 1993 to 1997, and in 1999, and 2003, African American families had higher median earnings than Latino families.

References

Avila, Jose Luis; Fuentes, Carlos and Tuirán, Rodolfo (n.d.) *Mujeres Mexicanas en la Migración a Estados Unidos*, Consejo Nacional de Población, pp. 151–72. Available online, www.conapo.gob.mx/publicaciones/migra3/08.pdf.

Brown, Irene (ed.) (1999) *Latinas and African American Women at Work*, New York: Russell Sage Foundation.

Camarota, Steven A. (2004) 'A Jobless Recovery? Immigrant Gains and Native Losses', Backgrounder, October, Center for Immigration Studies, Washington, D.C.: CIS.

Catanzarite, Lisa (2003) 'Wage Penalties in Brown-Collar Occupations', *Latino Policy and Issues Brief*, UCLA Chicano Studies Research Center, No.8, September. Available online, www.chicano.ucla.edu/press/siteart/LPIB_08Sept2003.pdf.

Durand, Jorge and Massey, Douglas S. (2003) *Clandestinos, Migración México-Estados Unidos en los albores del siglo XXI*, México, D. F.: Miguel Ángel Porrúa.

Fernandez-Vega, Carlos (2005) 'El trabajo barato sostiene la economía, aunque Fox no lo crea', *La Jornada*, 3 March: 28.

Gamio, Manuel (1969) *Mexican Migration to the United States*, New York: Arno Press.

INEGI (Instituto Nacional de Estadística, Geografía e Informática) (n.d.). Available online, www.inegi.gob.mx.

Lazear, Edward Paul (2004) 'The Plight of Immigrants from Mexico', *The Daily Report*, Hoover Institution. Available online, http://72.14.207.104/search?q=cache:BD0hrAbgH50J:www.hoover.org/pubaffairs/we/2004/lazear11.html+Lazear,+Edward+%E2%80%98The+Plight+of+Immigrants+from+Mexico%E2%80%99&hl=en&gl=ca&ct=clnk&cd=1.

Levine, Elaine (2001) *Los Nuevos Pobres de los Estados Unidos: los Hispanos*. Mexico, D. F.: Miguel Angel Porrúa and IIEc. and CISAN-UNAM.

Lowell, Lindsey (2004) Human Capital and the Economic Effects of Mexican Migration to the United Status, Paper presented in the Seminar 'Migración México, Estados Unidos: Implicaciones y retos para ambos países', México, D.F., 1 December.

Martinez, Fabiola (2004) 'En la economía informal, 62% de los empleos de México: OIT', *La Jornada*, 12 June: 33.

Ortiz Rivera, Angela (2003) 'Hijos del salrario Mínimo', *El Independiente*, 15 August: 4–5.

Passel, Jeffrey S. (2005) *Unauthorized Migrants: Numbers and Characteristics*, Washington, D.C.: Pew Hispanic Center.

Polaski, Sandra (2004) Perspectives on the Future of NAFTA: Mexican Labor in North American Integration, Paper presented at the Colloquium El Impacto del TLCAN en México a los 10 años, UNAM, 29–30 June.

Presidencia de la Republica (2004) *Cuarto Informe de Gobierno, Anexo Estadístico*, México, D.F.: Gobierno de los Estados Unidos Mexicanos.

Rendón, Teresa (2003) *Trabajo de Hombres y Trabajo de Mujeres en el México del siglo XX*, México, D.F., Universidad Nacional Autónoma de México.

Romero, José and Puyana, Alicia (2004) Evaluación integral de los impactos e instrumentación del capítulo agropecuario del TLCAN, Paper presented at the Colloquium El Impacto del TLCAN en México a los 10 años, UNAM, 29–30 June. Available online, www.sice.oas.org/geograph/westernh/NAFTA_AGRI.pdf.

Salas, Carlos (2003) 'El contexto económico de México', in Enrique de la Garza and Carlos Salas (coords.) *La Situación del trabajo en México*, México, D. F.: Plaza y Valdés, pp. 37–53.

Sassen, Saskia (1998) *Globalization and Its Discontents*, New York: The New York Press.

Sum, Andrew *et al.* (2002) Immigrant Workers and the Great American Job Machine: The Contribution of New Foreign Immigration to the National and Regional Labor Force Growth in the 1990s, Prepared for National Business Roundtable, Washington, D.C., August.

Suro, Robert and Passel, Jeffrey S. (2003) *The Rise of the Second Generation: Changing Patterns in Hispanic Population Growth*, Washington, D.C.: Pew Hispanic Center.

Thomas-Breitfeld, Sean (2003) 'The Latino Workforce', Statistical Brief No. 3, Washington, D.C.: National Council of La Raza.

US Census Bureau (2004) Current Population Survey, Annual Social and Economic Supplement, Ethnicity and Ancestry Statistics Branch, Population Division. Available online, www.census.gov/population/socdemo/hispanic/ASEC2004/20.

—— (2005) Statistical Abstract of the United States 2004–2005, Washington, D.C.: USGPO.

US Department of Labor (2004) *Employment and Earnings*, January, Washington, D. C.: Bureau of Labor Statistics.

—— (2005) *Employment and Earnings*, January, Washington, D. C.: Bureau of Labor Statistics.

Vernez, George and Mizell, Lee (2001) 'Goal to Double the Rate of Hispanics Earning a Bachelor's Degree', Santa Monica, CA: RAND Education, Center for Research on Immigration Policy.

Woo, Ofelia (2001) *Las Mujeres también nos vamos al Norte*, Guadalajara: Universidad de Guadalajara.

5 The problem of social reproduction under neoliberalism

Reconfiguring the male-breadwinner model in Australia

Ray Broomhill and Rhonda Sharp

Introduction

Throughout the world neoliberal restructuring has wrought complex changes in both capital accumulation and social reproduction. These are often viewed as separate or unconnected, but, at the most basic level, economies cannot survive without the reproduction of individuals, societies and the human race. Frequently, awareness of this important principle is not reflected in policy agendas until a crisis emerges. Throughout history though, commentators have stressed the interdependence between the economic and social spheres. Karl Polanyi, in his classic 1944 work *The Great Transformation,* points out that scientific significance is diminished when an understanding of the social implications of the market economy is excluded from the analysis. Polanyi also posited that capitalism is continually engaged in the internal struggle between the demand of capital accumulation on the one hand and the need for social sustainability and reproduction on the other (Polanyi 1957). In the present era of neoliberalism, the potential for capital accumulation to be pursued at the cost of social reproduction was encapsulated in a recent media headline warning of the potential for Australia to become a 'beautiful economy (but) with a dysfunctional society' (Steketee 2005: 10). Of course, the 'problem' of social reproduction extends beyond the abstract level of theory to shape the daily lives of people and the choices available to them. The everyday lives of men, women and children are currently affected by many challenges that constrain social reproduction.

In Australia, Canada and other Anglo-American societies the male-breadwinner model has been an enduring means of organizing social reproduction. This model, while never uniform or static, has been subjected to further changes under neoliberalism. Nancy Folbre (1994) notes the dilemma this raises and argues that, while the male-breadwinner model was never fair, it was partly functional in the sense that it underpinned social reproduction. Its potential demise raises the question of who is now going to take care of the kids, the sick and the elderly (ibid.: 10). In this chapter we assess what is happening to the male-breadwinner model in Australia under neoliberal restructuring. We argue that while many aspects of these traditional gender arrangements remain intact, they have been profoundly disrupted by restructuring within the labour market, the decline of the nuclear family and other socioeconomic changes affecting the gender division of labour within households. Gender arrangements also have been affected by contradictory government policies in relation to social reproduction. These changes have led to increased complexity and diversity as well as a growing polarization in the gender roles and arrangements within different socioeconomic groups in society. The winners and losers from the impact of economic and social restructuring are frequently engaged in quite different strategies of adjustment, resulting in both changed and reinforced versions of the traditional male-breadwinner model. The forces of global restructuring are dramatically restructuring class, gender and social arrangements – and in so doing are also restructuring social reproduction. However, rather than producing a new gender order, the restructuring process is producing increased social instability and gender (dis)order.

Our framework

We utilize the notion of a 'gender order' to examine the structural changes and continuities that are emerging in the processes of social reproduction in Australia under neoliberalism. Of course, while endeavouring to identify the impact of broader socioeconomic forces on people's lives it is also vital to be sensitive to the role of individual and collective agency in determining patterns of behaviour. The question of the primacy of structure versus agency in framing the response of the individual is a matter of longstanding debate and is the subject of much contention between feminists adhering to materialist or poststructuralist tendencies. Our view is that while gender relations are structured within a number of contexts, including for example within the institutions of the labour market and the state, the impact of these structures are negotiated and interpreted by 'changing and flexible gendered subjects' (Crompton 1999: 7–8). As Sylvia Walby puts it:

> Women make choices about their participation in paid work and involvement in various forms of household and thus may be considered to possess individual agency. However, they do not make such choices in circumstances of their own making, since they face structures which pre-date their own actions and which are sedimentations of the actions of others over a long period.'
>
> (2001: 183).

The challenge is to develop an analysis that effectively explores the complexities, and contradictions in the ways that individuals negotiate the gendered structures they are presented with. The term 'gender order'[1] is used to describe the power relations between men and women embedded in the formal and informal institutions, cultural norms and social practices that contribute to social coherence and change in different societies. To some degree a 'male-breadwinner' gender order was embedded in the major institutions of all post-Second World War capitalist societies, especially in the institutions of the welfare state and via the structures and processes of labour market and employment regulation.

We draw upon the typology developed by Birgit Pfau-Effinger (1999) that distinguishes different household models of male-breadwinner and dual-breadwinner arrangements according to the gender division of labour in both employment and the care work of households. However, Pfau-Effinger also recognizes that the postwar male-breadwinner gender order was also defined by more informal forms of social regulation, including specific gender norms, values, social patterns and cultural behaviours. Importantly these informal forms of social regulation included what men and women considered as 'normal' or desirable forms of gender relations and the gender division of labour (ibid.: 61–2). Such gender cultures and ideologies certainly influence power relations within a household quite apart from the reality of men and women's employment arrangements. We would add that the gender arrangements that are found at any time and place are also profoundly affected by the policies and actions of the state. Therefore, the formal and informal processes of social regulation together constitute the gender order and both have been crucial in defining and securing the pattern of social reproduction that seemed unusually stable during the postwar era – at least until the early 1970s.

Two forms of the male-breadwinner family are identified by Pfau-Effinger – the male-breadwinner/female home-carer model and the male-breadwinner/female part-time worker and carer model.[2] The male-breadwinner model therefore encompasses both 'traditional' and 'modern' versions. In the more traditional model, men are regarded as breadwinners who earn income for the family in the public sphere while women are primarily responsible for work in the private household. In the 'modernized' version, women participate on a part-time basis in the labour market but men are still viewed as the primary breadwinners. Pfau-Effinger also identifies two other modern household forms in which women are not only more fully integrated into the labour market but in which the tasks of breadwinning and household responsibilities are not as rigidly defined and separated. Increasingly, there has emerged a new household form where both partners' financial contributions are equally important. As a result, it may be possible to identify a new 'dual-breadwinner' household model. The first version of this model is a dual-breadwinner/state-carer form. Here both partners are full-time income earners and share, more or less equally, the task of financial provisioning. However, the task of caring for children is perceived not as the female's responsibility alone but to a considerable extent the task of the state. We would expand Pfau-Effinger's category further by the inclusion of market-provided care as an alternative, or additional, option to state-provided care in this type of household. However, it is also important to note that in some of these dual-earner households that utilize state or market-provided care the female remains primarily responsible for organizing that care and for other domestic labour. The second version of the 'dual-breadwinner' household model identified by Pfau-Effinger is the 'dual-breadwinner/dual-carer' model. This form is characterized by a 'symmetrical and equitable' sharing of breadwinning and household/caring provisioning. In particular, childrearing is seen as the equal responsibility of both partners (even if some proportion is delegated to the state or to the market). Consequently categorizing the current state of the breadwinner model involves considering not only the different distributions of both paid labour and unpaid care work between men and women but also the allocation of care work between the market, the state and men and women in households.

While a form of a male-breadwinner gender order was characteristic of all post-Second World War welfare states at some stage, the nature of the model existing in different countries varied greatly in form and intensity (Gottfried 2004, Pfau-Effinger 1998, Walby 2001, Crompton 1999).[3] Consequently, the usefulness of the concept of the male-breadwinner model for understanding comparative changes to social reproduction under neoliberal restructuring is enhanced if historically specific factors contributing to differences in the structuring of the gender order across countries is taken into account. Our approach therefore is to uncover the complexity and national specificity of the structuring of gender relations with respect to employment, household arrangements and government policies. In particular, we seek to address the following questions:

- Has a new 'gender order' emerged under neoliberal restructuring in Australia?
- Is any new or emerging 'gender order' fair?
- Will the gender order foster stable social reproduction, that is, will it provide the 'institutional fix' necessary to underpin social reproduction and the sustainability of neoliberalism?

Australia's postwar gender order

It has generally been perceived that from the late 1940s to the mid-1970s Australian gender structures and arrangements were based upon a relatively strong version of the male-breadwinner model (Gilding 1991, Cass 1998, Murphy 2002). While there is debate about the high point of the male-breadwinner model in Australia, the period of postwar prosperity, for the first time in the twentieth century, made full employment for males a reality.

In a study based upon interviews with men and women who had been young parents in the 1950s, Probert (2002) found a coherent pattern of beliefs about the role of men as 'breadwinners' and women as 'mothers and homemakers'. There was almost universal acceptance of the view that women were, and should be, financially dependent upon their male partner. The belief that children should be cared for in the home, by their mother, was very strongly held. Gender relations between men and women were fundamentally construed in terms of male power and female dependency. The dominant pattern within the gender order comprised strictly gendered divisions of labour in the household and in the labour market. Men's sphere of activity was primarily the workplace while women's was clearly the family even though an increasing number of married women were entering the labour market. At the outset of the postwar period, female labour market participation was relatively low, especially for married women. Most female workers were unmarried (Hargreaves 1982: 18–19). In 1947 married women made up only 4.4 per cent of the total workforce and by the mid-1950s they were still only 7 per cent. Gradually, however, women increased their level of paid employment and by 1966 married women represented 14 per cent of the labour force (Murphy 2003, Richmond 1974).

Australian governments played an important role in supporting the male-breadwinner model in the Keynesian postwar period. During the period 1949–1972 Australia was governed by a Liberal/Country Party coalition that, though implementing liberal Keynesian economic policies, was deeply conservative in social policy areas. The postwar Australian wage-earner welfare state overwhelmingly protected male workers. The male-breadwinner model itself was entrenched in 'all aspects of public policy, social and political culture' (Cass 1998: 42). Policies including taxation, employment, wage fixation and social security reflected assumptions about the predominance of the male breadwinner. For example, a dependent spouse taxation deduction strongly favoured a family model 'built around a male breadwinner and female homemaker' by providing strong disincentives for married women not to participate in paid work (Murphy 2003: 101).

Of particular importance in the Australian postwar regulatory framework was the evolution of a centralized industrial relations system built around the gendered concept of a minimum family wage for male workers and reduced wages for women. The 1907 Harvester Judgment established the principle that the male 'family wage' should be sufficient for a male breadwinner to support a dependent family (Watson *et al.* 2003). While at one level the family wage might be seen as protecting married women from having to seek paid work in the open market, in practice it played a critical role in blocking women's options in paid employment. Women's exclusion from the labour market was also reinforced by low levels of state intervention in the areas of maternity, parental leave and childcare policies (Murphy 2003: 101).

Nevertheless, the shape of the Australian postwar gender order was far from static. Although remaining fundamentally based upon a nuclear family structure and a male-breadwinner norm, it experienced significant changes during the 1950s and 1960s. Throughout the period women were increasingly drawn into the labour market. This was mainly due to the increasing demand for labour resulting from the extended economic growth that accompanied postwar capitalist development in Australia. However, changing child-bearing trends and changing attitudes to women's role in society were also important. Women's increasing labour market participation was due in part also to the increasing role of the state in providing services that were previously women's family responsibilities. While state economic intervention, during the 1950s and 1960s in particular, was not generally motivated by a conscious desire by policy makers to improve the economic and social position of women, in significant ways women's ability to participate in the labour market was enhanced by state interventionist policies. Governments also provided a growing welfare-state structure that underpinned individual and family welfare and social reproduction where the family failed or could not cope.

Clearly, women's increased participation in the labour market was not on equal terms with men's. Furthermore, the dominant gender culture ensured that women also remained primarily responsible for social reproduction within the home and the society. Thus postwar capital accumulation and social reproduction were both constructed upon a quite unequal division of labour – in the labour market and in the household. Nevertheless the changes that occurred to women's role and to gender relations during the latter part of the 'long boom' had a profound effect on the existing gender order. The male-breadwinner model was challenged by the increasing participation of women in the paid labour market, the increasing financial independence of women (from men at least if not from the state) through changes to the welfare system and the transforming influence of the women's movement on gender attitudes and culture. The latter included a shift in the politics of identity for women with 'women as mothers' were being gradually replaced by 'women as workers and breadwinners.' Ann Firth argues this latter transformation was an important factor in challenging the postwar economic policy-makers' vision of Australian society that gave centrality to the male breadwinner (Firth 2004: 507).

Restructuring the Australian gender order?

The multifaceted, and sometimes contradictory, arrangements that comprised the 'male-breadwinner' gender order during the 'long boom' are now further under challenge as a result of profound changes that have occurred in Australian society over the past two decades. Three dynamic processes have contributed to these changes. Firstly, labour market restructuring has profoundly affected women's and men's relationship to work. Secondly, these changes in turn have interacted with significant changes in the structure of families and households with profound implications for gender relations at all levels. Thirdly, the old 'father and Ford' social compact (McDowell 1991) that existed between the market, the Keynesian welfare state and the household has been shaken by neoliberal policies that have transformed institutional and informal arrangements for care work and social reproduction. Our concern here is to examine whether, as a result of changes within these three spheres, the male-breadwinner/female-carer model of gender relations within Australian households is indeed undergoing profound transformation and the extent to which a new 'gender order' is emerging.

Labour Market Restructuring

Global restructuring has undoubtedly had a major impact on the labour market experiences of both men and women but the impact of labour market restructuring on the gender order has been complex and often misinterpreted. Recently, the Australian Bureau of Statistics (ABS) argued that as a consequence of the dramatically higher labour force participation of women aged 24–54 years there has been the 'pervasive abandonment' of the traditional cultural norm that viewed a man's role primarily as 'breadwinner' and a woman's as 'home-maker' (ABS 2000a: 8). Certainly, there is evidence that the typical male-breadwinner household structure

Table 5.1 Australian couple families with children and labour force status June 2002

| *Female's labour force status* | *Male partner's labour force status* | | | |
	Employed full-time	*Employed part-time*	*Unemployed*	*Not in the labour force*
Employed full-time	19.2	1.7	0.4	1.2
Employed part-time	33.9	2.2	0.6	1.1
Unemployed	1.8	0.2	0.5	0.2
Not in the labour force	28.1	2.2	2.0	4.5
Total	83.0	6.3	3.5	7.0

Source: Australian Bureau of Statistics (2000) *Australian Social Trends 2003*, Canberra: Australian Bureau of Statistics, Catalogue 4102.0: 41.

has undergone enormous change. As Table 5.1 shows, in 2002 the percentage of Australian families in which the male was a full-time worker with a female partner not in the workforce represented only 28 per cent of all couple families with children under 15 years. A clear majority (57 per cent) of these families were those in which both parents were employed. However, the nature of this change may not be as profound as it first appears. In fact, these families were more likely to have a father employed full-time and a mother employed part-time than for both to be employed full-time (34 per cent compared with 19 per cent). The ABS has subsequently acknowledged that men are more likely to remain the primary earner even when their partners work (ABS 2003: 41).

Women's labour market participation has certainly steadily increased while men's has declined but the overall picture is more complex than it may appear. Certainly, at the aggregate level, women's labour market participation rate in Australia increased significantly between 1981 and 2004 from 45 per cent to 56 per cent. By June 2004, women represented 45 per cent of the total Australian workforce compared to 37 per cent in 1981 and 31 per cent in 1966 (ABS 2004c, ABS 1987). The labour market experiences of Australian men also have undergone fundamental changes over the past three decades. The male labour market participation rate has declined significantly from 81 per cent to 72 per cent in the period 1976–2004. Of most significance, however, male full-time employment has dropped dramatically over the period 1976–2004 from 75 per cent to 58 per cent of the adult (aged 15 years and above) male population.

However, aggregate figures showing women's ever-increasing and men's ever-decreasing participation in the labour market disguise other important trends. Significantly, as shown in Table 5.2, the percentage of adult women in full-time employment has actually remained steady at around 26–29 per cent over the period 1966–2005. On the other hand, the percentage of adult women in part-time employment increased from 8.5 per cent to 25.1 per cent between 1966 and 2005. In August 2005, 46.0 per cent of all women workers in Australia were in part-time employment compared to 33.5 per cent in August 1976. In spite of increasing numbers of men working part-time, the great majority of all part-time

Table 5.2 Female and male full-time and part-time employees as a percentage of all females and males aged 15 and over, Australia 1966–2005

	Females in the labour force as a % of all females aged 15+			Males in the labour force as a % of all males aged 15+		
	Full-time employees (%)	Part-time employees (%)	All females in the labour force* (%)	Full-time employees (%)	Part-time employees (%)	All males in the labour force* (%)
Aug 1966	26.9	8.5	36.3	79.9	3.1	84.0
Aug 1971	28.9	10.0	40.0	79.0	2.5	82.5
Aug 1976	26.8	13.5	43.0	73.4	3.4	80.0
Aug 1981	26.5	14.7	44.4	69.8	4.0	77.5
Aug 1986	27.1	16.5	47.6	64.7	4.6	75.1
Aug 1991	27.9	19.3	51.6	60.3	6.1	74.0
Aug 1996	28.2	20.9	53.4	59.0	7.8	73.2
Aug 2001	28.2	23.4	55.1	57.0	9.8	71.7
Aug 2005	29.4	25.1	57.4	59.0	9.9	72.5

Sources: Australian Bureau of Statistics (2004c) *Labour Force Australia*, ABS Cat. 6202.0, Australian Bureau of Statistics (1987) *Labour Force Australia: Historical Summary 1966 to 1984*, Canberra: Australian Bureau of Statistics, Catalogue 6204.0.

* Those classified as being 'in the labour force' include all full-time, part-time and unemployed workers.

workers remain female. Overall, 72 per cent of all Australian part-time workers in August 2005 were women.

Therefore, while Australian women continue to be increasingly drawn into the labour market, the so-called 'feminization of work' is almost totally based upon increasing levels of part-time employment – much of which is casual and insecure. The labour market, which formerly provided mostly permanent forms of employment, is characterized increasingly by part-time and more precarious forms of work – including casualized and contract jobs (Watson *et al.* 2003: 62–83). In this respect Australia contrasts sharply with other countries and has consistently experienced a higher rate of part-time employment than other industrialized economies (ILO 2002: 189). For example, only 20 per cent of Australian women with children are employed full-time compared to 40 per cent in the USA[4] (Bittman *et al.* 2003).

However, these general trends also obscure significant variations in the experience of different socioeconomic groups within society. It is important to recognize that, for both women and men, inequalities within the labour market increased dramatically during the 1970s, 1980s and 1990s. A variety of studies have demonstrated that income inequalities substantially increased during this period as a result of labour market changes (Harding 1997, Pappas 2001, Keating 2003). Table 5.3 shows that the full-time earnings of both male and female low-wage workers declined quite significantly relative to median earnings between 1975 and 2000. On the other hand, over the same period the relative earnings of both male and female high-wage workers increased substantially.

Table 5.3 Distribution of earnings for full-time adult non-managerial workers 1975–2000

	(earnings as a % of median earnings)			
	Lowest decile	*Lowest quartile*	*Upper quartile*	*Highest decile*
Males				
1975	76.0	85.6	121.1	141.2
1980	73.8	84.0	123.2	150.4
1985	72.5	80.7	125.7	154.1
1990	69.5	80.6	126.0	156.3
1995	67.7	79.4	127.8	160.7
2000	65.0	77.5	128.2	162.9
Females				
1975	80.2	88.8	115.3	136.5
1980	81.8	88.0	119.3	142.8
1985	78.6	87.3	121.2	147.9
1990	74.9	84.1	123.1	147.6
1995	73.4	84.1	125.3	152.0
2000	71.5	82.1	126.3	151.8

Source: Keating 2003: 376 (Using data from Norris and McLean 1999, and Australian Bureau of Statistics (2000b) *Employee Earnings and Hour*, Canberra: Australian Bureau of Statistics, Catalogue 6306.0).

In Australia in February 2004 women working full time earned (including over-time payments) an average of only 81.4 per cent of full-time working men – a slight increase from the situation in 1994 and compared to 77.6 per cent in 1984. However, for all women workers (including both full-time and part-time), total take home earnings dropped from 66.5 per cent to 65.7 per cent compared to men's between 1984 and 2004. These figures show that, under restructuring, women's total real earnings overall have fallen relative to men's in spite of a nominal improvement in comparative wage rates.

From the mid-1970s, rates of unemployment and underemployment rose well above the low levels experienced during the earlier long boom. At the same time, hours of work and work intensity for those in employment have increased (Watson *et al.* 2003: 84–106). The overall impact of restructuring on the Australian labour market has been summarized as creating a polarization of households into work rich and work poor – with many households having access to several jobs and working long hours in total and an increasing number of others having little or no work (Borland *et al.* 2001: 4). A recent study by the Australian Centre for Industrial Relations and Teaching reported that both mothers and fathers are working exten-sive amounts of overtime and up to two-thirds of fathers work more than 41 hours a week (Buchanan and Thornwaite 2001). There have also been more persons holding multiple jobs – an increase of 66 per cent in the past decade. An ABS study showed that over half of multiple job holders are now women and over 40 per cent of multiple job holders worked full-time in one of their jobs (ABS 2000a: 116–17). Invariably, increased stress resulting from increasing hours of work is particularly severe for women as a result of their double workload (Wooden 2001: 42,

Table 5.4 Female and male full-time and part-time employees' preferences for hours of work, Australia, November 2001

	Females			Males		
	Full-time employees %	Part-time employees %	Total female employees %	Full-time employees %	Part-time employees %	Total male employees %
Prefer more hours	4.8	30.5	16.1	8.0	49.1	13.8
Prefer less hours	32.7	6.5	21.3	28.2	3.0	24.6
Satisfied with hours	62.4	60.4	61.5	63.8	44.8	61.1
Not known	0.1	2.6	1.1	0.0	3.1	0.5
Total	100.0	100.0	100.0	100.0	100.0	100.0

Source: Australian Bureau of Statistics (1988) *Forms of Employment*, Canberra: Australian Bureau of Statistics, Catalogue 6359.0.

Broomhill and Sharp 1999, Pocock 2003). Table 5.4 shows the percentages of male and female full-time and part-time employees who would prefer to work more or less hours. It suggests that 21 per cent of female workers and 25 per cent of male workers are 'over-employed' (in regard to their preference) while 16 per cent of female workers and 14 per cent of male workers are 'under-employed'. Over 32 per cent of female full-time workers and 28 per cent of male full-time workers see themselves as working more hours than they would prefer.

During the key period of neoliberal restructuring, the most important variable influencing the labour market experience of Australian women and men was their class and socioeconomic position. A national study of urban neighbourhoods using census data found that for the bottom 70 per cent of neighbourhoods (categorized by socioeconomic status),[5] average household incomes fell in absolute terms between 1976 and 1991. Household incomes in high-status neighbourhoods, however, increased markedly. The income gap between the top and bottom 5 per cent of neighbourhoods increased by 92 per cent (Gregory and Hunter 1995: 5).

Differences in the experiences of different socioeconomic groups have been most extreme in the case of women. The pattern of employment change for women living in high-status socioeconomic neighbourhoods during restructuring was radically different from women in low-status socioeconomic neighbourhoods. In fact, all the aggregate growth in female labour force participation occurring between 1976 and 1991 was experienced by women who resided in the top 50 per cent of neighbourhoods. The proportion of employed women in the top 50 per cent of neighbourhoods increased by 10 per cent. For women living in the remaining (less affluent) half of all Australian neighbourhoods, the level of employment fell by 40 per cent. Therefore, while many women from high-status neighbourhoods increased their labour market participation as a result of opportunities created by economic restructuring, working-class women's opportunities to gain paid work drastically shrunk. Between 1976 and 1991 the mean annual income of women in the highest-status five per cent of neighbourhoods increased six-fold

more than the increase for women in the lowest-status five per cent of neighbourhoods (ibid.: 8–9). The labour market position of men also has been strongly influenced by their class position. Men in poorer socioeconomic neighbourhoods have
experienced significantly higher unemployment rates than men in higher-status
areas (Centre for Labour Research 1998). Between 1976 and 1991 the mean
annual income of men increased only in the top 20 per cent of neighbourhoods
(Gregory and Hunter 1995: 8). The labour market participation rate for men fell
across all neighbourhoods but the decline in the poorest neighbourhoods (42 per
cent) was more than double that of the most affluent neighbourhoods (ibid.: 14).

In our own recent study of neoliberal restructuring within a large Australian city
we found important differences in the experiences of women and men in different
socioeconomic neighbourhoods. Table 5.5 shows all 16 local government areas
(LGAs) of the South Australian capital city of Adelaide in ascending order
according to socioeconomic status (based on a range of socioeconomic variables
used by the ABS's Index of Advantage/Disadvantage) between the 1991, 1996 and
2001 censuses. In general, women's participation rates in poorer socioeconomic
suburbs were lower in 1991, fell substantially between 1991 and 1996 and then
either remained static or rose slightly again by 2001. In more affluent suburbs

Table 5.5 Changes in labour market participation, males and females, 16 Adelaide Metropolitan Local Government Areas 1991–2001

(Local Government Areas ranked from low to high levels of socio-economic status using the ABS index of Advantage/Disadvantage)

	Males			Females		
	1991	*1996*	*2001*	*1991*	*1996*	*2001*
Playford	72.9	66.6	63.3	44.4	42.7	42.5
Port Adelaide/Enfield	63.9	59.1	58.8	43.2	41.8	44.1
Charles Sturt	66.7	62.0	61.3	47.3	46.3	47.7
Salisbury	78.5	72.5	69.1	54.4	50.9	50.6
Onkaparinga	79.4	73.6	70.5	58.6	54.1	54.2
West Torrens	66.2	61.1	62.3	47.3	46.9	49.5
Marion	69.8	65.5	64.8	49.3	48.4	50.3
Campbelltown	71.7	65.7	64.0	52.3	50.1	50.1
Holdfast Bay	64.8	61.4	62.4	46.6	45.0	48.0
Tea Tree Gully	80.4	76.7	73.9	59.9	58.7	58.3
Prospect	69.2	67.8	70.1	52.5	54.7	58.1
Norwood, Payneham, and St Peters	67.0	64.4	64.2	49.8	50.3	53.1
Adelaide	61.9	57.7	55.1	50.1	49.1	47.1
Unley	71.2	68.0	69.1	57.2	54.7	56.2
Mitcham	70.2	66.4	67.2	54.1	51.1	54.0
Burnside	66.5	65.5	66.7	49.0	50.3	52.4
Australian average	72.2	68.9	67.3	50.7	51.2	52.2

Source: Australian Bureau of Statistics (2002) *Time Series Profiles, 2001 Census*, Canberra: Australian
Bureau of Statistics, Catalogue 2003.0.

women's participation rates were considerably higher in 1991, and then either fell marginally or increased in the period 1991–1996 and increased quite markedly again by 2001.

For men, similarly, there is a very clear correlation between lower socioeconomic suburb and falling labour market participation rates. In Adelaide's poorer suburbs the fall in participation rates in most cases is fairly dramatic, whereas in more affluent suburbs the decline in male participation rates over the period 1991–2001 is much less – and in some case the participation rate for men actually increased in these suburbs.

These very different experiences of labour market restructuring have had profoundly different consequences for the 'gender order' in different socioeconomic households. Women provided an increasingly important component of household income in working-class areas, not because their incomes actually increased but rather because working-class men's employment levels and incomes dropped dramatically. While the male-breadwinner is under threat in these households, it does not appear that any alternative, more equal, model is emerging. On the other hand, in more affluent areas the increased earnings of women have contributed substantially to household incomes (Gregory and Hunter 1995: 11). In these areas, women's economic role appears to have strengthened even though men's work role does not appear to have decreased in importance. There may be some evidence, therefore, of a shift towards a more symmetrical breadwinner model amongst some more affluent Australian households.

In summary, the labour market experience of women and men in a restructuring Australian economy is one of significant change, but with an uneven distribution of the gains and losses. The number of men in full-time employment has declined substantially while the number of women in part-time employment has risen. Despite the increasing commodification of women's labour, there seems little evidence that a new gender order is emerging based upon increased equality for women in the labour market. While more women have undoubtedly gained part-time employment opportunities, an assessment of these gains needs to take into account the problems associated with part-time and precarious forms of work. Significant also is the impact of restructuring on women's wages, working conditions and their unpaid workload. It appears, on the whole, that restructuring and the so-called feminization of the labour market has been a liberating experience for only those women who have gained access to the core labour market and who also have been able to benefit from changes in the household sphere. Mostly, these are women from already privileged households. Although continuing to occupy relatively segmented positions in the labour market, men and women overall appear to be experiencing more similarity in working conditions as a result of the restructuring of the Australian labour market. This does not so much reflect any significant improvement in women's position but rather perhaps a 'harmonizing down' process whereby the decline in men's overall position has made many men's jobs more like women's jobs, with both incorporating less protection from decommodifying influences.

Household restructuring

The different and unequal labour market outcomes for different groups of men and women under restructuring needs to be understood in the broader context of changes occurring within the organization of family life and households. Gender arrangements within households comprise an important component of the gender order in any society. Gender relations socially structure the work of households and the relationships between households and the formal economy. In general, however, the 'private' realm of the family and household is taken as a given and not subjected to scrutiny by conventional economic analyses of restructuring or by policy-makers.[6] Among other things, the organization of the family and households has a marked impact on the capacities of men and women to participate in paid work. Being disproportionately responsible for the unpaid activities of households, women enter the labour market with 'domestic baggage' with the result that the 'labour market is no level playing field' (Humphries 1998: 223). Understanding of the impact of restructuring on men and women in the 'public sphere' of paid work will be very limited without an equal focus on the profound changes simultaneously occurring in the 'private' spheres of the household and gender arrangements. An examination of what is happening to gender roles within the household, therefore, tells us something about the capacity of the society to sustain both capital accumulation and social reproduction.

The unpaid reproductive and productive work undertaken by Australian households, although difficult to measure, is clearly significant in size and remains, as elsewhere in the world, highly gendered. A national time use study conservatively estimated unpaid household activities and voluntary and community work in 1997 at 48 per cent of the value of total measured GDP. Unpaid work grew 15 per cent from the previous national time use study in 1992 (ABS 1997: 4–16). Particularly telling is Duncan Ironmonger's calculation that the volume of labour hours used in the household economy is 40 per cent greater than that for the formal economy (1996: 47).[7] National time use studies show that between 1992 and 1997 women and men's relative unpaid work contribution overall has remained relatively unchanged. Women contributed 65 per cent and 64 per cent of unpaid work activities in 1992 and 1997 respectively (ibid). Men have increased their hours of childcare and while different groups of men have different patterns of unpaid work, overall men's hours of unpaid work have not changed markedly. The main source of change in the gender division of labour between 1987 and 1997 occurred as a result of women doing less (on average), rather than men doing more (Bittman and Pixley 1997: 90, Baxter 2002: 420). Aggregate time use data indicates that any household adjustments between paid work and unpaid household labour have been made primarily by women without any significant challenge to the traditional gender model. In other words, women substitute their time by buying market services, or simply not doing the housework, as they seem either unable or unwilling to negotiate substantial increases in men's unpaid work. This suggests that restructuring has reinforced women's 'double shift' with women being responsible for developing strategies for combining paid and unpaid work. Moreover it is women, both married and single parents, who combine full-time work with family responsibilities that have the longest load of paid and unpaid working hours. As a result, neoliberal policies that 'refamilialize' or re-privatize social reproduction tend to increase women's unpaid work burdens and undermine the capacity and resilience of households to carry out their productive and reproductive roles.

A more nuanced analysis of changes in aggregate time use statistics for unpaid household work indicates that while gender relations in Australian households may appear relatively unchanged, they are nevertheless being subjected to important restructuring pressures. A study by Bittman and others (2003) comparing bargaining and household time use in Australia and the USA concluded that women's paid work and increasing income in both countries gave them greater bargaining power with women decreasing their household work as their earnings rose. However, where Australian men were earning less than their wives the response was often for the wife to compensate for the 'gender deviance of female breadwinning' by undertaking substantially more housework. In the USA case the husband reduced his housework slightly (ibid.: 209). Time use data points to a gender order in Australia that is underpinned by men's participation in housework being 'impervious to their wives' earnings' (ibid.: 207). While the reasons for this remain unresolved, this data does point to the resilience of a strong male-breadwinner culture in Australia.

An important pressure for change in the gender arrangements of Australian households is the series of demographic changes in the structure of Australian families that have accompanied labour market restructuring. Census data shows that one of the features of recent changes in demographic trends has been a decline in the marriage rate from 7.2 per 1,000 in the population in 1986 to 5.3 in 2001 (ABS 2003: 36). Other important changes include a rise in divorce rates, an increase in the average age for the birth of a woman's first child and a declining fertility rate. The result has been a dramatic decline in the typical family structure comprising a married couple with children. As shown in Table 5.6 the number of persons living in couple families with dependent children declined substantially during the 1990s – from 59 per cent of the population in 1991 to 52 per cent in 2001. At the same time, persons living in couple relationships without children have increased in number by 28 per cent over this period. However, lone person households and one-parent families are the fastest growing types of household in Australia. Persons living in one-parent families in Australia increased by 34 per cent from 1991 to 2001 while lone person households increased by 42 per cent. This increase was largely associated with an increase in the number of separated and divorced persons (ibid.: 37–9). These trends indicate a significant decline in traditional families. In 2001 the total population living in a couple family with children household still comprised a majority but one that is rapidly declining.

Australian Bureau of Statistics projections indicate that the traditional breadwinner family structure is likely to further decline over the next few decades.[8] Whereas at the time of the national census in 2001 couple families with children comprised around one-third (33.8 per cent) of all households, by 2026 these are projected to decline to less than one-fifth (18.6 per cent) of all households – a

Table 5.6 Persons in family, group and lone person households, Australia 1991–2001

	1991 %	1996 %	2001 %	% change in number of persons 1991–2001
One family household:				
Couple family with children	59.2	54.6	52.2	-1.8
Couple family without children	17.2	18.7	19.8	+28.1
One-parent family	9.3	10.1	11.2	+34.2
Lone person household	7.8	9.3	10.0	+42.1
Group household	3.8	3.8	3.6	+3.7
Other	2.7	3.5	3.2	
Total	100.0	100.0	100.0	+11.3

Source: Australian Bureau of Statistics (2002) *Time Series Profiles, 2001 Census*, Canberra: Australian Bureau of Statistics, Catalogue 2003.0.

decline of almost 20 per cent. Couple households without children will have increased in number by 73 per cent. Single parent households are projected to increase by 63 per cent. Lone person households are projected to more than double in number and to represent over one-third of all households in Australia.

The rise in gay and lesbian households and cohabiting heterosexual couple households since the 1980s also potentially provides a challenge to the traditional male-breadwinner/female-carer household structure. As marriage rates steadily decline there has occurred an accompanying increase in the number of cohabiting couples. These relationships have increased from less than 1 per cent in 1971 to 12 per cent in 2001 (de Vaus *et al.* 2003: 13, Borland *et al.* 2001: 124). The percentage of persons aged 15 and over cohabiting increased from 3 per cent to 7 per cent between 1981 and 2001 while the percentage married decreased from 60 per cent to 52 per cent (de Vaus 2003). While these figures partially reflect an increasing trend to cohabitation prior to marriage, the length of time spent living together before marriage has also increased as has the number of enduring cohabitations. While detailed estimates of the numbers of same-sex cohabiting relationships are not yet available, the actual numbers are likely to be increasing. Recent Australian studies 'have consistently found that around 10 per cent of young people aged 14 to 18 are sexually attracted to the same sex' (Hillier and Walsh 1999: 23). Because of the increasing degree of social acceptance of same-sex relationships it is highly likely that over the next decade a more accurate statistical picture of the number of gay and lesbian relationships will be possible – revealing further evidence of the decline of the traditional breadwinner family structure.

The extent of these new household forms does in itself present an important challenge to the old postwar gender order. A study by Lindsay (1999) of the domestic labour arrangements in Australian heterosexual non-married relation-ships showed that many cohabiters shared the domestic labour, and most of these men did more domestic labour than their married counterparts. Significantly also, traditional ideas about women's and men's work were not used to justify domestic labour arrangements. However, it is far less clear that these changes herald a paradigm shift towards increased gender equality. The study also found that partners who took fully equal shares of household work were still relatively rare and there was little evidence of an alternative discourse of gender equality in most households.

The decline in traditional families implies that women will spend less time over their life course engaged in household work (Baxter 1998: 59). The decline in the fertility rate, from 2.9 per cent to 1.7 per cent between 1971 and 2001, has reflected the tension faced by Australian women between a family caring role and a worker role (ABS 2004a: 7–10, Pocock 2003). In Lois Bryson's view, globalisation has absorbed mothers into the labour market and allowed them to survive without male economic support. It has also changed the basis of the construction of a couple relationship (Bryson 2001: 19). She argues that traditional family values are becoming less central in women's lives. However, the additional freedom and greater equality that has come with declining fertility and women's increased access to paid work has not brought with it a cultural change to the 'public' sphere, which continues to privilege masculine values and roles. The ongoing cultural ambivalence about women's proper role, reinforced of course by a neoliberal political and economic culture, has served to increase divisions between women. In particular, those women who pursue primarily a homemaker/carer role pay considerable economic and social penalties (ibid.: 21). Consequently, the challenge to the male-breadwinner gender order that arises from these demographic changes has not led to the emergence of more equitable alternatives. There is as yet little evidence of a widespread cultural change that would allow women or men to make a choice to adopt a homemaker and carer role without experiencing economic and social disadvantage.

Young people's perceptions of their future paid and unpaid work and childcare plans suggest gender inequalities in the sharing of unpaid work are likely to persist among future couple households in the absence of significant institutional and policy changes supportive of social reproduction. Barbara Pocock's 2004 study of 10–18 year olds from high to low socioeconomic groups in both urban and rural locations in Australia concludes that most of the young people assumed they would live in a dual earner couple household with childcare being shared with their partner. Ostensibly this could be expected to contribute to the continued decline in the traditional male-breadwinner household. However there were significant mismatches in the young men and women's plans with respect to the division of labour between paid work and childcare. Young men were much more likely to favour the structure of the male-breadwinner work and care arrangements (ibid.: 17). Resistance to domestic work was strongly demonstrated among the young men. While the young women expressed a commitment to sharing, they knew that they would have to 'start strong and stay strong' to persuade their partners to share (ibid.: vii). In Pocock's view the capacity for these young people to pursue their choice of a dual income earner model will depend on the introduction of policies that support parenting and labour market participation: parental leave, flexible work arrangements, affordable and quality childcare.

Nevertheless, there is evidence of significant differences emerging in household gender arrangements according to place, class and other socioeconomic factors. Australian qualitative research on the impact of labour market changes on gender relations within households has emphasized the importance of class. In a study of Melbourne households Belinda Probert has shown that the social reproductive activities of households and strategies for survival under restructuring vary signifi-cantly by social class, reflecting a growing polarization of experience within different households (Probert 1996: 44). Working-class households in which the male breadwinner is in a low skilled job and the female is engaged in full-time unpaid household work appear to be holding on to a pattern of gender arrange-ments based upon a strict sexual divisions of labour. Children remain the focus of identity also for many working-class women engaged in paid work and the care of children is perceived as their responsibility. In contrast, further up the socioeco-nomic scale, women are more likely to engage in a degree of negotiation around household work and caring responsibilities, resulting in a less rigid sexual division of labour. In short, it is evident that different households are engaged in different strategies of adjustment in response to the impact of restructuring. In particular, it appears that the scope for transforming the male-breadwinner model of gender relations underpinning men and women's paid and unpaid work within working-class households is frequently less than their higher social status counterparts.

The values associated with motherhood appear central in explaining some of the continuities and changes in Australia's gender order. In a more recent qualita-tive study Probert (2002), while acknowledging that there are many elements of the Australian gender culture, concluded that the values associated with motherhood are central in explaining the ongoing role of gender culture in the gender order. She compares the gender culture of two groups of men and women – one that had young children in 1956, and another that had young children in 1996. In Australia in the 1990s, in sharp contrast to the 1950s, the dominant cultural assumption was that mothers should work in paid employment. This is reflected in the fact that women, particularly married women, are increasingly participating in the labour market, and indeed are likely to express a preference for paid work. However, the view that women should undertake paid work co-exists with another, more tradi-tional, view that caring work should be done in the home. Probert argues that these contradictory aspects of gender culture are interpreted in different ways by different households.

Policy re-structuring

The negative impact of neoliberal policies on the potential to achieve gender equity in households has been well documented (Bakker 2003, Rakowski 2000, Bryson 1995). The examples are numerous: the lack of recognition of women's unpaid contributions; the difficulties of achieving gender equality in the paid and unpaid divisions of labour; the inadequacy of publicly provided services for children, the disabled, mentally ill and the aged; the quality and cost of market provided care services; the low levels of training, pay and working conditions of those who provide care; and the problematic experience of domestic migrant labour. An analysis of the care provisions in Australian policy in the late 1990s led Bettina Cass to conclude that while some important historical assumptions about women's difference and dependency associated with marriage and 'naturalness' of women as carers have been overturned in social policy, the policy direction has been towards a modified male-breadwinner model rather than a dual-bread-winner model. The unequal division of care work in the household combined with limited access to paid maternity/parental leave and family leave means that a deep tension remains between the private and public responsibilities in the area of social reproduction (1998: 56–63).

Neoliberal policies also produce dual and contradictory movements towards increased marketization of some social reproductive activities on the one hand and 'refamilialization' of others on the other hand. In Australia some policies have contributed to the market provision of many reproductive activities, including aged income support, education and health. In other cases many caring activities such as care of the disabled, mentally ill and childcare have been reassigned to the realm of the family and household – that is, refamilialized. The changes to childcare benefits in recent years are illustrative of such contradictions. The modest means tested childcare subsidy for families using formal approved childcare has been associated with the removal of government operating subsides for not-for-profit childcare centres and the growth of private childcare centres, higher fees and significant shortages in the supply of childcare places relative to demand, particularly in lower income localities. However, a family tax benefit provides financial assistance to single-income couples 'choosing' to have one parent remain at home. As this benefit is only means tested on the second earner's income, over 30,000 couple families on incomes in excess of $100,000 per annum received the benefit in 2002/3 (Sex Discrimination Unit 2005: 107). In 2005/6 new financial assistance for childcare will be provided to working parents who are in the position to access a 30 per cent tax rebate for childcare up to the value of $4000 for out of pocket childcare expenses. Such policies foster refamilialization by advantaging the (usually male) breadwinner in high income households while the use of tax expenditures increase the affordability of marketized childcare for those parents who are in higher taxation brackets.

Such contradictory policies can be partly explained by the trend to restore what Joan Acker terms 'non-responsibility' for reproduction by both capital and the state under global neoliberal restructuring (Acker 2004: 27). Because business interests in the now dominant finance and service sectors have been so intently focused upon achieving their own short-term economic goals in the restructuring process they have largely discarded previous concerns for the maintenance of a stable workforce and the need to socially reproduce that labour force. On the contrary, capital has been far more interested in enforcing greater labour market discipline within the economy, in particular by removing decommodifying safety net and welfare provisions that were so important in underpinning the increasing bargaining power of workers, trade unions and other groups (including women) during the postwar boom. Hence, under pressure from private capital, the state too has greatly reduced its traditional support for social welfare and reproduction resulting in the refamilialization of responsibility for many of the tasks previously performed in the state sector. As neoliberal policies increasingly result in the withdrawal of support for social reproduction, those high income households and professional women who can afford to purchase increasingly privatized childcare, education, health and elder care services, do so. Less well-off women use family networks of aunts and mothers or neighbours. In short, neoliberal restructuring has resulted in a 'growing polarization' of experience and gender attitudes particularly between the rich and poor (Probert 1996: 44).

Conclusion: the end of the male-breadwinner gender order?

While a strong version of the male-breadwinner/female carer model remained an important component of the gender order in the post-Second World War era in Australia, albeit one that was neither static nor uniformly experienced, there have been significant changes to the model in the past few decades. In general it is clear that the traditional male-breadwinner/female-carer household form has further declined to the point that it represents only a relatively small minority of Australian households. However, the number of households containing two full-time income earners has hardly increased at all. While the number of genuinely dual-bread-winner/dual-carer households may have increased somewhat, especially in some socioeconomic groups, this increase is the result of a change of gender culture amongst some men and women rather than the result of more women gaining access to full-time paid work. The most significant change, however, appears to be a substantial increase in the number of male-breadwinner/female part-time worker and carer households as women have increased their labour market participation in part-time employment.

However, the impact of these changes has been complex and even contradictory. In this chapter we have sought more fully to recognize the complexity and diversity existing within restructuring gender arrangements. Importantly, these changes and continuities in the patterns of household gender relations have not been experienced evenly. Some of the differences in these experiences can undoubtedly be explained by individual choice. However, there is clear evidence of the role of place, class, culture and other socioeconomic differences in structuring those experiences. In some households opportunities and benefits for women and positive changes in gender relations have arisen as a result of labour market and social changes. Those that can afford to buy childcare, elder care, education and so on in the marketplace may have increased opportunities and choices. In these cases, there is some evidence of the emergence of a more symmetrical set of gender arrangements. However, for many, the burden of social reproduction has shifted back to the household and to women. The combined impact of economic restructuring and neoliberal state policies has put enormous pressures on the capacity of these households to effectively undertake productive and reproductive activities. In some of these households the traditional male-breadwinner model continues to exist, and perhaps has even been reinforced. The winners and losers from the impact of recent economic, social and political changes are frequently engaged in quite different strategies of adjustment, resulting in both changed and reinforced versions of the traditional male-breadwinner model.

The male-breadwinner model remains an important but less dominant component of this more complex gender order. However, the cultural and ideological dimensions of the traditional male-breadwinner model also remain particularly influential within the public spheres of the labour market and the state's public policies. The neoliberal agenda that attempts either to marketize social reproduction responsibilities or to force responsibility for them back onto already stressed households remains a major impediment to attempts to achieve a new, more equitable, gender order. In this context, the sustainability of social reproduction in the long run under a neoliberal regime remains problematic. The neoliberal agenda that relentlessly pursues the marketization of every aspect of human life may not be capable of adequately ensuring a sustainable set of social arrangements, even as a 'temporary fix'. This uncertainty ensures that a space will continue to exist for challengers to neoliberal globalism to pursue alternative strategies to support sustainable structures of social reproduction both within and outside the state.

Notes

1   The terms 'gender order' (Connell 1987, Brenner 2002), 'gender system' (Duncan 1995), 'gender contract' (O'Reilly and Spee 1998, Gottfried 2000), 'gender settlement' (Junor 2000) and 'gender regime' (Walby 2001) have all been used. However, none of these terms fully acknowledge the ongoing process of change to which gender relations are subject. Neither do they fully acknowledge the differences that exist in gender arrangements within each society along class and other lines. Hence in this article, while utilizing the term 'gender order', sometimes we find it more meaningful to speak of the various 'gender arrangements' that exist within a society.

2   Actually, Pfau-Effinger also identifies another form of the breadwinner model that she calls 'the family economic gender model'. We have not incorporated this category here because it fundamentally describes a traditional European family model from a previous era in which men and women worked together in a farm or craft enterprise. Here the male was clearly defined as the decision-maker and the care of children did not consume a substantial proportion of the woman's time since they are treated as members of the family economic unit as soon as they are physically able to work (Pfau-Effinger 1999: 62).

3   The existing literature on the male-breadwinner model suffers somewhat from a tendency to theorize based upon analysis at an aggregated national level. We agree with Angelique Janssens (1998: 22) who calls upon historians and social scientists to undertake empirical research in order to identify differences within and between societies in their changing gender patterns. One of the limitations of existing debates about the male-breadwinner model has been the tendency to assume that uniform versions of the model exist within each particular nation. The impact of changes on the male-breadwinner model under neoliberal restructuring has not been deeply analysed in Australia. This is reflected in the notable absence of explicit discussion of this issue in spite of extensive work by Australian researchers on recent changes affecting gender relations in both the labour market and the household (Watson *et al.* 2003, Pocock 2003, Keating 2003, Buchanan and Thornwaite 2001, Papas 2001, Borland *et al* 2001, Wooden 2001, Harding 1997, Ironmonger 1996, Gregory and Hunter 1995).

4 While the USA is at the opposite extreme to Australia, most OECD countries are much closer to the US model than to Australia in their rates of part-time employment (ILO 2002).

5 This study based its categorization of neighbourhoods on the ABS's Index of Relative Advantage. The variables used by the ABS to construct this index include family income, educational qualifications, occupation, and housing standards etc. (Gregory and Hunter 1995).

6 Understandings of global restructuring have been dominated by neoliberal analyses and policy prescriptions that are notable for their narrow and 'economistic' view of the impact of restructuring on a community. While the discourse of neoliberalism has been particularly successful in giving unprecedented primacy to the market and its values in economic, social and political life, many other analyses of restructuring also privilege both the public sphere and economic explanations of social change. As a result, these approaches can be criticized for containing 'conceptual silences' in relation to significant sectors of both the economy and society (Bakker 1994: 1; and 2003). Economistic perspectives of global restructuring are particularly limited in their capacity to uncover the gendered nature of 'globalization'.

7 Ironmonger used the 1992 National Time Use Survey to calculate that 380 million hours of work per week were undertaken on an unpaid basis in households. He used the regular ABS Population Survey to calculate that 272 million hours per week of work were undertaken in the market economy. Thus the Australian unpaid household economy used 108 million more labour hours per week – 40 per cent greater than the official SNA measure of the market economy of business and government.

8 The ABS actually developed three scenarios based upon different assumptions about changes in families in Australia. The scenario chosen here is based upon the plausible assumption that the rate of change in family structures from 1986 to 2001 continues to 2026 (ABS 2004b: 6–7).

References

Acker, Joan (2004) 'Gender, Capitalism and Globalisation', *Critical Sociology*, 30, 1: 17–41.

ABS (1987) *Labour Force Australia: Historical Summary 1966 to 1984*, Canberra: Australian Bureau of Statistics, Catalogue 6204.0.

—— (1988) *Forms of Employment*, Canberra: Australian Bureau of Statistics, Catalogue 6359.0.

—— (1997) *Unpaid Work and the Australian Economy*, Canberra: Australian Bureau of Statistics, Catalogue 5240.0.

—— (2000a) *Australian Social Trends*, Canberra: Australian Bureau of Statistics, Catalogue 4102.0.

—— (2000b) *Employee Earnings and Hours*, Canberra: Australian Bureau of Statistics, Catalogue 6306.0.

—— (2002) *Time Series Profiles, 2001 Census*, Canberra: Australian Bureau of Statistics, Catalogue 2003.0.

—— (2003) *Australian Social Trends*, Canberra: Australian Bureau of Statistics, Catalogue 4102.0.

—— (2004a) *Australian Social Trends*, Canberra: Australian Bureau of Statistics, Catalogue. 4102.0.

—— (2004b) *Household and Family Projections 2001 to 2026*, Canberra: Australian Bureau of Statistics, Catalogue 3236.0.

—— (2004c) *Labour Force, Australia*, Canberra: Australian Bureau of Statistics, August, Catalogue 6202.0.

Bakker, Isabella (ed.) (1994) *The Strategic Silence: Gender and Economic Policy*, London: Zed Books.

—— (2003) 'Neo-liberal Governance and the Reprivatization of Social Reproduction: Social Provisioning and Shifting Gender Orders', in I. Bakker and S. Gill (eds) *Power, Production and Social Reproduction*, Basingstoke UK: Palgrave Macmillan, pp. 66–82.

Baxter, Janeen (1998) 'Moving towards Equality? Questions of Change and Equality in Household Work Patterns', in M. Gatens and A. Mackinnon (eds) *Gender and Institutions: Welfare, Work and Citizenship*, Cambridge: Cambridge University Press, pp. 55–74.

—— (2002) 'Patterns of Change and Stability in the Gender Division of Labour in Australia, 1986–1997', *Journal of Sociology*, 38, 4: 399–424.

Bittman, Michael and Pixley, Jocelyn (1997) *The Double Life of the Family: Myth, Hope and Experience*, Sydney: Allen & Unwin.

Bittman, Michael; England, Paula; Folbre, Nancy; Sayer, Liana and Matheson, George (2003) 'When Does Gender Trump Money? Bargaining and Time in Household Work', *American Journal of Sociology*, 109, 1: 186–214.

Borland, Jeff; Gregory, Bob and Sheehan, Peter (2001) 'Inequality and Economic Change', in J. Borland, B. Gregory and P. Sheehan (eds) *Work Rich, Work Poor: Inequality and Economic Change in Australia*, Melbourne: Centre for Strategic Studies, Victoria University, pp. 1–20.

Brenner, Johanna (2002) Feminism in the New Gender Order: Restructured Capital, Reconstructed Identities, unpublished paper. Available online, www.igc.apc.org/solidarity/atc/97Brenner.html.

Broomhill, Ray and Sharp, Rhonda (1999) 'Restructuring Our Lives: Engendering Debates about Social and Economic Policies in South Australia', in J. Spoehr (ed.) *Beyond the Contract State: Policies for Social and Economic Renewal in South Australia*, Adelaide: Wakefield Press, pp. 132-55.

Bryson, Lois (1995). 'Two Welfare States: One for Women, One for Men', in A. Edwards and S. Magarey (eds) *Women in a Restructuring Australia: Work and Welfare*, Sydney: Allen & Unwin, pp. 60–76.

—— (2001) 'Motherhood and Gender Relations: Where to in the Twenty-First Century?', *Just Policy*, 24, December: 12–23.

Buchanan, John and Thornwaite, Louise (2001) *Paid Work and Parenting: Charting a New Course for Australian Families*, Sydney: ACIRRT, University of Sydney.

Cass, Bettina (1998) 'The Social Policy Context', in P. Smyth and B. Cass (eds) *Contesting the Australian Way: States, Markets and Civil Society*, Cambridge: Cambridge University Press, pp. 38–54.

Centre for Labour Research (1998) *South Australian Labour Market Briefing*, 2, 2, September, Adelaide: University of Adelaide.

Connell, Bob (1987) *Gender and Power*, Cambridge: Polity Press.

Crompton, Rosemary (1999) 'The Decline of the Male Breadwinner: Explanations and Interpretations', in R. Crompton (ed.) *Restructuring Gender Relations and Employment: The Decline of the Male Breadwinner*, Oxford: Oxford University Press, pp. 1–25.

de Vaus, David; Qu, Lixia and Weston, Ruth (2003) 'Changing Patterns of Partnership', *Family Matters*, 64: 10–15.

Duncan, Simon (1995) 'Theorizing European Gender Systems', *European Journal of Social Policy*, 5, 4: 263–84.

Firth, Ann (2004) 'The Breadwinner, his Wife and their Welfare: Identity, Expertise and Economic Security in Australian Postwar Reconstruction', *Australian Journal of Politics and History*, 50, 4: 491–508.

Folbre, Nancy (1994) *Who Pays for the Kids: Gender and the Structures of Constraint*, London and New York: Routledge.

Gilding, Michael (1991) *The Making and Breaking of the Australian Family*, Sydney: Allen & Unwin.

Gottfried, Heidi (2000) 'Compromising Positions: Emergent Neo-fordisms and Embedded Gender Contracts', *British Journal of Sociology*, 51, 2: 235–59.

—— (2004) 'Gendering Globalisation Discourses', *Critical Sociology*, 30, 1: 9–15.

Gregory, Robert George and Hunter, Boyd (1995) *The Macro Economy and the Growth of Ghettos and Urban Poverty in Australia*, ANU Centre for Economic Policy Research Discussion Papers, No. 325.

Harding, Ann (1997) 'The Suffering Middle: Trends in Income Inequality in Australia 1982 to 1993–94', *Australian Economic Review*, 30, 4: 341–58.

Hargreaves, Kaye (1982) *Women at Work*, Melbourne: Penguin.

Hillier, Lynne and Walsh, Jenny (1999) 'Abused, Silent and Ignored: Creating More Supportive Environments for Same Sex Attracted Young People', *Australian Institute of Family Studies: Youth Suicide Prevention Bulletin*, 3: 23–7.

Humphries, Jane (1998) 'Towards a Family-friendly Economics', *New Political Economy*, 3, 2: 223–40.

ILO (2002) *Key Indicators of the Labour Market 2001–2002*, Geneva: International Labour Office.

Ironmonger, Duncan (1996) 'Counting Outputs, Inputs and Caring Labor: Estimating Gross Household Product', *Feminist Economics*, 2, 3: 37–64.

Janssens, Angelique (ed.) (1998) *The Rise and Decline of the Male Breadwinner Family? An Overview of the Debate*, New York: Cambridge University Press.

Junor, Anne (2000) 'Permanent Part-time Work: Rewriting the Family Wage Settlement', *Journal of Interdisciplinary Gender Studies*, 5, 2: 94–113.

Keating, Michael (2003) 'The Labour Market and Inequality', *The Australian Economic Review*, 36, 4: 374–96.

Lindsay, Jo (1999) 'Diversity but not Equality: Domestic Labour in Cohabiting Relationships', *Australian Journal of Social Issues*, 34, 3: 267–83.

McDowell, Linda (1991) 'Life without Father and Ford: The New Gender Order of Post-Fordism', *Transactions of the Institute of British Geographers*, 16, 4: 400–19.

Murphy, John (2002) 'Breadwinning: Accounts of Work and Family Life in the 1950s', *Labour & Industry*, 12, 3: 59–76.

—— (2003) 'Reply to Humphrey McQueen', *Labour & Industry*, 13, 3: 99–103.

O'Reilly, Jacqueline and Spee, Claudia (1998) 'The Future of Regulation of Work and Welfare: Time for a Revised Social and Gender Contract?', *European Journal of Industrial Relations*, 4, 3: 259–81.

Pappas, Nick (2001) 'Family Income Inequality', in J. Borland, B. Gregory and P. Sheehan (eds) *Work Rich, Work Poor: Inequality and Economic Change in Australia*, Melbourne: Centre for Strategic Studies, Victoria University, pp. 21–39.

Pfau-Effinger, Birgit (1998) 'Culture or Structure as Explanations for Differences in Part-Time Work in Germany, Finland and the Netherlands?', in J. O'Reilly and C. Fagan (eds) *Part-time Prospects: An International Comparison of Part-time Work in Europe, North America and the Pacific Rim*, London: Routledge, pp. 177–96.

—— (1999) 'The modernization of family and motherhood in Western Europe', in R. Crompton (ed.) *Restructuring Gender Relations and Employment: The Decline of the Male Breadwinner*, Oxford: Oxford University Press, pp. 60–79.

Pocock, Barbara (2003) *The Work/Life Collision*, Sydney: Federation Press.

—— (2004) Work and Family Futures: How young Australians Plan to Work and Care, Discussion Paper No 69, Canberra: The Australian Institute.

Polanyi, Karl (1957) *The Great Transformation: The Political and Economic Origins of our Time*, Boston: Beacon Hill.

Probert, Belinda (1996) 'The Riddle of Women's Work', *Arena Magazine*, 23: 39–45.

—— (2002) 'Grateful Slaves or "Self-made Women": A Matter of Choice or Policy?' *Australian Feminist Studies*, 37: 7–18.

Rakowski, C. A. (2000). 'Obstacles and Opportunities to Women's Empowerment under Neoliberal Reform', *Perspectives on Global Development and Technology*, 16, 1: 115–38.

Richmond, K. (1974) 'The Workforce Participation of Married Women in Australia', in D. Edgar (ed.) *Social Change in Australia: Readings in Sociology*, Melbourne: Cheshire, pp. 267–304.

Sex Discrimination Unit (2005) Striking the Balance: Women, Men, Work and Family, *Discussion Paper 2005*, Sydney: Human Rights and Equal Opportunity Commission.

Steketee, Mike (2005) 'A Dysfunctional Society in a Beautiful Economy', *The Australian*, Sydney: News Limited National Newspaper, August 18: 10.

Walby, Sylvia (2001) From Gendered Welfare State to Gender Regimes: National Differences, Convergence or Re-Structuring?, Paper presented to Gender and Society Group, Stockholm University. Available online, www.sociology.su.se/cgs/workshop.html.

Watson, Ian; Buchanan, John; Campbell, Iain and Briggs, Chris (2003) *Fragmented Futures: New Challenges in Working Life*, Sydney: Federation Press.

Wooden, Mark (2001) 'The Growth of "Unpaid" Working Time', *Economic Papers*, 20, 1: 29–44.

Part II

Remapping gendered spaces

6   Masculinity and masculinism under globalization

Reflections on the Canadian case

Satoshi Ikeda

Two historical processes in the past several decades – the feminist movement and globalization – have affected broader cultural understandings of masculinity and masculinism. The former is a social movement that achieved success in the 1970s and 1980s while the latter is a socioeconomic restructuring process, which, beginning in the 1980s, has been pushed by the powerful capitalist states for the benefit of the rich, the investors, and the major corporations. The feminist movement in North American societies challenged the patriarchal power structure associated with the postwar male-breadwinner model of gender relations. This movement succeeded in advancing gender equality, especially in the workplace, establishing women's reproductive rights, and politicizing violence against women. But was there any significant change in masculinity? Was there a change in masculinism, an ideology that justifies male domination and women's subordination? The historical process of globalization, even though it was a response to the crisis of accumulation (profit squeeze), also affected the trajectory of masculinity and masculinism. Did globalization cause a crisis of male-breadwinner model masculinity? What were the responses of diverse groups of men situated differently in the global political economy? To answer these questions, this chapter first examines the changes in masculinity under globalization and then examines the Canadian case. The chapter also offers a new interpretation of the changes in masculinism that have occurred in the postwar era. The chapter concludes with a suggestion for future action to overcome masculinist oppression.

Globalization and the crisis and response of masculinity

This section reviews the literature on masculinity and the transformation of masculinity under globalization. Although feminist political economists have written extensively about the impacts of globalization on women in both the North and the South, little attention has been devoted to the impacts of globalization on the daily lives of men or on broader social conceptions of masculinity. Of course, the question of what has happened to men under globalization is both evasive and complex. It is evasive because neither men nor women form a homogeneous category in theory or daily experience. The assumption of homogeneity of men and women is betrayed by countless differences among and between these social categories related to, among other things, race, ethnicity, age, religion, sexual orientation, and nationality. These differences preclude any firm conclusions about the experience of men under globalization. However, it is possible to examine the broader historical contours of masculinism – the ideology that justifies male domination – and the masculinist institutions that endorse masculinism while keeping in mind that masculinism in concrete cases would be best analyzed in its intersection with other stratification/discrimination attributes such as race and ethnicity (Stasiulis 1999).

Neoliberal globalization was ushered in during the early 1980s by the administrations of Margaret Thatcher in the United Kingdom and of Ronald Reagan in the United States. Their policies included, among other things, taxation policies that favoured the rich at the expense of the middle class and the poor, the privatization of public services, labour union bashing, and the reduction or elimination of labour and environmental regulations on corporate activities. These core neoliberal policies were soon imposed on the Third World countries through the structural adjustment programmes of the International Monetary Fund (IMF) and World Bank and through bilateral and multilateral trade agreements involving industrialized countries. Canada, for example, signed the Canada-US Free Trade Agreement (FTA) in 1987 and the North American Free Trade Agreement (NAFTA) in 1993. At the same time, corporate activities, as a result of trade and financial liberalization, became increasingly global in character, as evidenced by a significant expansion in the transborder movement of goods, services, finance, workers, and information (McBride and Shields 1997). In the peripheral countries, or the so-called 'developing' countries of the global South, the project of national economic development of the postcolonial period was replaced by the globalization project (McMichael 2004). The role of government was increasingly reduced to luring foreign investment, largely through low wage policies and lax labour and environmental standards. In the process, manufacturing jobs were 'exported' from core countries to peripheral countries, causing job insecurity and lower wages for heretofore privileged 'white' male workers in the core countries. The consequences of global economic restructuring were even more pronounced for non-white males already marginalized by racism. Some men, however, enjoyed rising incomes in growth sectors such as finance, trade, information technology, and resource extraction. This is the historical backdrop, which, I argue, brought about a crisis and reformulation of masculinity.

Masculinity is culturally and historically constructed on norms that regulate male identity and behaviour. Together with femininity, masculinity provides the basis for gender role assignment. The typical 'traditional' male role of 'breadwinner' for a household typified the post-Second World War (or postwar) nuclear family where the male 'head' of household was responsible for earning income for the entire family (postwar male-breadwinner model). Such role assignment in turn prescribed cultural norms about who was a 'man' and how he should behave (such as being tough both physically and emotionally). Male gender role assignment provided a power base for male domination, and together with the cultural message of dominant masculinity, it produced and reproduced male domination in family, community, and society.

In postwar Canadian society, the male-breadwinner model became the norm that defined masculinity. According to this model, the male 'head' of household was responsible for earning income outside the home while his wife engaged in unpaid household reproductive labour. The unwaged nature of housework, in turn, was the basis of lower wages for women when they entered the labour market, while institutionalized discrimination against working women justified the division of labour between men and women in the household. Economic power held by men formed the basis of patriarchal oppression, and thus equality in employment (in terms of both wages and opportunities) became one of the primary objectives of the feminist movement. A successful feminist movement, together with an anti-racism movement, created more opportunities for women and racial minorities in the workplace, and open sexism and the display of sexist attitudes increasingly became less acceptable. While the feminist movement challenged the male-breadwinner model, it was global economic stagnation, beginning in the mid-1970s and the neoliberal response to overcome the crisis of accumulation, that transformed the economic foundations of this model of gender relations.

Corporations sacrificed employees to secure investor value, by such means as union busting, wage cuts, cuts in fringe benefits, downsizing, and plant relocation to low cost countries. Life-long careers accompanying postwar industrialization were replaced by casual forms of employment (part-time, seasonal or term contract and self-employment). To make ends meet, an additional income source became necessary for households, thus the male-breadwinner model was replaced as the predominant household model by one-and-a-half or dual income earner model (Broomhill and Sharp *in this volume*). There were many significant social changes that accompanied this shift which caused the crisis of masculinity. Women's advancement in the labour market, although largely in low-paying service sector jobs, weakened their dependence on male income. The feminist movement broadened women's choice of relationships, and changed prevailing attitudes toward the family, childbearing and rearing, and divorce (Whitehead and Barrett 2001: 9). These conditions in turn led to a crisis of masculinity, which some argue have contributed to a growing mental health crisis among men (Coyle and Morgan-Sykes 1998).

Loss of steady jobs for middle-class males, however, did not mean that women achieved equality with men. As demonstrated with Canadian examples later, the male advantage over women in employment remained intact. Just as the postwar industrialization process offered men opportunities to advance their power and domination over women, the globalization process in the 1980s and onward provided opportunities for some men to maintain their domination in newly expanded areas such as international finance, information technology, and the global deployment of extractive industries. The proper characterization of the crisis of 'breadwinner model masculinity' is that a downwardly mobile male population faced the crisis but those who were upwardly mobile transformed the breadwinner model masculinity with the neoliberal rhetoric of the market. The new upper class included entrepreneurs, upper level managers in emerging sectors, corporate lawyers and accountants, and financial speculators. Connell labels the masculinity exhibited by such international businessmen as 'transnational business masculinity' which, he argues, is the hegemonic masculinity in the contemporary global era (2001a).

Hegemonic masculinity is 'the configuration of gender practice which embodies the currently accepted answer to the problem of the legitimacy of patriarchy, which guarantees (or is taken to guarantee) the dominant position of men and the subordination of women' (ibid.: 38–9). Transnational business masculinity is associated with the global corporate executives who exhibit egocentrism, very conditional loyalties, and a declining sense of responsibility for others (Connell 2001b: 369). By depriving access to economic wealth, this masculinity subordinates working-class men in the core and the general population in the periphery. Transnational business masculinity subjugates women to market 'discipline' and justifies male domination and the exploitation of women. It does so by using the neoliberal rhetoric that ongoing gender discrimination is simply a natural consequence of the invisible hand of the market which is assumed to be gender neutral, efficient, and just. In addition to justifying gender discrimination, transnational business masculinity endorses and justifies commodification of women's bodies on a global scale.

In North America, the breadwinner model of masculinity was, it appeared, accompanied by stronger Christian morality that discouraged commodification of women's bodies in the form of pornography and prostitution. Transnational business masculinity, in contrast, fully endorses prostitution. Hotels where business conventions and meetings are held routinely offer pornographic videos. Night life involving prostitutes is often an important business practice and, in some countries, international businessmen are 'served' by a well developed prostitution industry (ibid.: 370). Under globalization, prostitution has been legalized in many countries such as Holland and Australia (Economist Global Agenda 2003). The International Labour Organization, the longest standing international institution for the protection of worker rights, moreover, has endorsed prostitution as an important industry for economic development (Lim 1998, cited in Raymond 2004: 1162). The flourishing prostitution industry under globalization has been fuelled by illegal migration of women who are often the victims of kidnapping.

International NGOs which oppose trafficking are divided into two camps – one opposing trafficking of women but supporting prostitution and the other opposing both trafficking and prostitution. The latter views both practices as a form of violence against women. Raymond, for example, questions the difference between prostitution and behaviours that otherwise would be regarded as abusive and violent.

> It is the exchange of money in prostitution that serves to transform what is actually sexual harassment, sexual abuse, and sexual violence into a "job" known as "commercial sex work," a "job" performed primarily by racially and economically disadvantaged women in the so-called first and third worlds,

and by overwhelming numbers of women and children who have been the
victims of childhood sexual abuse

(Raymond 1998: 2).

Transnational business masculinity has inherited the role of setting the
masculinist order from the previously hegemonic breadwinner model of masculinity in the West, as well as the traditional patriarchal masculinities of the global
South. This may be partly a result of the rise in feminist movement which
demanded equality with men and the elimination of violence against women both
at home and in society. Transnational business masculinity can be interpreted as a
mechanism of continuing male domination by justifying the unfair advantage that
certain men enjoy by arguing that market outcomes are fair and just. Transnational hegemonic masculinity may dominate the current era of globalization, but
there have been various responses by men who facing a crisis of masculinity.

The Promise Keepers movement, originating in the United States and imported
to Canada, employs religion (evangelical Christianity) to restore men's place in
marriages and families. In organized gatherings, men learn to express themselves
and to care for others including men from different races. Through the appeal of
godly manhood based on rational patriarchy, expressive egalitarianism (men's
liberationism), the tender warrior (poeticized manhood), and the multicultural
man (interracial masculinity), this movement expanded rapidly in the 1990s
(Bartkowski 2001). While this movement makes Christian men's masculinity more
expressive of emotions and caring and accepting of other races, it leaves the gender
and racial privilege of white men untouched (Heath 2003).

There also is a tendency to link masculinity to physical security. The expanding
activities of the National Rifle Association, for example, are a countermovement
designed to prevent erosion of frontier masculinity (Melzer 2004). Albers (2003)
argues that anti-UN (United Nations) paramilitary men use the dual ideologies of
hegemonic masculinity and nationalism to reinforce their identities. For them
paramilitarism sustains masculinity and anti-UN stance represents opposition to
globalization and a new global order. The UN is perceived as an entity that
threatens US sovereignty and has hosted several international conferences to
advance women's rights. In this sense, anti-UN sentiment expresses, in addition to
US unilateral nationalism, resentment toward women's equal rights and any gain
women have made toward equality both nationally and internationally.

The most brutal expression of such masculinist resentment toward women is
violence against women (VAW) which has become widespread under globalization
(Erchak and Rosenfeld 1994, Levinson 1989, Michalski 2004). The 1993 United
Nations World Conference on Human Rights defined violence against women as
'any act of gender-based violence' resulting or likely to result in harms to women,
and occurring in the family, within the general community, and perpetrated or
condoned by the state (Hester 2004: 1433). Barzilai summarizes that:

(d)espite some success of feminism inside and outside the courtroom, basic
practices of male-dominated societies against women – marginalization,

domestication, discrimination, subjugation, displacement, underpresentation, sexual exploitation, and violence – have not significantly been altered even when globalization has generated expectations of liberal egalitarianism

(2004: 870).

Globalization was accompanied by the increased possibility of international–global feminist cooperation, but massive economic and social change affected violence against women within a context of patriarchal domination (Hester 2002, 2004). VAW in Germany, for example, is high among the lowest socioeconomic class, especially the young unemployed (Kury *et al.* 2004) and violence among intimate partners is underreported but high in Japan (Kury and Yoshida 2003).

Violence against women (VAW) takes various forms, but it is necessary to include 'control through fear' as a category related to VAW even though instances may not involve physical assault. Such forms include stalking (Barzilai 2004) and verbal harassment (Robinson 2005). Stalking is prevalent in the US (Barzilai 2004) and American women cannot enjoy carefree outdoor activities due to fear of male attack (Wesely and Gaarder 2004). Sexual harassment is a means of maintaining and regulating hierarchical power relationships involving gender, race and class (Robinson 2005), and financially vulnerable people, especially women, are the victims of unwanted touches and invasion of personal space (Ugge and Blackstone 2004). Sexual harassment as a mechanism to subordinate women is prevalent in North American universities (Litwin 1998) and UK primary schools (Skelton 1997). Workplace harassment is often serves as the means whereby men put down a female competitor for job advancement (Lee 2000).

Data from Canada seem to conform to these broad international trends. A study from the province of Quebec, for example, found that poverty is related to VAW, although VAW spans all socioeconomic groups (Rinfret-Raynor *et al.* 2004: 721). Another study reports that Canada ranks the highest among 27 North American and European countries in physical violence against women with 13.1 per cent of women reporting experience of physical violence and 7.9 per cent sexual violence in the previous five years. Roughly one-quarter of Canadian women reported experiencing one or more types of physical violence by their partners at some point in their relationship (Randall and Haskell 1995, Weir 2000, Michalski 2004).

A crisis of masculinity also leads to violence against women in the global South. Neoliberal policies imposed in many indebted peripheral countries upset the middle-class expectation of inheriting their parents' economic standing. Kimmel suggests that the displacement of men from traditional roles, expectations, and power relations may be a factor underlying many forms of male violence in contemporary politics, particularly the rise of terrorism.

It is the lower middle class – that stratum of independent farmers, small shop-keepers, craft and highly skilled workers and small-scale entrepreneurs – who have been hardest hit by the processes of globalization. This has resulted in massive male displacement – migration, downward mobility. And it has been felt the most not by the adult men who were the tradesmen, shopkeepers and skilled workers, but by their sons, by the young men whose inheritance has been seemingly stolen from them. They feel entitled and deprived – and furious. These angry young men are the foot soldiers of the armies of rage that have sprung up around the world

(2003: 605).

Religious fundamentalism, be it the Muslim version or the born-again Christian version, can be interpreted as a male response to stall the global gender revolution (Giddens and Hutton 2000, Whitehead and Barrett 2001) or else a misogynist response to the crisis of masculinity and loss of patriarchal male domination (Kimmel 2003: 616). Traditional masculinist cultures are re-emerging or reinforced as a response to global corporate and US military domination. When traditional masculinities are threatened, partly due to an eroding economic base or to the imposition of liberal gender policies by the United Nations or World Bank, the response is to reaffirm local gender orthodoxies and hierarchies. Thus masculine fundamentalism is a common response in gender politics (Connell 2001b: 370).

Violence against women predates globalization as does oppressive masculinism. Globalization shook up the economic base of male-breadwinner model masculinity, and there emerged transnational business masculinity as a hegemonic form of masculinity that justifies masculinism with the rhetoric of the market. Under globalization masculinist oppression continues involving violence against women. Do we see continued male advantage and masculinist oppression in Canada? Let us turn to the examination of these issues in Canada.

Male advantage and masculinist oppression in Canada

Discussions of the crisis of masculinities under globalization make several assumptions about negative employment trends for men. It is commonly argued, for example, that, in the global North, well-paid manufacturing jobs for men have been replaced by low-paid service jobs for women This section examines Canadian employment data to determine whether these developments characterize the contemporary labour market. We first examine data on wages. Unless otherwise stated, the data used are from Statistics Canada's CANSIM electronic database.

The female-to-male wage ratio (which measures hourly wage differences) for all employees in all industries decreased from 81.2 per cent in 1997 to 80.6 per cent in 2000, then increased to 83.3 per cent in 2004. The other measure of gender inequality is the female-to-male earning ratio. Earnings are derived by multiplying wage by hours of work. The female-to-male earning ratio increased from 63.5 in 1981 to 72.4 in 1995. The ratio went through big ups and downs in the 1990s, settling at around 70 per cent from 2000. In the twenty-first century male advantage appears to have declined slightly (2.76 per cent narrowing in the wage gap). However, a huge male advantage still remains with respect to the wage gap (20 per cent) and especially with respect to earning (30 per cent).

The gender wage gap in Canada appears to be narrowing over the long term. Some researchers, in fact, are optimistic that male and female hourly wages will

Table 6.1 Female-to-male earning ratio by cohorts (%)

	1983	1993	2003
15 to 24 years old in 1993		90.2	74.4
15 to 24 years old in 1983	79.6	74.9	72.8
25 to 34 years old in 1983	73.1	71.5	67
35 to 44 years old in 1983	62.9	67.3	68.6
45 to 54 years old in 1983	59.4	69.5	

Source: Calculated based on figures in Statistics Canada CANSIM electronic database

converge as women acquire a similar education and length of training profile as men in the future (Rathje 2002). Others, however, contend that the gap will remain due to the institutional practice of discrimination against women (Canada 2002). Shannon and Kidd (2001) predict that the gender wage gap will persist until at least 2031 even after women achieve educational equality. Canadian women are underrepresented in high paying jobs such as senior managers of goods-producing companies (11:1 in favour of men) and female senior managers earn only 56 per cent of the wage earned by their male counterparts doing the same work according to the 1998 Census data (UNPAC).

Despite the trend in hourly wage equalization, institutionalized discrimination practice continues in the labour market. In addition to gender discrimination in workplaces, the fundamental problem that creates a large gender earnings gap lies outside the workplace.

To underscore male advantage in earnings, the female-to-male earning ratio was traced for the same cohorts for the previous two decades. Table 6.1 summarizes the results.

Table 6.1 indicates that the female-to-male earning ratio tends to converge around 70 per cent. For younger people in recent years, the ratio tends to be higher, such as 90.2 per cent in 1993. But after ten years, the same female group only earned 74.4 per cent of male earnings. Likewise, the ratio declined for those at 15 to 24 years in 1983 over the 20 years. Those in the middle age category in 1983 experienced a rise in the ratio, but it remained under 70 per cent. Overall, men maintained advantage over women even though the gap for the younger cohorts narrowed. The persistence of this gender earnings gap in part reflects the unequal division of household reproductive labour. Women do more housework than men in Canada (Silver 2000) reflecting the persistent influence of the masculinist idea that household duty is women's role. The contemporary younger generation is presumably enjoying employment equality, which was a victory won by feminists over many years. But the statistics suggest that their earning ratio dropped as they enter childbearing and childrearing age (a drop of earning ratio from 90.2 per cent in 1993 to 74.4 per cent in 2004 for those who were 15 to 24 years old in 1993). It is safe to assume that this is a result of a combined 'reality' that the male partner could earn more income than the female partner and that it is still the social norm for women to engage in more housework. A lack of daycare in Canada also forces many female workers into part-time employment so that they can meet childcare needs. Baxter (2002: 419) reports that, in the case of Australia, women 'do about two-thirds of childcare tasks, at least three-quarters of the routine everyday indoor housework tasks, and spend about three times as many hours as men on the latter'. In Canada women do 75 per cent of housework according to the 1980s data (Baxter 1997). This women's 'duty' at home leads to disadvantage for women in the labour market.

> It is women, not men, who tend to utilize parental leave and work part-time. It is women, not men, who therefore have work interruptions to rear children and lowered work experience, labour force attachment, and on-the-job training. And those things matter: they increase women's economic reliance on men within marriage, and leave women much more economically vulnerable than men when marriages end ...
>
> (Burkhauser *et al.* 1990, cited by Bianchi *et al.* 1999: 31).

The Gender Job Segregation Index (GJSI) illustrates the glass wall phenomenon, that is, gender segregation by occupation. I have calculated the GJSI as the weighted sum of male-to-female employment ratio where the weight is the sector's share of total employment. If the numbers of male and female employees are the same in all industries, the index becomes one. The higher the GJSI, the greater is gender segregation. There are two types of statistics available from CANSIM electronics database for the derivation of GJSI. The North American Industry Classification System (NAICS) offers industry-based employment statistics and the National Occupational Classification for Statistics (NOC-S) offers occupation-based employment statistics. The industry-based GJSI increased from 2.16 in 1987 to 3.20 in 2003. Gender job segregation by industrial category has steadily expanded. The occupation-base GJSI also increased from 1.42 in 1987 to 1.60 in 2004. These findings suggest that male advantage in the form of gender job segregation is significant and that glass wall remains; in fact, the gender job segregation gap is widening.

One of the alleged impacts of globalization is the relocation of manufacturing activities from the global North to the global South and accompanying replacement of goods-producing sector employment with service-sector employment in the global North. In Canada, employment in the goods-producing sectors (manufacturing, agriculture, mining, utilities, etc.) slightly increased between 1981 (2.7 million men and 787,000 women) and 2004 (3 million men and 942,000 women). Employment in the service-producing sector has increased markedly in the same period (from 3.8 million men and 3.8 million women in 1981 to 5.4 million men and 6.5 million women in 2004). In terms of the share in total employment, the goods-producing sectors lost share for men (from 42 per cent in 1981 to 36 per cent in 2004) and for women (from 17 per cent in 1981 to 13 per cent in 2004), while service-producing sectors expanded for men (from 58 per cent in total male employment to 64 per cent) and women (from 83 per cent to 87 per cent). There was a decline in the goods-producing sector employment in terms of the share in total employment, but the absolute number in employment increased nonetheless for both men and women. The service-producing sectors, on the other hand, increased male and female employment both absolutely and relatively. The impact of globalization on sectoral employment, therefore, can be expressed as 'a rapid expansion in service-producing sector jobs while employment in goods-producing sector increased only slightly'.

Canadian employment in the durable manufacturing sector increased by 300,000 between 1993 and 2000. This is largely because US automobile manufacturers expanded their Canadian operations under NAFTA to take advantage of lower labour costs and the declining value of the Canadian dollar in the 1990s. In a sense, this is an indication that Canada occupies a peripheral position *vis-à-vis* the US since Canada is a recipient of US manufacturing jobs that were exported to low cost countries. Canadian status as US car manufacturing base, however, is not stable. US automakers started reducing the size of their operation in Canada in 2005 because of the rising value of the Canadian dollar (as a result of oil price increase), Canada's cost disadvantage against countries with lower production costs (such as Mexico), and the loss of market share to non-US carmakers. Under globalization, it may not be possible for an oil-rich semiperipheral country such as Canada to escape the path of de-industrialization.

It has been alleged that globalization has replaced well-paid manufacturing jobs with low-paying service sector jobs. Has that been the case in Canada? To answer this question, I have rank ordered average wages in 2004 by industry sector for both men and women. The lowest-paying sector for both men and women was 'accommodation and food services' with an hourly wage of $11.29 for men and $9.86 for women, in contrast to the highest – 'utilities' – with an hourly wage of $29.13 for men and $24.17 for women. I ranked 16 sectors according to the average hourly wages, and classified them into three categories, i.e., poorly-paid, medium-paid, and well-paid. Between 1981 and 2004 employment increased by 1.9 million for men and by 2.9 million for women. Table 6.2 shows the percentage of each sector's contribution to total employment increase (a sector's employment increase divided by total employment increase times 100) together with the wage class status.

The service-producing sector contributed to 92 per cent of the increase in male employment and 95 per cent of the increase in employment for women during these years. In the service-producing sector, 'professional, scientific and technical service' contributed to 21 per cent of male employment increase followed by trade (19 per cent). The former is well-paid while the later is poorly-paid for men. Among the service-producing sector, well-paid sectors contributed to 28 per cent, medium-paid 20 per cent, and poorly-paid 44 per cent of the employment increases for men. This implies that not all service sector jobs were poorly-paid. However, male job expansion was more prominent in the poorly-paid sectors while well-paid jobs in the goods-producing sector declined. Therefore, there was a replacement of well-paid goods-producing jobs with poorly-paid service-producing jobs for Canadian men, while some men enjoyed expanded employment opportunities in well-paid service sectors. For women, well-paid service sectors contributed to 48 per cent, medium-paid 14 per cent, and poorly-paid 33

Table 6.2 Sectoral contribution to total employment change (%), 1981–2004, wage class in 2004

	Male	Male wage Ccass	Female	Female wage class
Goods-producing sector	7.88	Medium-paid	5.31	Medium-paid
Agriculture	-5.53	Poorly-paid	-0.60	Poorly-paid
Forestry, fishing, mining, oil and gas	-4.12	Well-paid	0.26	Well-paid
Utilities	-0.39	Well-paid	0.44	Well-paid
Construction	11.66	Medium-paid	1.50	Medium-paid
Manufacturing	6.27	Medium-paid	3.72	Medium-paid
Services-producing sector	92.12	Medium-paid	94.69	Medium-paid
Trade	18.96	Poorly-paid	14.29	Poorly-paid
Transportation and warehousing	5.75	Medium-paid	2.70	Medium-paid
Finance, insurance, real estate and leasing	7.41	Well-paid	5.24	Medium-paid
Professional, scientific and technical services	20.63	Well-paid	8.91	Well-paid
Business, building and other support services	11.96	Poorly-paid	7.28	Poorly-paid
Educational services	2.06	Well-paid	10.59	Well-paid
Healthcare and social assistance	5.93	Medium-paid	23.52	Well-paid
Information, culture and recreation	7.98	Medium-paid	5.74	Medium-paid
Accommodation and food services	8.70	Poorly-paid	8.32	Poorly-paid
Other services	4.68	Poorly-paid	3.37	Poorly-paid
Public administration	-1.95	Well-paid	4.74	Well-paid

Source: Calculated based on figures in Statistics Canada CANSIM electronic database

per cent of the employment increases. This implies that nearly half of the employment expansion occurred in well-paid sectors and one-third occurred in poorly-paid sectors, leading to polarization in women's wages. Also, even though employment in well-paid service sectors increased more for women than men, the overall wage gap between men and women remains high (20 per cent). This is because female-to-male wage ratio is 73 per cent in the professional, scientific and technical services sector where male employment increased the most (20.6 per cent) while women's employment expansion in this sector was a modest 8.9 per cent. The healthcare and social assistance sector shows the fastest growth for women's employment (23.5 per cent) but the female-to-male wage ratio is still 91 per cent even though this is a well-paid sector for women. Male advantage in employment is maintained through gender job segregation and a significant gender wage gap in 'male' jobs.

Another alleged trend in employment is 'casualization'. This implies a shift in employment forms from full-time to part-time, or from institutional employment to self-employment, and precarious employment which involves frequent job loss.

What was the trend in part-time employment and self-employment? 'Part-time' in Statistics Canada data implies shorter working hours (less than 30 hours per week). 'Self-employed without paid help' is expected to include 'casual' employment (as opposed to the self-employed with paid help who can be considered entrepreneurs). The share of self-employed without paid help in total employment increased from 7.4 per cent in 1976 to 12.28 in 1999, then declined slightly. The share of part-time employment also increased from about 7 per cent in the early 1980s to about 11 per cent in recent years. The combined 'casual employment' share (part-time plus self-employed without paid help) increased from 13 per cent in 1976 to 22.5 per cent in 2004 for men. Put differently, the number of Canadian men in casual employment increased from one in every eight employed men to one in every four.

The growth in the part-time share has been quite high for women as compared to men, and it kept increasing from 23.61 per cent in 1976 to 29.41 per cent in 1997. Between 1998 and 2004 it remained at about 27 per cent level. Self-employment without paid help also increased until 1998. The share of female casual employment (part-time plus self-employed without paid help) increased from 28 per cent in 1976 to 35 per cent in 2004. The degree of 'casualization' has been more pronounced for women than men, involving one in every three employed women. Casual employment for women is particularly high in accommodation and food services (44.5 per cent in 2004), retail trade (41.9), other services (34.4), agriculture (32.0), and educational services (30.0). Out of 21 sectors, 12 sectors recorded more than 20 per cent casual employment for women. In contrast, only two sectors (accommodation and food services at 34.1 per cent and retail trade at 23.6 per cent) recorded above 20 per cent casual employment for men. Seen as part of the overall trend, male privilege over females in the form of full-time jobs versus part-time jobs continues. Also, the larger proportion of part-time women workers depresses average wages, thus contributing to a persistent gender wage gap.

Is male advantage continuing in areas other than the workplace? Education plays a critical role both in personal career development and in stratifying workers in post-education employment. In Canada women workers with university degrees increased steadily from 12.9 per cent in 1990 to 21.4 per cent in 2004. The rapid increase in women workers with university degrees was not matched by men (14.6 per cent in 1990 to 20.0 per cent in 2004). This, on the surface, may indicate an erosion of male educational advantage. But not all university degrees guarantee high-paying jobs or generate similar future income. Despite the fact that the disciplinary door is open to those qualified, clear gendered educational paths still exist. In order to examine 'educational glass wall', I calculated the female-to-male enrolment ratio for 31 university degree programmes between 1992/3 and 2001/2 academic years (data from CANSIM electronic database). The female-to-male ratio for the entire university degree programmes has increased from 1.25 to 1.35, reflecting a larger enrolment figure for women than men. Out of 31 programmes 17 programmes were 'female dominated' in 1992/3 (the ratio was larger than 1.0, or more than one female students for every male student), the highest being

'French language/literature/letters' with 3.32 followed by 'psychology' (3.19), 'public administration and services' (3.09), 'library science'(3.03) and 'foreign languages, literatures, and linguistics' (2.90). In 10 years, all of 17 programmes remained female dominated and the ratio increased in 10 programmes, implying that 'female' fields are increasingly 'feminized'.

There were 14 programmes that were male dominated (the ratio was smaller than 1.0) in 1992/3, the lowest (or most male dominated) being 'military technologies' (0.16) followed by 'engineering' (0.20), 'computer and information sciences' (0.31), 'physical sciences' (0.41), and 'mathematics' (0.59). Between 1992/3 and 2001/2, four programmes out of 14 became 'female dominated', that is, the ratio exceeded 1.0 in 2001/2 for 'business, management, marketing' (from 0.98 to 1.09), 'parks, recreation, leisure and fitness studies' (from 0.93 to 1.49), 'natural resources and conservation' (from 0.78 to 1.11) and 'agriculture, agricultural operations' (from 0.76 to 1.21). The ratio decreased in only one programme (philosophy and religion), but the degree of 'male domination' remained intact in the top five male dominated programmes, especially 'computer and information sciences' whose ratio increased only by 0.01. The choice of programme is, in theory, 'voluntary' since all fields are open to both men and women. But the existing gender culture practice both at home and in society (via mass media particularly) and instructional practice at primary and secondary schools, among many other factors, continue to create 'male' and 'female' fields. Bearing in mind the significant gap between expected income in male and female career paths, we can conclude that masculine domination is still reproduced in the Canadian school system.

As a university instructor of sociology courses, I usually ask those heterosexual female students who have, or intend to have, partners whether they will quit their jobs to raise children. Except for those who are flatly refusing to have children, most of them say whoever is making less money will quit work and engage in child raising. To them this is a rational economic choice. Their 'rational' choice, often accompanied by confidence that their relationship will last a lifetime, ignores the fact that engagement in housework benefits men at the expense of women's careers. As the statistics on employment show, one in three women enter casual employment partly to accommodate the demands of caring and domestic work. Male advantage in income earning activities is still significant despite the rise in two-income households. Such advantage is strengthened by the still significant glass wall and glass ceiling in the labour market.

In addition to continued male advantage in employment, masculinist oppression in the form of violence against women is prevalent in Canada. Statistics Canada conducted a nationwide survey in 1993. Compared to the previous studies that used police reports or limited case studies, this survey of 12,300 women aged 18 years and older was quite comprehensive and it established how widespread was VAW in Canada. Slightly more than half of the country's 10.5 million women have experienced some form of assault after age 16. Fully 51 per cent of the women surveyed, it found, have been kicked, choked, raped or otherwise assaulted in their adult lives (Brady 1993). This study also tracked the incidence of intimate partner violence.

According to the reported data, three in 10 Canadian women (currently or previously married or coupled) have experienced at least one incident of physical or sexual violence by their partner, violence that is consistent with legal definitions of these offences and hence against the law: 63 per cent of women who had been assaulted by a current or past partner had been victimized on more than one occasion, 32 per cent more than 10 times. One in every three women assaulted by their partners feared for their own lives at some point during the abuse. Women who reported having a violent father-in-law were at three times the risk of abuse (36 per cent) as women with non-violent fathers-in-law (12 per cent). (Nason-Clark 1996: 519)

Many victims of domestic violence, despite suffering from violence repeatedly, do not report the incident to authorities. Only 26 per cent of wives that were assaulted by their husbands reported to police (Nason-Clark 1996: 519). This finding suggests that three out of four VAW cases are not reported.

The frequency of VAW varies among different ethnic groups. In the native communities, four out of five women are victims of abuse. Living in isolated communities, these women do not have police or shelter services. The offenders were often victims of sexual and physical abuse in the residential school system created by the Canadian government and administered by the Catholic and Protestant Churches (Allen 1992). Immigrant women often face different sets of problems because of language, cultural and institutional barriers. It is difficult for immigrant women from India to seek help because of patriarchal culture, difficulty in communicating and the harsh reality waiting for them if their husbands are arrested. More awareness of the complicated situations of migrant women is needed (Shirwadkar 2004). In addition, some women become victims of religious cults that exploit women sexually with violence (Allen 1992).

The Montreal Massacre which occurred in 1989 when a misogynist male student shot and killed 14 women brought the issue of tighter gun control to public consciousness in Canada. While women's groups had long been deeply involved in the issue of violence against women, men began to become active as well. The male organized White Ribbon Campaign was one of the most successful of these (Kaufman 2001). But prevalence of VAW in Canada did not change as Figure 6.1 shows.

According to Figure 6.1, the number of VAW cases in Canada rapidly increased from 1983 (11,932 cases) to 1993 (34,754 cases). After that the number declined until 1999. From 2000 the number remained steady at between 23,000 and 24,000. No systematic research has revealed the causality between economic hardship and VAW or between the feminist movement and VAW. But it is possible to interpret that the tripling of incidents in the ten years between 1983 and 1993 as related to economic stagnation in the initial stage of globalization and the crisis of masculinity experienced by those who are negatively affected. It is also possible that the success of the feminist movement encouraged more women to report VAW. A widespread campaign against VAW in the 1990s that was triggered by the Montreal Massacre could not, however, prevent the incidence from rising until 1993 partly because the movement targeted gun control and not masculinist

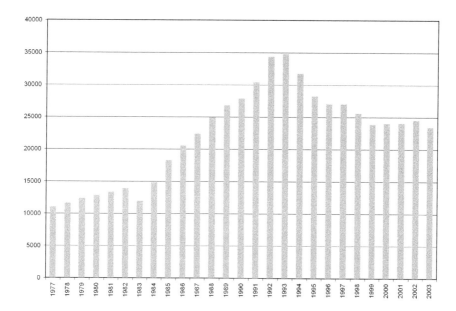

Figure 6.1 Number of reported cases of violence against women in Canada

Source: Prepared based on figures provided by Statistics Canada's *CANSIM* electronic database

domination. But since then the number declined partly as a result of economic recovery accompanying NAFTA. The number of incidents in the past several years remains quite high at about 24,000 a year. And if three out of four VAW incidents are not reported, then there would be 100,000 cases of VAW committed every year. As Michalski (2004: 655) states, despite awareness campaigns, violence against women is still prevalent.

Masculine oppression also appears in the form of neoliberal rollback in the welfare state. Improvement in welfare provisions for women and children was achieved in the last quarter of the twentieth century because of a successful feminist movement. Neoliberal globalization (Cohen and Clarkson 2004) has turned the clock back. Decline in the welfare state (McBride and Shields 1997) resulted in the curtailment of protection for women and children (Caragata 2003). By replacing state intervention with market solutions, the welfare state was transformed into a re-invented masculinist state under the veil of neoliberalism.

New regime of masculinism

The starting premise of this chapter has been that there are two historical processes shaping masculinity and male domination today. They are the feminist movement and globalization. In this section, I would like to attempt a historical and sociological reinterpretation of the transformation of masculinism. I propose the concept of the 'regime of masculinism' that encompasses the socioeconomic and political institutional practice of male domination together with the ideology for justifying such domination. In order to analyze regime change I suggest focusing on the forms of male domination and the expression of masculinist ideology in public and private spaces. By public space, I mean the domain of public discourse such as the political arena and mass communication. The labour market, although formally in the private sector, also occupies critical public spaces. Private space is the domain that is usually hidden behind walls, such as the home, unless the parties involved reveal what is happening there. Corporations belong to private space because events happening within corporations are usually concealed as corporate secrets.

Patriarchy is the practice and culture of male domination and/or female subordination based on the unequal distribution of power between men and women at various levels in a social organization, including the home, workplace, and political arena. Under the male-breadwinner model, economic power in a household tended to be in the hands of a male breadwinner, and this power was the base of male domination. Patriarchal attitudes were embedded in institutionalized discrimination against women in both public and private spaces. This breadwinner regime of masculinism was challenged by the postwar feminist movement, which protested, among other things, male discrimination in employment and political participation, lack of reproductive freedom, and violence against women. By the late 1980s, gender equality legislation was established in many countries, women became represented in most aspects of public life, and blatant sexist comments made in public space were frowned upon.

These anti-sexist achievements, however, were often symbolic and were not duplicated in private space such as the home, family, interpersonal relationships, and many corporate workplaces. Participation in housework remained unmasculine especially among lower-class males, and the use of verbal harassment and physical violence together with rape were still widespread. Even though women's labour force participation was rising in the 1980s, the gender wage gap and discrimination in private sector were prevalent. In other words, the rise of the feminist movement challenged the blatant discrimination written into the postwar gender regime but did not disrupt it.

As discussed earlier, globalization brought a crisis to the masculinity of the breadwinner model of masculinism as single male income became insufficient to sustain households. globalization also provided disproportionate opportunities to men to succeed in the transnational business community. Male domination in the Canadian workplace is still intact despite women's advancement into universities and the labour market. Continued male domination is supported by the neoliberal ideology that the outcomes of the free market are efficient and just. The regime of masculinism under globalization can be called the market regime of masculinism. Male domination is justified under the market regime of masculinism using the rhetoric that individuals are free to choose their actions and they have to bear the burden of the consequences of their actions. State intervention, according to neoliberal doctrine, distorts the market, and this argument is used to reduce welfare spending or to employ 'market' mechanisms in welfare dispensing. Big business, however, continues receiving government subsidies and enjoying protection and/or promotion. The celebration of the market is based on the utterly unrealistic assumption that no one in the market holds capacity to influence the price. Also ignored is the inequality at the start of the competition game. By ignoring inheritance or the presence of big players in the market, the neoliberal market ideology serves the interest of those already holding power.

Under the new regime of masculinism, the rhetoric of the market is used to justify the public practice of gender oppression and exploitation. Prostitution, a form of violence committed against women, is endorsed in this regime because it is 'market' transaction and it provides 'market income' for women. Transnational business masculinity, the hegemonic masculinity under globalization according to Connell (2001a), commodificates women's bodies. Discrimination against women in the workplace is also justified using the rhetoric of the market. Thus, male domination is legitimized under the guise of market transaction, leading to the continued practice of male domination in private space. Domestic violence, harassment in the workplace and schools, and rape by intimate partners are continuing features under the market masculinism, and male domination in the form of an unequal division of housework continues laying the foundation of women's disadvantage and men's advantage in the labour market.

Conclusion

The feminist movement and globalization have been integral historical processes for the transformation of masculinity. Economic restructuring under globalization with expanded women's awareness and rights brought about the crisis of the masculinity of the male-breadwinner model. Under globalization Canadian women had expanded employment opportunities, but the significant gap in earnings continues due, in part, to an unequal division of housework and the glass wall and glass ceiling in the labour market. The erosion of male advantage pushed by feminists has been stalled under globalization as neoliberal doctrine and transnational business masculinity gained acceptance. The masculinism of the male-breadwinner model where a single income served as the foundation of male domination was replaced by a new form of masculinism where male domination is justified using the rhetoric of the market.

The rise of the regime of market masculinism can be interpreted as a counter-movement to the Western feminist movement. The rise of market masculinism is a consequence of globalization which is a 'counter-revolution' of capitalists against those who caused the erosion of profit, such as unionized workers and the women who demanded equal wages and opportunities. The mainstream feminist movement in the global North focused on equality in the labour market and in public places such as politics. Despite successes, or because of their success, capitalists of the powerful countries (that is, shareholders, investors, financiers, and executives of major corporations) with the aid of powerful states reallocated the jobs and rewards within and across countries. Led by major corporations, there emerged hegemonic transnational business masculinity which is justified by the neoliberalism or a belief of the efficiency and fairness of the invisible hand of the market. However, the invisible hand is that of powerful men.

To end continued male domination, it is necessary to challenge both market masculinism and powerful international business interests. To counter market masculinism, it is necessary to challenge both the ideology of the market and the practice of private patriarchy. Masculinism is an expression of a man's weakness or deficiency that he needs an oppressed 'other' in order to be a complete person. For men to overcome this dependency and addiction, they need to unlearn masculinist ideology and practices they inherited from the generations of masculinist parents. A new round of feminist activism needs to focus on educating and changing masculinist men in addition to educating and changing women who are condoning and endorsing male domination at home and in society. It is also necessary to challenge big corporations for their continuing monopolization of economic power. In order to counter the coalition of masculism and capitalism, new imagination is required in order to create an egalitarian future free from masculinist and capitalist oppression.

References

Albers, Benjamin D. (2003). The Militia Movement, Masculinity, and the UN, Paper presented at Southern Sociological Society (SSS), Charlotte, North Carolina.

Allen, Glen (1992) 'Silent Suffering', *Maclean's*, 105, 22, 1 June: 12–13.

Bartkowski, John P. (2001) 'Godly Masculinities: Gender Discourse among the Promise Keepers', *Social Thought and Research*, 24, 1–2: 53–87.

Barzilai, Gad (2004) 'Culture of Patriarchy in Law: Violence from Antiquity to Modernity', *Law and Society Review*, 38, 4, December: 867–83.

Baxter, Janeen (1997) 'Gender Equality and Participation in Housework: A Cross-National Perspective', *Journal of Comparative Family Studies*, 28, 3, Autumn: 220–48.

—— (2002) 'Patterns of Change and Stability in the Gender Division of Household Labour in Australia, 1986–1997', *Journal of Sociology*, 48, 4: 399–424.

Bianchi, Suzanne M.; Casper, Lynn M. and Peltora, Pia K. (1999) 'A Cross-National Look at Married Women's Earnings Dependency', *Gender Issues*, 17, 3, Summer: 3–33.

Brady, Diane (1993) 'A New Measure of Violence', *Maclean's*, 29, 106, 48: 19.

Broomhill, Ray and Sharp, Rhonda (2006) 'The Problem of Social Reproduction under Neoliberalism: Reconfiguring the Male-Breadwinner Model in Australia' *in this volume*.

Burkhauser, Richard; Duncan, Greg J.; Hauser, Richard and Bernsten, Ronald (1990) 'Economic Burdens of Marital Disruptions: A Comparison of the United States and the Federal Republic of Germany', *Review of Income and Wealth*, 36, December: 319–33.

Canada (2002) 'Gender Pay Differentials: Impact of the Workplace', *The Daily*, Statistics Canada, Wednesday 19 June. Available online, www.statcan.ca/Daily/English/020619/d020619b.htm.

Caragata, Lea (2003) 'Neoconservative Realities: The Social and Economic Marginalization of Canadian Women, *International Sociology*, 18, 3, Sept: 559–80.

Cohen, Marjorie Griffin and Clarkson, Stephen (eds.) (2004) *Governing under Stress: Middle Powers and the Challenge of Globalization*, London: Zed Books.

Connell, R.W. (2001a) 'The Social Organization of Masculinity', in Stephen M. Whitehead and Frank J. Barrett (eds) *The Masculinities Reader*, Cambridge, UK: Polity Press, pp. 30–50.

——— (2001b) 'Masculinity Politics on a World Scale', in Stephen M. Whitehead and Frank J. Barrett (eds.) *The Masculinities Reader*, Cambridge, UK: Polity Press, pp. 369–74.

Coyle, Adrian and Morgan-Sykes, Caroline (1998) 'Troubled Men and Threatening Women: The Construction of "Crisis" in Male Mental Health', *Feminism and Psychology*, 8, 3, August: 263–84.

Economist Global Agenda (2003) 'Sex for Sale, Legally', 11 June. Available online, www.economist.com/index.html.

Erchak, Gerald M. and Rosenfeld, Richard (1994) 'Societal Isolation, Violent Norms, and Gender Relations: A Reexamination and Extension of Levinson's Model of Wife Beating', *Cross-Cultural Research*, 28: 111–33.

Giddens, Anthony and Hutton, Will (2000) 'In Conversation', in Anthony Giddens and Will Hutton (eds) *Global Capitalism*, New York: New Press: 1–51.

Heath, Melanie (2003) 'Soft-Boiled Masculinity: Renegotiating Gender and Racial Ideologies in the Promise Keepers Movement', *Gender and Society*, 17, 3, June: 423–44.

Hester, Marianne (2002) 'Patriarchal Reconstruction and Witch-Hunting', in D. Oldridge (ed.) *The Witchcraft Reader*, London: Routledge, pp. 276–88.

——— (2004) 'Future Trends and Developments: Violence against Women in Europe and East Asia', *Violence against Women*, 10, 12, December: 1431–48.

Kaufman, Michael (2001) 'Building a Movement of Men Working to End Violence against Women', *Development*, 44, 3, September: 9–14.

Kimmel, Michael S. (2003) 'Globalization and its Mal(e) Contents: The Gendered Moral and Political Economy of Terrorism', *International Sociology*, 18, 3, September: 603–20.

Kury, Helmut and Yoshida, Toshio (2003) 'Wie warden Opher von Straftaten gesehen? Zur Stigmatisierung von Verbrechensopfern' ('How are crime victims looked at? On the stigmatization of crime victims'), *Hokkaigakuen Law Journal*, 38: 811–64.

Kury, Helmut; Obergfell-Fuchs, Joachim and Woessner, Gunda (2004) 'The Extent of Family Violence in Europe: A Comparison of National Surveys', *Violence against Women*, 10, 7, July: 749–69.

Lee, Deborah (2000) 'Hegemonic Masculinity and Male Feminisation: The Sexual Harassment of Men at Work', *Journal of Gender Studies*, 9, 2, July: 141–55.

Levinson, David (1989) *Family Violence in Cross-Cultural Perspective*, Newbury Park, CA: Sage.

Lim, Lin Lean (1998) *The Sex Sector: The Economic and Social Bases of Prostitution in Southeast Asia*, Geneva, Switzerland: International Labor Office.

Litwin, Ken J. (1998) A Conceptual Scheme for Sexual Harassment as an Assertion of Hegemonic Masculinity, Paper presented at American Sociological Association (ASA), New York, NY.

McBride, Stephen and Shields, John (1997) *Dismantling a Nation: The Transition to Corporate Rule in Canada*, Halifax: Fernwood Publishing.

McMichael, Philip (2004) *Development and Social Change: A Global Perspective*, 3rd edn, Thousand Oaks: Pine Forge Press.

Melzer, Scott A. (2004) 'The National Rifle Association: Conservative Politics and Frontier Masculinity', *Dissertation Abstracts International, A: The Humanities and Social Sciences*, 65, 4: 1545-A.

Michalski, Joseph H. (2004) 'Making Sociological Sense Out of Trends in Intimate Partner Violence: The Social Structure of Violence against Women', *Violence against Women*, 10, 6, June: 652–75.

Nason-Clark, Nancy (1996) 'Religion and Violence against Women: Exploring the Rhetoric and the Response of Evangelical Churches in Canada', *Social Compass*, 43, 4: 515–36.

Randall, Melanie and Haskell, Lori (1995) 'Sexual Violence in Women's Lives: Findings from the Women's Safety Project, A Community-Based Survey', *Violence against Women*, 1: 6–31.

Rathje, Kelly (2002) Male Versus Female Earnings – Is the Gender Wage Gap Converging? *Economica Ltd. The Expert Witness Newsletter*, 7, 1, Spring. Available online, www.economica.ca/ew71p2.htm.

Raymond, Janice G. (1998) 'Prostitution as Violence against Women: NGO Stonewalling in Beijing and Elsewhere', *Women's Studies International Forum*, 21, 1: 1–9.

—— (2004) 'Prostitution on Demand: Legalizing the Buyers as Sexual Consumers', *Violence Against Women*, 10, 10, October: 1156–86.

Rinfret-Raynor, Maryse; Riou, Ariane; Cantin, Solange; Drouin, Christine and Dube, Myriam (2004) 'A Survey on Violence against Female Partners in Quebec, Canada', *Violence against Women*, 10, 7, July: 709–28.

Robinson, Kerry H. (2005) 'Reinforcing Hegemonic Masculinities through Sexual Harassment: Issues of Identity, Power and Popularity in Secondary Schools', *Gender and Education*, 17, 1, March: 19–37.

Shannon, Michael and Kidd, Michael P. (2001) 'Projecting the Trend in the Canadian Gender Wage Gap 2001–2031: Will an Increase in Female Education Acquisition and Commitment Be Enough?' *Canadian Public Policy/Analyse de Politiques*, 27, 4, December: 447–67.

Shirwadkar, Swati (2004) 'Canadian Domestic Violence Policy and Indian Immigrant Women', *Violence against Women*, 10, 8, August: 860–79.

Silver, Cynthia (2000) 'Being There: The Time Dual-earner Couples Spend with their Children', *Canadian Social Trends*, 57, Summer: 26–9.

Skelton, Christine (1997) 'Primary Boys and Hegemonic Masculinities', *British Journal of Sociology of Education*, 18, 3, September: 349–69.

Stasiulis, Davia K. (1999) 'Feminist Integrational Theorizing' in Peter Li (ed.) *Race and Ethnic Relations in Canada*, Don Mills, Ontario: Oxford University Press Canada, pp. 347–97.

Ugge, Christopher and Blackstone, Amy (2004) 'Sexual Harassment as a Gendered Expression of Power', *American Sociological Review*, 69, 1, February: 64–92.

UNPAC (UN Platform for Action Committee Manitoba) (n.d.), 'Women's Economic Inequality: The Wage Gap: Men/Women and the 10 Highest/Lowest Paid Occupations in Canada', *Women and the Economy*. Available online, www.unpac.ca/economy/wagegap3.html.

Weir, E. (2000) 'Wife Assault in Canada', *Canadian Medical Association Journal*, 163: 328.

Wesely, Jennifer K. and Gaarder, Emily (2004) 'The Gendered "Nature" of the Urban Outdoors: Women Negotiating Fear of Violence', *Gender and Society*, 18, 5, October: 645–63.

Whitehead, Stephen M. and Barrett, Frank J. (2001) 'The Sociology of Masculinity', in Stephen M. Whitehead and Frank J. Barrett (eds) *The Masculinities Reader*, Cambridge, UK: Polity Press: 1–26.

7 Indigenous peoples and the topography of gender in Mexico and Canada

Isabel Altamirano Jiménez

Introduction

The deepening of the globalization process, including the emergence of quasi-constitutional forms of economic integration such as the North American Free Trade Agreement (NAFTA) and the Free Trade Agreement of the Americas (FTAA), has fuelled new conflicts over the control of the world's strategic natural resources. Since many of the areas of greatest resource diversity are located within Indigenous territories, they are currently the sites of new struggles over the right to control lands and resources as well as to limit the impact of neoliberal globalization on Indigenous peoples, particularly women. Around the world, Indigenous peoples are mobilizing for the recognition of their status as nations and for the implementation of some form of self-government and political autonomy aimed at giving them control over how, and by whom, their lands and resources are exploited.

In this chapter, I explore the main connections between globalization, the rise of Indigenous nationalism and gender in both Mexico and Canada. I argue that Indigenous nationalist movements in these countries represent political responses to the uneven geography of globalization and its contradictory and intertwined economic development. However, globalization also encourages and enables the formation of new political and economic alliances that go beyond place and identity. Although Indigenous nationalisms are constructed as a real liberation from the capitalist system and as a way of controlling the impact of globalization within Aboriginal communities, Indigenous control over resources and self-government is leading to new integrative processes, forms of class stratification and the intensification of the experience of gender. Indigenous peoples' agency and cultural alternatives have evolved over time and are linked to their abilities to negotiate rights and their position in the global economy.

Globalization, indigenous peoples and the geography of development

In recent decades, Indigenous peoples have struggled to keep control of their lives and lands in the context of complex networks that traverse the boundaries between the state, the market and civil society. The growing importance of international corporations and global flows of capital, the expansion of global media networks and the rise of environmentalist and human rights movements and discourses have altered Indigenous peoples' strategies for surviving and retaining the autonomy they still exercise. On the one hand, Indigenous peoples are expressing their resistance against the uneven appropriation of their natural resources by others. On the other, Indigenous peoples' internal social reproduction is being dissolved by a stronger integration into the larger system, which has positioned some Indigenous peoples as central economic players.

Neoliberalism and globalization have drastically changed rural landscapes, produced new regional discrepancies, and reinforced old patterns of urbanization. These changes are tied to the social, spatial and ecological conditions that existed long before neoliberalism became hegemonic. Most countries are characterized by extreme internal regional differences that have led to high levels of mobility and urbanization. The geographies of globalization express these older inequalities and, at the same time, reinforce new patterns and trends that deepen economic interconnections and the locality of globalization (Chase 2002: 6).

In North America, regional economic integration has involved transformations that are not only economic but also dramatically political (Macdonald 2002: 187). While neither Canada nor Mexico's close relationship with the US economy is new, the intensification of these relationships, and especially the neoliberal reforms that have accompanied continental integration, have redefined how people relate to each other, to resources and to the state. In this context, relationships between the state and Indigenous peoples also have been transformed and new forms of governance negotiated. In both Mexico and Canada, Indigenous peoples are the most economically marginalized groups, if we understand 'marginal' as signifying a low degree of sharing in a country's products, materials and social resources (Weaver 1996). Many Indigenous rural communities in both countries subsist on a mixed economy characterized by a household economy, which combines traditional activities such as hunting, fishing, trapping, gathering, foraging and craft-making, with cash income from part-time or full-time wage-paying work (Hicks and White 2000). However, traditional economic practices have been thrown into question as national governments bind themselves to new global economic treaties that have pushed for the opening of Indigenous lands and resources to national and international investment and development.

Many Indigenous lands sit on the 'frontlines' of the expansion of globalization, and some of these frontlines have so far remained untapped. These territories are abundant in bio-diversity, forest, mineral, water and energy resources, all of which are in demand by a growing international market, particularly a growing North American market. As a result of their interests in binding international agreements and opening up Aboriginal lands to development, both the Mexican and Canadian governments have undertaken a series of policies aimed at redefining their relationship with Aboriginal peoples. This redefinition is usually shaped in controversial ways because it both undermines collectivities and emphasizes market-oriented development (Steward-Harawira 2005: 179).

Although neoliberal globalization's influence in both Mexico and Canada has been differentiated, segmented and uneven, the governments of each country have focused on the implementation of similar 'certainty policies' intended to transform Indigenous lands into open, business-friendly economic spaces. These strategies combine the creation of 'safe' contexts and the liberalization necessary to encourage long-term investment within Indigenous territories according to corporate demands (Globerman 2001, Ratner *et al.* 2003). Nevertheless, as Mexico and Canada's positions in the global economy differ, the contexts of the implementation of these policies also differ.

As discourses have political and material impacts, they contribute to the constitution of specific topographies (Katz 2001a, 2001b). In both Mexico and Canada, government policies are framed within a discourse of rights and restitution as well as on assumptions, values and positions rooted in long-standing notions of civilization and progress. As such, these policies are constructed as providing Indigenous peoples with the means to access modernity and the global market and to reach self-sufficiency. The primary purpose of these policies, however, is to remove obstacles to capital and especially foreign investment. As Wendy Russell (2004) has argued, development enters communities as an institutionalized and apolitical solution to problems disguised by its seemingly natural and mutual goals.

In Mexico, the implementation of these policies has resulted in the liberalization of Indigenous peoples' control over their communal lands and the consequent eruption of a strong Indigenous nationalist movement, which has challenged the very nature of Mexico's insertion into the global system. In Canada, on the other hand, certainty policies have been designed to solve Indigenous territorial demands through the signing of modern treaties aimed at responding to corporate needs. Both approaches suggest that the global localization of economies for Indigenous peoples is far from being homogeneous, but is shaped by regional and national characteristics determining Aboriginal peoples' historical experience and contemporary engagement with the national state (Stewart-Harawira 2005: 178).

Globalization and the geography of gender inequality

During the past few decades, feminists have made gender inequality internationally visible, and women's claims have been recognized as legitimate by a broad range of policy actors. In the 1970s, women's issues were increasingly considered in development and in the policies formulated in the welfare state. However, the imposition of neoliberal globalization as the new form of governance has impacted upon state–society relationships and, particularly, upon gender relations in complex and contradictory ways. These contradictions have led some scholars to see positive changes with regard to women's empowerment and the demise of patriarchalism (Castells 1997, 1998).

The increasing presence of women in paid work does not mean that gender inequalities have disappeared. Neither has women's entry into the paid labour force been translated into the demise of patriarchalism. Women's increasing participation in economic production is governed by institutional rules, norms and conventions that have powerful material effects on people's lives. Neoliberal governance is associated with discourses oriented to genderless individuals and to self-sufficiency. However, gender continues to be a key organizing principle in the distribution of labour and resources. Unequal gender relations are legitimized through ideas of difference and inequality that embody assumptions about the 'nature of femininity and masculinity' (Kabeer 2003).

Institutions set up the rules by which society and people's relationships are governed. These rules may be written or unwritten; explicit or implicit; codified in laws; mandated by policy; upheld by religion, tradition or convention; or embodied in the standards of family, community and society. They play a powerful role in constructing human behaviour and gender roles and identities in terms of what is permitted and what is prohibited. Historical and culturally diverse constructions of gender identities and roles intensify distinctive regional patterns in labour-force participation and gender inequality, especially when the neoliberal state has undermined the relevance of gender.

While institutions themselves are abstract concepts, they take concrete form in organisations and groups such as the state, markets, civil society and/or community and especially kinship and family. Families and kinship are different from other institutions because of the nature of the relationships within them. These forms of organization are usually based on intimate ties of blood, marriage and adoption, in contrast to the more impersonal relationships of contract and statute found in the market and state. Family and kinship are also generally 'gender-ascriptive'. Family identities strongly overlap with gender roles and biological sex. In many Indigenous societies, women are associated with the functions of care and maintenance including rearing children and most of the activities necessary to the survival and wellbeing of the family members.

Women, with few exceptions, assume the weight of the unpaid work of social reproduction.

Women's roles in social reproduction thus are critical elements in understanding the nature of gender inequality within different societies and among different social groups. However, as Kabeer (2003) argues, the contemporary era is marked by different geographies of gender. These geographies reflect systematic regional differences as well as the intensification of the experience of gender in the everyday lives of women, particularly the poor and the marginalized in both the global North and South.

The scope of women's agency and their access to socially valued resources influence the extent to which women play a critical role in production. Indigenous men and women often relate to and use resources in different ways, both in their everyday lives and according to their cosmologies and traditions. These differences are usually muted or ignored when models of economic development are designed because women are often seen as peripheral contributors to the economic viability of a community (Nuttall 2005). More is known about men's than women's relation to land and use of resources, and men's rather than women's knowledge is incorporated into the planning and implementation of economic development within Indigenous lands. While some of these inequalities may be the result of community norms, determining roles, access to resources and education, the silencing of women's knowledge is perpetuated by government institutions.

From this perspective, Indigenous women's participation in economic production can be characterized as being influenced by many of the uneven landscapes of economic globalization, including institutions such as the state and family, household patterns and customary rules, which determine the gendered division of labour and the distribution of resources, responsibilities, agency and power within Indigenous societies. The hybrid components conditioning Aboriginal women's participation in the labour force reveal the complexity of contemporary global, national and local developments and the different contexts for normalizing postcolonial relations among Indigenous peoples.

Indigenous traditionalism and women

Indigenous lands and resources have historically been an important element of the global accumulation process. Increasing global interconnections among countries and regions have provided Indigenous peoples with unprecedented opportunities to engage with states, regions and the global economy. However, since this process of engagement is shaped by neoliberal globalization and market forces, it is embedded in contradictions that have given rise to struggles to redefine identities and interactions among individuals, communities, Indigenous peoples, corporations and national states (Stack 1985: 5).

The rise of Indigenous nationalist movements is related to globalization and the insertion of Indigenous communities into the global market. Indigenous nationalist movements are constructed as a way of controlling the impact of or to benefit from globalization through autonomy and self-sufficiency. In this sense, Indigenous nationalist ideologies can be understood as an important strategy in the struggle for the reproduction of the local through representation. What is represented both to the local society and to the outside world is a claim to a history that differs from the national history, and which is useful to assert further claims in the fields of economy and politics. This construction of history is a strategy of creating identity out of re-making history and is linked to the present political interests involved in its creation (Shröder 2003: 437). Although Indigenous nationalisms are represented as egalitarian, homogeneous and liberating movements, they are, in fact, gendered projects perpetuating ideals concerning the 'proper' place of women and men within Indigenous society.

Territorial claims are based on genderless, collective memories emphasizing the reversal of colonization and conquest. Nevertheless, social differentiation and specialization in spheres of social and economic activity mean that Indigenous knowledge systems and experiences are gendered. In the case of Mexico, Indigenous nationalism emerged in response to the negative effects of neoliberal globalization for Indigenous communities and their land tenure system, but little is said about how women have been further marginalized. In contrast, in Canada, the construction of traditionalist ideologies has developed in response to the historical open access to Aboriginal lands and resources and the possibilities of negotiating treaties focusing mainly on men's concerns.

Since identity is created in the political process of constructing consensus through mythic or empirical means, identity itself is a politicized frame of reference, and its deployment in the service of politics too often produces essentialism, which leads to intra-group contestation over who is 'real' and what practices are 'traditional'. This contestation has the effect of silencing and making invisible the presence and aspirations of women (Smith 1999: 72). Furthermore, contemporary legal and political approaches to Indigenous rights and land titles are embedded in a context influenced by the commodification of labour and resources as well as the capitalist system, as I will show in the following sections.

Mexico

In Mexico, global economic integration was embedded in the negotiation and implementation of NAFTA. For over a decade, this trade agreement has had a strong impact on Mexico's domestic politics, particularly on the Indigenous peoples–government relationship. The Indigenous uprising in the southern state of Chiapas, Mexico, is commonly recognized as a movement linking globalization to the resistance of Indigenous peoples. The rebel group known as the Zapatista Army of National Liberation (EZLN), or the 'Zapatistas', timed its armed uprising against the Mexican state to coincide with the first day of NAFTA's implementation, on January 1, 1994. The Zapatistas, calling NAFTA a 'death sentence for Indigenous peoples', issued a list of demands calling for democracy, economic and social justice, and later, for the recognition of Indigenous political autonomy.

Several authors (Tarrow 1998, Harvey 1999, Nash 2001) have shown that the Mayan communities in Chiapas and other regions were forced into the global economy even before NAFTA, through the oil boom of the 1970s, which was followed by a severe economic crisis and later on by the implementation of structural adjustments in the 1980s. The economies of Indigenous communities were impoverished by government's interference through programmes and policies directed specifically at assimilating Indigenous peoples, while only superficial action was ever taken to strengthen their local economies. As J. Peter Brosius (1997) and Dan Jorgensen (1999) have argued about the Malaysian and New Guinean cases, respectively, developmental projects in Mexico were manipulated to include some locally articulated Indigenous goals. However, small-scale, subsistence or land-based Indigenous economies continue to be linked to pressures to dismantle national services and to remove subsidies for Indigenous subsistence. Liberation movements such as the Zapatistas exposed the uneven geography and unwanted consequences of economic development.

The neoliberal reforms implemented in Mexico, including the privatisation of state-owned industries, and the end of state protection for agricultural products, deepened the already vulnerable economies of Indigenous communities. Furthermore, in the countryside, these transformations were expressed in the reform of constitutional Articles 4 and 27 in 1991 and 1992, respectively. The reform of

Article 4 recognized the pluri-cultural nature of Mexican society and framed identity politics as a politics of symbolic recognition.

Article 27 had protected Indigenous communal lands, known as 'ejidos,' from being sold and gave communal assemblies a special collective legal status. The 1992 modification of this article emphasized the privatization of Indigenous lands by loosening Indigenous control and allowing new forms of association between private investors and *ejido* land-holders (Harvey 1999: 187). What is even more relevant for the purpose of this chapter is that the agrarian counter-reforms in Mexico did not provide the joint parcelling and titling of land for married or conjugal partners nor did they prioritize the claims of single female households as other Latin American countries have done as part of their neoliberal reforms. Rather, the modifications to Article 27 eliminated the inheritance rights enjoyed by Indigenous women in Mexico before the reform (Deere and León 2001, Hamilton 2001), thus legalizing Indigenous discriminatory practices that have, in many cases, prevented women from holding land. In the laws of the market, women, particularly Indigenous women in rural Mexico have lost all legal access to land, unless they can afford to buy it outright (Vázquez García 2002: 95). The modification of Article 27 thus not only threatened the very existence of Indigenous communities as collective entities, but also encouraged a model of economic development in which Indigenous peoples were forced to enter new global market-oriented networks and in which Indigenous women's use of resources and roles in production were muted or ignored (Momsen 1991).

Some observers (Díaz Polanco 1992, Fox 1992, Hindley 1996) have noted that the Indigenous policy that the Mexican government implemented in the context of the NAFTA negotiations in the late 1980s was contradictory and aimed at remaking the national culture by strengthening civil society's participation in fighting poverty. As Hindley (1996: 231–2) has argued, this policy spoke of overcoming poverty as a matter of justice irrespective of people's ethnicity and gender. This perception was consistent with the neoliberal restructuring process that the government was implementing to bring Mexico into the global order and economy.

Ironically, while NAFTA revealed the dark side of globalization with its negative impact on the living conditions of Indigenous peoples, it also legitimized the use of a human rights discourse by Indigenous peoples (Jung 2003). Although the implementation of certainty policies such as the modification of Articles 27 and 4 was aimed at securing and providing certainty for corporate access to Indigenous lands, these actions had, paradoxically, the opposite effect. On the one hand, the reform of Article 27 fuelled Indigenous alienation; on the other, Article 4 recognized Indigenous peoples' distinctive status, legitimizing Indigenous demands and, to some extent, the Zapatista uprising.

Since these neoliberal policies affected Indigenous peoples' control over their material and social reproduction, the Zapatistas and, later, other Indigenous movements, articulated a traditionalist discourse that reified tradition and pre-colonial interpretations of Indigenous relations of production and power. This process contrasts with the diminishing importance of traditional forms of social relations in contemporary Indigenous societies (Shröder 2003: 438).

While emphasizing Indigenous traditions, the Zapatista movement also portrayed itself as an inclusive movement concerned with Indigenous rights, democratic demands and Indigenous women's demands. Almost simultaneously with the Zapatista uprising, a strong national Indigenous women's movement emerged to question the Indigenous nationalist project by emphasizing gender discrimination and inequality and demanding land property rights. As place-specific and knowledge-situated, Indigenous women's political response in Mexico focused not only on supporting the Indigenous struggle against the negative impact of globalization but also on emphasising women's different experiences.

An extensive literature has documented the social context in which Indigenous women's rights and political participation have been ignored or undermined and how customary law has eroded women's property rights in most Indigenous communities (Casa Chousal 1994: 16–21, Goetze 1995, Rojas 1995). Little attention, however, has been paid to how the state itself has perpetuated unequal gender relations within Indigenous communities. Gendered patterns according to tradition, social norms and cultural values determined women's actual ownership and control of land before the reforms. The current legal framework and institutionalized discrimination, however, have rendered Indigenous women increasingly vulnerable to dispossession and disinheritance (Hamilton 2001: 120).

This problem is a clear example of gender inequity reinforced by tradition, national laws and prejudices rooted in ideology and culture and, specifically, in the gendered ownership of land. The right to access land is one of the most important Indigenous women's demands but this issue was omitted in the San Andrés Accords – an agreement between the federal government and the Zapatista Army of National Liberation signed in February 1996. This omission is ironic considering both that land has been central to the Indigenous struggles and that the Zapatistas were the first to recognize in a position paper that land should be distributed in an egalitarian form to men and women and that 'women must be included in tenancy and inheritance of land' (Rojas 1995: 251). Subsequently, the federal government failed to honour these accords recognizing Indigenous autonomy, and the outcomes expected from the reform of Article 27 have not been achieved. As Hamilton (2001: 139) notes, despite the increasing difficulties of sustaining rural livelihoods, the massive selling of *ejidal* plots that the Mexican government planned has not yet occurred. Instead, migration to urban and border areas has increased and women's income-producing work has diversified.

When NAFTA was being negotiated, three million producers, or 40 per cent of all Mexicans working in agriculture, cultivated corn, which was Mexico's most basic and important produce. Mexico's corn producers were hit the hardest by NAFTA, not the least because Mexico's borders were opened ten years ahead of schedule to allow for cheaper imports of corn and beans from the US and Canada. As a result, small, poor farmers who produced for the local markets were unable to compete with cheaper imports. According to the Mexican Agricultural Ministry (SAGARPA 2001), 81.5 per cent of the rural population in Mexico in 2001 lived in poverty in contrast to approximately 64 per cent in 1994, the year NAFTA was implemented. In only ten years, the proportion of workers employed in agriculture shrunk by 10 per cent, and 80 per cent of rural families have at least one member living outside the community, including the United States. Those living in rural areas, mainly Indigenous peoples, are increasingly insecure and increasingly relying on survival strategies including migration, informal economy, and the formation of cooperatives (Henriques and Patel 2004: 2.). Unlike the migrant population of previous decades, the heterogeneous population of migrants of the past decade have included Indigenous women and men from regions such as Chiapas, which had not experienced massive migration flows before 1994.

In a study of the creation of the flexible worker, Lynn Stephen (2001) found that migrant Indigenous families are caught in a labour market segmented by gender. While agro-export companies provide relatively stable, low-wage employment for women and their children on the Mexican side of the border, men are pushed to assume the risks of US immigration (Zabin and Hughes in Stephen 2001: 6). As a result, families have been divided.

Change also characterizes the traditional migration pattern in which males go to the US, and women remain in their local communities. Increasingly, women have become more involved with agricultural and community activities. Indigenous women's responsibilities as the head of single-parent households have increased and include assuming the religious and community posts of their absent husbands and male relatives. Nonetheless, these changes have not necessarily resulted in women's empowerment. Rather, women have been forced to assume new responsibilities in order to maintain absent men's membership within their communities. In addition, in order to fulfil their families' needs, women are increasingly participating in the wage economy and informal economy as vendors of handcrafts and other non-agricultural products (Hamilton 2001: 131).

Indigenous women are also migrating to urban areas where as domestic workers they do not receive benefits, contracts or healthcare. The racial, class and urban–rural divides have been intensified in the last decades. According to the Census 2000, domestic work is the third most important source of income for poor women, with Indigenous women accounting for 80 per cent of all domestic workers (Instituto Nacional de Estadística Geografía e Informática 2000). This work, however, is not recognized as an integral part of the economy.

Indigenous women are also found in large numbers in maquiladoras where low wages, flexibility and few benefits are common. Although women's participation in the maquiladora industry is not restricted to Indigenous women, young Indigenous women are preferred as they are more likely to accept the poor working conditions. As well, Indigenous women who previously practised agriculture are now working for Mexican agribusiness, where a racial divide exists. Deborah Barndt (1999: 165) has shown that whereas Indigenous women of all ages are relegated to the fields, young *mestiza* women (that is, of mixed Indigenous and Spanish origin) get the jobs in the packing plants. Local mestiza women are hired mainly for the harvest period while Indigenous migrant women are transported from plant to plant and have become a kind of moving *maquila*. As Gabriel and Macdonald (1996: 167) contended, 'the mobility of international capital is predicated on the politics of race and gender'. In their constant search for cheaper labour, multinational and national corporations and companies competing in the international market take advantage of deeply ingrained and institutionalized sexist and racist divides.

Indigenous women's insertion into the informal economy, nonetheless, has resulted in social activism. Stephen (2005) has shown that Indigenous women's responses to increased economic globalization do not involve only individual solutions, but also generate localized political responses. In order to avoid intermediaries, for example, Indigenous women have organized handcraft cooperatives and entered the fair trade system. In doing so, women's cooperatives have been able to make alliances with other non-Indigenous actors and also organize political responses to economic globalization.

Canada

Unlike Mexico, there does not appear to be such a clear link between the implementation of economic integration agreements such as NAFTA and policies affecting Indigenous peoples in Canada. As a white settler society, Canada's political economy has always been linked, both directly and indirectly, to the political economy of Aboriginal peoples. As Clarkson (2000) suggests, Canada's political, social and economic reality was part of globalization trends even before they were noticeable elsewhere. Although the internationalization of Canada's economy has a long tradition, neoliberal globalization has deepened the trend and produced new regional discrepancies.

The very development of Canada's resource-based economy and the expansion of international trade have depended upon the dispossession of Aboriginal land and resources. In the late nineteenth century, Canada promoted a free-entry system emphasizing developers' and prospectors' rights and privileges. This system is characterized by its unrestrictive access to Crown minerals, free acquisition of title and the right to develop and mine (Barton 1993 in McPherson 2003: xix). The timing, the context and the way in which Canada developed during its origins resulted in the establishment of treaties between some Indigenous peoples and Euro-Canadians and, later, in the transformation of treaty relations into relations of domination (McPherson 2003: xx).

Through the 1960s and beyond, the scope and pace of global economic integration and the development of new technologies placed renewed pressure on the search for energy and mining resources, a search which targeted untapped Indigenous territories (Saladin d'Anglure and Morin 1992: 14). The federal and provincial governments reacted positively to global economic trends by encouraging stake claims, surveys and occupation of Aboriginal lands for mineral and energy exploration and development. Since most Aboriginal lands were considered geographical and social hinterlands, much of this economic activity gave Indigenous peoples little or no benefit, thus contributing to growing Aboriginal resentment. At both the national and international levels, the Inuit of the Arctic, the Dene of the Northwest Territories, the Indigenous peoples in the Yukon, the peoples of the northwest coast, and the Cree of Quebec, among others, began to assert their territorial sovereignty and their right to self-determination by drawing attention to the negative impact of economic development on their traditional way of life. By the 1970s, Aboriginal territorial claims were one of the major political challenges confronting Canada's economic and political strategists (Raunet 1984: 161).

During the era of Prime Minister Pierre Elliot Trudeau (1968–1984), aboriginal policy was shaped by a liberal conception of equality and individual rights (Abele *et al.* 1999: 259). For instance, Indigenous poverty and marginalization were considered to be an issue of exclusion requiring a mix of economic development and inclusion into a citizenship regime. The Trudeau government's 1969 'Statement on Indian Policy' commonly known as the 'White Paper' was one of the cornerstones of this policy. It recommended parcelling out reserve lands on the basis of individual ownership and eliminating 'Indian status'. At the same time, the White Paper sought to eliminate obstacles to development and exploration of resources within Aboriginal regions, particularly the North. However, strong Indigenous mobilization contributed to the withdrawal of this initiative. Aboriginal peoples mobilized on different fronts, including the United Nations Working Group on Indigenous Rights, the Supreme Court of Canada and the political arena, to claim nationhood and collective rights.

Starting in the 1970s, various judicial decisions confirmed the existence of Aboriginal land titles in Canada and helped to legitimize Aboriginal demands for self-determination and sovereignty. This new-found legitimacy, however, threatened Canada's right to access and develop Aboriginal lands and to provide the 'right to explore' for minerals in much of this country's territory without Native consent (McPherson 2003: xviii-xix). McPherson (2003) has argued that developers and investors played a significant role in pressuring the government to seek a lasting solution through the implementation of land claim negotiations guaranteeing that economic development operations would be carried out with certainty and confidence within Aboriginal territories. As a result, the Canadian government started to redefine its relationship with Aboriginal peoples based on the reproduction of colonizing practices within a decolonizing framework, or what has been termed 'deep colonizing' (Bird Rose 1996). This concept refers to the complex and contradictory practices involved in reversing colonization through processes such as land claims. On the one hand, processes like this reverse colonization by returning land to Aboriginal peoples. On the other, the marginalization and silencing of women and the negotiation of development-oriented land claims perpetuate colonizing practices and resource appropriation.

From this perspective, the most basic aspect of the land claim negotiations was the embrace of 'finality' or once-and-for-all settlement of claims. The principle of 'finality' responded to developers' needs but, at the same time, it positioned some Aboriginal leaders as economic players. From a developers' perspective, the unsettled rights of access to land and resources is one of the factors creating the most uncertainty for long-term economic projects (Globerman 2001: 157). Arguably, developers have influenced not only the Canadian government's decision to solve

Aboriginal territorial claims but also the type of solution. Thus, a direct relationship exists between signing modern treaties and opening Indigenous lands to development.

In the early 1990s, the federal government formalized its 'certainty policy' by openly linking the negotiation of modern treaties finalizing land claims with the promotion of economic development. The implementation of this policy coincided with neoliberal reform emphasizing deregulation and devolution as well as with the negotiation of economic agreements such as NAFTA. The basic assumption behind this government policy was that development would provide new opportunities and jobs for Aboriginal peoples while removing their dependence on state programmes (Ratner *et al.* 2003: 218). Accordingly, the self-sufficiency of Aboriginal peoples, as advanced through land claim agreements, is dependent on the major commercial exploitation of natural resources and on emphasizing self-government as a means of transmitting capitalist values to this population (Slowey 1999: 118).

In contrast to Mexico, Canada has invested major financial resources in the signing of modern treaties with the intention of compensating Aboriginal peoples for the surrender of their lands and encouraging Aboriginal participation in the global economy. Nonetheless, the implementation of this particular certainty policy has not benefited equally all Aboriginal peoples or all members of Aboriginal communities. Because the scope of each treaty is determined, to a large extent, by the type of natural resources found within Indigenous territories and by investors' interests, these types of arrangement have been completed on a case-by-case basis, producing very different substantive outcomes (Wotherspoon and Satzewich 2000: xxv). Moreover, since government institutions tend to prioritize men's concerns whenever treaties are negotiated, women's roles in production and women's environmental knowledge remain ignored.

Although some Aboriginal peoples have entered into modern land claim negotiations, others are either still confronting Canadian ownership over what they consider to be their traditional lands or refusing to sign the treaties offered by the government. This situation continues to subsume the uneven and contradictory impacts of economic development among the different Aboriginal regions and to produce socially and spatially uneven processes. In many poor Aboriginal communities where the primary income comes from inadequate government transfers and social welfare programmes, any alternative offering an increased standard of living is likely to be welcome. Unfortunately, the modern treaty style directly links economic development and Aboriginal self-sufficiency with initiatives that rely heavily on large-scale natural resource development. Under these circumstances, Aboriginal–state relations in Canada are based upon a hegemonic strategy that replaces the Indian Act's coercive paternalistic relations with forms of neoliberal Aboriginal self-governance aimed at creating an economic regime that Rata (1999: 233) has termed 'tribal capitalism'. This term refers to the articulation of exploitative social class relations of production and a neo-traditionalist ideology aimed at reviving communal relations within a social formation structured by a capitalist regime of accumulation. Nevertheless, the crucial difference between tribal capitalism and capitalism is the absence of privatized ownership of the means of production, because under the former, the Aboriginal group rather than the individual is the legal owner of the lands, waters and knowledge. Thus, class relations of production are reified as communal social relations within a neo-traditionalist ideology.

Under the conditions of tribal capitalist accumulation, Aboriginal élites use their position as intermediaries between the state and the Aboriginal population to appropriate the majority of the profits derived from Aboriginal-owned resources and communally operated businesses for the benefit of themselves and their allies. In effect, a system of local inequality has emerged that resembles a class system. These pragmatic deals appeal to many Aboriginal leaders, some of whom are already positioned to earn financial rewards by entering partnerships with corporations and banks eager to access the natural, human and financial resources (Anderson 1997: 1490). The eventual capitalization of Aboriginal lands, water and other resources as means of production, effectively controlled by a new 'Aboriginal bourgeoisie' introduces wage labour among the lower-ranked kin, thus creating class polarization (Rata 1999: 233).

In recent years, male Aboriginal leadership insufficiently inclusive of women, but claiming to represent its entire constituencies, has been accused of being co-opted when negotiating modern treaties and of enshrining male patriarchy. With the élite controlling the economic benefits and the political agenda, little attention has been paid to pressing social issues such as alcoholism, domestic violence and the creation of mechanisms providing women with the space and funding to articulate their concerns (Fontaine 2002). Gerdine Van Woudenberg (2004: 6) has pointed out that the contemporary interface between discourses of law, politics and identity in the negotiation of Aboriginal rights and title create a 'colonial full circle'. She argues that inaccurate colonial representations of women as landless and domestically placed is being increasingly accepted and perpetuated. By merging gender categories under the notion of collective rights, the female category is submerged under the male.

Two crucial examples of this situation involve matrimonial property rights and the construction of land use and occupancy as male-centred. Despite continuous national and international criticism, Canada has failed to provide women living on- and off-reserve with equivalent matrimonial real property rights. Spouses living on-reserve do not have legal recourse to obtain interim exclusive possession of the family home equivalent to that available to all spouses living off-reserve. In Canada as elsewhere, neoliberalism has eroded the political and social visibility of gender in everyday life and in the policy-making process. Since the 1960s, Aboriginal women have challenged the male leadership through local responses and national organizations. However, gendered struggles against colonialism are often constructed as struggles for individual rights by both the formal male leadership and the federal government. Aboriginal women's organizations have not only been underfunded, but in recent years, such funding has decreased as the Canadian government offers support only on a project-by-project basis.

Although rarely recognized as such, when dealing with land title the government has focused on the identification of the key activities attached to the continuing land use and occupancy of the areas claimed. This approach has emphasized what traditionally is considered as the male sphere of activities such as hunting, fishing and trapping which, in turn, has become the core of Aboriginal cultures. The marginalization of women, moreover, is perpetuated by the state's institutions, which do not require that men and women be equally involved in preparing and presenting land claims. As Bird Rose (1996: 13) observes, the erasure of women's power and presence in the context of land claims involving the cultural and social bases of land ownership is a form of violence that obscures and nullifies the living presence of women in their social, moral and cultural complexity. This process disadvantages women not only because of the knowledge and history they are unable to present but also because the results serve legally to disenfranchise them.

The indirect consequences of the gendered land claims negotiation process extend beyond the actual contents of a land claim. The bodies mandated to hold and distribute the compensation funds provided through an agreement do not guarantee equal representation of women and men nor ensure that women have equal access to these funds. For instance, as part of the land claims the Tungavik Federation of Nunavut (TFN) negotiated wildlife income support with the North-west Territories government; the TFN agreed to narrow the focus of the programme from the 'household' to the 'hunter'. This agreement fits within an existing government initiative that provides hunters (primarily men) with small amounts of funds to subsidize gas and repairs to machines used for harvesting (Archibald and Crnkovich 1999: 8). The shift from the 'household' to the 'hunter' not only valued men's activities as opposed to women's but also provided them with unequal material compensation. The gendered bias land claims should not suggest that Aboriginal women no longer interact with land. Rather, the negotia-tion of land title and Aboriginal rights is embedded in a context influenced by the commodification of labour and resources as well as by the capitalist system (Van Woudenberg 2004: 6).

Women's inequality is a likely outcome of land claims that focus on large scale resource development, for employment opportunities are promoted mainly in male-dominated areas such as mining, forestry and fishing. In addition, as most development projects require relocation from communities to distant worksites for long periods, Aboriginal women seldom benefit from employment opportunities as women have to fulfil most of the family responsibilities (Archibald and Crnkovich 1999: 17). The increasing differentiation among Indigenous peoples in terms of their abilities and their material rewards is threatening to exacerbate the existing gap between the employed and unemployed, particularly between men and women.

Increasingly, young Aboriginal women are migrating to urban settings, but adjustment to urban life often means living on the margins of urban society. Racism as well as disadvantages in education and training exacerbate social exclu-sion (Western Landscapes 2001). Young Aboriginal women, for example, are over-represented and exploited in the sex trade. Prostitution has become one means to which Aboriginal women have resorted in order to provide for their families

(PACE Society 2000: 82). In this context, the off-reserve women's employment rate is higher than that of on-reserve women but lower than that of non-Aboriginal women. As well, 44 per cent of the Aboriginal population living off-reserve lives below the poverty line and 47 per cent of Aboriginal persons living on-reserve have an annual income of less than $10,000. Women are over-represented in this category (Canada 2001: 258, National Anti-Poverty Organization 1999).

Although important variations exist among Aboriginal women in Canada, an increasing number of working women, particularly First Nations women, are employed on a casual, part-time basis in the marginal labour force, where wages are low and job security is non-existent (White *et al.* 2003). In this respect, the experience of Aboriginal women is very similar to their counterparts in Mexico. Moreover, although these women are increasingly represented in the wage economy, and their households depend upon their financial contribution, the burden of performing household duties continues to fall solely on them. As the Royal Commission Report on Aboriginal Peoples emphasized, under current conditions and approaches to development, little prospect for a better future is envisioned for Indigenous women (Canada 1996: Vol. 2, Part 2, Ch 5).

Neoliberal globalism has not only affected the Aboriginal peoples–state relationship but also deepened gender inequalities. Although, at the rhetorical level, Canada commits itself to promoting gender equality among Aboriginal peoples, the government also perpetuates and creates gender inequalities. In recent years the treaty style pursued by the government has focused on securing large-scale economic development and on promoting male dominated employment sectors. This government policy may be considered as a means of co-opting Aboriginal organizations and leaders because the debate at the negotiating table is now focused on how much of the 'pie' Aboriginal people will get rather than on the kind of development people want (Archibald and Crnkovich 1999: 12). With the Aboriginal political élite controlling the economic benefits and the political agenda, and with the state undermining the experience of gender, little attention has been paid to women's complex role in the social reproduction of their communities.

Conclusions

This chapter has focused on the relationship between globalization, Indigenous nationalism and gender in Mexico and Canada. I have argued that Indigenous nationalist movements in these countries represent political responses to the uneven geography of globalization and its contradictory and intertwined paths of economic development. However, globalization also encourages and enables the formation of new political and economic alliances that go beyond place and identity, fostering place-specific political responses either to counteract globalization or to deepen economic assimilation.

Neoliberal globalization has socially and spatially uneven material effects in multiple locations. Places, from this perspective, are distinct because of their historical and contemporary linkages to broader political and economic processes.

Neoliberal globalization's footprints in both Mexico and Canada have been differentiated, segmented and uneven. The governments of both countries, however, have focused on the implementation of similar 'certainty policies' intended to transform Indigenous lands into open, business-friendly spaces. These strategies promote the creation of 'safe' contexts and the liberalization necessary to encourage long-term investment within Indigenous territories while Indigenous peoples are constructed as self-sufficient, genderless, market-oriented actors pursuing their own interests.

Globalization affects Indigenous peoples in specific ways and thus harms women in gender specific forms. The impact on Indigenous women's knowledge and role in primary production is particularly clear in both countries. Indigenous men and women often relate to and use resources in different ways, both in their everyday lives and according to their traditions. These differences are often muted or ignored when models of economic development are being designed because women are often perceived as secondary contributors to the economic viability of a community.

In Mexico, the certainty policies were implemented through the modification of constitutional Article 27, which was aimed at privatizing Indigenous communal lands and opening the possibility of creating partnerships between Indigenous individual landowners and private investors. Moreover, the reform of Article 27 eliminated the inheritance rights enjoyed by Indigenous women, legalizing discriminatory practices that have, in many cases, prevented women from holding land. Paradoxically, the massive selling of *ejidal* plots and the economic development that the Mexican government planned has not yet occurred. Instead, a far-reaching Indigenous movement emerged articulating Indigenous nationalism as an alternative to economic globalization. At the same time, Indigenous migration to urban and border areas has increased while Indigenous women have entered the labour force in order to maintain the precarious rural livelihood. This situation is exacerbating the racial, class and urban–rural divides.

Canada, in contrast, has historically implemented a free-entry system, characterized by its unrestrictive access to Crown minerals, free acquisition of title and the right to develop and mine. During the 1970s, Aboriginal nationalist movements and the various judicial decisions, which confirmed the existence of Aboriginal land title, challenged this country's right to access and develop Native lands without these peoples' consent. Later, in the context of neoliberal globalization and as a result of developers' pressure, the Canadian government implemented policies based on land claim negotiations and the construction of Native lands as open lands, friendly to development. Unlike Mexico, Canada has provided financial compensation for the extinction of Aboriginal title, which has helped to position some Aboriginal communities as economic players and accelerated economic assimilation. Because many Aboriginal peoples believe that development will take place with or without negotiations, the debate at the negotiating table focuses on how much of the development benefit Aboriginal people will get.

In this process, the living presence of women in their social, economic and cultural complexity has been undermined. The merging of gender categories under the notion of collective rights and the inaccurate colonial representation of women as landless and domestically placed have resulted in severe disadvantages for Aboriginal women. The indirect consequences of the gendered land claims negotiation process extend beyond the actual contents of a land claim and are expressed in the lack of substantial property rights, employment opportunities for women and support for their traditional activities. Similar to Mexico, the Canadian state continues to construct and perpetuate gendered rights and access to resources and employment. Aboriginal women both in Canada and Mexico are increasingly employed on a casual, part-time basis in the marginal labour force, where wages are low and job security non-existent. Under the current conception of economic development within Indigenous lands, little prospect for a better future for women is envisioned.

Notes

1 Mexico's population is ethnically divided in the Indigenous population and the *mestizo* population. The latter is the mainstream population and is not considered to be Indigenous even though *mestizos* have Indigenous and Spanish backgrounds.

References

Abele, Frances; Graham, Katherine A. and Maslove, Allan M. (1999) 'Negotiating Canada: Changes in Aboriginal Policy over the Last Thirty Years', in Leslie Pal (ed.) *How Ottawa Spends 1999–2000*, Ottawa, ON: Carleton University Press, pp. 251–92.

Anderson, R. B. (1997) 'Corporate/Indigenous Partnerships in Economic Development: The First Nations in Canada', *World Development*, 25: 1483–504.

Archibald, Linda and Crnkovich, Mary (1999) 'If Gender Mattered: A Case Study of Inuit Women, Land Claims and the Voisey's Bay Nickel Project'. Available online, www.swc-cfc.gc.ca.pubspr/0662280024/199911_06622800_e.pdf.

Barndt, Deborah (1999) 'Women Workers in the NAFTA Food Chain', in Mustafa Koc, Rod MacRae, Luc J.A. Mougeot and Jennifer Welsh (eds) *For Hunger-Proof Cities: Sustainable Urban Food Systems*, Ottawa: International Development Research Centre, pp. 162–66. Available online, www.idrc.ca/openebooks/882-1/.

Barton, Barry J. (1993) Canadian Law of Mining, Calgary: University of Calgary Faculty of Law.

Bird Rose, Deborah (1996) 'Land Rights and Deep Colonising: the Erasure of Women', *Aboriginal Law Journal*, 3, 85: 6–14.

Brosius, J. Peter (1997) 'Prior Transcripts, Divergent Paths: Resistance and Acquiescence to Logging in Sarawak, East Malaysia', *Society for Comparative Study of Society and History*, 39, 1: 468–509.

Canada (1996) *Report on the Royal Commission on Aboriginal Peoples: People to People, Nation to Nation*, Economic Development, Ottawa: Ministry of Supply and Services. Available online, www.ainc-inac.gc.ca/ch/rcap/sg/sgmm_e.html.

— (2001) *Aboriginal Women A Profile from the Census 2001*, Indian and Northern Affairs Canada, Ottawa: Ministry of Supply and Services. Available online, www.ainc-inac.gc.ca/pr/pub/abw/figu_e.html.

Casa Chousal,Yoloxochilt *et al.* (1994) 'Causas de la marginacion de las mujeres chiapanecas', *Fem*, 18, April: 16: 16–21.

Castells, Manuel (1997) *The Information Age: Economy, Society and Culture, Vol. II: The Power of Identity*, Oxford: Blackwell.

—— (1998) *The Information Age: Economy, Society and Culture, Vol. III: End of Millennium*, Oxford: Blackwell.

Chase, Jacquelyn (2002) 'Introduction: The Spaces of Neoliberalism in Latin America', in Jacquelyn Chase (ed.) *The Spaces of Neo-liberalism in Latin America. Land, Place and Family in Latin America*, Bloomfield: Kumarian Press: pp. 1–21

Clarkson, Stephen (2000) 'The Multi Level State: Canada in the Semi-Periphery of both Continentalism and Globalization'. Available online, www.envireform.utoronto.ca/publications/stephe.clarkson/multi-level-state.pdf.

Deere, Carmen Diana and León, Magdalena (2001) 'Institutional Reform of Agriculture under Neoliberalism: The Impact of the Women and Indigenous Movement', *Latin America Research Review*, 36, 2: 31–63.

Díaz Polanco, Hector (1991) *Autonomía regional: La autodeterminación de los pueblos indios*, Mexico City: Siglo Veintiuno Editores.

Fontaine, Nahanni (2002) 'Aboriginal Women's Perspective on Self-Government', *Canadian Dimension*, 36, 6: 10–11. Available online, www.canadiandimension.mb.ca/v36_6nf.htm.

Fox, Jonathan (1992) *The Politics of Food in Mexico: State Power and Social Mobilisation*, Ithaca, New York: Cornell University Press.

Gabriel, Christina and Macdonald, Laura (1996) 'NAFTA and Economic Restructuring: Some Gender and Race Implications', in Isabella Bakker (ed.) *Rethinking Restructuring: Gender and Change in Canada*, Toronto: University of Toronto Press, pp. 165–86.

Globerman, Steven (2001) 'Investment and Capital Productivity', in Roslyn Kunin (ed.) *Prospering Together: The Economic Impact of the Aboriginal Settlement in BC*, 2nd edn, Vancouver: The Laurier Institution, pp. 139–68.

Goetze, Diana (1995) 'The Zapatista Women: the Movement from Within' in *Zapatistas, Documents of the New Mexican Revolution*, New York: Autonomedia. Available online, www.actlab.utexas.edu/~geneve/zapwomen/goetze/thesis.html.

Hamilton, Sarah (2001) 'Neoliberalism, Gender and Property rights in Rural Mexico', *Latin America Research Review* 37, 1: 119–43.

Harvey, Neil (1999) *Chiapas Rebellion: The Struggle for Land and Democracy*, Durham, NC: Duke University Press.

—— (2001) 'Globalisation and Resistance in Post-Cold War Mexico: Difference, Citizenship and Bio-Diversity Conflicts in Chiapas', *Third World Quarterly* 22 ,6, pp. 1045–61.

Henriques, Gisel and Patel, Raj (2004) 'NAFTA, Corn, and Mexico's Agricultural Trade Liberalization,' Americas Programme, Silver City, NM: Interhemispheric Resource Center, February 13. Available online, http://americas.irc-online.org/pdf/reports/0402nafta.pdf.

Hicks, Jack and White, Graham (2000) 'Nunavut: Inuit Self-Determination through a Land Claim and Public Government?', in Jens Dahl, Jack Hicks and Peter Jull (eds) *Inuit Regain Control of Their Lands and Lives*, Copenhagen: International Work Group for Indigenous Affairs, pp. 30–115.

Hindley, Jane (1996) 'Towards a Pulticultural Nation: The Limits of Indigenism and Article 4', in Rob Aitken, Nikki Craske, Gareth A. Jones, and David E. Stansfield (eds) *Dismantling the Mexican State?*, New York: St. Martin's Press, pp. 225–43.

Instituto Nacional de Estadística Geografía e Informática (2000) XII Censo de Población Y Vivienda. Available online, www.inegi.gob.mx/est/contenidos/espanol/proyectos/censos/CPV2000/muestracensal.

Jorgensen, Dan (1999) The Conquest of Nena: Property, Identity and the Politics of Mining in Papua, New Guinea, Paper presented at the Annual Meeting of the American Ethnological Society, March 1999, Portland, Oregon, US.

Jung, Courtney (2003) 'The Politics of Indigenous Identity: Neoliberalism, Cultural Rights and the Mexican Zapatistas', *Social Research*, 70, 2, Summer: 433–63.

Kabeer, Naila (2003) *Gender Mainstreaming in Poverty Eradication and the Millennium Development Goals: A Handbook for Policy-makers and Other Stakeholders*, London: Commonwealth Secretariat, International Development Research Centre. Available online, http://web.idrc.ca/openebooks/067-5/.

Katz, Cindi (2001a) 'Vagabond Capitalism and the Necessity of Social Reproduction', *Antipode*, 33, 4: 709–28.

—— (2001b) 'On the Grounds of Globalization: A Topography for Feminist Engagement', *Signs: A Journal of Women in Culture and Society*, 16, 4: 1213–34.

Macdonald, Laura (2002) 'Governance and State Society Relations: The Challenges', in George Hoberg (ed.) *Capacity for Choice: Canada in a North America*, Toronto: University of Toronto Press, pp. 187–223.

McPherson, Robert (2003) *New Owners in Their Own Land: Minerals and Inuit Land Claims*, Calgary: University of Calgary Press.

Momsen, J.H. (1991) *Women and Development in the Third World*, London: Routledge.

Nash, June (2001) *Mayan Visions: The Quest for Autonomy in an Age of Globalization*, New York: Routledge.

National Anti-Poverty Organization (1999) *Poverty in Canada: Some Facts and Figures*, Fact Sheet, April, Ottawa, Canada.

Nuttall, Mark (2005) 'Gender, Indigenous Knowledge and Development in the Arctic', Danish Polar Center, Copenhagen, Denmark. Available online, www.pc.dk.PolarPubs/Technical/No5papers/Nuttall.html.

PACE Society (2000) 'Violence against Women in Vancouver's Street Level Sex Trade and the Police Response', Vancouver, BC, Canada.

Rata, Elizabeth (1999) 'The Theory of Neo-Tribal Capitalism', *Review*, 22: 231–88.

Ratner, R.S.; Carroll, William K. and Woolford, Andrew (2003) 'Wealth of Nations: Aboriginal Treaty Making in the Era of Globalization', in John Torpey (ed.) *Politics and the Past: On Reparing Historical Injustices*, New York: Rowan and Littlefield Publishers, pp. 217–47.

Raunet, Daniel (1984) *Without Surrender without Consent. A History of the Nishga Land Claims*, Vancouver: Douglas and McIntyre.

Rojas, Rosa (ed.) (1995) *Chiapas ¿y las mujeres qué?, Vol. I*, Mexico City: Ediciones la Correa Feminista.

Russell, Wendy (2004) 'The People Had Discovered Their Own Approach to Life: Politicizing Development Discourse', in Mario Blaser, Harvey A. Feit and Glenn McRae (eds) *In the Way of Development: Indigenous Peoples, Life Projects and Globalization*, London: Zed Books, pp. 130–52.

SAGARPA (Centro de estadística Agropecuaria) (2001) Información Estadística de la Producción Agrícola en México, Mexico: Secretaría del Gobierno Federal, May.

Saladin d'Anglure, Berbard and Morin, Françoise (1992) 'The Inuit People, between Particularism and Internationalism: An Overview of their Rights and Powers in 1992', *Inuit Studies*, 16, 1–2: 13–19.

Shröder, Ingo W. (2003) 'The Political Economy of Tribalism in North America: Neo-Tribal Capitalism?', *Anthropological Theory*, 3, 4: 435–56.

Slowey, Gabrielle Anne (1999) 'Neo-liberalism and the Project of Self-Government' in Dave Broad and Anthony Wayne, *Citizens or Consumers? Social Policy in a Market Society*, Halifax: Fernwood Publishing, pp. 116–128.

Smith, Linda Tuhiwai (1999) *Decolonizing Methodologies: Research and Indigenous Peoples*, London: Zed Books.

Stack, J. John (ed.) (1985) *Ethnic Identities in a Transnational World*, Westwood: Greenwood Press.

Stephen, Lynn (2001) 'Globalization, the State and the Creation of Flexible Indigenous Workers: Mixtec Farm Workers in Oregon', Working Paper 36, The Centre for Comparative Immigration Studies, University of California, San Diego.

—— (2005) 'Women's Weaving Cooperatives in Oaxaca: An Indigenous Response to Neoliberalism', *Critique of Anthropology*, 25, 3, Spring: 253–78.

Stewart-Harawira, Makere (2005) *The Indigenous New Response to Imperial Globalization Order*, London: Zed Books and Huia Publishers.

Tarrow, S. (1998) *Power in Movement: Social Movements and Contentious Politics*, New York: Cambridge University Press.

Van Woudenberg, Gerdine (2004) 'Placing Gender in the Mediation of Aboriginal Resource Claims and Conflicts', *Reserches amérindiennes au Quebec*, 34, 3: 75–86.

Vázquez García, Veronica (2002) 'Native Women and State Legislation in Mexico and Canada: The Agrarian Law and the Indian Act', in Tamara Hunt and Micheline R. Lessard (eds) *Women and the Colonial Gaze*, New York: New York University Press and Palgrave, pp. 91–103.

Weaver, Thomas (1996) 'Mapping the Policy Terrain: Political Economy, Policy, Environment, and Forestry Production in Northern Mexico', *Journal of Political Ecology*, 3: 37–68.

Western Landscapes (2001) *Urban Aboriginals: Opportunities and Challenges*, Summer. Available online, www.turtleisland.org/news/WLSummer2001.pdf.

White, Jerry *et al.* (2003) 'Labour Force Activity of Women in Canada: A Comparative Analysis of Aboriginal and Non-Aboriginal Women', *Canadian Review of Sociology and Anthropology*, 40, 4: 391–415.

Wotherspoon, Terry and Satzewich, Vic (2000) *First Nations: Race, Class and Gender Relations*, Regina: Canadian Plains Research Centre.

Zabin, Carol and Hughes, Sallie (1995) 'Economic Integration and Labor Flows: Stage Migration in Farm Labor Markets in Mexico and the United States', *International Migration Review*, 29, 2: 395–422.

8 Women's activism and the marketing of the nonprofit community

Randi Drevland

Introduction

Women's activism in semi-peripheral nations is framed by conditions related to diminishing access to public services, eroding employment standards and the increasing casualization of labour (ILO 2004: 7). For many women increased economic insecurity and political marginalization means having to adjust to economic restructuring at the level of both the household and the workplace. This dual nature of restructuring by necessity leads women's groups to be involved in increased activism between the boundaries circumscribing their so-called private and public lives.

A case in point is the recent type of activism that characterizes women within the United Steelworkers of America, activism that arises out of their everyday life experiences. The women 'developed and used "in-between" movement spaces to create a feminism more responsive to their multiple political interests as workers, as women, and as citizens' (Fonow 2003: 2). The intersections between women's lived experiences and identities, as existing between public and private dimensions of everyday life, challenge normative political views and highlight the linkages between women's political activism, their association to voluntary sector organizations and social movements. In Canada, women's resistance to neoliberal policy change occurs within the nonprofit sector in response to an environment of increasing vulnerabilities and diminishing opportunities. But also, the neoliberal trend is beginning to encroach upon this sector such that women's access to this sector itself is in jeopardy (O'Neill 1994: 1–2). It is in this nonprofit sector where women's public and private lives are directly affected by neoliberal policies because it is here where women are engaged as paid and unpaid workers, are recipients of services and function as political actors.

Currently, within the Canadian nonprofit sector women are the majority of employees (74 per cent) and more are employed on a temporary (14 per cent) and a part-time basis (26 per cent), which is representative of gender trends occuring in the workforce as a whole (Scott 2003: 168). In addition to these numbers are the countless women who volunteer their unpaid labour to support various organizations within this sector.

The voluntary sector or nonprofit sector is variously referred to as the social economy, the nonprofit sector, the voluntary sector, the civic sector, the third sector and the independent sector. The working definition of the voluntary and nonprofit sector (despite slight differences), which I will be treating as one sector, integrates the following set of social, political and economic criteria.[1]

1 It is based on a primacy of social objectives.
2 It includes a range of organizations, from enterprises that are self-reliant and generate their revenues from a variety of sources, including commerce and membership fees, to those that are supported by governments and private donors.
3 It is highly dependent on volunteerism.
4 Surplus earnings are used to strengthen the organization and improve its services.
5 The net assets of organizations are analogous to a social dividend passed from generation to generation.
6 Democratic control based upon one-member/one vote is a fundamental feature.
7 It also includes a network of informal groups that are not 'registered' within 'recognized' charity or volunteer categorizations.
8 It is generally conceived as autonomous from formal government administration and serves people in a multitude of capacities.

With the rise of neoliberal policy reform that has negatively affected the welfare states, there has been a corresponding growth and interest in the voluntary sector as a moderating influence on neoliberal policy, one that acts as a buffer between the state and market forces.

> Globalization clearly has important implications for nonprofit-governmental relations [considering the scope of] international agreements such as the General Agreement on Tariffs and Trade (GATT) and the North American Free Trade Act (NAFTA), and World Trade Organization (WTO) rulings … Such forms of global governance have spawned a new generation of transnational nonprofits as well as local sites of resistance and oppositional associations.
>
> (Wolch 2003: 190)

Women's organizations are prominent actors in the nonprofit community and are known especially for their stand on the protection of and need for advocacy within this sector. Shifting power imbalances surfacing around issues of race, class, labour and gender relations provide a collective convergence of motivations within voluntary organizations around such issues as advocacy and their shared determination to engage with the state. This engagement with the state is not unproblematic, however. Feminist critiques about the depolitization of the women's movement within Canada have emphasized the peril of viewing the state as an unchanging neutral entity. Although the necessity for autonomy from the state has been a hallmark of contemporary feminist activism, this has not meant political disengagement from the state (Briskin 1991: 24–40). The autonomy of women's movements and organizations is challenged, however, as neoliberalism and market ideology creates an environment that compels the need for a strengthening of government relationships. It is therefore timely to reconsider the way in which the state is engaged by feminist and voluntary sector organizations to understand the depth of changes taking place within liberal democratic societies. The main challenges involve the way that the nonprofit sector itself is affected by neoliberal reforms.

Integrating women's social protest as political movement

Historically, voluntary sector organizations within communities have provided a venue for women's political presence and extraparliamentary activity allowing them to transit societal constraints such as gender roles, class, racial and cultural differences. This has positioned some women in potentially powerful political roles as protectors and advocates of public welfare, particularly by coupling the 'ability to link the practical and the effective delivery of services to larger political questions … making the local and community-based dimension of municipalities an important component' (Andrew 1992: 114). However, should corporations and market forces gain dominance within the voluntary sector, a critical space for democratic public participation and resistance will be stifled with disastrous implications for many as labour and human rights become marginalized.

Women and their organizations in the nonprofit sector are playing a substantive role in support of a socially responsible state through women's extraparliamentary activism. This is clearly evident through the work and activism of individual women and women's organizations, including those within 'gender neutral' organizations, such as Marie Clarke-Walker, Executive Vice President of the Canadian Labour Congress, Maude Barlow, the National Chairperson of the Council of Canadians, the largest citizen's advocacy organization in Canada, and until her recent death, Jane Jacob's commitment to promoting the development of sustainable Canadian cities. Organizations such as the Canadian Women's Health Network (CWHN), Canadian Research for the Advancement of Women (CRIAW), Canadian Women's Foundation (CWF), Native Women's Association of Canada (NWAC), National Organization of Immigrant and Visible Minority Women (NOIVMWC), and the Disabled Women's Network (DAWN) are all lobbying and acting on behalf of diverse communities, challenging the state to promote equitable social governance. But when women's social protest and political dissidence is categorized under the umbrella 'women's movement', it masks their community roots and political diversity.[2]

Women's involvement in urban and grassroots social movements has spanned a diversity of issues and yet 'the impact of women's participation in various forms of resistance and protest has remained largely unnoticed or taken for granted [thereby] concealing women as active agents of sociopolitical changes' (Fairhurst *et al.* 2004: 208). As a result, the reciprocity and crosscutting nature of issues that have relevance for diverse segments of society are often obscured from public scrutiny. These social movements are often represented as 'transient' phenomena, emerging in a temporary response to an issue. Their participants are generally depicted as sexless and genderless members of an organized interest group. The labelling of some social movements as transient phenomena representing special interests leaves 'the specific presence of women and men in the political field ... denied' (West and Blumberg 1990: 8). In this way the differences and similarities between groups is neutralized and so too is the idea of collective political action and consciousness.

Representing social movements as entities in themselves depoliticizes the vital political communities and actors that come together to form these groups, rendering invisible the complex interconnections between local community organizations, neighbourhoods and participants, which define their political engagement as anything but transitory. These groups, organizations and participants, working and living within neighbourhoods, create political communities within the voluntary sector, raising critical consciousness by establishing networks of support and information sharing, which, at times, can serve to activate mass social mobilizations.[3] An example of this type of networking is the 16th International AIDS Conference in Toronto, 'Time to Deliver' 2006. This conference brought together 300 African and Canadian grandmothers and others, from communities ranging from Coquitlam, British Columbia, Canada, to representatives of villages in Zimbabwe and South Africa, in a campaign known as 'Grandmothers to Grandmothers'. The organization, Greater Vancouver Gogos (*gogos* is the Zulu word for grandmother), in support of the Stephen Lewis Foundation, is represented by Barbara Clay who is active in outreach work concerning AIDS awareness and the consequences of inaction by pharmaceutical corporations and governments.

Urban and grassroots social movements draw attention to 'scales beyond local' while making visible the 'dynamics of local struggle' and give meaning to the diverse vocalizations of contestations worldwide by situating 'localised forms of action within a globalised context' (Hamel *et al.* 2000: 2). Despite the diverse issues and communities these movements represent they share common qualities because they arose from the processes that relate to specific issues and places. These processes involve interaction with the state because, as Janet Conway notes, 'communities are formed, in significant part, by their relation to policy categories and funding relationships' (2004: 49).

Women's social movements politicize the often hidden practices and consequences of neoliberal capitalism from diverse community perspectives and forge local strategies of resistance to neoliberal treatment (Fairhurst *et al.* 2004: 203). As neoliberal policy frameworks attempt to decentralize government, local politics operating through the nonprofit sector are providing discursive political space for confrontation and negotiation. For some, social movements also represent an opportunity not only for exposing the system's glaring crises, but also offering a mediating influence within the sphere (Hamel *et al.* 2000: 5).

Although women are significant political actors within communities, municipal politics and transnational activism, this activism, until recently, has been largely

invisible (Conway 2004: 39). Women do want recognition as a distinct and legitimate social group to redress inequalities in power and under-representation in
political arenas (Phillips 2003: 264). Women's engagement with the state and the
socioeconomic structural biases which underpin governance challenge the normative construction of politics and power as a masculine enterprise built upon
conceptualizations of the public and private spheres and women's place within
them. Similarly, women have had to wrestle with acknowledging diversities
amongst themselves.

Women's presence as engaged political actors in communities therefore seem
rather paradoxical in light of women's exclusion and struggles. However, the sepa-
ration of genders into public and private identities are continuously subject to strategic social, economic and political manipulation, often allowing women's
reproductive and productive labour to be devalued, exploited and commodified.
By extension, communities and the nonprofit sector are socially and politically
constructed as 'feminine' and related to 'women's work' owing to their association
with societal reproduction and wellbeing. The voluntary sector can thus be alienated from the state, devalued and exploited, permitting the state to off-load many
social responsibilities to this sector as it restructures. Through this process 'the
work of women in the community is quietly assumed and practically confirmed
[and] in this way community work takes a gendered character' (Dehli 1990: 47).
Nevertheless, Canadian women's groups are organizing within the voluntary
sector to oppose the deteriorating conditions of women's lives as a consequence of
neoliberal government changes to public services, programmes and social policies.
This process has been accompanied by the emergence of the voluntary/nonprofit
sector operating in a dual capacity: as an essential public service and as a site of
resistance.

The Canadian voluntary sector

As the gap between rich and poor is expanding and welfare mechanisms and
public services are shrinking the Canadian voluntary sector, feminist organizations
as well as countless others, are taking on an increasing share of the burden and
responsibility for providing services and support normally provided by the Canadian welfare state. In the *Report Card on Child Poverty in Canada*, it states that a 'deep
inequality [has been] entrenched through economic growth [and] Canada's top 10
per cent richest families with children had average incomes that were more than 13
times higher than the bottom 10 per cent' (Campaign 2000 2005: 1). Paradoxically, in a climate of decreased funding to the voluntary sector, eroded public
services and increased need, more is being expected from the voluntary sector.

Voluntary sector agencies and organizations are placed in a precarious situation
where their resources are stretched to capacity as new responsibilities are transferred to them by a government that is increasingly redefining their relationship as
a corporate partnership based on contractual arrangements. The already beleaguered voluntary sector finds itself in an administrative nightmare, as efficiency
and accountability become new guidelines for management. Cash strapped

agencies find it difficult to fulfil their mandates as more time is spent on paperwork for funding proposals and strategies. Facing severe disadvantages in a growing hierarchal environment many of the more socially committed organizations are being excluded as the rest of the sector is depoliticized. The reciprocity, albeit imperfect, developed between government and the voluntary sector in the Keynesian state based upon a mixed welfare economy that underscored relations of mutual social support and provision for public benefit is being dismantled.

As government recedes from its social obligations – retooling state–societal relations on a set of principles touted as private–public partnerships – international capital and market fundamentalism is stepping in, reshaping the voluntary sector as a new growth industry. With seemingly benign schemes such as social marketing, corporations are gaining entry into the voluntary sector even though they donate less than one per cent of their profits to charity. The voluntary sector is, then, recreated as a site of production, consumption and entrepreneurialism and competitiveness in the delivery of public services becomes the new maxim while people become clients and consumers as social services become commoditized. This change in redistributive and social justice provision has led voluntary organizations to reconsider their relationship with the Canadian state in the face of neoliberal reforms.

The voluntary/nonprofit sector of the Canadian economy has been described as the 'invisible economy' (Hirshhorn 1997) and its significance has been largely ignored.[4] It provides a complex scaffolding that underpins a host of services and programmes which support the needs of Canadians, but it is also a significant economic contributor to Canada in terms of employment, revenue and infrastructure. Because of this there has been revived interest in the sector by government and industry to tap into its enormous market potential.

> Despite the moniker 'voluntary' the sector employs more than 1.3 million Canadians, one in every 11 jobs. Charities already pay out salaries and benefits of more than $40 billion a year; most of the other 50 billion that passes through the sector goes to programme delivery (65 per cent) and administration (15 per cent) and they are repeatedly touted as a principal growth area in the so-called 'new economy' … This does not include the approximately 1.6 million people who do voluntary work, a contribution valued at 12 billion a year … with a value of assets at approximately $109 billion.
>
> (Picard 1997: 3)

With renewed enthusiasm the government has turned fresh eyes to a previous archaic regulatory framework. In the space of two years a Voluntary Sector Initiative (2000) was established which was followed by a Canada Volunteerism Initiative (2001) and a Minister Responsible for Voluntary Sector was appointed in 2002. A framework of re-regulation between the Government of Canada and the voluntary sector was designed based upon an Accord between the Government of Canada and the Voluntary Sector, supplemented by the Code of Good Practice on Funding and a Code of Good Practice on Policy Dialogue (Association Xpertise

Inc. 2005). As of March 2004, it was announced that the Canada Revenue Agency in consultation with the voluntary sector had instituted 72 regulatory improvements to the Income Tax Act concerning charities. But some anticipated changes have cast a pall over some agencies within the nonprofit sector (Brock 2003: 5). As the lines between government and the sector, and business and government blur, 'the social contract is changing, the relationship between citizens and government is changing and civic engagement is changing' (Picard 1997: 6).

Significantly, with the implementation of neoliberal reforms, the nonprofit sector was one of the first to face devastating cutbacks affecting service delivery in education, welfare and health in organizations such as food banks, women centres, homeless and battered shelters, nursing homes and crisis centres, to name a few. Those organizations that collected revenue through fees such as universities have covered the shortfall of government funding by increasing user fees thereby reserving access to services and programmes to those who can afford these increases. Other public services were downsized, costs increased and unions came under attack as privatization gained a foothold in the sector.

However, resistance to these reforms is simmering beneath the surface, even in some of the more conventional circles of the sector. Agnes G. Meinhard's and Mary K. Foster's (2003) national survey of 351 women's voluntary organizations and 294 'other' (gender neutral) organizations within the third sector asked the question: 'What motivates organizations to seek collaborations and partnerships?' The responses were as follows. Out of a list of eight items presented to the respondents, three key motivating factors for both groups are the same: gaining attention for causes through strength in numbers, achieving greater community involvement, and providing more integrated services. The item 'becoming more independent of government' is ranked lowest as a motive for collaboration for both groups (ibid.: 383).

The voluntary sector has been slow to respond to the changing environment, preferring instead to believe that the past partnership with the government could be restored. Even as the pace of demands accelerated and funding contracted a Voluntary Roundtable was convened to initiate a proactive interface with government. The sector has actively sought recognition and a place in the discussions about changes to social policy with both federal and provincial governments. However, the coordination amongst voluntary organizations across the country is embryonic and considerable ambiguity exists about the relationship to government (White 2004: 125).[5] The ideological approaches of government and the voluntary sector could not be more different as government pushes for marketization, professionalization and regulation of the third sector, and the voluntary sector prioritizes social capital, cohesion and responsibility or a social economy, in short. As Bob Jessop notes, the proponents of a social economy 'aim to re-embed the organization of the economy in specific spatio-temporal contexts oriented to the rhythms of social reproduction rather than to the frenzied circulation of digitalised capital' (2000: 94). Resistance to the corporatist approach of governance within the voluntary sector is occurring at all levels, from the municipal to the national and international.

A politically crucial contention between the voluntary sector and government revolves around the issue of advocacy. The imposition of a corporatist governance framework as the basis for state–societal relations is foreclosing the principle of participatory citizen engagement with government, a foundational cornerstone of democracy. As the state recedes from its social obligations there has been an accompanying 'political backlash against public participation as it historically has been practiced' thus creating an environment of distrust and suspicion on one hand and a curtailing of politics on the other hand (Graham and Phillips 1998: 13). In the third sector this has created a climate of fear and uncertainty, particularly concerning the government's monitoring of advocacy by voluntary agencies.

> In an era where lobbyists are an accepted part of the political process, and where governments provide funding for various groups to advocate on behalf of consumers, charities still risk losing their status if more than 10 per cent of their receipted donations are spent on advocacy.
>
> (Picard 1997: 7)

Many organizations are, in effect, being silenced by regulatory means, especially those that depend on government contracts and funding for their existence. Smaller organizations are particularly vulnerable because of their dependency on government and the lack of resources to aggressively fundraise and compete with larger agencies that effectively garner the lion's share of financial support. Hospitals, colleges and universities receive 80 per cent of fund transfers (60 per cent goes to hospitals) which leaves only 20 per cent to other agencies and organizations in the nonprofit sector (Canada 2004: 7, 9). This poor distribution of funding has resulted in the proliferation of autonomous, informal civic organizations which sometimes act as the voice for those registered charities that cannot be seen to heavily engage in activism and advocacy.

However, with the formation of national voluntary forums, issues concerning the direction of activism and advocacy are becoming a focus of contention. In the 1998 Canadian Leader's Forum on the voluntary sector, 'Advancing the Dialogue', speakers on behalf of organizations emphasized the importance of their relationship with federal and provincial governments, the necessity to include agencies in policy development and the need for continuing financial support. At the same time they were particularly critical of intrusions, by both public and private funders, into their social mandates and responsibilities.

> Funders (both public and private) are holding voluntary organizations to account for their activities and finances, and are requiring that they provide more information about how funds are being raised, managed and expended; as a consequence, voluntary organizations are being pressured to change their mandates to conform to funder's expectations; they may, for example, be required to reduce or abandon their efforts to improve their client's situations

through advocacy for change, or to deliver the kind of services their clients need …

(Public Policy Forum 1998: 6)

Primarily, accountability of this nature is problematic because many funders may seek to look after their own class interests and the organizations that support them rather provide services to needier, broader segments of society (Brock 2003: 4–7). The contradictory and compromising nature of regulatory intervention underway in Canada is undermining agency mandates and service delivery. However, owing to the strength of nonprofit/voluntary sector convictions around issues of advocacy, various agencies have demanded and established an Advocacy Working Group (2001) within the Voluntary Sector Initiative to mediate a framework of discussion with government (Non-Profit and Voluntary Sector Affairs Division), establishing a national counter-position to corporatist agendas. The acceptance of this initiative is subject to intense debate as many voluntary/ nonprofit organizations maintain that this is a move to co-opt and pacify the voluntary sector and compromises their overall legitimacy with the public. An important factor in these discussions is the economic and political variability among provinces to neoliberal policy entrenchment.

The Case of British Columbia

British Columbia (BC) provides a rich, nuanced provincial resource, both historically and contemporaneously, for women's activism and voluntary sector organizing in connection to neoliberal policy reform. In BC restructuring has resulted in a dramatic backlash of social protections that target women's and advocacy organizations by implementing severe funding cuts such as those that led to the closure of women's centres, nursing homes, legal aid access and outreach crisis lines. The depth of these reforms brought condemnation internationally from the United Nations Committee on the Elimination of Discrimination against Women (CEDAW) and the International Labour Organization (ILO) because their implementation is viewed as a contravention of international rights. This situation stands in sharp contrast to a province that was recognized in '[the] early twentieth-century [as] creating a rights-based programme for women that was more inclusive than any other in Canada and most others in the United States' (Little 2002: 188).

When federal transfer payments to the provinces for social and public programmes were sharply reduced in 1995 it initiated cascading effects at provincial and municipal levels across Canada. However in BC transference of provincial governance from the New Democratic Party of BC to the Liberal Party of BC brought extensive changes to acts and regulations between 2001 and 2005. The passing of several bills dealing with labour and revisions to welfare and disability assistance led many civic groups within British Columbia to suggest that a legislated 'third-worlding' of labour and marginalized populations is taking place, one that establishes a low wage economy and promotes exploitation of workers, children and vulnerable segments of society. The fallout from neoliberal policy implementation has been accompanied by an increase in homelessness in the province covering a more diversified population (SPARC 2005: 1, Wallace *et al.* 2006: 14). The solution of the provincial government has been to offload responsibility to an already beleaguered nonprofit/voluntary sector undergoing funding cuts and advocacy limitations by directing people to foodbanks, shelters and other charities within the sector.

January 17, 2002, was labelled 'Black Thursday' by labour unions and other organizations across British Columbia because of Liberal government announcements of a programme of job and spending cuts, implicating major changes to the Labour Relations Code, Employment Standards Act, the Employment and Assistance Act and the Workmen's Compensation Act. These legislative changes to social protections and assistance limited access to welfare benefits sharply impacting single-parent families, the majority of which (88.5 per cent) are headed by women in BC. The amendments implemented constraints such as time limitations on the receipt of aid insisting that women are 'employable' when their youngest child reaches three years of age, deducting child support payments from fathers from income assistance benefits, and disallowing women who attend an educational programme, while in need of support, ineligible for assistance. Overall, the government cut 20,000 jobs in the public sector (75 per cent held by women), weakened employment standards, cut childcare, reduced access to educational services for marginalized populations and eliminated proactive measures such as pay equity (Creese and Strong-Boag 2005: 2). Restructuring in British Columbia also took place organizationally within government as specific ministries were collapsed in one with the creation of the BC Ministry of Community, Aboriginal and Women's Services. This move effectively integrated and sidelined three sectors of the public known for their proactive advocacy work.

British Columbia is also presently the only province in Canada not to have a Human Rights Commission, as a result of successive legislative changes taking place in BC, 'removing a central institution relied on by women and other vulnerable members of British Columbian society to articulate and defend their right to equality, and to prevent its perpetuation' (BC CEDAW Group 2003: 7). In short, the government no longer has a statutory obligation to provide redress for human rights complaints. Additionally, further funding cuts to legal aid eliminated poverty law assistance and curtailed access to legal representation in family law matters. The Law Society of British Columbia passed a non-confidence resolution against the Attorney General of BC in 2002 and afterwards the President of the society remarked 'How cynical is it to create legal rights and then deny the poor any means to assert those rights? The government is making a mockery of equality before the law' (ibid.: 10). Access to justice for many British Columbians has become an illusory concept.

The province of British Columbia has been taken to task by international bodies for the inequitable implementation of neoliberal provincial policies. First, labour agitation has led to censure by the United Nations through the International Labour Organization (ILO) for the province's deemed illegal actions concerning labour legislation and the contravention of collective bargaining rights. Second, the agitation of a plurality of women's organizations acting in concert brought the province under condemnation by the United Nations Committee on the Elimination of Discrimination against Women (CEDAW) for the attenuation of women's rights and the precipitous erosion of social conditions. Canada as a signatory to United Nations conventions in relation to these issues finds itself in contravention of internationally accepted agreements due to actions taken by provincial governments. What emerges in British Columbia is a regulatory, civic framework supported by neoliberal economic policy initiatives, creating a network of constraints and controls over both public services and labour domains to the benefit of business interests rather than domestic populations. The primacy of the market based upon a process of privatization, deregulation and/or re-regulation and liberalization is dictating social, environmental, labour and other public policy to the detriment of all else creating vast social deficits. The first groups affected were those most vulnerable: women, the working poor and unemployed, the disabled, immigrants and indigenous peoples. This in turn has put increasing pressure on the voluntary sector's capacity to deliver services in an environment that also seeks to constrain them.

As the Canadian government has developed and 'signed-on' to increasingly complex trade and investment treaties, it has, almost simultaneously, initiated a process of downloading of social services that includes the dismantling of national health, education and welfare standards. This downloading of responsibility has fallen first to provincial governments, then to municipal governments, and now, in British Columbia at least, to community-based nonprofit agencies and individual families (Vancouver Status of Women 2004: 20).

As legislative changes were implemented, British Columbia's third sector reacted sharply with a proliferation of protests from various labour unions representing health, welfare and education, which, in turn, were joined by welfare activists, women's groups, environmentalist groups and poverty groups amongst others. Women were in the front lines of these political protests, as leaders, organizers and participants. As the socio-political climate in British Columbia continues to undergo change, more people, disproportionately represented by women and children, are becoming reliant on voluntary organizations to stave off the effects of diminishing social security. A number of voluntary organizations representing disaffected populations are engaged in forming counter-responses and alternatives. Whether through acts of social protest or in more formalized venues such as debates at roundtable forums, the meaning of democracy is being contested.

Conclusion

The underpinnings of neoliberal globalism are embedded in the dynamics of male privilege within capitalism. Women can be systemically excluded from decision-making and yet their labour remains pivotal for the progression of economic globalization. However, markets as the institutional bearers of gender also reflect the 'tensions, contradictions and potential for change which is characteristic of any pattern of gender relations, no matter how unequally power is distributed' (Elson

1999: 612). Women have taken up this challenge and by doing so have exposed the contingent and relational nature of global capitalism's control of power. In Canada and other semi-peripheral countries the nonprofit/voluntary sector is emerging as a political social force for change guided by the strong representation of women in this sector as leaders, workers and volunteers.

The formal political representation of women in Canada remains minimal and with the increasing pace of neoliberal globalism this under-representation has facilitated the reversal of previous gains in many semi-peripheral countries. Until women gain more significant political representation, it is important for women's organizations to focus on creating more autonomous and communitarian funding practices so that government control or influence does not affect their actions. So far it appears that many women's and voluntary organizations have become embroiled in competitive funding while trying to shore up the previous relationship with government. Instead, a programme that redoubles efforts towards a model of collaboration that expands networks of representation throughout the sector would expand activism beyond issue-specific cooperation. Women's organizations within government, such as Status of Women Canada, have been slow to respond to the neoliberal environment whose 'cuts and changes have been targeted in such a way as to seriously erode women's organizations and the necessary supports that ensure a coordinated inter-sectoral response' (Morrow *et al.* 2004: 360). Most pointedly, the adoption of project funding over core funding for groups has facilitated the weakening of women's and voluntary organizations, and allows the marketization of services to gain a foothold. In the report of the Standing Committee on the Status of Women in May 2005, chaired by Anita Neville, MP, the Committee 'heard that the move from core funding has made it difficult to sustain a women's movement in Canada and made it increasingly difficult for the women's movement to advocate on behalf of women' (Neville 2005: 6). Until a collective sector response is developed, inclusive of strong national representation of both women's and voluntary organizations, they will remain caught between placating government and the need for action. If they hesitate any longer to take a definitive stand the opportunity to stem the intrusion of market forces into the voluntary sector will be lost and advocacy will become a resounding silence.

Notes

1   The first six are based on Jack Quarter's definition with the seventh and eighth being my added elements (Quarter 1992: 11–12).
2   bell hooks makes this point noting 'I drop the definitive article rather than speaking of "the" feminist movement. When we do not have a definite article, we are saying that feminist movement can be located in multiple places, in multiple languages and experiences' (Childers and hooks 1990: 68).
3   Such was the case for mobilizations which occurred on November 30, 1999, in Seattle, Washington, protesting the WTO trade roundtable. Maude Barlow was prominent in the struggle for social protections to hedge the impact of trade regulations that benefit corporations and not people (Aaronson 2004).
4   This part of the economy covers such diverse organizations as universities and hospitals (although these institutions are viewed as quasi-governmental), recreation centres, cultural centres, daycares, food banks, churches, foundations and an endless list of charitable and voluntary associations,

amongst others, that provide assistance and services to diverse segments of the public. Lester Salamon (1995: 54) separates the various organizations into: funding agencies or fund-raising intermediaries (e.g. United Way), member serving organizations (e.g. trade unions), public benefit organizations (e.g. daycares, cultural institutions, social services), and religious organizations (e.g. churches).

5 Quebec has opted out of this social union process of provincial–federal negotiations over distributions of resources and responsibilities concerning social policy.

References

Aaronson, Susan Ariel (2004) *Taking Trade to the Streets: The Lost History of Public Efforts to Shape Globalization*, Ann Arbor: The University of Michigan Press.

Andrew, Caroline (1992) 'The Feminist City', in Henri Lustiger-Thaler (ed.) *Political Arrangements: Power and the City*, Montreal, New York: Black Rose Books, pp. 109–17.

Association Xpertise Inc. (AXI) (2005) *New Canada Not-For-Profit Corporations Act and Its Impact on Charitable and Non-profit Corporations*, Guest Article prepared by Jacqueline M. Connor, Terrance S. Carter and assisted by D. Ann Walters. Available online, www.axi.ca/tca/Jan2005/guestarticle_3.shtml.

B. C. Committee on the Elimination of Discrimination against Women (CEDAW) Group (2003) *British Columbia Moves Backwards on Women's Equality*, Vancouver: BC CEDAW Group.

Briskin, Linda (1991) 'A New Approach to Evaluating Feminist Strategy', in Jeri Dawn Wine and Janice L. Ristock (eds) *Women and Social Change: Feminist Activism in Canada*, Toronto: James Lorimer and Company, pp. 24–40.

Brock, Kathy L. (2003) 'The Nonprofit Sector in Interesting Times: An Introduction Plus', in Kathy L. Brock and Keith G. Banting (eds) *The Nonprofit Sector in Interesting Times: Case Studies in a Changing Sector*, Montreal and Kingston: McGill University Press, pp. 1–16.

Campaign 2000 (2005) *Decision Time for Canada: Let's Make Poverty History: 2005 Report Card on Child Poverty in Canada*, Toronto: Campaign 2000.

Canada (2004) *Satellite Account of Nonprofit Institutions and Volunteering (1997–1999)*, Report prepared by Mingyu Yu, Karen Ashmas, Malika Hamdad, Sophie Joyal, and Catherine Van Rompaey, Ottawa: Statistics Canada.

Childers, Mary and hooks, bell (1990) 'A Conversation about Race and Class', in Mirianne Hirsch and Evelyn Fox Keller (eds) *Conflicts in Feminism*, New York: Routledge.

Conway, Janet M. (2004) *Identity, Place, Knowledge: Social Movements Contesting Globalization*, Halifax: Fernwood.

Creese, Gillian and Strong-Boag, Veronica (2005) *Losing Ground: The Effects of Government Cutbacks on Women in British Columbia, 2001–2005*, Report prepared for the BC Coalition of Women's Centres, University of British Columbia Centre for Research in Women's Studies and Gender Relations and BC Federation of Labour, March 5, Vancouver: British Columbia Federation of Labour.

Dehli, Kari (1990) 'Women in the Community: Reform of Schooling and Motherhood in Toronto', in Roxanna Ng, Gillian Walker and Jacob Muller (eds) *Community Organization and the Canadian State*, Toronto: Garamond Press, pp. 47–64.

Elson, Diane (1999) 'Labor Markets as Gendered Institutions: Equality, Efficiency and Empowerment Issues', *World Development*, 27, 3: 611–27.

Fairhurst, Joan; Ramutsindela, Maano and Urmilla, Bob (2004) 'Social Movements, Protest, and Resistance', in Lynn A. Staeheli, Eleonore Kofman and Linda J. Peake (eds) *Mapping Women, Making Politics: Feminist Perspectives on Political Geography*, New York, London: Routledge, pp. 204–17.

Fonow, Mary Margaret (2003) *Union Women: Forging Feminism in the United Steelworkers of America*, Minneapolis: University of Minnesota Press.

Graham, Katherine A. and Phillips, Susan D. (eds) (1998) *Citizen Engagement: Lessons in Participation from Local Government*, Toronto: The Institute of Public Administration of Canada.

Hamel, Pierre; Lustiger-Thaler, Henri and Mayer, Margit (2000) 'Introduction: Urban Social Movements – Local Thematics, Global Spaces', in Pierre Hamel, Henri Lustiger-Thaler and Margit Mayer (eds) *Urban Movements in a Globalising World*, London, New York: Routledge, pp. 1–22.

Hirshhorn, Ronald (ed.) (1997) *The Emerging Sector: In Search of a Framework, CPRN Study No. 1*, Canadian Policy Research Networks (CPRN), The Nonprofit Research Initiative, Ottawa: Renouf Publishing.

International Labour Organization (ILO) (2004) *Economic Security for a Better World*, ILO Socioeconomic Security Programme, Geneva: International Labour Organization Office.

Jessop, Bob (2000) 'Globalisation, Entrepreneurial Cities and the Social Economy', in Pierre Hamel, Henri Lustiger-Thaler and Margit Mayer (eds) *Urban Movements in a Globalising World*, London, New York: Routledge, pp. 81–100.

Little, Margaret Hillyard (2002) 'Claiming a Unique Place: The Introduction of Mothers' Pensions in British Columbia', in Veronica Strong-Boag, Mona Gleason and Adele Perry (eds) *Rethinking Canada: The Promise of Women's* History, Don Mills, ON: Oxford University Press, pp. 187–202.

Meinhard, Agnes G. and Foster, Mary K. (2003) 'Differences in the Response of Women's Voluntary Organizations to Shifts in Canadian Public Policy', *Nonprofit and Voluntary Sector Quarterly*, 32, 3: 366–96.

Morrow, Marina; Hankivsky, Olena and Varcoe, Colleen (2004) 'Women and Violence: The Effects of Dismantling the Welfare State', *Critical Social Policy*, 24, 3: 358–84.

Neville, Anita (2005) *Funding through the Women's Program: Women's Groups Speak Out*, Report of the Standing Committee on the Status of Women, Ottawa: House of Commons, pp. 1–21.

O'Neill, Michael (1994) 'The Paradox of Women and Power in the Nonprofit Sector', in Teresa Odendahl and Michael O'Neill (eds) *Women and Power in the Nonprofit Sector*, San Francisco: Jossey-Bass Publishers, pp. 1–16.

Phillips, Anne (2003) 'Recognition and the Struggle for Political Voice', in Barbara Hobson (ed.) *Recognition Struggles and Social Movements: Contested Identities, Agency and Power*, Cambridge: Cambridge University Press, pp. 263–73.

Picard, Andre (1997) *A Call To Alms: The New Face of Charities in Canada*, Toronto: The Atkinson Charitable Foundation.

Public Policy Forum (1998) *The Voluntary Sector Advancing the Dialogue: The Canadian Leader's Forum Summary of Discussions and Outcomes*, Ottawa: Public Policy Forum.

Quarter, Jack (1992) *Canada's Social Economy: Co-operatives, Non-profits, and Other Community Enterprises*, Toronto: James Lorimer & Company.

Salamon, Lester M. (1995) *Partners in Public Service: Government–Nonprofit Relations in the Modern Welfare State*, Baltimore: John Hopkins University Press.

Scott, Katherine (2003) *Funding Matters: The Impact of Canada's New Funding Regime on Nonprofit and Voluntary Organizations*, Ottawa, ON: Canadian Council on Social Development.

Social Planning and Research Council of BC (SPARC) (2005) *Homeless Count, 2005: On Our Streets and in Our Shelters ... Results of the 2005 Greater Vancouver Homeless Count*, Vancouver: SPARC.

Vancouver Status of Women (2004) *A New Era: The Deepening of Women's Poverty*, Women and Welfare Project, Vancouver: Vancouver Status of Women.

Wallace, Bruce; Klein, Seth and Reitsma-Street, Marge (2006) *Denied Assistance: Closing the Door on Welfare in BC*, Vancouver: Canadian Centre for Policy Alternatives (CCPA) and Vancouver Island Public Interest Research Group (VPIRG).

West, Guida and Blumberg, Rhoda Lola (eds) (1990) *Women and Social Protest*, New York and Oxford: Oxford University Press.

White, Deena (2004) 'The Voluntary Sector, Community Sector and Social Economy in Canada: Why One Is Not the Other', in Annette Zimmer and Christina Stecker (eds) *Strategy Mix for Nonprofit Organizations: Vehicles for Social and Labour Market Integration*, New York and Dordrecht: Kluwer Academic and Plenum Publishers, pp. 117–41.

Wolch, Jennifer (2003) 'State, Subject, Space: Silences in Institutionalist Theories of Nonprofit-Government Relations', in Helmut K. Anheir and Avner Ben-Ner (eds) *The Study of the Nonprofit Enterprise: Theories and Approaches*, New York and Dordrecht: Kluwer Academic and Plenum Publishers, pp. 187–98.

9 Canada's Three Ds

The rise and decline of the gender-based policy capacity

Janine Brodie[1]

Introduction

In 2005, Status of Women Canada (SWC), the principal agency responsible for gender-based policy analysis and advocacy within the federal government, launched a nation-wide consultation on gender equality in Canada. This stock-taking, the first since the mid-1980s, coincided with a number of significant milestones in the unfinished struggle for women's equality in Canada. Thirty-five years had passed since the release of the agenda-setting Royal Commission on the Status of Women (Canada 1970) and it had been 30 years since Canada, along with other UN member states, declared 1975 as the International Year of Women (IYW), and the beginning of the UN Decade of Women. Moreover, it had been ten years since Canada had enthusiastically endorsed the 1995 Beijing Platform for Action, which invited governments to mainstream gender into the development and implementation of all policy initiatives. Although gender equality had been on the federal government's legislative agenda for more than three decades, SWC reported that progress toward this goal was uneven and, in some cases, reversing. Just as disconcerting, SWC observed, was a growing perception, especially among women's organizations, that Canada's governments were not taking 'its commitments to women seriously' while many other Canadians had the false impression that 'gender equality had been achieved' (2005: 1). The Canadian experience, it would appear, parallels the Australian case, where Anne Summers, a former head of the Australian Office of the Status of Women, recently lamented 'we have come to the end of equality' (Summers 2003: 6).

This chapter describes how, over the course of a generation, Canadians have witnessed both a remarkable rise and a precipitous decline in the importance attributed to gender in public policy and in the pursuit of the broader social goals of gender equality and inclusive citizenship. In the 1970s and early 1980s, Canada was widely regarded as a leader in the international community with respect to the formal affirmation of women's equality rights, the development of gender-based policy capacity within government, and the creation and maintenance of linkages to both local and national women's organizations. Beginning in the mid-1980s, however, gender has been progressively erased as a critical factor in the development of Canadian public policy. The degendering of politics and public policy across Anglo-American democracies during these years has been attributed to many different factors, including the apparent cyclical or 'wave-like' history of the organized women's movement, the institutionalization of the women's movement, the neoconservative backlash against second wave feminism, and the ascendancy of neoliberal governance (Sawer 2006). While each of these factors helps situate, in different ways, the politics of gender in the contemporary era, this chapter focuses on the capacities of gender-based policy machinery, within the Canadian federal government and in the provinces, to influence the development and implementation of gender sensitive public policy. As this chapter describes, the progressive erasure of gender can be tracked through three interrelated processes – the delegitimization of feminism, the dismantling of gender-based policy units, and the disappearance of the gender subject of public policy. Before describing how these three Ds have unfolded in the Canadian case, the chapter first describes how gender-based policy capacity was built up within Canadian government in the 1970s and early 1980s.

Building gender-based policy capacity

The development of gender-based policy units within the Canadian federal government has a long history, dating back to the establishment of the Women's Bureau within the Ministry of Labour in 1953. Following the lead of the International Labour Organization (ILO), the Women's Bureau tracked women's participation in the paid labour force and was instrumental in the development of equal pay legislation in 1956 and maternity leave legislation in 1971 (Burt and Hardman 2001: 201–2). As Table 9.1 demonstrates, however, the structuring and restructuring of federal gender-based policy machinery occurred during two periods – first in the early 1970s and, again, in the mid-1990s. During both periods, Canadian institutional capacity-building corresponded to and interacted with key initiatives undertaken by the United Nations, especially those arising from the UN International Decade of Women (1975–1985) and the Beijing Platform for Action (1995).

In the early 1970s, Canada emerged as a leader among developed countries with respect to the development of policies and agencies designed to enhance the status of women in all sectors of society and to provide them with points of entry into the policy-making process. The 1970 Report of the Royal Commission on the Status of Women (RCSW) was instrumental in this process. The idea of establishing such a commission had been pushed by a national coalition of women's groups during the 1960s, especially after a similar taskforce was appointed in the United States by the Kennedy administration. In 1966, the Pearson government appointed journalist Florence Bird to head a Royal Commission and directed it to 'recommend what steps might be taken by the Federal Government to ensure for women equal opportunities with men in all aspects of Canadian society' (Canada 1970: vii). In all, the Commission made 167 recommendations, some 122 of which were exclusively federal responsibilities. The RCSW is widely recognized as having

Table 9.1 Building federal gender-based policy machinery

1953	Women's Bureau (Department of Labour)
1970	Royal Commission on the Status of Women
1971	Office of Coordinator for Status of Women (Privy Council Office)
1972	Women's Program (Secretary of State)
1973	Canadian Advisory Council on the Status of Women (CACSW)
1976	Status of Women Canada
	Minister Responsible for the Status of Women
1993	Women's Bureau moved (to Strategic Policy Branch HRDC)
1995	Canada Commits to Beijing Platform
	CACSW disbanded
	Women's Program integrated into Status of Women Canada
	Minister of State Responsible for the Status of Women downgraded to Secretary of State
1995	Beijing Platform for Action
1996–2000	'Setting the Stage for the Next Century: The Federal Plan for Gender Equity'
1999	Gender-based Analysis Directorate
2000–2005	Agenda for Equality

Source: Status of Women Canada 2002, pp. 8–13, Burt and Hardman 2001, pp. 201–22.

set much of the political and legislative agenda for the Canadian women's movement for the 1970s and beyond (Brodie 1995: 42–4).

One unintended outcome of the Royal Commission was the consolidation of a growing and increasingly politicized women's movement, especially in English Canada, which fixed its eyes firmly on the federal government and its promise of breaking down legislative and social barriers to women's equality. In 1972, an *ad hoc* committee of prominent feminists organized the 'Strategy for Change Conference', which saw the formation of Canadian feminism's key frontline organization, the National Action Committee on the Status of Women (NAC). This conference as well as launching the NAC reflected a collective resolve that a women's organization outside the federal government was needed to pressure the federal government to implement the recommendations of the RCSW and monitor its progress. During the 1970s, NAC and other women's organizations popularized women's issues, conducted research, organized public forums and repeatedly lobbied state actors to make public policy, especially social policy, more responsive to their conception of women's needs. In fact, NAC officials met with the Prime Minister and top federal officials annually to discuss this goal. In what Findlay describes as the 'consultative period', the federal government also invited the organized women's movement to consult on a broad spectrum of issues, ranging from pay equity to sexual assault to divorce reform (1988). In the process, feminist activists developed political acumen and policy expertise as well as a strong support base among Canadian women who were increasingly willing to rate Canadian political leaders and their parties on the basis of what they were saying about and doing for women as a distinct political constituency with specific policy needs.

Another immediate impact of the Royal Commission was the development of gender-based policy machinery inside the federal government –one of the most elaborate in the world at the time (see Table 9.1). In 1971, the Office of the Coordinator for the Status of Women was established within the Privy Council Office (PCO) and a year later the Women's Programme was set up within the Citizenship Branch of the Secretary of State. Its mandate was 'the development of a society in which the full potential of women as citizens is recognized and utilized' (Burt 1994: 216). This mandate reflected the prevailing governing philosophy at the time that state funding of disadvantaged groups enriched both Canadian democracy and the public policy by making them more responsive to community needs and priorities.

Guided by this commitment, federal funding for the Women's Programme grew from a meagre $233,000 in 1973 to $12.4 million in 1987, leaving in its wake a mosaic of national feminist organizations with the resources to generate research on women's issues, lobby government and hold it accountable, as well as a vibrant mix of grassroots women's organizations that provided education, shelters and services to women marginalized by, for example, violence, immigrant status, and poverty (Burt and Hardman 2001: 204). In 1973, this gender-based infrastructure was further elaborated with the establishment of the Canadian Advisory Council on the Status of Women (CACSW), an arm's length organization, designed to provide policy advice to the federal government and to liaise with the organized women's movement. The CACSW, in turn, interacted with a network of provincial advisory councils. In 1976, the Office of the Coordinator was moved out of the PCO and expanded into an interdepartmental coordinating agency – SWC – and linked into the federal cabinet through the creation of a Minister Responsible for the Status of Women. Although the SWC was the hub of gender-based policy machinery within the federal government, it was not given a legislative mandate to advance gender equality goals within the federal government or to hold the government accountable for policies that might disadvantage Canadian women generally or specific subpopulations such as Aboriginal women or immigrant women. In a few cases, overtly discriminatory policies were challenged in the courts, especially after the equality provisions in the Charter of Rights came into effect in 1985 but the results of this strategy were mixed.

By 1975, International Women's Year, the Canadian federal government had already built up an intricate national machinery to advocate for women's equality within government – something that the United Nations Plan for Action for the UN Decade of Women had called on member states to do. Indeed, by the end of the decade, approximately two-thirds of UN member states had established their own national machineries, many of which emulated the models already provided by such leader-countries as Canada and Australia (Sawer 2006). Canada's 'feminist state' had built within it:

1   a gender unit mandated to empower civil society groups to educate, provide services, and make their demands known to government (through the Women's Programme);

2   a semi-autonomous agency, designed to link academic, provincial and
    community policy networks to the federal government, to advocate on
    women's issues, and to provide policy advice (through the CACSW);
3   a designated agency within the federal bureaucracy to coordinate policy initia-
    tives (SWC) and inform a Minister Responsible for the Status of Women who
    held a seat at the cabinet table.

During these years, many Canadian provinces also followed the federal example
and set up some form of gender-based policy machinery or advisory mechanism.
By the mid-1980s, most provinces had two, if not three, vehicles for policy advice.
First, most provinces had some form of advisory council, which was generally
created through provincial legislation, comprised of appointees supported by
permanent employees or civil servants, and funded by government (in the earlier
years, both provincial and federal). These advisory mechanisms predominantly
reported either to the provincial executive office or to a Minister Responsible for
the Status of Women. Many of the provinces, especially during the 1980s, also
developed policy machinery inside provincial bureaucracies in the form of a
women's bureau, directorate or secretariat. British Columbia was unique in
Canada, however, because in 1993 this province established a line department, the
Ministry of Women's Equality. A self-standing gender-focused ministry is considered to be an optimal organizational strategy to pursue gender equality goals
(Sawer 2006).
    In these early years, Canada's gender-based policy machinery ranked high on
practitioner and academic assessments of best practices with respect to advancing
gender equality within government. For the most part, it gender units were:

- centrally located in an interdepartmental agency as well as in key departments
  and able to monitor the gender impacts of all kinds of policies;
- backed by authority, fortified by a Royal Commission report, and able to draw
  on the influence of the federal PCO and Cabinet, and, at the provincial level,
  the Premier's Office or Executive Council;
- goal congruent with broader governing philosophy of citizenship equality and
  inclusiveness;
- organizationally-linked to community groups and the growing second wave of
  the Canadian women's movement, nationally and provincially (Sawer 2006,
  Teghtsoonian 2004, Summers 2003).

With the hindsight of history, it is now clear that the mid-1980s marked the apex
of political influence for the Canadian women's movement both inside and outside
the state. In only a few years, it had witnessed an exponential growth in the number
of women elected to political office, a proliferation of federal and provincial initiatives that advanced a gender equity agenda, the constitutional entrenchment of a
sexual equality clause in the new Charter of Rights and Freedoms, and unprecedented access to political leaders and the federal bureaucracy. The fact that the
federal party leaders participated in a nationally televised debate on women's

issues, organized by NAC, during the 1984 federal election, was another indicator of the legitimacy accorded to women's equality claims in mainstream politics. However, almost as quickly as these political gains and policy infrastructures were realized, they were eroded by broader social and political forces, beginning with the election of an unapologetically neoliberal federal government in 1984. The erasure of gender as focus of public policy began with the delegitimization of feminist voices, indeed of virtually all equality-seeking groups as relevant claims-makers in the policy process. This anti-feminist politics also eroded the legitimacy accorded to gender units inside government. Often viewed as a backlash against second-wave feminism, this phase was followed by the dismantling of much of the gender-based policy capacity within the federal government and in many of the provinces. Ironically, it was argued that these units had been surpassed by gender mainstreaming across the government but, in practice, it meant that gender was everywhere in rhetoric and nowhere in substance. Finally, the gendered subject was disappeared in policy discourses and practices. These three interrelated processes are described below.

Delegitimization

As already noted, the progressive delegitimization of a 'women's voice' in Canadian policy process began in the mid-1980s and coincided with the ascendancy of neoliberal governing practices as well as a broader wave of social conservatism that swept over many western democracies during these years. In Canada, a newly elected Progressive Conservative government of Brian Mulroney (1984) rather quickly ran into political opposition from the organized women's movement, especially its flagship the National Action Committee on the Status of Women (NAC), which loudly objected to the new government's legislative agenda of reducing the state, dismantling universal social programmes, empowering the market, and, later in its mandate, striking a free trade deal with the United States.

These conflicts reflected a fundamental incompatibility between the tenets of neoliberal governance and the orientations and practices of the dominant current of the Canadian women's movement during these years. Since the early 1970s, it had consistently linked the achievement of women's equality to state intervention whether through social spending, the courts, or regulation of the economy and the private sector. Key feminist demands, constitutive of the public face of the women's movement, such as universal and affordable daycare, income security for sole mothers and elderly women, action on violence against women, and pay and employment equity, all called for more not less government. This friction between the agendas of the women's movement and neoliberal fundamentalists left little room for compromise.

Later in the 1980s, feminism and feminists were regularly disparaged in political debate and in the popular media, and, along with other equality-seeking groups, labelled as 'special interest groups'. According to this construction, 'special' interests stood outside of and in opposition to the interests of 'ordinary' Canadians while federal funding of such groups only served to skew policy priorities and to waste scarce (and undeserved) public resources (Brodie 1995). It was argued that so-called 'special interest' organizations should be funded, not by the public, but by the private constituencies that they represented (Dobrowolsky 2004: 187). In other words, equality-seeking groups were considered as lobbyists and should be treated as such. The rhetoric of special interests, largely imported from the American social conservative movement, veiled a broader backlash against feminism, which was articulated in Canada by such groups as REAL (realistic, equal, active, for life) Women. Labelling itself as 'Canada's Alternative Women's Movement', REAL Women's motto is 'women's rights but not at the expense of human rights' (REAL Women of Canada). This socially conservative group argued that those women's organizations such as NAC, which received the bulk of its operating funds from the federal government, did not represent the interests of the silent majority of Canadian women and could not speak for them in the policy process. As a result of their intensive lobbying, combined with the support of some government backbenchers and members of the Reform Party (a regionally-based social conservative party), the government changed the eligibility rules of the Women's Programme, allowing for the funding of groups that promoted traditional roles for women as well as patriarchal family values (Dobrowolsky and Jenson 2004: 164–6).

While the organized women's movement was progressively sidelined and delegitimized as the voice of Canadian women, the increasingly unchallenged construction of special interests also indirectly contributed to the waning influence of gender-based agencies within the federal bureaucracy. The relationship between state agencies and women's groups and community organizations, so carefully cultivated across the previous decade, was represented as a 'cosy conspiracy' between feminists inside the bureaucracy and rent-seeking special interests who were milking government coffers and taxpayer dollars for more than they deserved because they neither represented the interests of ordinary Canadian women nor wielded electoral clout. Sawer reports that this discourse of 'special interests' similarly accompanied the rise of neoliberalism in Australia (Sawer 2006).

As a result, from the mid-1980s onward, federal funds designated to improving the status of women were progressively cut back and previously established gender equality targets began to disappear. Between 1987 and 1990, for example, Women's Programme funds, designated for community groups, shelters and targeted services were cut by approximately 30 per cent (Burt and Hardman 2001: 205). Any injections of new funding were largely confined to the Canadian Panel on Violence against Women (1991) as well as related educational and infrastructural initiatives following the 1990 Montreal Massacre of 14 women engineering students. Yet, even in the face of this tragedy and the obvious need for support services for battered women, in Canada and elsewhere, there also was a growing backlash against what was dismissively termed as 'victim feminism', which allegedly cast all women as an exploited economic underclass or as the prey of batterers and rapists (Brush 2002: 179).

Dismantling

The delegitimizaton of gender-based citizenship claims on the state was soon followed by the dismantling of much of the federal government's gender-based policy capacity, especially after the election of the new Liberal government in 1993. It had its eye firmly set on eliminating the federal deficit, devolving responsibilities to the provinces, and reducing its longstanding financial commitments in the social policy field. The Canadian Advisory Council on the Status of Women (CACSW) was closed in 1995. Similarly, the federal government's Women's Programme, which was charged with providing operational and project funding to women's organizations, was folded into Status of Women Canada (Dobrowolsky 2004: 176–82). In 1995, the Minister Responsible for the Status of Women was downgraded to the lower status of a Minister of State Responsible for the Status of Women and, thus, a designated space for the articulation of women's interests around the federal cabinet table was lost.

This 1995 reorganization contradicted a central recommendation of the Beijing Platform for Action that the federal government was preparing to endorse. Paragraph 201 of that document recommended as a best practice that national gender units be located at the highest possible level in federal systems and that these units have access to the forums where the federal division of powers is negotiated (Sawer 2006). In Canada, these locations are unequivocally the executive offices of the Prime Minister and the Premiers and a seat in the inner cabinet of the governing party. During these same years, SWC was progressively downsized and shifted to the margins of federal power, most recently being housed under the umbrella of the Department of Canadian Heritage, which has a grab bag of responsibilities, including arts, sports, diversity and identity. Gender, it would appear, is now coded as just one of many identities that make up the Canadian multicultural mosaic, rather than as a fundamental structuring principle informing the daily lives and opportunities of all Canadians.

This dismantling process can also be clearly tracked at the provincial level, especially in Canada's richest provinces, that adopted the most stringent neoliberal social assistance regimes and welfare-for-work programmes during the 1990s. Alberta was the first to eliminate its gender-based policy machinery, when, in 1996, it exercised a sunset clause in its initiating legislation, and eliminated the Alberta Advisory Council on Women's Issues. This arbitrary action met considerable resistance, both from provincial women's groups and opposition parties in the legislature (Harder 2003). The government's response to these objections was characteristic of the kinds of arguments that have been raised in Canada and elsewhere by governments determined to dismantle their gender-based policy machinery. One typical response has been that women's organizations have matured and strengthened to the point where they no longer need public support to maintain their capacity to speak to government. As Alberta Minister for Community Development Gary Mar stated at the time:

Regarding the disposition of the Advisory Council of Women's Issues, I would note that even the federal Liberal government has reached the same conclusion that we have in Alberta; namely that times have changed, women's groups have multiplied and grown in strength, and they can and want to speak for themselves to government without a publicly funded intermediary.

(Alberta Assembly Debates: March 27, 1995)

The other typical argument rallied against women's policy agencies was that women are too diverse a constituency to be represented by a single agency. Again, Minister Mar expressed this position during the Alberta legislative debate on the fate of the Alberta Advisory Council:

the chair of that advisory Council herself has said that women in the province of Alberta speak with many voices; they do not speak with one voice. I happen to agree. As a consequence, it is the strongly held view of this government that women cannot be heard and cannot be represented by a single agency. Rather, very clearly women would choose to represent themselves and speak with their own voices.

(Alberta Assembly Debates: March 25, 1995)

Unlike Alberta, the election of the neoliberal Harris government in Ontario in 1995 did not see the elimination of the Ontario Women's Directorate (OWD) but, instead, a dramatic downsizing and restructuring of this once large and active gender unit. Established in 1983 and housed in the Office of the Premier, the OWD immediately saw a reduction in its staff, budget and influence in the early days of the Harris administration. In 1996, its mandate was changed from the advocacy of women's equality writ large to two policy areas – violence against women and women and economic development with a special focus on women's entrepreneurship. According to Malloy, the OWD was effectively transformed 'into an unmistakable public administration entity with a mandate to "manage" women's issues, rather than provide an entryway into government for women's movements and their demands' (Malloy 2003: 88, 106).

In British Columbia, one of the first acts of the newly (neo) Liberal Campbell government in 2001 was to eliminate the province's Ministry of Women's Equality, while over 30 women's centres that had been funded by the provincial government for more than a decade had their funding withdrawn. As Teghtsoonian explains, 'women lost their voice' (2005: 324). The province's gender-based policy capacity has since been confined to Women's Equality and Social Programmes, a small subunit of the Ministry of Community, Aboriginal and Women's Services (CAWS). During the same period, the new provincial government also exacted debilitating cuts to childcare – slashing funding to childcare centres and subsidies to low income parents and eliminating training programmes for daycare workers. The government subsequently assigned responsibility for childcare to the Minister Responsible for the Status of Women, thus ensuring that this office would be only partially focused on women's issues. Teghtsoonian has dubbed this strategy as a 'gender diluting function' wherein diverse policy respon-sibilities are subsumed within gender-based units and the gender-specific focus of a portfolio or unit is diffused and undermined (ibid.: 320).

The fate of gender-based units federally as well as in Alberta, Ontario and British Columbia appears to support Dobrowolsky's claim that 'there is no doubt then that the neoliberal state diminished political space for women, metaphorically and liter-ally' (2004: 188). The gender units of other provinces, which have not so sharply turned toward neoliberal governance, have also shared a number of common expe-riences in recent years. First, they report that their budgetary allocations have decreased or remained virtually frozen across the past decade. The 2004 Report of the Women's Advisory Council of Newfoundland and Labrador underlines the implications of a decade and more of fiscal restraint. 'The concern from women's equality-seeking organizations', the report notes, 'is whether the provincial govern-ment will continue with its fiscally driven agenda or listen to the concerns of women and equality-seeking women's organizations' (PACSW 2004). Second, in many provinces, once autonomous advisory councils have either been folded into the permanent bureaucracy, or communicate with government through actors in the permanent bureaucracy. Finally, many provincial units report the increasing tendency for provincial governments to demand business plans that effectively narrow the range of their research and consultation activities. The end result is that the channels that were developed between Canada's governments and women's organizations and community groups have all but disappeared.

The downsizing of the federal government's gender units coincided with the now infamous 1995 federal budget, which, in the name of deficit reduction, brought dramatic cuts to federal transfers to the provinces for social programmes and a pronounced contraction in the federal bureaucracy and in programme spending. For example, the operating budget of Human Resources Development Canada (HRDC), which was responsible for many social and employment programmes for women, was slashed by 35 per cent over three years (Yalnizyan 2005: 29–30). In addition, approximately 14 per cent of jobs in the federal public service, the vast majority held by women, were eliminated. While SWC also expe-rienced cuts, the dismantling and reorganization of the federal government's gender units in 1995 was not generally attributed to government's seemingly singular focus on eliminating the deficit. Instead, according to official rhetoric, this reorganization reflected the federal government's renewed commitment to gender equality, which would now be advanced through gender mainstreaming, as prescribed by the 1995 Beijing Platform for Action and the Federal Plan for Gender Equality, released in the following year. The Beijing Platform prescribes, that, with respect to all policies and programmes, 'before decisions are taken, an analysis is made of the effects on women and men'. In keeping with its international commitment, the federal plan also prescribed an encompassing implementation of gender-based analysis (GBA) in the development of policies, programmes and legislation (Status of Women Canada 2002: 1–3).

Many feminist activists and academics caution that there are both opportunities and constraints associated with gender mainstreaming. For example, while gender-based analysis (GBA) promises to insert gender into all policy fields and at every stage of the policy process, it is a relatively blunt policy instrument that promotes a one-dimensional focus on gender equality. GBA evokes a vision of the liberal abstract woman, and thus is insufficiently attentive to the needs and priorities of women differently situated by family status, race, sexuality, ethnicity, or class (Hankivsky 2005: 83). Neither can GBA effectively engage with the assumptions informing new policy initiatives (Burt and Hardman 2001: 208–11). If a social problem is framed, however inaccurately, as a problem of children, families, or individuals rather than being lodged in unequal gender structures, the capacity of GBA to advance women's equality is diminished. GBA also is conducted as an in-house and technocratic exercise that erodes the link between government agencies and the broader community.

Although these critiques are clearly relevant, raising gender to the centre of the full range of public policy remains an essential piece in the complicated task of achieving gender equality. As with most policy reforms, however, fewer problems arise with the goals of GBA than with its operationalization and implementation. Policy reform can have unintended and undesirable outcomes. Not the least, as Sawer observes, too often the new language of gender mainstreaming has been used by governments, less than sympathetic to gender equality, to legitimate the dismantling of units with expertise in promoting equal opportunity for women and designated groups (2006). In such cases, gender mainstreaming effectively means that gender-based analysis is both 'everywhere and nowhere' in government.

This 'everywhere and nowhere' metaphor is especially appropriate in describing the fate of gender-based analysis in the Canadian case. In 1995, Status of Women Canada was given primary responsibility for building capacity within the federal bureaucracy for GBA and, in conjunction with the GBA Directorate established in 1999, developed a six-point strategy for implementing the federal plan. This strategy consisted of training, tool development, policy case studies, research and education, evaluation and accountability and coordination (Canada 2005: 7). Although the federal government reconfirmed its commitment to GBA in its *Agenda for Gender Equality* in 2000, a 2005 Report of the House of Commons Standing Committee on the Status of Women found that, after a decade of implementation, GBA is not being implemented evenly or effectively across federal departments. The report concludes that:

> The committee was disheartened to hear about the significant challenges still working against the effective application of GBA at the federal level. Despite ten years of effort … GBA is still not being systematically incorporated into policy-making in all government departments.
>
> (Canada 2005: 31)

This assessment, in fact, underestimates the obvious failure to embed GBA in policy formulation and evaluation in the past decade. The committee highlighted a number of fatal weaknesses in this alternative to gender-based policy units. First, although Status of Women was giving responsibility for GBS capacity building, the onus of establishing GBA units was left to individual line departments and no mechanisms were set in place to ensure that they did so. The Standing Committee found that the departments did not want to take on the responsibility for gender mainstreaming, preferring that it be done through Status and the GBA Directorate, and did not want the extra workload that an effective GBA would necessarily involve. Moreover, in the handful of departments that did take tentative steps to implement GBA, the job was often taken up by 'individuals who champion gender equality'. Departments, moreover, had few incentives to replace such individuals when they moved on or when a department was restructured (ibid.: 11). Moreover, the Department of Finance, which shapes the single most important policy document in Canada, the federal budget, has no GBA unit (ibid.: 32). In interviewing various highly placed federal bureaucrats, the committee found that there was:

1   a widespread assumption that gender equality already had been achieved;
2   little shared understanding of the GBA process;
3   confusion about best practices, accountability, and measures of success;
4   no mechanism to ensure compliance (ibid.: 26). The committee concluded that, after a decade of implementation, there was, in fact, 'a decreased interdepartmental capacity to ensure gender equality' (ibid.: 2).

Gender mainstreaming was promoted as a preferred alternative to gender-based policy units because it promised to inject the issue of gender equality in all policy sectors and at each stage in the policy process, from formation, to implementation, to evaluation. However, after a decade, it is clear that this strategy to put gender everywhere has left it nowhere. This experience is not unique to Canada but has been replicated in many other countries that have adopted gender mainstreaming. In Australia, for example, Sawer notes that the restructuring of its gender-based policy machinery in the past decade has:

•   devalued gender-based expertise in favour of management skills;
•   deemed it more difficult to evaluate policies at source for gender impacts and to audit gender outcomes of government activity;
•   contributed to an ongoing loss of corporate memory, making it more difficult to sustain the capacities required for the long-term project of advancing gender equality;
•   decreased the visibility of gender units, both inside and outside of government;
•   eroded community education functions and severed engagement with community organizations (Sawer 2006).

Disappearance

The final of this chapter's three Ds is the disappearance of women as an analytic category in public policy development and, in turn, the erosion of women's equality as a central goal of Canadian governments. The progressive erasure of

gender in governmental discourses, public policy, budgetary priorities, and institutional machinery in the past decade stands in stark contrast to the commitments
undertaken by the federal government in signing the Beijing Platform for Action
(1995), which was elaborated in *Setting the Stage for the Next Century: The Federal Plan for
Gender Equality* (1996) and, again, in the *Agenda for Gender Equality* in 2000. The
current invisibility of gender is the outcome of an amalgam of factors that have
already been discussed in this chapter, among them, the rise of social conservatism
and the attendant delegitimization of feminist and all equality-seeking groups as
'special interests', the 'everywhere and nowhere' underpinnings of gender
mainstreaming, the dismantling of gender-based policy machinery, and the
erosion of a broader-based women's movement with strong links to the state.

Although the disappearance of the gendered subject can be tracked through
social policy reform, so-called active welfare policies, at the provincial level as well
as in the fiscalization of social policy, the final section of this chapter will focus
briefly on the elevation of the child (and family) as the priority constituency for new
federal funding and for social policy reform, especially in the past decade. As
McKeen documents, the ascendancy of the child as the iconic subject of social
policy reaches back to the late 1980s when the federal government, following a
growing international trend, pledged to end child poverty by the turn of the millennium. Following the ratification of the UN's Convention on the Rights of the Child
in 1991, the Mulroney government embarked on what it termed its 'child's
agenda', concentrating its energies particularly on 'children at risk' (2003: 94–
101). The federal government's almost singular concern with the child and children's poverty intensified during Chrétien years, especially after the introduction
of the National Child Benefit in 1997. In subsequent years, child policy has been
enriched and expanded to include, among other things, a Child Disability Benefit.

The displacement of the gendered subject and a gender equality agenda by the
genderless child involves what Lister calls 'the politics of renaming' (2004). As
Dobrowolsky and Jenson rightly remind us, an exploration of the politics of
renaming is neither an academic exercise nor simply a matter of talk. 'Representa-
tional adjustments to the names of claimants is significant' (2004: 172) in understanding how social policy is framed, which social actors are considered as
legitimate claimants, what kinds of policy interventions are considered appropriate
and by whom. It is important to underline, however, that although contemporary
social problems may be framed and analyzed as if gender is no longer relevant, the
gendered underpinning of these same social problems do not disappear. On the
contrary, they tend to intensify (Bakker and Gill 2003, Brodie 2006).

The disappearance of the gendered subject of social policy can be clearly tracked
through federal policy discourses and new spending initiatives in recent years,
which effectively cast the child as the focal point of social policies. A textual analysis
of Speeches from the Throne (SFT) across the past two decades, for example,
provides one way to chart the disappearance of both women as subjects of social
policy interventions and the goal of gender equality in official discourses. In the
1980 SFT, social policies and programmes were discussed in the context of
equality for women and there was explicit discussion of sexual discrimination and

violence against women. There was also recognition of the structural impediments to employment facing equality-seeking groups such as natives, young people, women and the disabled. A similar emphasis on women as a focus of policy reform is reflected in the throne speeches throughout the 1980s. By 1991, however, the SFTs began to focus on children as 'the most vulnerable members of our society', while the family was identified as 'the most fundamental building block of Canadian society'. By 1994, the social security system and its reform was emphasized and linked to violence against women and children.

During this period, the problem of violence against women was progressively renamed and policies reformulated as one of 'family violence' and funding targeted to women's groups doing anti-violence work was cut substantially. A modest reinvestment in the federal government's Family Violence Initiative in late 1990s, moreover, focused on offenders as well as First Nations (Weldon 2004). It is important to note that violence against women did not disappear in these years – in fact, the number of women reporting violence and seeking shelter increased. However, federal policy increasingly conveyed the message, both in rhetoric and practice, that the pervasive social problem was confined to the perpetrators of violence or to particular communities. This politics of renaming veiled an ongoing social need and shifted resources away from those whose lives had been upset by violence. As Weldon reports, between 1998 and 2002 the number of women's shelters increased by only two per cent, while the number of admissions to existing shelters increased by 20 per cent (ibid).

By 1997, the federal government had tamed its deficit and indicated that it was prepared to reinvest in Canadians, especially the child and families. 'Social policy renewal', according to the 1997 SFT, identified Canada as 'a country that has decided to invest in its children', and whose 'objectives as a country' were to 'ensure that all Canadian children have the best possible opportunity to develop their full potential'. The speech asserted that 'while families have the greatest responsibility in the nurturing and development of our children, they are not alone'. Within this policy frame, the federal government announced its National Child Benefit (NCB), which, as discussed below, constitutes the federal government's largest new social policy expenditure since its budget cutting exercise of the mid-1990s. This approach to social policy reform was consolidated in the Throne Speech of 1999 with the introduction of the National Children's Agenda and the Government's objective to reach agreement on 'a national action plan to further support parents and families'. By 2004, the SFT identified children as the most important social 'investment' for the federal government and the National Child Benefit was singled out (along with Medicare) as Canada's most significant social programmes. In sum, across the past decade, progressively from one SFT to the next, we witness the virtual erasure of women and gender-based equality claims from official policy discourses.

The NCB embodies many of the contradictions and inequities that can arise from the politics of renaming. The NCB is comprised of two initiatives – the Canadian Child Tax Benefit (CCTB), which provides a refundable tax credit to all families with children, below a specified income level, and the National Child Benefit

Supplement (NCBS), which provides additional support for low income families. Under the new programme, however, the provinces are allowed to reduce their social assistance payments to families on social assistance by the amount provided by the NCBS and use these savings to provide new benefits and services for low income families. The problem with this 'clawback' scenario is that female lone parent families are disproportionately and negatively affected. According to recent statistics (2003), fully 38 per cent of female-headed one-parent families are poor compared to 13 per cent of male-headed one-parent families and 7 per cent of two-parent families with children (Townson 2005: 2). The federal government's Policy Research Initiative includes lone parents (a category not disaggregated by sex of the parent) as one of the five groups in Canada that are 'persistently poor' (the others being the disabled, recent immigrants, Aboriginals off-reserve, and the older unattached) (Hatfield 2004). However, the category 'lone parent' is not gender neutral. In 2001, single parent mothers accounted for 85 per cent of all single parent families in Canada and over 90 per cent of all poor single parent families (National Council of Welfare 2005).

The issue of whether and how provinces clawback the NCBS and the extent to which these savings are reinvested, if at all, in new services for the poor differs from province to province. However, as the National Council of Welfare points out, the NCBS 'discriminates against welfare families and especially single parent families on welfare. Most poor single parent families are headed by women, so the clawback also discriminates against women.' According to the Council's estimates, over one-half of families with children on welfare or 11 per cent of the 1.3 million Canadian families eligible to receive the NCBS are denied this benefit. The Council concludes that the 'clawback and the current funding arrangements for welfare are blatant and long-standing examples of bad social policy, and bad social policy almost inevitably produces bad results' (ibid.: 15, x).

The goal of eliminating child poverty in Canada is both overdue and necessary but, in many ways, the elevation of the abstract 'poor child' as the focus of social policy reform incorrectly specifies the policy problem. As poverty groups have underlined time and again, the feminization of poverty is a root cause of child poverty but the gendered structures of inequality in Canada's labour markets and in society do not enter into a child-centred policy frame (Dobrowolsky and Jenson 2004: 174). Rather, this politics of naming effectively sets up an opposition between the child and other disadvantaged groups – as a dichotomy between the deserving and undeserving poor as well as between child and parent. Moreover, these policy discourses depict the poor child as a homogeneous category, veiling over considerations of how all children are themselves differently configured by, among other things, gender, race, ethnicity, sexuality and national origin. As Lister observes, the ascendancy of the homogenized and decontextualized category of child sidesteps structural social divisions that consistently correlate with official definitions and lived experiences of poverty. Among all these structural determinants of poverty, Lister argues, 'gender constitutes the most profound differentiating division. A gendered analysis of poverty reveals not simply its unequal incidence but also that both cause and effect are deeply gendered' (2004: 54–5).

Canada's children's agenda fails to acknowledge the inescapable fact that, in the vast majority of cases, poor children live with poor women who experience poverty in many different ways. Clearly, gender is a critical factor in the child poverty story. Although women may be erased from the analysis, as Brush reminds us, most mothers, whether single or not, continue to pay a child penalty (2002: 175). Women's disproportionate share of domestic work and childcaring tasks correlates with labour market discrimination and subsequent inequalities in pay, benefits and the quality of jobs (Stratigaki 2004: 31). Inadequate provision for social care means that many mothers must fashion their labour force participation to accommodate their caring responsibilities. They are often found working part time in precarious 'feminized' sectors of the labour force that offer few cushions if personal circumstances change, for example, if a relationship breaks down. Many female lone parents who cannot rely on a second wage earner have little alternative other than to rely on the minimal income provided by provincial and territorial social assistance programmes, at least until their children reach school age. In sum, then, the unequal structure of gender, and increasingly race, weaves through both the incidence and the experience of child poverty. The erasure of systemic considerations from social policy analysis, however, does not diminish their persistent effects. In the absence of policies and programmes addressing the structural bases of women's poverty, a child-centred agenda will not reduce child poverty and, as currently configured, may aggravate the feminization of poverty.

Conclusion

This chapter has traced the remapping of gender through the policy machinery of the Canadian federal government. The mutually reinforcing processes of delegitimization, dismantling and disappearance of gender have not occurred in isolation but are an integral part of the reinvention of the Canadian state and public policies to better correspond to the requisites of neoliberal governance. At the very least, this governing strategy disregards both claimsmaking on the state by structurally disadvantaged groups and the broad goal of social citizenship equality. As this chapter describes, gender has been progressively erased from policy formation in recent years, but it continues to frame the daily lives of Canadians, albeit in very different ways than was the case even a generation ago. The past two decades have seen remarkable changes in the way that most Canadian women organize their daily lives and sustain themselves and their families. The postwar male-breadwinner model that consisted of a single male earner and dependent wife and children has virtually disappeared over the span of three decades. Fully 72 per cent of Canadian families have two income earners compared to 33 per cent in 1965. The employment rate for women with children under 16 was 72 per cent in 2003 compared to 39 per cent in 1976. Still, women constitute 70 per cent of all part-time workers and women workers remain concentrated in such traditional pink ghettos as teaching, nursing, sales and services. Among full-time workers, the female-to-male earnings ratio has remained stuck at around 70 per cent since the early 1990s. These years have also seen the number of female-headed lone-parent families double to one-fifth of all families in Canada (Townson 2005).

These statistics should send strong signals to policy-makers that the current practice of trying to make gender disappear from their policy calculations is fraught with contradictions and, by any measure, is bad policy practice. It is also unsustainable. As Canadian women increasingly enter the workforce or take on the task of forming families alone, the problem of work–life balance has become pronounced for both Canadian employees and employers. Lacking a policy frame-work that recognizes the growing demands on women to engage in paid labour as well as maintain primary responsibility for domestic and caring work, many Cana-dian women now find themselves forced into a series of unsustainable trade-offs. Issues of time, health and quality of life are rapidly becoming the new feminine mystique – in the late Betty Friedan's terms 'the problem with no name' (1963). Rather than erasing gender from the calculations and strategies of governing in the contemporary era, many social policy reformers, especially in Europe, are now calling for the negotiation of a new gender contract, involving public policies that would better enable women to strike a sustainable balance between paid labour and the multiple and gendered demands of social reproduction (Esping-Anderson *et al.* 2002). The current child-centred focus of Canadian social policy has effec-tively excised women and gender concerns from the policy process, while gender mainstreaming, whatever its initial intent, has served to dismantle and diffuse the capacity of government to engage in meaningful policy research which recognizes both the diversity of experiences of Canadian women and the complexities and constraints of gender. As this chapter demonstrates, the politics of renaming is rife with contradictions and the author of public policies that do not speak to the lived realities the vast majority of Canadian women and men. In sum, gender, in all its complexities, must be remapped onto the state.

Notes

1 Support for this research was provided by the SSHRC-funded MCRI project, Neoliberal Glob-alism and its Challengers as well as by the Canada Research Chair Programme in which I hold a Tier 1 Chair in Political Economy and Social Governance.

References

Alberta Assembly Debates (n.d.). Available online, http://isys.assembly.ab.ca.
Bakker, Isabella and Gill, Stephen (2003) 'Global Political Economy and Social Reproduc-tion', in Isabella Bakker and Stephen Gill (eds) *Power, Production, and Social Reproduction*, London: Palgrave, pp. 3–16.
Brodie, Janine (1995) *Politics on the Margins: Restructuring and the Canadian Women's Movement*, Halifax: Fernwood Publishing.
—— (2006) 'Putting Gender Back In: Women and Social Policy in Canada,' in Y. Abu-Laban (ed.) *Gendering the Nation State: Canadian and Comparative Perspectives*, Vancouver: UBC Press, *forthcoming*.

Brush, Linda (2002) 'Changing the Subject: Gender and Welfare Regime Studies', *Social Politics*, 9, 2: 161–86.

Burt, Sandra (1994) 'The Women's Movement: Working to Transform Public Life', in James Bickerton and Alain Gagnon (eds) *Canadian Politics*, 2nd Edn, Peterborough, Ontario: Broadview Press, pp. 207–23.

Burt, Sandra and Hardman, Sonya (2001) 'The Case of Disappearing Targets: The Liberals and Gender Equality', in Leslie Pal (ed.) *How Ottawa Spends, 2001–2002: Power in Transition*, Toronto: Oxford University Press, pp. 201–22.

Canada (1970) *Report of the Royal Commission on the Status of Women*, Hull: Information Canada.

—— (1996) *Setting the Stage for the Next Century: The Federal Plan for Gender Equality*, Ottawa: Status of Women Canada.

—— (2000) *Agenda for Gender Equality*, Ottawa: Status of Women Canada.

—— (2005) *Report of the Standing Committee on the Status of Women, Gender-Based Analysis: Building Blocks for Success*, Ottawa: Communications Canada.

Dobrowolsky, Alexandra (2004) 'The Chrétien Liberal Legacy and Women: Changing Policy Priorities with Little Cause for Celebration', *Review of Constitutional Studies*, 9, 1–2: 171–98.

Dobrowolsky, Alexandra and Jenson, Jane (2004) 'Shifting Representations of Citizenship: Canadian Politics of "Women and Children"', *Social Politics*, 11, 2: 154–80.

Esping-Anderson, Gosta; Gallie, Duncan; Hemerijck, Anton and Myers, John (2002) *Why We Need a New Welfare State*, Oxford, UK: Oxford University Press.

Findlay, Sue (1988)'Feminist Struggles within the Canadian State 1966–1988', *Resources For Feminist Research*, 17, 3, September: 5–16.

Friedan, Betty (1963) *The Feminist Mystique*, New York: Random House.

Harder, Lois (2003) *State of Struggle: Feminism and Politics in Alberta*, Edmonton: University of Alberta Press.

Hatfield, Michael (2004) 'Vulnerability to Persistent Low Income', *Horizons: Policy Research Initiative*, 7, 2: 19–33.

Hankivsky, Olena (2005) 'Gender vs. Diversity Mainstreaming: A Preliminary Examination of the Role and Transformative Potential of Feminist Theory', *Canadian Journal of Political Science*, 38, 4: 977–1002.

Lister, Ruth (2004) *Poverty*, Cambridge U.K.: Polity Press.

McKeen, Wendy (2003) *Money in Their Own Name: The Feminist Voice in Poverty Debate in Canada*, Toronto: University of Toronto Press.

Malloy, Jonathan (2003) *Between Colliding Worlds: The Ambiguous Existence of Government Agencies for Aboriginal and Women's Policy*, Toronto: University of Toronto Press.

National Council of Welfare Report (2005) *Poverty Profile 2001*, Ottawa: Minister of Public Works and Government Services.

PACSW, Newfoundland and Labrador Advisory Council on the Status of Women (2004). Available online, www.pacsw.com/index.htm.

REAL Women of Canada (n.d.) Canada's Alternative Women's Movement. Available online, www.realwomenca.com>.

Sawer, Marian (2006) 'From Women's Interests to Special Interests: Reframing Equality Claims', in Louise Chappell and Lisa Hill (eds) *The Politics of Women's Interest*, Abingdon, UK: Routledge, pp. 111–29.

Status of Women Canada (2002) *Canadian Experience in Gender Mainstreaming 2001*, Ottawa: Status of Women Canada. Available online, www.swc.gc-cfc.gc.ca/resources.

—— (2005) *Resources: Gender Equity Consultation*. Available online, www.swc-cfc.gc.ca/resources/consultations/ges09-2005/intro e.html.

Summers, Anne (2003) *The End of Equality: Work, Babies and Women's Choices in the 21st Century*, Sydney: Random House.

Stratigaki, M (2004) 'The Cooptation of Gender Concepts in EU Policies: The Case of "Reconciliation of Work and Family"', *Social Politics: International Studies in Gender, State & Society*, 11, 1: 30–6.

Teghtsoonian, Katherine (2004) 'Neoliberalism and Gender Analysis Mainstreaming in Aotearoa/New Zealand', *Australian Journal of Political Science*, 39, 2, July: 267–84.

—— (2005) 'Disparate Fates in Challenging Times: Women's Policy Agencies and Neoliberalism in Aotearoa/New Zealand and British Columbia.' *Canadian Journal of Political Science*, 38, 2: 308–33.

Townson, Monica (2005) Poverty Issues for Canadian Women, Prepared for Gender Equality Consultations, Ottawa: Status of Women Canada (August).

Weldon, Laurel (2004) Citizens, Victims, Deviants: Restructuring Government Response to Violence against Women in Canada, Paper presented at the Annual Meeting of the American Political Science Association, Chicago, Illinois, USA.

Yalnizyan, Armine (2005) *Canada's Commitment to Equality: A Gender Analysis of the Last Ten Federal Budgets (1995–2005)*, Ottawa: Canadian Feminist Alliance for International Action.

Part III

Surviving and resistance
Strategies and action

10 Reordering globalism?

Feminist and women's movements in the semi-periphery

James Goodman

As globalism reorders gender, patriarchy is redefined, and with it, women's movements and feminism. But what kinds of feminist forces are brought into play, and
how do these develop? Feminisms are embedded in the particular gender order, a
product of interactions between circumstance and consciousness, as well as
between experience and action. Feminism, as a social movement, involves the
construction of a collective social actor with a shared awareness and a particular set
of practices geared to pursuing common aspirations. The aspirations, practices,
consciousness, awareness – indeed the very categories to be constructed and mobilized – reflect the ways in which patriarchal antagonisms are played out. In other
words feminisms are situated in experience and in the specificity of patriarchy.
Against the universalizing disembodied logic of globalism, feminist praxis asserts
the embodied experience of gender orders in a dialectical relationship with globalism. This chapter seeks to enter into this dialectic, exploring the dynamics of
feminism under globalism from the vantage-point of the global semi-periphery.

Feminist social movements are often said to have passed through two phases,
from a 'first wave' centred on extending existing citizenship rights to women, to a
'second wave' centred on constructing new social rights and entitlements
addressing the specific experience of women. Where the first politicized patriarchy
in the already-existing public realm, the second did so in ostensibly private and
domestic spheres, such as in businesses and households or 'private' spheres of life.
The first wave gained momentum through the late nineteenth and early twentieth
centuries, in tandem with a stronger state authority, primarily within industrial-
izing societies. The second wave emerged from late-industrial society, in tandem
with a widespread revolt against social conformity and mass consumerism, again
primarily in the industrial West.

As globalism has reordered gender hierarchies, and recast the political arena,
the second wave has been redefined. New channels and sites for feminist politics
have emerged, forcing a new series of debates and dialogues to the centre of feminist praxis. Some characterize the resulting dialogic mode of feminism as a 'third
wave'. Whether or not it is seen as a qualitative shift, there are strong continuities
with past 'waves'. From the outset the second 'wave' was concerned with the need
for dialogue across differences (Petman 1996). What seems to be new is the extent
to which these dialogues have extended beyond the industrialized West, thereby

shifting the centre of gravity for feminist praxis. As women's and feminist movements produce very different 'context dependent' agendas, dialogue comes to play
a constitutive role in defining what it means to be feminist (Bryson 2003: 250).

In Northern contexts, globalism has forced feminism beyond any assumed identification or agenda (Arneil 1999). A key driver is the increased commoditization of
Northern societies, and the emergence of an explicit neoliberal state, that has
systematically distorted and hollowed-out the policy advances of the 'second
wave'. The result is a shift into the politics of the everyday, with a more pluralist or
even individualized feminism, which may be understood primarily as a form of
collective self-expression (Burgmann 2003). As Bagguley (2002) notes, in many
Northern contexts the result is a movement forced onto the margins, and into
'abeyance'. But rather than demobilizing feminist agency, the personalization of
feminist identification can radicalize feminist subjectivity, and form a key part of
the generalized revolt against market-life. As borne-out in various counter-
globalist movements, these revolts are most clearly manifested in context-bound
local mobilizations of women targeting specific forms of marketization. At the
same time, excluded from policy-making, more instrumental feminist approaches
may become more directly critical of public policy orientations. Feminisms radicalized by marketization may then find new grounds, for instance, in exploiting
discontinuities between patriarchal and marketizing forces. The confrontation
between the mythic nuclear family and the flexibilization of formal labour, manifested in the work–life collision and in an intensely-fought 'politics of care', is just
one dimension.

Such radicalization may be spurred by parallel shifts in Southern contexts.
Increasingly, Northern feminisms are engaged with waves of increasingly visible
Southern feminisms, also driven in many respects by the fall-out from market globalism. A feminization of poverty, especially in the South, has seen feminists enter
the political field as key agents for global justice. These feminisms prioritize livelihoods and living environments, against patriarchal structures within postcolonial
cultural hierarchies. Just as Northern feminisms are mapped across both North
and South, so too are the more livelihood-centred approaches. Importantly, as
globalism creates *global* Souths and *global* Norths, Southern feminisms spill over
into Northern contexts, informing agendas for broader counter-globalist social
movements. Across both contexts there are multiple efforts at constructing and
asserting the claim to personal and social 'wellbeing' against the logic of
marketization (Rowbotham and Linkogle 2001: 5).

In addressing neoliberal globalism, then, feminism addresses the effects of the
global market. Strategy emerges from specific places and along specific lines of
antagonism. Initiatives are defined against the gender order of corporate globalism, and pursue agendas that are embedded within, and make a claim on,
national, local and communal identifications. The central question addressed by
this chapter is how such contexts shape strategy. The focus is on the 'local' or the
'national', and on how it comes into play with the 'global' through feminist praxis.
Discussion centres on dichotomies between particularity and universality, and on
how feminists address the resulting tensions, imbricating one with the other in the

struggle to contest globalism. Feminist inclusivity is thus mapped as a spatial strategy, grounded in particular places where interactions between various forms of feminism are played out. As the chapters in this book describe, the specific experience of semi-peripheral societies is particularly revealing. Such societies reflect a combination of both peripheral Southern and core Northern dynamics. The assertion of an unqualified cosmopolitical worldview, from the heartland, the global core, comes into conflict with the assertion of difference, as the necessary politics of the subordinated, on the global periphery. The deep divisions between social formations, in a global hierarchy of wealth, lifestyle and status, thus move to the foreground of feminist praxis. The contending pressures meet and are played out in particular national and local contexts: the specificity of these contexts becomes central, shaping the potential for leverage, and the logic of contestation.

Section one of this chapter focuses on feminist trajectories under globalism, especially difference debates and the tensions between transnationality, and national specificity. From here, the second section takes up specific experiences of women's movements and feminisms in semi-peripheral contexts. The cases are drawn from women's and feminist movements in Canada, Mexico and Australia. In all three a double tendency is traced, of a more sharply critical and more diverse engagement with national state authorities, hand-in-hand with highly focused sub-state women's mobilizations against globalism. In Canada the National Action Committee on the Status of Women took a lead role in the campaign against the North American Free Trade Agreement, whilst in Quebec, the Federation des Femmes du Quebec played a central role in the Global March for Women. In Mexico the national women's NGO lobby was strengthened with the move away from authoritarianism, while maquiladora and Zapatista women's organizations took a central role in prioritizing opposition to globalism. In Australia, feminists challenged patriarchal nationalism in the Republic debate and politicized the work–life collision at national level. These struggles were, in turn, bolstered by local-level challenges to outworking and to the marginalization of migrant and indigenous women.

Trajectories

From difference to situation

Globalism, as a diffused gender order, recasts patriarchy to feminize poverty. The process, though, is profoundly uneven and deeply stratified. In contesting globalism, feminisms are, then, in the first instance driven by a concern with the different situations of women. In doing so they foreground an awareness that emerged with both the first and second 'waves', that the collective experience of patriarchy can be radically different, reflecting the happenstance of everyday existence, and the variety of class positions, racialized and cultural locations and sexual orientations. The antagonism of patriarchy, as the focus for feminism, is thus embedded in circumstance. In different ways universality is balanced with particularity. Recognizing and bridging particularity, addressing rather than settling differences, becomes the key issue. The result is a recasting of feminism as a relational practice, centred on drawing strength from difference, rather than from assumed similarity. The process may be thought of as a form of 'solidarity-with-recognition', an ethic of solidarity that establishes frameworks for living and acting together, to become a founding-stone of feminist politics.

In the context of globalism, these dilemmas of constructing counter-patriarchy across ideological, national and sociocultural contexts rise to the top of the agenda. In this spirit, for instance, Women's Studies International Forum has argued that 'developing strategies for global cooperation involves working towards an understanding of differences rather than simply recreating new versions of "sisterhood"'; this was the necessary first step for 'resolving the power imbalances between different feminists in the global arena' (Flew *et al.* 1999: 401–2). Clearly, if pushed to its logical end-point, such difference politics can empty-out antagonism, reducing the social movement to a social gathering. The risks are clear: on the one hand feminism risks implosion as universal claims are exposed as domination; on the other it risks losing the mobilizing power of collectivist feminist ideology, in a slide into individualism. Feminist subjectivity – the consciousness of feminism itself – may, then, be said to rest on a knife-edge between the universal and the particular.

Implosion may be averted, though, not so much through balancing as through situating. Here gender as a practice is imbricated with other modes of stratification and identity, forcing recognition of the multi-faceted character of feminist antagonism. As Chilla Bulbeck argued in *One World Women's Movement*, this ideological interaction or 'dialogue' involves recognition that the context, or experience, of patriarchy requires widely varying responses: 'experience may be shared, but the responses vary'; thus 'the world's women's movement need not be "one", but can be many', unified by a common commitment to challenging gender subordination (1988: 150, 153). Several writers view this as a form of 'transversal' politics, a term that defines a politics of dialogue across difference, in which different points of departure are acknowledged, and mutually traversed, to permit common understanding (Yuval-Davis 1997: 125).

Feminists have sought pathways beyond unitary feminism and fragmented women's movements – beyond 'mystified notions of similarity and difference' – through engaged action (Kaplan 1994: 148). The process has been called 'rooting' and 'shifting' – being rooted in your own context, while shifting to understand the roots of other women's positions (Charlesworth and Chinkin 2000). These modes of action are caught between deconstruction and reconstruction: the move to embrace difference, as a deconstructive moment, directly implies or requires reconstruction in the form of action. The tensions between such moves are reflected in disputes between deconstructive post-modernism and reconstructive 'standpoint feminism', with various cross-accusations of one or the other of dominating the social process.

Power divides and solidarity

Beyond the deconstruction/reconstruction bifircation, the relational model for mobilization reflects broader social transformations under globalism where feminist movements have been forced to engage with each others' differences, and not just within the rich West. As Gamble (2000) notes, the themes reflect longstanding internal debates amongst feminists, brought to the fore by globalizing pressures. A key driver, forcing engagement, is the logic of neoliberalism and globalism in politicizing the gender order. As Peterson argues, globalizing pressures 'aggravate women's subordination and divisions among women, but they also politicize the interaction of gender, ethnicity and race in the contemporary divisions of labour' (1996: 12).

Under globalism women have become enmeshed in myriad special economic zones, free trade areas and maquiladoras, while also constituting a growing proportion of the migrant contract, homeworking and the urban poor workforce. In different contexts globalism has thus brought a combined process of proletarianization and informalization of women's work: Dunaway characterizes this status as 'semi-proletarianized household labour' (2001:23). In this respect women are positioned at the core of the world system; the political response, through feminism, thus acquires central transformative significance.

Such significance is only realized in political action, where dialogue draws people together, to form collectivities. Solidarity – and the possibility of collectivity – requires recognition 'not only of differences, but also the relational nature of those differences' (Brown 1997: 275). Both dominant and subordinate histories exist simultaneously, often in an inter-dependent dialogue with each other; their logics are separate but related. The historian Elsa Brown refers to jazz music to help conceptualize this idea, in which musicians weave their different melodies, exploring points of divergence and difference as much as convergence and similarity. Such explorations are embedded in power relations. Rather than be 'power evasive' and reduce differences 'to a conglomerate of discursive entities', the focus must be on overcoming power hierarchies (Moreton-Robinson 2000: 347). In this way, any commitment to inclusivity has to be overlaid with a commitment to addressing power divides: as Alexander and Mohanty argue, 'in place of relativism, this critical application of feminist praxis in global contexts would substitute responsibility, accountability, engagement and solidarity' (1997, xix). Reflecting this, they point to a variegated 'transnational feminism' rather than a relatively unified 'global sisterhood' as the foundation for feminism.

Locality and trans-localist action

Sensitivity to power relations forces action and analysis into locality and specificity. Globalism frames localities, pitting them one against each other. As Connell argues, the agents of globalism – transnational corporations, inter-state institutions, global consumerisms – articulate local gender orders with and against one another (2002). Feminisms emerge within and across localities, to contest the ways in which gender orders are constructed and manipulated. Such feminisms are profoundly localized, but are also embedded in cross-local contestations: in this respect they offer both diversity and unity. For Connell, these 'interactions between local gender orders' constitute one of the two 'basic arenas of struggle for democratization' (the other being within globalizing institutions) (ibid.: 146).

The key task, then, becomes one of mapping and contesting specific experiences in their systemic context. Appeals for such approaches have proliferated. Dunaway (2001) for instance argues for commodity-chain analysis as a way of rematerializing the systemic logic of contemporary capitalism. Freeman (2001) likewise argues for bridges connecting localized embodied materiality with system-wide logics, for locally-sensitive accounts of gender within the analysis of macro global dynamics. Mohanty also argues for contextual localization, borrowing the term 'place consciousness' to emphasise the centrality of *in situ* struggles under globalism (Dirlik 1999 as cited in Mohanty 2003: 514). Globalism thus foregrounds the question of cross-cultural feminist solidarity, and produces intense debates about understanding differences as the basis for solidarity (Heywood and Drake 1997). The crucial aspect is specificity: modes of 'transnational feminism ... operate on the assumption that global gender categories are historically located and socially and culturally constructed' (Ifekwunigwe 1999: 209). Struggles become more embedded in local or national contexts and differences, while at the same time entering trans-local and transnational frameworks, constructing 'bridge identities' (Ferguson 1998). Any common positions emerge from differences, and create connections across communal, local or national identifications, rather than simply between them. The result is thus more transcommunal than intercommunal, translocal than interlocal, transnational than international, and to borrow a phrase from Samir Amin (1997), the dynamic is more multipolar than multilateral.

A range of tensions open up between these feminist connections and more exclusivist identifications, whether communalist, localist or nationalist. The tensions, though, are productive, forcing mutual reassessments and realignments (Bulbeck 1998). In this, feminism reflects a much wider tendency amongst social movements, where the interaction between specificities drives a reformulation of aspirations and action (Goodman 2006). Central to such possibilities is the recognition of specificity, not as secondary or residual, but as central to the process of feminist praxis. Specificity is not trumped by universality, but, paradoxically, viewed as constitutive of it.

We are, then, brought full circle from Northern particularity to assumed universality and back to particularity. Common action becomes genuinely translocal, or transnational, in both affirming local or national contexts, and crossing them. Such action, as Mackie argues, is based on linkages not similarities, embedded in imagined feminist communities (2001). Key issues here are issues of spatiality – of territory, place, locality and nationality – and the engagement with spatial frameworks for identification and action. Within this nexus the question of the 'national' is central.

The place of the national

Feminist struggles traditionally challenge the exclusion of women from the defini-tion of the 'national'. Under globalism this process of engaging the national remains as urgent as ever in both the North and the South – anti-statism is not an option. As Bagchi argues,

> There is an illusion among some activists that the disempowering of the national state is always a good thing. However, in poorer countries, it is ulti-mately the state which can provide universal primary education, primary healthcare, basic sanitation, and food security for the poor, and protect common property resources. Getting the state to make these provisions is part of the democratic struggle throughout the world.
>
> (2003: 117)

Feminisms thus remain critically engaged with national states. In making national claims they define themselves against patriarchal manifestations of nationalism and in the process may prefigure (if not in fact argue for) alternative modes of national belonging. Indeed, in some contexts, explicitly anti-nationalist feminism can be disempowering, especially in postcolonial contexts where such a stance can play into the hands of those who define feminism as 'Western', and nationalism as 'authentic' (Mohanty *et al.* 1991). Rather than accepting a dichotomy between national culture and feminism, women actively 'contest the nation' as a key site of power. As Narayan argues, 'if nations are "imagined communities" then bigoted or distorted nationalisms must be fought with feminist attempts to reinvent and re-imagine the national community that is more genu-inely inclusive and democratic' (1997: 406).

There is, then, no leap from the national, but equally, there is no enclosure within it. The dynamic is best illustrated by feminist engagement with the process established under the United Nations (UN) Conference on Women. First at the 1993 Vienna World Conference on Human Rights and then most forcefully at the 1995 Beijing UN Conference on Women, feminists and other women's move-ments 'move[d] from being bit players on the world's stage to main stage actors' (Stienstra 2000). Here they participated in the creation of global norms, forging an inter-state declaratory position. These commitments though, were primarily directed at the national realm – they were used to legitimate feminist demands and to hold governments to account, to 'finally force the full inclusion of women as part of the democratic community at nation-state level' (Dickenson 1997: 118). The model was a simple one, and reflected broader UN practice, of asserting rights as universal, but confining claims for justice and equality to the national unit (Otto 1996). All hinged on – and was directed at – enlarging the capacity to exert leverage on the national context.

Reflecting this, the Beijing Platform was premised on the assumption that states had not only the will, but also the capacity to respond. In many contexts the Plat-form was implemented, but proved inadequate. An early assessment of the Beijing process stressed that despite implementation of formal commitments, the status of women was deteriorating. Neoliberal structural adjustment that made women the 'shock absorbers for structural change' was the prime culprit (WEDO 1998). In 2000, the UN's own five-year review of the Beijing commitments and their implementation came to a very similar conclusion, arguing: 'the globalisation process has, in some countries, resulted in policy shifts in favour of more open trade and financial flows, privatisation of state-owned enterprises and in many cases lower public spending, particularly on social services'. It concluded that 'in a large number of countries, particularly in developing and least developed countries, these changes have also adversely impacted on the lives of women and have increased inequality … aggravating the feminization of poverty' (United Nations 2000: para 34). The ten-year review, which came in 2005, developed a similar perspective. WEDO Report to the Beijing plus 10 Conference, 'Beijing Betrayed', demonstrated how women had used the Platform for Action to push governments into taking action, albeit with limited results. The Report found the continued pursuit of market-driven policies, along with heightened militarism and fundamentalism had ensured that 'many women in all regions are actually worse off now than they were 10 years ago' (WEDO 2005: 2).

Hopes vested in the Beijing agenda had 'proved to be an illusion', and primarily because of the lack of leverage against neoliberalism at the national governmental level. In response, feminist organizations became more radicalized, in terms of targeting the agents of corporate globalism, and constructing North–South linkages. Eschle points to an 'intensification of transnational feminist organising during and after the UN Decade for Women, in which black and third-world feminist arguments about the inequalities of global capitalism became increasingly influential', feeding an 'explosion of feminist theorizing and practice around "development"'(2005: 11). There is, as a result, a deepening of the transnational feminist agenda – beyond a relatively formalized rights-based framework as reflected in the Beijing commitments – to a more diffuse focus on collective priorities in the context of globalization (Stienstra 2000).

Semi-peripheral themes in the Asia-Pacific

The dynamics of transnational and national strategizing in contemporary women's and feminist movements draw attention to spatial specificity and positionality. Here, the scope for specificity is set by a three-country comparison – of Mexico, Australia and Canada – understood as semi-peripheral societies with radically different histories, yet with shared experiences. Semi-peripheral states have emerged as relatively marginal in relation to dominant centres of power, yet have acquired autonomy in the world political economy primarily through nationalist mobilization and state intervention, including by subordinating more peripheral sites and populations (Cohen and Clarkson 2005). In the later decades of the twentieth century these societies have been profoundly affected by doctrines of neoliberal marketization and globalization and in many such contexts there has been a radical reorientation of state power. The consequences, in terms of a shift in public policy and state ideology, and in terms of the reformulation of feminism, are instructive.

A key starting point is that context matters. Macdonald for instance contrasts the different ways in which Canadian, Mexican and US-based feminist movements contested the North American Free Trade Agreement (NAFTA), highlighting the importance of national-level political institutions and political traditions in shaping the response, and the degree of leverage such movements could acquire (2002). Importantly, the US-based 'peak' group, the National Organization for Women, failed to address the issue; in contrast, the Canadian National Action Committee on the Status of Women (NAC) took up a leading position in the anti-NAFTA campaign. Although the NAC had limited impact on the Agreement itself, which was negotiated behind closed doors, NAC nonetheless played a key role in building an anti-free trade movement in Canada (Sparke 1996: 634).

Born as a centrist women's rights organization in the 1970s, the NAC had been radicalized through the 1980s and into the 1990s. This directly related to the sharpening of the Canadian gender order in the 1980s with deepened globalism and the imposition of neoliberalism. The shift of focus for NAC came first from 1985 with the effort to prevent the signing of a Canada–US Free Trade Agreement, which failed with the re-election of a conservative government in 1988 (and which led to the partial axing of NAC funding, along with other public interest groups). But radicalization continued, as the NAC continued to highlight the impact of neoliberalism on women. Funding cuts and an increasingly hostile government had enabled the NAC 'to take up more autonomous positions', notably on NAFTA (ibid.: 628). In the early1990s the NAC anti-NAFTA campaign marshalled English-Canadian feminists into the 'Pro-Canada' campaign against the Agreement, using its autonomy to play a key role in the anti-NAFTA movement, and thereby 'affirmed a feminist form of national imagining' (ibid.: 626). At the same time new transnational linkages were forged, for instance amongst feminists in the Canadian and Mexican labour movements, who became significantly more engaged through the joint campaign against NAFTA, and in the process created new dialogues, addressing the historical legacies of North-South subordination in Canada–Mexico trade union relations (Gabriel and Macdonald 1994). In Canada, as elsewhere, globalism had the effect of dismantling the model of state-sponsored social inclusion, disaggregating civil society and the public sphere, the primary 'organizing ground' of second wave feminism (Caragata 2003: 576). With that, though, came new constituencies of the marginalized, and the possibility of constructing and legitimizing new explicitly 'counter' publics. In some respects this is what the NAC did in the aftermath of the signing of NAFTA, with a deeper engagement with migrant and indigenous women, and a stronger willingness to take up wider international political agendas as feminist agendas (Gottlieb 1993). In the 1990s the NAC leadership shifted to reflect these new orientations, developing what was seen as a more 'engaged feminism' (Rebick and Roach 1996). In the face of 'anti-terrorist' militarism from 2001 the NAC officially took a traditional pro-peace stance, although at the same time defended anti-racist and anti-war positions (Nadeau 2002).

An important contrast within Canada is the Quebecois feminist movement, which in 2000 embarked on a remarkable experiment in global feminist solidarity through the 'World March for Women'. Here, the Federation des Femmes du Quebec (FFQ) conducted a grassroots initiative to mobilize women against the global feminization of poverty, and against violence against women. The process began with the formation of local groups across Quebec, building into demonstrations and rallies, including in a 30,000-strong demonstration in Montreal. These developed across Canada, with a set of concrete measures – 68 in all – developed and elaborated as a federal policy platform (Canadian Women's March Committee 2000). The March attracted participation from 5,500 feminist groups in 163 countries and produced a women's 'global charter' movement, with a relay march across 65 countries, from Brazil to Burkina Faso. The March culminated at the UN on October 17, 2000, the international day for the eradication of poverty, which effectively became a global day of action.

In part, the success of the FFQ Global March reflects the specificity of feminist engagement with nationalism within Quebec. The FFQ and other Quebecois feminist organizations had largely grounded their legitimacy within the Quebec policy-making context (Chappell 2000). In 1995, as the Quebec government developed programmes addressing the status of women, the FFQ moved to promote critical support for Quebec independence. That support was questioned from the late 1990s as the Quebec Government implemented neoliberal programmes, undermining health, education and social services. The movement became more deeply engaged against the feminization of poverty and violence against women within Quebec society. At the same time there was growing engagement with North–South alliances of women against globalism. The March, then, marked a 'new phase in the Quebec women's movement' in both grounding the movement and reaching out to similarly-affected women worldwide (Schoenwandt 2001).

The importance of local context is also clear when we shift our focus to Latin American politics during these years. Latin America's 'twin transitions … to political democracy and economic neoliberalism' had a central impact on feminisms in the region (Alvarez *et al.* 2003: 354). Where the first opened up access to the policy process for feminist organizations to act as 'gender experts' or 'surrogates for civil society', the latter involved widespread contracting out of service provision, offering opportunities for feminist service providers, enabling a 'feminist NGO "boom"' in the region (Alvarez 1999). These developments created sharp tensions between 'insider' advocates and 'outsider' mobilizers, the first increasingly professionalized, constituted in its engagement with state and inter-state authorities and with international foundations, the latter more markedly embedded in communities of women marginalized and alienated by both the political process and the turn to neoliberalism. Deep power imbalances thus opened up within the movements, forcing divisions and differences onto the agenda, and producing a shift from 1998 to a much more explicit concern for diversity within the movement, especially in terms of age, culture or ethnicity and sexuality (Alvarez *et al.* 2003).

Reflecting this background, in Mexico there had been a flowering of feminist policy advocacy especially since the shift away from the PRI hegemony to a more transparent system of political representation from 1997. From the 1970s the movement had centred on a women's rights agenda, from 1976 through the 'Coalition of feminist women', and later, in 1979, through the 'National front for women's rights', precipitating a loosely associated multisectoral women's movement in the 1980s. Here, the issues for poor women were subsumed into a wider women's movement that 'depended implicitly on the universality of women's oppression' (Marcos 1999). 1999 saw a revival of this approach, with the formation of a new national feminist lobby, the 'Consortium for Parliamentary Dialogue and Communication toward Equality' (El Consorcio).

Similarly, a tradition of grassroots feminist and women's movements has also been invigorated. With deepening social divides under neoliberalism, there has been an upsurge in grassroots women's movements and feminist-inspired movements, embedded in communities marginalized by neoliberalism. As in Canada, women have borne the brunt of neoliberal marketization; neoliberalism has also has seen 'increased incorporation of women into the labour force both in the maquiladoras ... and in the informal sector', offering new sources of mobilization (Macdonald 2002: 166). The most obvious responses were from indigenous women's movements, especially Chiapas-based Zapatista *campesina* groups, and maquiladora women's organizations, based in the Northern Mexican export platforms.

Indigenous women's organizations, in particular, appeared as key players from the 1994 announcement of the 'Women's Revolutionary Law' by Zapatista women and Tojobal, Chol, Tzotzil and Tzeltal women. The law is said to have had great symbolic importance for indigenous women in Mexico, leading to the formation of the 'National Coordinating Committee of Indigenous Women' three years later, with the participation of 20 indigenous communities from across Mexico. These indigenous feminisms have had a direct influence on urban feminist formations. As Castillo argues, unlike the 'urban feminist movement in Mexico, indigenous women have maintained a double militancy': this challenges indigenous organizations to address gender issues, and feminists to address issues of cultural inequality (2002: 3). An embrace of sub-national or non-national particularity has thus proceeded hand-in-hand with a shift into international contexts; these fronts dovetail with local strategies, around specific concerns, such as reproductive health and campaigns against violence (Marcos 1999).

The spatial themes in Canada and Mexico, of contesting nationalism while doing feminism, are also well illustrated by experiences in Australia. Mainstream second-wave feminism in Australia had similarities with its Canadian counterpart, in likewise being focused on state policy. As Yeatman notes, 'there was barely a moment in Australia when this movement was not being shaped and constituted by the state' (1994: 183). Feminists developed a 'femocrat' strategy centred on policy-making, leading to the 'professionalization' of feminist ideology. This strategy resulted in several major achievements in the 1970s and 1980s but many of these gains have since been lost. First with neoliberal Labor administrations in the early 1990s, and then with an explicitly conservative government from 1996, there was a wholesale downgrading of official commitments.

This turnaround marked a 'crossroads' for Australian feminism (Curthoys 1996). Something of an altered direction emerged in the latter half of the 1990s with dual attempts at 'domesticating' international gender norms and an intensified challenge to Australian nationalist rhetoric. Attempts at deploying international norms had limited effect, and in some respects rebounded. In the immediate aftermath of Beijing, feminist organizations found a new confidence in facing an increasingly anti-feminist political climate in Australia (Mitchell and Pradham 1997). The United Nations process, though, was important more as a means of shaming the government than as a means of forcing policy change. At the 1997 meeting of the United Nations Committee on the Elimination of Discrimination against Women (CEDAW), for instance, Australian feminist NGOs successfully recruited the weight of international opinion to their cause. The Committee was highly critical of the Australian Government, and NGOs successfully drew negative comparisons with other state signatories of the CEDAW, especially those not falling into the 'western' category, exposing the myth of Australian gender equality. The government response, though, was profoundly negative. In 2000, in response to criticisms from the UN Human Rights Commission on a range of issues, including from the CEDAW committee, the Government announced it would take a more 'robust and strategic approach' and would seek to 'ensure adequate recognition of the primary role of democratically elected governments and the subordinate role of non-government organizations' at UN human rights committees (Downer, Williams and Ruddock 2000). In 2000 the Australian Government failed to submit its periodic report to the CEDAW committee; a combined fourth and fifth Periodic Report was finally submitted in 2003, and a ten-page update was submitted in 2006. On both occasions Australian-based feminist organizations prepared a 'shadow report': the 2006 NGO report for instance, was submitted by the Women's Rights Action Network on behalf of 103 women's and feminist organizations (WRANA 2005). The CEDAW committee continued to criticize the Australian Government for its failure to implement earlier recommendations, and outlined a series of issues that required 'priority attention', stating it expected the forthcoming 2008 report to outline 'implementation actions' to address them (United Nations 2006). The criticisms, though, had little immediate impact, either on the Australian public sphere, or on public policy.

With the emergence of a Federal Government significantly more hostile to feminist NGOs and to UN interventions, there has been a sharpened contest over the definition of the national interest, and over national identity. The subordination of feminist demands to the government's 'competitiveness' drive emerged with growing strength from the late 1990s, pre-dating the election of the Howard administration in 1996 (Johnson 1996). Subsequently, feminist priorities have not simply been subordinated, but also directly confronted by an increasingly hostile and avowedly nationalist conservatism. As in Canada, feminists have contested these dominant agendas, challenging masculinist versions of what it means to be Australian, and patriarchal definitions of the 'national interest'. Such contestations are not necessarily new – feminists in Australia have always contended with nationalism (Lepervanche 1989) – but under globalism have become more critical as its effects have been brought into sharper relief.

Challenges to nationalism emerged for instance with feminist critiques of the 'republic debate', from 1996 to 1999. These highlighted the gendered definition of Australian nationalism, and challenged the legitimacy of those claiming to speak for the 'national interest', whether republican or monarchist (Hoorn and Goodman 1996). There were feminist re-writings of 'the national story', such as the Penguin paperback, *Creating a Nation 1988–1990*, through which the authors sought a 'reconstruction of the nation' (Grimshaw *et al.* 1996: 314). There were also direct interventions into the political debate, for instance through the 1998 Women's Constitutional Convention (WCC), which attempted to set the agenda for the national Convention on the Republic (Reynolds 1998). The WCC placed gender equality at the centre of the national constitution, arguing for a Bill of Rights that would secure substantive equality in both the public and private spheres.

A similar claim on national identity was made with the 'Women for Wik' campaign, which campaigned against government proposals to expropriate indigenous land rights. In October 1997 the group made a submission to the Joint Parliamentary Committee on the government's Native Title Amendment Bill, endorsed by 50 women's organizations. It asserted that 'Women for Wik represents a phenomenal groundswell of mainstream opinion in support of Native Title ... one of the most powerful national grassroots women's movement since the Vietnam war', arguing that 'to ignore this is to ignore the opinion of the so-called silent majority – the women voters' (Women for Wik 1997). Like the WCC intervention, a collective women's voice was asserted as the voice of national conscience demanding to be heard above the fray of party politics. In both cases, feminists were challenging the delimitation of women's concerns, and in doing so, mapping an alternative agenda for Australian national identification.

The feminist challenge to nationalist rhetoric has gathered more momentum as the government's social conservativism has deepened. Perhaps most intense has been the feminist challenge to exclusivist nationalist categories, and their application in migrant, asylum-seeker and refugee policy, and in intermittent attacks on cultural difference and on indigenous identity. The articulation of a culturally-homogenous Australian identity has been especially challenged by feminists organising from within affected communities. Asian Women at Work has systematically (and successfully) campaigned for homeworkers' rights, through the 'Fair Wear' campaign for instance, which was set up in 1996 with participation from relevant trade unions and community organizations (Sutherland 2004). Immigrant Women's Speak-out, founded in 1985, likewise has maintained a powerful presence in challenging government attacks on migrant women, and politicizing questions of migration and domestic violence (IWSO 2000). There are parallel and related collaborations in responding to media and governmental vilification of Muslim women, with Muslim women's organizations finding ways of 'answering back' rather than being silenced by what has become a barrage of prejudice (Dreher 2003).

At the same time, national debates over the politics of care have surfaced, with sharp tensions between the neoliberal orthodoxy and 'family values'. In the early 2000s the intensification of women's work, along with a rolling-back of the social wage, was producing a crisis in care provision. A series of national debates ensued, with something of a moral panic over the fate of the nuclear family and of 'community'. During the 2004 Federal election, for instance, party leaders sought to outbid each other in offering 'baby bonus' payments, primarily directed at women. These debates placed key feminist priorities at the centre of public policy, with concerns about the fate of 'social capital' and of the impact of the 'work–life collision' offering openings for feminist intervention to address the gendering of care (Pocock 2003). An example is the 'What Women Want' programme launched by a group of relatively conservative alliance of women's organizations, welfare agencies, churches and trade unions, brought together by the National Foundation for Australian Women. The group presented a report in 2005 that was highly critical of the Government's proposed industrial relations and welfare reforms, and used commissioned research to show that women would be 'disproportionately affected by the proposals [and] will translate into lower wages and poorer conditions for women' (National Foundation for Australian Women 2005).

Conclusions

In 1998 four members of the Canadian NAC wrote a strategic assessment of the implications of neoliberal globalism for feminists. The authors asserted the resilience of feminism, arguing that 'ideas about eliminating women's subordination have been advanced over long periods of time, in the face of extraordinary odds and against the self-interests of the most powerful in society. For this reason, that is the ability to succeed despite overwhelming odds, feminists are well-placed to advance the ideas for egalitarian projects internationally in the twenty-first century' (Cohen *et al.* 2002: 9). The experiences discussed here, drawn from Mexico, Australia and Canada underline the resilience and adaptability of women's and feminist movements in the face of globalism.

Feminist and women's movement projects in the three countries have been reconfigured by globalism. Their experiences suggest there is much to be gained from re-embedding feminism in the experience of women marginalized by marketization, hand-in-hand with women more strategically positioned to force gender into the policy-making process.

The cases discussed here are also suggestive of the strategic importance of experiences on the global semi-periphery. Within these contexts globalism appears to both deepen and broaden the feminist agenda. In the first instance the feminization of poverty creates new grassroots forces, which emerge to claim a central role in feminist praxis. At the same time the state has remained a key focus for women's movements and for feminists. In the different contexts the process of challenging dominant definitions of national belonging and national identity has remained an important means of achieving changes in state policy. As they claim the right to speak for or from within the nation, however, such challenges also invoke and engage with international gender norms, and operate as part of broader global justice social movement configurations. In the process, feminists are explicitly engaged in fusing cosmopolitan and national perspectives to exploit the growing contradictions and vulnerabilities of globalist politics.

The resulting dialogues between national policy-focused feminists and grass-roots community feminists have moved to the centre, deepening engagement across the divides between women, especially across class and cultural divides.

In many respects these engagements become central to the definition and redefinition of feminist programmes, projects and visions. Such a politics offers a possible antidote to the process of neoliberal globalism that so successfully disempowers peoples. These forms of praxis deploy embedded experiences against the disembedding forces of globalism, they marshal deeply-felt identifications to construct alternative feminist subjectivities. Perhaps most important, they challenge depoliticization and demobilization with invigorated forms of participatory agency, asserting and enacting forms of deep democracy against the disempowering logic of globalism. In this respect women's and feminist movements have had much to share with other social movements, as part of the generalized reassertion of popular priorities and popular participation against the disciplines and dictates of neoliberal globalism.

References

Alexander, M. Jacqui and Mohanty, Chandra (eds) (1997) *Feminist Genealogies, Colonial Legacies, Democratic Futures*, New York: Routledge.

Alvarez, Sonia E. (1999) 'Advocating Feminism: The Latin American Feminist NGO "Boom"', *International Feminist Journal of Politics*, 1, 2: 181–209.

Alvarez, Sonia E.; Friedman, Elisabeth Jay; Blackwell, Maylei; Chinchilla, Norma Stoltz; Lebon, Nathalie; Navarro, Marysa and Tobar, Marcelo Ríos (2003) 'Encountering Latin American and Caribbean Feminisms', *SIGNS: Journal of Women in Culture and Society*, 28, 2: 537–79.

Amin, Samir (1997) *Capitalism in the Age of Globalisation*, London: Zed Books.

Arneil, Barbara (1999) *Politics and Feminism*, London: Blackwell.

Bagchi, Amiya Kumar (2003) 'The Parameters of Resistance', in J. Foster and R. McChesney (eds) *Pox Americana: Exposing the American Empire*, New York: Monthly Review Press, pp. 106–28

Bagguley, Paul (2002) 'Contemporary British Feminism: A Social Movement in Abeyance?', *Social Movement Studies*, 1, 2: pp. 169–85.

Brown, Elsa Barkley (1997) '"What has happened here": The Politics of Difference in Women's History', in L. Nicholson (ed.) *The Second Wave: A Reader in Feminist Theory*, London: Routledge, pp. 272–87.

Bryson, Valerie (2003) *Feminist Political Theory*, New York: Palgrave.

Bulbeck, Chilla (1988) *One World Women's Movement*, London: Pluto Press.

—— (1998) *Re-orienting Western Feminisms: Women's Diversity in a Postcolonial World*, Cambridge: Cambridge University Press.

Burgmann, Verity (2003) *Power, Profit and Protest: Australian Social Movements and Globalisation*, Sydney: Allen & Unwin.

Canadian Women's March Committee (2000) 'It's Time for Change! Demands to the Federal Government to End Poverty and Violence Against Women', World March of Women in the Year 2000, September. Available online, www.marchofwomen.org/en/demands/demands_eng.html.

Caragata, Lea (2003) 'Neoconservative Realities: The Social and Economic Marginalization of Canadian Women', *International Sociology*, 18, 3: 559–80.

Castillo, R. Aida Hernández (2002) 'Zapatismo and the Emergence of Indigenous Feminism, *NACLA Report on the Americas*, 35, 6, May/June: 39–43.

Chappell, Louise (2000) 'Interacting with the State: Feminist Strategies and Political Opportunities', *International Feminist Journal of Politics*, 2, 2: 244–75.

Charlesworth, Hilary, and Chinkin, Christine (2000) *The Boundaries of International Law*, Manchester: Manchester University Press.

Cohen, Marjorie; Ritchie, Laurell; Swenarchuk, Michelle and Vosko, Leah (2002) 'Globalisation: Some Implications and Strategies for Women', *Canadian Woman Studies*, 21.22, 4/1, Fall: 6–14.

Cohen, Marjorie and Clarkson, Stephen (eds) (2005) *Governing Under Stress: Middle Powers and the Challenge of Globalisation*, London: Zed Books.

Committee on the Elimination of Discrimination against Women (CEDAW) (1997) *Third Periodic Report: Australia*, Seventeenth Session, Rapporteur, Aurora Javate de Dios, New York: CEDAW.

Connell, Raewyn (2002) *Gender*, Cambridge: Polity Press; Malden: Blackwell Publishers.

Curthoys, Ann (1996) 'Australian Feminism and the State, in Paul James (ed.) *The State Question: Transformations of the Australian State*, Sydney: Allen & Unwin, pp.138–61.

Dickenson, Donna (1997) 'Counting Women in Globalisation, Democratisation and the Women's Movement', in A. McGrew (ed.) *The Transformation of Democracy? Globalisation and Territorial Democracy*, Cambridge: Polity Press, pp. 97–120.

Dirlik, Arif (1999) 'Place-Based Imagination: Globalism and the Politics of Place', Review, *Journal of the Ferdinand Braudel Center for the Study of Economics, Historical Systems, and Civilizations*, 22, 2: 151–87.

Downer, Alexander, Williams, Daryl and Ruddock, Phillip (2000) '*Media Release*', Office of the Ministers for Foreign Affairs and for Immigration and Multicultural Affairs, Australia, 29 August.

Dreher, Tanja (2003) 'Speaking Up and Talking Back: News, Media Interventions in Sydney's "Othered" Communities', in L. Jacka and L. Green (eds) *The New Others: Media and Society Post-September 11*, Media International Australia, 109, November, pp. 131–3.

Dunaway, Wilma A. (2001) 'The Double Register of History: Situating the Forgotten Woman and her Household in a Capitalist Commodity Chains', *Journal of World Systems Research*, 7, 1, Spring: 2–31.

Eschle, Catherine (2005) '"Skeleton Women": Feminism and the Anti-Globalisation Movement', *SIGNS: Journal of Women in Culture and Society*, 30, 3, Spring: 1741–60.

Ferguson, Ann (1998) 'Resisting the Veil of Privilege: Building Bridge Identities as an Ethico-politics of Global Feminisms', *Hypatia*, 13, 3: pp. 95–113.

Flew, Fiona; Bagilhole, B.; Carabine, J.; Fenton, N.; Kitzinger, C.; Lister, R. and Wilkinson, S. (1999) 'Introduction: Local Feminisms, Global Futures', *Women's Studies International Forum*, 22, 4: 393–403.

Freeman, Carla (2001) 'Is Local: Global as Feminine: Masculine? Rethinking the Gender of Globalisation', *SIGNS: Journal of Women in Culture and Society*, 26, 4: 1007–37.

Gabriel, Christina and Macdonald, Laura (1994) 'NAFTA, Women and Organising in Canada and Mexico: Forging a Feminist Internationality', *Millenium*, 23, 3: 535–63.

Gamble, Sarah (2000) 'Postfeminism', in Sarah Gamble (ed.) *Critical Dictionary of Feminism and Post-feminism*, New York: Routledge, pp. 43–54.

Goodman, James (2006) 'Reflexive Solidarities: Reframing the Local, National, Global Divides', in James Goodman and Paul James (eds) *Nationalism and Global Solidarities: Alternative Projections in the Globalising World*, London: Routledge, pp. 187–204.

Gottlieb, Amy (1993) 'What About Us? Organizing Inclusively in the National Action Committee on the Status of Women', in Linda Carty (ed.) *And Still We Rise: Feminist Political Mobilizing in Contemporary Canada*, Toronto: Women's Press, pp. 368–85.

Grimshaw, Patricia; Lake, Marilyn; McGrath, Ann and Quartly, Marian (1996) *Creating a Nation* (first published in 1994 by McPhee/Gribble), Melbourne: Penguin.

Heywood, Leslie and Drake, Jennifer (1997) *The Third Wave Agenda: Being Feminist, Doing Feminism*, University of Minnesota Press: Minneapolis, U.S.

Hoorn, Jeannette and Goodman, David (eds) (1996) Vox Republicae: Feminism and the Republic, *Journal of Australian Studies*, Special Edition, 47, Melbourne: La Trobe University Press.

Ifekwunigwe, Jayne O. (1999) 'Borderland Feminisms', in Mrinalini Sinha, Donna Guy, and Angela Woollacott (eds) *Feminisms and Internationalism*, Oxford: Blackwell, pp. 51–82.

Immigrant Women Speak-out (IWSO) (2004) *Living without Violence 2000*, video, Sydney: IWSO.

Inder, Brigid (2003) 'The Women's Report Card', *On the Record*, 52.

Johnson, Carol (1996) 'Negotiating the Politics of Inclusion: Women and Australian Labour Governments, 1983–1995', *Feminist Review*, 52, Spring: 102–17.

Kaplan, Gisela (1994) 'Women in Europe and Australia: Feminisms in Parallel?', in Norma Grieve and Alisa Burns (eds.) *Australian Women: Contemporary Feminist Thought*, Melbourne: Oxford University Press, pp. 40–52.

Lepervanche, M. (1989) 'Woman, Nation and State in Australia', in N. Yuval-Davis and F. Anthias (eds) *Woman-Nation-State*, London: Macmillan, pp. 36–57.

Macdonald, Laura (2002) Globalisation and Social Movements: Comparing Women's Movements Responses to NAFTA in Mexico, the USA and Canada, *International Feminist Journal of Politics*, 4, 2: 151–72.

Mackie, Vera (2001) 'The Language of Globalization, Transnationality and Feminism', *International Feminist Journal of Politics*, 3, 2: 180–206.

Marcos, Sylvia (1999) 'Twenty-five Years of Mexican Feminisms – A History', *Women's International Studies Forum*, 22, 4, 8, July: 431–3.

Mitchell, S. and Pradham, R. (1997) *Back to Basics from Beijing: An Australian Guide to the International Platform for Action*, Australian Council for Overseas Aid Development Dossier 39, Canberra: Australian Council for Overseas Aid (ACFOA).

Mohanty, Chandra Talpade; Russo, Ann and Torres, Lourdes (eds) (1991) *Third World Women and the Politics of Feminism*, Indianapolis: Indiana University Press.

Mohanty, Chandra Talpade (2003) '"Under Western Eyes" Revisited: Feminist Solidarity through Anti-capitalist Struggles', *SIGNS, Journal of Women in Culture and Society*, 28, 2, Winter: pp. 499–535.

Moreton-Robinson, Aileen (2000) 'Troubling Business: Difference and Whiteness within Feminism', *Australian Feminist Studies*, 15, 33, December 21: pp. 343–52.

Nadeau, Mary-Jo (2002) 'Towards "A Peaceful Solution": NAC and the Politics of Engagement', *Canadian Woman Studies*, 22, 2: 48–55.

Narayan, Uma (1997) 'Contesting Cultures: "Westernisation", Respect for Cultures, and Third World Feminists', in Linda Nicholson (ed.) *The Second Wave: A Reader in Feminist Theory*, London: Routledge, pp. 369–414.

National Foundation for Australian Women (2005) 'What Women Want – Is a Guarantee of No Disadvantage', *Press Release*, Canberra, 23 August.

Otto, Dianne (1996) 'Holding up half the sky, but for whose benefit? A Critical Analysis of the Fourth World Conference on Women', *Australian Feminist Law Journal*, 6: 7–28.

Peterson, V. Spike (1996) 'The Politics of Identification in the Context of Globalisation,' *Women's Studies International Forum*, 19, 1-2: 5–15.

Petman, Jan Jindy (1996) 'Second-class citizens? Nationalism, Identity and Difference in Australia', in Barbara Sullivan and Gillian Whitehouse (eds.) *Gender, Politics and Citizenship in the 1990s*, Sydney: UNSW Press, pp. 2–24.

Pocock, Barbara (2003) *The Work-Life Collision*, Sydney: Federation Press.

Rebick, Judy and Roach, Kiké (1996) *Politically Speaking*, Vancouver: Douglas and McIntyre.

Reynolds, Margaret (1998) Is the Federal Government Meeting its International Obligations to Australian Women?, Speech to the Women's Constitutional Convention, January.

Rowbotham, Sheila and Linkogle, Stephanie (2001) 'Introduction', in Sheila Rowbotham and Stephanie Linkogle (eds) *Women Resist Globalization: Mobilizing for Livelihood and Rights*, London: Zed Books.

Schoenwandt, Jeanne (2001) 'A Fire of Unity: From Feminist Nationalism to Global Feminism in Quebec', *World and I*, 16, 5, May: 194.

Sparke, Matthew (1996) 'Negotiating National Action: Free Trade, Constitutional Debate and the Gendered Geopolitics of Canada', *Political Geography*, 15, 6–7: 615–39.

Stienstra, Deborah (2000) 'Making Global Connections amongst Women 1970–99', in Robin Cohen and Shirin M. Rai (eds) *Global Social Movements*, Athlone Press: London, pp. 62–82.

Sutherland, Elissa (2004) 'In-the-field politics: Multiple Voices of Outworkers and Researcher', *Australian Geographer*, 35, 2: 161–8.

United Nations (2000) Report of the Ad Hoc Committee of the 23rd Special Session of the General Assembly, New York.

—— (2006) *Concluding Comments of the Committee on the Elimination of Discrimination against Women*, 16 January to 3 February 2006, CEDAW 34th Session. Available online, www.un.org/womenwatch/daw/cedaw/cedaw34/statements/Chair_closing%20remarks.pdf .

Yuval-Davis, N. (1997) *Gender and Nation*, London: Sage.

Women's Constitutional Convention (1998) *Outcomes*, 29 January, Canberra: WCC.

WEDO (Women's Environment and Development Organisation) (1998) *Mapping Progress: Assessing Implementation of the Beijing Platform for Action*, WEDO: New York.

—— (2005) *Beijing Betrayed: Women Worldwide Report that Governments Have Failed to Turn the Platform into Action*, New York: WEDO.

Women for Wik (1997) Submission to the Joint Parliamentary Committee on the Native Title Amendment Bill 1997, October, Sydney: Women for Wik.

WRANA (2005) Australian NGO Shadow Report on the Implementation of the Convention on the Elimination of all forms of Discrimination Against Women (CEDAW), Melbourne: Women's Rights Action Network Australia.

Yeatman, Anna (1994) 'Women and the State', in Kate Pritchard Hughes (ed.) *Contemporary Australian Feminism*, Melbourne: Longman Cheshire, pp. 177–92.

Yuval-Davis N. (1997) Gender and Nation Sage, London.

11 Engendering accountability in government budgets in Mexico

Jennifer Cooper and Rhonda Sharp

Introduction

During the past decade Mexico, like several other middle-power countries, has introduced gender-responsive budget initiatives. But how effective are gender-responsive budget initiatives in making governments accountable for the gender impacts of their budgets in an era of neoliberal governance? This chapter assesses the gender-responsive budget initiative that has emerged in Mexico under neoliberalism as a strategy for increasing the national government's accountability for the gender impacts of its budget. In particular, the chapter examines three aspects of the Mexican initiative that international experience indicates are important in contributing to the accountability of governments for the gender impacts of their budgets. They are:

1   the ability of gender-responsive budget initiatives to connect with and bring about changes in the budgetary process;
2   the contribution of women's non-government organizations in putting political pressure on governments to be accountable for their budgetary impacts on gender equality;
3   the capacity of these initiatives to contest the macroeconomic framework of the budget from a gender perspective.

We argue that an examination of these aspects of the Mexican initiative shows that, in the face of other spaces closing for gender equality strategies, gender-responsive budget initiatives have had a significant measure of success in providing a new terrain for demanding gender equity and women's rights. However, the chapter also argues that some of these spaces may be compromised with the government's outsourcing to non-governmental organizations (NGOs), including feminist NGOs, while political contestation of budgets has been reduced because neoliberalism limits the notion of fiscal accountability. The chapter concludes with discussion of ways that the Mexican gender-responsive budget initiative might continue to expand the political spaces for promoting gender equality by fostering fiscal democracy as well as the limitations to this process.

Neoliberal fiscal policy and gender-responsive budgets

Globalization has been accompanied by fundamental shifts in policy relating to government revenues and expenditures. These global changes in the budgetary activities of government form part of an overall reconceptualization and rational-ization of the roles of the government, markets, households and the not-for-profit sectors. This policy approach, referred to variously as the 'Washington consensus' or 'neoliberalism' is characterized by an emphasis on market liberalization and contains within it the broader objective of a substantially changed role of the state.[1] Neoliberal fiscal policies in Mexico and elsewhere have involved cuts in public expenditure, particularly on health, education and welfare, the privatization and contracting-out of public service delivery, the introduction of user-pays fees and regressive consumption taxes to raise revenues, the downsizing of the public sector workforce and the priortization of low inflation and balanced budgets over other macroeconomic goals such as full employment and equitable distribution. An important lubricant in the fiscal stance of the 'Washington consensus' has been the transfer of budgetary and management processes and techniques developed in the private sector context to the public sector, along with the accompanying account-ability discourses of transparency, participation and performance measurement.[2]

The fiscal policy practices and discourses of a country are an important determi-nant of the budget's impact on different groups. In this regard the Organisation for Economic Co-operation and Development (OECD) has aptly described the government budget as a financial mirror of the economic and social choices of a society (2001). The social choices and policy priorities invoked in fiscal or budgetary policy are, however, rarely neutral. Because women and men usually engage in different types and combinations of paid and unpaid economic activities, are subjected to different socioeconomic norms, and tend to occupy different economic and social positions, budgets are unlikely to impact on them in similar ways. Neither does public spending have a uniform impact on women: class, regional and ethnic differences condition access to government services and underpin differences in needs.

The experience of Australia with respect to gender budgeting is instructive here. The notion of 'gender non-neutrality' appeared formally in the Australian budget processes in the mid-1980s. Under pressure from the women's movement and particularly the feminists or 'femocrats' within the state, Australian federal, state and territory governments introduced the first initiatives to make budgets more gender responsive. They aimed to systematically assess policies and programmes and to foster structures and processes within government to influence budgetary decision-making and make governments accountable for their gender equality commitments. However, as neoliberal policies and discourses progressively took hold throughout the 1990s, these Australian 'women's budget' initiatives floun-dered. A climate of expenditure cutbacks, particularly in the areas of welfare and women's policy machinery, the introduction of regressive taxes and political discourses that emphasised market accountability rather than accountability to women and men as citizens, made it increasingly difficult to maintain the momentum of the Australian gender-responsive budget initiatives (Sharp and Broomhill 2002, Sawer 2003).

As the Australian women's budget initiatives were being scaled back the idea of making governments accountable for the gender impacts of their budgets was gaining support at an international level.[3] In the mid-1990s there were two important sources of momentum for the introduction of gender-responsive budget initiatives worldwide. One was the United Nations Beijing Platform of Action recommendations (S345, 346 and 358), which stated that an understanding of the impact of government budgets on gender equality outcomes requires assessments to be undertaken as well as changes to budgets and access to services to be made in the light of these assessments. These recommendations recognized that following the money is critical because government policy promises for gender equality are frequently not adequately resourced and, as such, remain paper promises. The other force for the expansion of gender-responsive budgets was the interest taken by international organizations and donors. This began in 1996 with the Commonwealth Secretariat pilot programme on gender budget initiatives in Commonwealth countries, which spread to national aid agencies, UN organizations and a variety of other international donors and foundations (Sharp 2003: 7–8). Important outcomes of this process were the development of networks among the participants, the sharing of experiences and expertise, the development of technical tools and capacity and a growing research literature.

The spread of gender-responsive budget initiatives over 60 countries, including Mexico, has been an example of how actions for gender justice can be facilitated by globalization.[4] Paradoxically, as Diane Elson notes, this engagement with government budgets for their gender impacts is occurring at the same time as other market liberalization and globalization policies in trade, investment and finance have come into force, which has put pressure on governments to introduce neoliberal fiscal polices that tend to have significant negative impacts on gender justice. She argues that gender equality and the empowerment of women will require the establishment of 'fiscal democracy'. At a minimum, it requires that budget processes are transparent, accountable and participatory and that all citizens have an equal voice in budget decision-making processes (2004: 639).

Gender-responsive budgeting in Mexico

Mexico's gender-responsive budget initiative has its origins in the women's non-government sector.[5] A turning point was the consolidation of the activities and agendas of some 80 NGOs during the preparations for the International Conference on Population and Development (ICPD) held in Cairo in 1994 (Espinosa, Paredes and Rodríguez 1999). A national network of NGOs (Foro Nacional de Mujeres y Políticas de Población) was formed to monitor the Cairo Programme of Action in Mexico, which became a focus of feminist concerns for an adequately funded and holistic approach to reproductive health. The initial review of Mexico's Programme of Action in 1999 by a group of Foro researchers was a

208 *Jennifer Cooper and Rhonda Sharp*

budget analysis focusing on trends in federal programmes and spending on reproductive health. The study found 'that between 1993 and 1996, federal expenditure in reproductive health dropped by 33 per cent in real terms, while government health expenditures in general dropped by an astounding 36 per cent' (Hofbauer 2002: 86).

A gender analysis of budget expenditures of all ministries gained momentum with the establishment of the National Institute for Women (Inmujeres) in 2001 by the Vicente Fox federal government. The President of the Republic appoints the director of the institute, which is ruled by an honorary consultative and social council constituted by women selected from the various political parties, civil associations and private organizations as well as academics. Inmujeres is a decentralized organization within the Federal Public Administration and has a policy-coordinating role among all government ministries. The National Programme for Equal Opportunities lays down guidelines for gender equality and mainstreaming as part of Mexico's National Development Plan 2001–2006. These guidelines require various ministries to allocate funds from their annual budget to activities specifically targeted at women and to collaborate with other ministries to carry these out under the supervision and recommendations of Inmujeres. The commitment of Inmujeres to institutionalizing gender, or gender mainstreaming, as recommended by the Beijing Platform of Action (1995), and the government's ratification of the International Convention for the Elimination of all forms of Discrimination Against Women (CEDAW) on June 15, 2002 has meant that a gender-responsive budget initiative has been given an official sanction within government circles. The initiative has largely been a response to the Mexican government's need for, and sensitivity to, international accountability for its gender commitments.

Connecting with and changing budgetary processes

Effective gender-responsive budgets need to connect with the budgetary process across the cycle of formulation, execution, implementation and audit, and insert changes that will foster a gender perspective (Sharp 2003: 69–70). Many international initiatives have been significantly constrained by their inability to connect to and effect a space for change in the budgetary processes. Neoliberal reforms to budgetary processes have taken place in many countries and the new discourses and practices have in some cases realigned the political spaces in budgetary decision-making in ways that create opportunities for gender-responsive budget initiatives. The Mexican initiative, for example, has benefited from, and utilized, changes in the budgetary processes that have fostered transparency. Transparency is usually defined as a functional element of accountability requiring that information about gender issues and the impact of policies and budgets is provided in an understandable and relevant form. Politically, transparency is best described as the capacity to 'inspect and establish the truthfulness of claims' (Bakker 2002: 290). Transparency is a prerequisite for raising awareness of gender issues in budgets and policies which in turn affects the capacity of gender budget initiatives to make governments accountable for their record on gender equality (Sharp 2003).

Access to budget documentation, by both government and civil society actors, is a prerequisite for transparency. One reform in Mexico, which served as an enabling force for the gender-responsive budget initiative, has been making the national budget available electronically. This has greatly facilitated the analysis of targeted spending on women. A technique has been developed using key words related to women, such as mujeres (women), género (gender), viudas (widows), ninas (girls), papanicolou (pap smear), and so on, against the names and funding of the previous year's programmes. Importantly, electronic access to the budget has enabled activists and Inmujeres to give press conferences on some of the gender implications of the proposed budget soon after the October budget is released. This is always a decisive political moment in the Mexican budget process.

In addition, careful monitoring and skillful scrutiny of the budget has identified non-transparent reallocations that have potentially significant and negative gender impacts.[6] In 2004, for example, funds assigned by the Health Ministry to combat AIDS were transferred in the course of the year to a 'right-to-life' group as a result of a unilateral decision of a legislative member of the government budget commission. Subsequently, the Health Minister was asked to justify his authorization of three million US dollars to non-government 'right-to-life' groups that, when audited, showed great irregularities in their finances (Ramirez Cuevas 2005). Because the minister's answer was unsatisfactory and no sanctions were applied to the accused legislative member and others involved, a 'citizen's tribunal' put them on trial publicly in April 2006. Academics and media personalities made up the jury. Undoubtedly, the enthusiasm for gender-responsive budget exercises is partly due to the political use of information previously not utilized as well as the capacity of gender analyses to generate relevant proposals for facilitating additional studies.

The establishment of Inmujeres and its budget programme has also opened up new spaces around the budget process for those NGOs and consultants who are able to respond to such openings. For example, some NGOs and consultants have entered into new relationships with government through delivering gender-budgeting training courses for government officials on behalf of Inmujeres. Inmujeres organized 16 workshops for 84 government officials from all ministries who had some responsibility for budgeting in 2003 (Instituto Nacional de las Mujeres 2004: 343). Also, close cooperation between the Health Ministry and NGOs led to the formation of a gender equity unit that both plans and monitors programmes within the health sector.

An outcome of these training sessions has been that Inmujeres, NGOs and consultants have gained valuable insights into the 'mind-set' of government officials and opportunities to contest such thinking about the gender impacts of budgets. Many government officials view the impacts of most government spending as being gender neutral. This has posed a great challenge to the success of the training and to the gender-responsive budget initiative. In one case a vociferous participant from the electricity commission would not budge from the argument that 'a light post is a light post, for men and women'. The facilitators pointed out that in Cuidad Juarez, where over 300 women, mainly maquiladora workers, have mysteriously disappeared or been killed, a key demand is for adequate lighting around the factories in the export processing zones. Other insights into the impact of gender differences in relation to the experience and perception of violence were obtained from the Ministry of Sport, which had noticed inexplicable rates of desertion and decline in the number of young girls participating in their programmes. It was suggested that, due to the violence, even rape, of young women in taxis known as *colectivos* and molestation on public transport, many parents were not willing to let their girls go into the street, let alone travel to sporting venues far from home. According to a National Survey on Violence, 70 per cent of women in Mexico have stopped going out at night (cited in Mejía Madrid 2004). The lack of public security has meant that many women in Mexico City are too frightened to venture into the streets, thus severely constraining their opportunities and lives. Violence towards women in Mexico is a factor that cannot be ignored when formulating and evaluating government programmes in transport, policing and infrastructure as well as health.

The government training and capacity-building courses have been an important awareness-raising strategy among government bureaucrats about specific conditions of women's lives and hence the non-neutral nature of most government expenditures. In particular, the Mexican gender-responsive budget initiative, through monitoring targeted spending on women's health, has pointed out the inconsistencies between the government's discourse on transparency and gender equity and its actual policies. The work of the gender equity unit in health, for example, resulted in the denouncing of right-to-life groups receiving funds for AIDS victims (referred to earlier) and the tracking of programmes and funds that had been earmarked to reduce maternal death rates, but had 'disappeared' in previous budgets.[7] The challenge, however, is to go beyond the prevalent idea among government officials that gender-responsive budget analysis only looks at expenditures earmarked for women and girls. Fostering transparency in the gender impact of all government expenditures is a necessary step for the Mexican gender-responsive budget initiative to ensure government accountability.

One of the objectives of the workshops has been to help participants fulfil their obligations contained in a budget amendment on transparency passed in December 2002 (Decreto Aprobatorio del Presupuesto de Egresos de la Federación para el ejercicio 2003, Artículo 54, fracciones I y IV). Ministries were asked to report the results of their programmes by October 15, 2003, using gender-disaggregated performance indicators as well as an analysis of the programme's impact on equity, equality and the welfare of women. The loophole in the legislation was that no sanctions were applied to those ministries that did not comply with the deadline. Even the members of the legislative budget committee for 2004 (90 per cent of whom are men) were not aware of the requirement, considerably weakening its enforcement. Nevertheless, the rationale and focus of gender-responsive budget training for government officials in 2003 arose from this law and these workshops went some way to countering the belief in gender neutrality. However, for the law to be used by the gender-responsive budget initiative some sort of sanction or official admonition may be necessary to ensure what Isabella Bakker calls the 'necessary power and authority relationships for accountability' (2002: 17).[8]

Inmujeres also sought to engage with the budgetary process by contracting consultants to draw up technical guides and develop analytical 'tool kits' to provide government ministries with frameworks and formats for reporting on the impact of their programmes and budget outlays on women and men. In 2003 Inmujeres' statistical unit used a standardized format designed to closely examine 21 service programmes (*programas con reglas de operacion*) operating with federal subsidies for their gender implications. The use of sex-disaggregated qualitative and quantitative performance indicators was proposed as part of the evaluation format (Instituto Nacional de las Mujeres 2003, 2004: 343). If this were implemented it would represent a key advance in fostering accountability that is in keeping with the strategy of many gender-responsive budget initiatives internationally of identifying performance indicators to provide evidence of the nature and beneficiaries of the transformation of gender relations. This strategy also has the potential to make connections with the performance budgeting reforms being introduced in Mexican budgetary processes.

Non-government organizations: accountability 'to whom' and 'for what'

The international experience points to the centrality of civil society groups in putting political pressure on governments to be accountable for the gender impacts of their budgets at various stages of the budget process. The new links forged with NGOs (and other independent institutions) under neoliberal globalism have been seen by some researchers as generating a fundamental shift in focus and re-alignment of accountability. Sonia Alvarez warns that, in the NGO world and increasingly in academia 'the privileged themes are determined by monies from international cooperation and the state' (1998: 16). Of concern here is to what extent Mexico's gender-responsive budget initiative, a current priority, represents the demands of a social women's movement for greater government accountability. Furthermore, what role have donors' money and their agendas of democracy, good governance and transparency (agendas now considered requisites for capital investment and development) played in shaping the politics of the Mexican initiative? Implicit in such questions are the broader concerns of transparency and accountability to whom and for what and how to achieve legitimacy when conducting gender-responsive budget exercises.

The gender-responsive budget initiative in Mexico has given rise to an upsurge of gender mainstreaming activity in limited circles of the bureaucracy, which has increased the accountability of the Mexican government for its international commitments to gender equality. However, the main non-government actors in this process – consultants contracted by Inmujeres and 'institutionalized' women's NGOs – can face significant constraints in their independence from government.

Some accounts of the gender-responsive budget initiative in Mexico have affirmed that there have been a range of actors involved including women's organizations actively engaged in advocacy (Hofbauer 2002: 63). However, this claim of diversity of actors in the Mexican initiative warrants further analysis because of the crucial role NGOs potentially play in the effectiveness of the initiative. Of particular interest here is the role of feminist-based NGOs in the Mexican gender-responsive budget initiative in fostering government accountability.

The feminist-based NGOs in Mexico (as opposed to multiple local and church-affiliated groups at the community level) emerged from grassroots feminist organizations in the 1980s. While they continue to have a strong identification with women's issues they no longer aim to build a mass autonomous women's organization. These feminist NGOs carry out a wide range of tasks from monitoring human rights and evaluating World Bank programmes to the construction of local health centres and training women to set up a cooperative or small business. Typically they are small, specialized organizations of professional women who receive their monies from international donors and are often used by government ministries as consultants.

Feminist NGOs in Mexico have undergone significant changes since the 1990s. During the 1980s, feminist NGOs in Mexico were involved in giving voice to the demands of working and marginalized urban poor women, part of the 'movimiento de las mujeres'. Today the presence of these feminist NGOs is maintained primarily through giving short-term courses on leadership or conducting surveys on the efficiency of poverty eradication programmes for the Mexican government, the World Bank or other international agencies.[9] Alvarez (1998) argues such institutionalization of the feminist movement in Mexico and the rest of Latin America has been a result of the minimalist state, characteristic of neoliberal economic policies, and the new policy agenda whereby governments are outsourcing their functions to NGOs, including evaluations of policies. She describes the consequences of this process for the women's movement as a loss to civil society:

> changing international donor and development policies, together with structural adjustment and the growing erasure of local States from the realm of social policy, may be propelling States and inter-governmental organizations (IGOs) to turn to some feminist NGOs as "experts on gender" rather than as citizens' groups advocating on behalf of women's rights.
>
> (ibid.: 1)

This loss to society may have implications for the effectiveness of the engagement of NGOs in gender-responsive budgeting. For example, the Mexican initiative has had limited input from grassroots women. The 'invited spaces' for political activity have been described as those being 'occupied by those grassroots and their allied non-governmental organizations that are legitimized by donors and government interventions' (Miraftab 2004). However this author points out that other 'invented spaces' exist that are 'occupied by the grassroots and claimed by their collective action, but directly confronting the authorities and the status quo'. Civil organizations in Mexico that are outside the 'invited spaces' have not participated in the gender-responsive budget initiative because most NGOs in Mexico today, including feminist ones, are not too far removed from the official structure of government.

One way of approaching legitimacy is to ensure that the transparency and accountability demanded of governments is also applied to NGOs on both the left and right of the political spectrum. In short, there needs to be greater clarity about the limitations of NGOs in representing women as they conduct their leadership courses, surveys and evaluations. There is reason to agree with Alvarez that there is nothing 'intrinsically wrong with feminist NGOs subcontracting their services as experts or executors of government programmes, especially when organizational survival and personal livelihoods are at stake' (1998: 16). However, the main strategy of the gender-responsive budget initiative has relied on an engagement between the institutionalized NGOs, government ministers and bureaucrats (Espinoza Damián 2004: 400). Governments must also be accountable to trade union women, poor and marginalized women and grassroots organizations. The voices of these women also need to be heard in relation to budgets. Debbie Budlender, drawing on the Southern African experience, suggests that one way of doing this is to conduct participatory research with their organizations and to encourage gender budget tools to be incorporated into their existing programmes and advocacy (2002: 83).

In the Mexican context there is little to be gained by nostalgically wishing for a vibrant, donor-free women's movement. The challenge is to engage critically with the government and those participating in the institutionalized spaces to make government accountable to the demands of all Mexican women across all social groups. This may have the advantage of contributing to policy advocacy and grass-roots organizing by making connections between gender budget analysis and the issues that bring people out into the streets in support (Borges-Sugiyama 2002: 33).

Contesting the macroeconomic strategy

Gender-responsive budget initiatives are a strategy for mainstreaming gender into macroeconomic policy, with fiscal policy as the entry point. It is argued that the integration of a gender perspective into fiscal policy through fostering efficiency and equity potentially promotes macroeconomic outcomes such as increased output in goods and services, greater participation in decision-making and reduced poverty (Commonwealth Secretariat 1999, Elson and Catagay 2000, Himmelweit 2002). However, the activities related to the gender-responsive budget initiatives in Mexico have been carried out within the dictates of the current government's economic policy framework. Gisela Espinoza describes this as 'concentrating on the part and ignoring the whole' (2004: 400). The macroeconomic policy frame-work and the economic theories that justify it have in the main been taken as given by most of the actors engaged in exercises related to gender-responsive budgets. While this has been the case for the vast majority of gender budget initiatives inter-nationally, our concern here is to examine the potential for greater scrutiny of macroeconomic policy in the context of neoliberalism in Mexico.

In Mexico, as in most developing countries, macroeconomic accountability under neoliberalism has been interpreted as the need to give a focus to 'the three Cs' of credibility, consistency and confidence, which reflect the needs of capital markets (Gill 1998). The Washington consensus outlined the means to foster such accountability for investment capital that included fiscal discipline in the form of balanced budgets, the introduction of user-pays principles and the privatization of government services.[10] In spite of the financial débâcle of December 1994, the ensuing economic crisis and the increase in the number of Mexicans classified as poor, particularly women and children, the official message has been that the macroeconomic policies of the Washington consensus are not flawed. The problem is defined as the corrupt environment that distorts policy implementation rather than the macroeconomic policy settings (Franco-Barrios 2003: 20).

In making the links with macroeconomic outcomes, gender-responsive budgets need to have as a core goal the widening of the governance and accountability structures of government by giving voice to those previously marginalized from fiscal policy decision-making (Bakker 2002: 12). The Australian experience demonstrated however that such budgetary accountability required considerable countervailing power on the part of women's groups and their allies (Sharp and Broomhill 2002). The difficulty of generating a greater voice for women in budgetary decision-making in many developing countries under neoliberalism should not be underestimated, as Isabella Bakker warns:

> the concentration of macroeconomic policy in the hands of central banks, finance and multilateral or bilateral donor agreements often 'locks out' elected representatives from key aspects of macroeconomic decision-making thus rendering them, ultimately, less accountable to poor people and women for these very international development commitments.
>
> (Bakker 2002: 13)

While taking the macroeconomic policy framework as a given is problematic for gender-responsive budgeting, the Mexican government also acknowledged the role of greater civil society participation and voice in the budget process and the increased fiscal transparency that this provided. For example, three days after taking office in 2000, breaking 50 years of hegemonic rule by the PRI party, the very first public decision of President Fox's government was to publish a Presidential Agreement to create the Inter-Ministerial Commission for Transparency and Against Corruption in the Federal Public Administration (World Bank 2004, Franco-Barrios 2003).[11] Known as the strategy of honest and transparent government, it established a 'homemade' index (IST) for evaluating government programmes for transparency.[12] In the international Corruption Perceptions Index 2002 Mexico ranks 57 out of a total of 102 countries (Transparency 2002). Some commentators give great credence to the strategy on the basis that the government was keen to improve Mexico's grades in both national and international corruption perception indexes as it was well aware that being denoted a high risk country was bad for business investment (Franco-Barrios 2003: 38).

Furthermore, the main political promises made by President Fox in his inaugural address were strengthening democracy, establishing a transparent and participatory relationship with civil society, and responsible control of public finances (Presidencia de la República 2001: 1).[13] Organized civil society groups responded positively to the political promises of the new government. Academics from the Centro de Investigación de Docencia Económica (CIDE) and Fundar (an NGO 'think tank'), for example, wrote manuals for popular audiences, gave training courses and carried out research on the budget (Guerrero and López 2000; Casar and Hérnandez 2000; Fundar 2000). While the external concerns took precedence over the government's objective to modify internal perceptions about its performance, transparency and participation discourses, nevertheless they created a climate that stimulated interest in, and opened spaces for, gender-responsive budget analysis.

One attempt to give voice to citizens of Mexico City that has provided some gender insights was a beneficiary survey by Cooper and Guzmán-Gallangos (2003). This study surveyed 1,500 people in Mexico City using face-to-face interviews, asking them to ascertain the benefits they received from different types of government expenditures.[14] The highest score was for education and public transport, with 35 per cent and 32 per cent of respondents respectively identifying these expenditures as having community benefits.[15] Relatively low levels of community benefit were perceived from outlays on finance for small businesses, aid to industry, public administration, national defence and electoral processes.[16] The main gender difference was in the ranking of 'benefits and assistance to poor families', with women more likely than men to indicate a preference for increased government expenditure in these areas. The use of beneficiary analysis by gender-responsive budget initiatives can contribute to greater government accountability by providing both an informed basis for change and a political agenda for policy makers. The survey revealed, for example, that public security was ranked in first place by all respondents, rich and poor, when asked where the government should be spending more money (ibid). This has the potential to provide broad political support for the government to do more in an area that traditionally significantly impacts on women.

Neoliberal budgetary accountability in Mexico has come with a concentration of power in the budget process and fiscal restrictions, both of which have limited the room for the gender-responsive budget initiative to engage in innovative manoeuvres (Fundar 2000, Cooper and Guzmán-Gallangos 2003, Espinoza Damián 2004: 400). The central planning authorities identify the programme objectives and actions, and money is allocated behind closed doors by the Treasurer and his functionaries. The centralization of policy formulation and institutional processes of economic governance tend to give more political weight to 'technocrats', 'that is neo-classical economists, financial administrators and central bankers, who may not be representative of broader societal interests' (Bakker 2002: 5).[17] Furthermore Mexican debt payments have severely restricted monies available for new programmes. By any standard, the $55 billion price tag attached to Mexico's bailout of the banks in 1999 was considerable (Mcquerry 1999) and an agreement was made to pay the annual cost of the rescue package out of each year's budget.[18] Between 1995 and 2000 an average of 16.6 per cent of total government expenditure was designated for financial services, similar to the total expenditure on education (Cooper and Guzmán-Gallangos 2003: 74). By 2002 58 cents of each revenue peso were earmarked for debt payments (mainly private bank debt taken over by the government) so only 42 per cent of total revenue was available for other budget items and subject to negotiation in that year (Pérez Silva and Garduño 2002).

While increases in the amount of money assigned to programmes do not guarantee that the target population benefits proportionally, restrictions in the amounts assigned or the transference of costs to the beneficiaries of a project undoubtedly limit the positive impacts of a project or action. As Gisela Espinoza Damián points out, insufficient funds allocated to public health do not guarantee the health of either men or women even in the event of gender equality in the distribution of the budget (2004: 400). In many cases issues of gender equality cannot be isolated from the need to increase the amount assigned public services and the redistribution of income. This issue is further illustrated by the Mexican government's policy of replacing the universalist approach to social security, health and education with user-pays models. This has taken place in a context where real wages have fallen drastically in the last decade with nearly half of the 'employed' Mexicans now in the informal, non-wage economy. As a result, large numbers of people cannot contribute to their own social security, health or education. This situation can be compounded by restrictions on access to the resources provided through the public budget. Focus group interviews with women in Mexico City have detected that due to the large demand for services many women are effectively being denied access. Incidents such as having to queue from 5 a.m. to get a number for a medical consultation, only to find that they have to come back the next day and try again because the numbers have run out, were commonly reported (Cooper and Guzmán-Gallangos 2003).

A survey of the impact of user-pays policies on women, analyzed using an index of marginalization for zones within the city, found that women at the two extremes of the socioeconomic spectrum were using targeted services far less than those in the middle. Only 0.5 per cent of the poorest compared to 1.9 per cent of the richest and 2.3 per cent in medium-marginalized zones reported using public childcare services (ibid.: 194). The better-off women had the means to pay for the private services, while the degree of marginalization of the poorest women is such that they often do not comply with the requirements imposed on the beneficiaries. In the case of government childcare centres, both washing one's children and disposable diapers are requirements for children to attend. A lack of available water means that poor children are not washed frequently and a lack of money means that disposable diapers are not available.[19] Even with their emphasis on participation, gender-responsive budgets cannot solve such systemic failures in service provision.

Nevertheless, neoliberal discourse on accountability for government services stresses that client–provider relationships through market transactions are the short, more direct route to accountability (World Bank 2004: 78). It is argued that clients experience first hand what is going on and can withdraw their custom if services are bad (ibid.: 64). But client empowerment (through consumption) relies on the assumption that articulated needs can and will be met (Davis *et al.* 1993: 199). If this is not the case then any demands of the poor for government accountability will fall on deaf ears. Allocation of resources among the poor rests on age-old classifications of deserving and undeserving, albeit in a more subtle form (Gordon and Spicker 1998, cited by Boltvinik 2004). Antipoverty programmes such as Oportunidades, in which all poor women are considered deserving, but not all poor men, use this moral approach. Furthermore, as one commenter notes, 'only those poor women who behave well receive this honourable classification which is earned by the sweat of their brow' (Boltvinik 2004: 18). Moreover, eligibility for a continuing place in the programme requires the women to fulfill certain community obligations. Additionally some mothers enrolled in Oportunidades report having been obliged to accept family planning methods if they wish to keep on receiving benefits (Escobar and Rocha 2002). In the Mexican context, however, in which citizens' basic socioeconomic rights once guaranteed by the Constitution have been replaced, in theory, by client power, poor women and men are likely to be excluded by such a macroeconomic framework. The political alternatives, or what the World Bank (2004: 48) terms the 'long route to accountability', are the space that gender-responsive budgets have yet to fully occupy. Gender-responsive budgets potentially expand the spaces for accountability, as these initiatives recognize that articulating needs is essentially a political issue of giving citizens a voice. Through making public the results of its evaluations and undertaking action research projects that enable women and their organizations to denounce the dysfunction and absence of public services, the Mexican initiative has had some impact on accountability by giving voice to women's concerns, including that of poor women.[20]

Conclusion

Gender-responsive budgeting is being enthusiastically embraced in Mexico as a result of the commitment of international donors and the development community as well as that of internal actors within civil society and the state. The three aspects of the Mexican gender-responsive budget initiative examined in this chapter show that the neoliberal context in which the Mexican initiative operates has provided both openings and restrictions in making the government accountable for the gender impacts of its budgets.

First, by utilizing the discourses and practices of transparency and performance budgeting, awareness of gender issues in national budgetary processes has been raised both inside and outside government. However this gender-based information and impact analysis has not systematically come with a capacity within government or civil society to enforce changes to budgetary decision-making. Second, the participation of NGOs has been a positive force in fostering gender-responsive budgeting. The neoliberal practices of outsourcing that have facilitated the growth of NGO consultancies in gender training and analysis also have the

218 *Jennifer Cooper and Rhonda Sharp*

potential to shift and dilute the government's accountability for gender equality. Accountability to civil society through the NGOs that represent it is in danger of being eroded as the increased collaboration of NGOs with the Mexican government makes it difficult for these NGOs to adopt a critical stance on government policies. Third, in a climate that is potentially far more democratic and sensitive to issues of accountability, the macroeconomic policy framework might be open to greater scrutiny. While these conditions do not guarantee the integration of a gender perspective in macroeconomic policy, fiscal democracy is unlikely to flourish without them. Macroeconomic policy success and accountability however has been defined in neoliberal terms of economic growth and maintaining credibility with global capital. Such a restrictive notion of accountability raises significant challenges for the gender-responsive budget initiative in Mexico. It requires, for example, a critical stance on the current neoliberal macroeconomic policies while simultaneously applauding the increased transparency in the current government's administration and performance budget initiatives. The dilemma is that the closer gender-responsive budget initiatives align themselves with these neoliberal conditioned frameworks the more problematic these gender justice initiatives become as a transformative mechanism. In order to maintain their transformative capacities and not be co-opted by neoliberalism, gender-responsive budget exercises will need to be vigilant in adapting their strategies and in critiquing budgetary policy, as well as proceeding with the development of new conceptual frameworks and theories of the economy and society.

Notes

1 The term 'neoliberal globalism' is used by Gerardo Otero (2004: 9) to refer to structural adjustment programmes, the Washington consensus and the New World Order. More recently, the term 'post-Washington consensus' has been used to describe a shift away from hardcore neoliberal policies to a recognition of the importance of institutions (including the state) and that persistent poverty cannot be eliminated through economic growth alone (Onis and Senses 2005).

2 Mexico's structural adjustment and stabilization policies of the early 1980s involved a major round of neoliberal reforms imposed by the World Bank and International Monetary Fund after Mexico declared a moratorium on the servicing of its large foreign debt. The country was required to restructure its economy to reduce the role for government and increase reliance on market forces for resource allocation. See Otero (2004) and Alvarez (2004) for a further discussion.

3 Accountability is a slippery concept and is used differently and applied with different meanings in the development, public administration and feminist economics literatures. In this chapter accountability is used as an umbrella term to convey a variety of ideas including a relationship (e.g. a financial relationship; a relationship with the power of enforceability; a performance relationship), issues of accountability (e.g. transparency, participation, answerability) and routes to accountability (market processes or political processes). For a discussion of accountability as a useful rubric see Bakker (2002), Goetz and Jenkins (2002) and World Bank (2004).

4 It is difficult to provide a precise estimate of the number of initiatives as the definition of what constitutes a gender-responsive budget initiative varies and it is difficult to get up-to-date information. Sharp (2005) builds on audits by Budlender (2002) and Rubin and Bartle (2005) and estimates that 62 countries had undertaken gender budget initiatives by 2004.

5 The history, methods and range of stakeholders involved in gender-responsive budget exercises in Mexico have been well documented by Helena Hofbauer (2002).

6   Further detailed accounts of other gender-responsive budget exercises by different NGOs are to be found in Espinoza Damián (2004) and Hofbauer (2002).
7   For an excellent and detailed account of this research see Freyermuth (2004).
8   The government might, for example, publish the results in a manner that identifies the complying and non-complying ministries in a way similar to that utilized by the Australian Affirmative Action Agency in the administration of the relevant legislation.
9   Alvarez describes this transformation of the role of the NGOs in relation to Sao Paulo's *favelas*. The description is also applicable to marginalized zones of Mexico City and rural areas.
10   Mexico and Chile have been described as the two Latin American countries that most faithfully followed the dictates of the Washington consensus (Estévez 2002). For example, between 1982 and 1990 approximately 875 or 76 per cent of all Mexican public enterprises were sold (Rogozinsky 1994). Between 1988 and 1999, countless macroeconomic programmes were introduced to continue liberalization. In spite of the signing of the North American Free Trade Agreement (initiated in January 1994) and a general optimism for the economic success of liberalization, Mexico suffered a devastating crisis in December 1994 and throughout 1995, when the peso devalued 100 per cent. The débâcle led to a massive bailout of the financial sector and the recommendations of the World Bank for a second generation of reforms. These were aimed particularly at making labour conditions and wages flexible along with the privatization of social security. 'Bad financial management' was the official cause of the 1994 crisis. Based on this analysis, the macroeconomic pillars of neoliberalism were left untouched (Dussel Peters 2000: 71), and in fact fortified, through the World Bank's recommendations to correct past policy distortions of liberalization.
11   In a climate where change was so desperately desired in Mexico, some on the left consciously advocated and exercized the 'useful vote' to help bring to office a president who was so obviously committed to big business and the Catholic Church. The rationale often presented was that after 50 years of the same party being in power any change was better than none at all.
12   These ideas have their origins in the early 1990s, when the 'General Programme for Simplification of the Federal Public Administration 1989–1994' was implemented. The broad aims of this programme were to empower citizens, deregulate public administration, build efficient institutions and strengthen social trust in government. Its specific objectives were oriented to: strengthen economic modernization; implement an administrative culture for improving efficiency and productivity in public management; fortify quality and transparency in public services; prevent and combat corruption; foster civil society's participation for improving trust in government; and implement public servants' performances based on honesty and efficacy (Franco-Barrios 2003).
13   These promises were detailed in the law for Transparency in the Use of Public Resources which was published in the government gazette on 11 June 2002 (el Diario Oficial de la Federación, 11 June 2002).
14   Responses were graded, with positive recognition being measured by the proportion of respondents nominating a reasonable amount or a lot of benefit in each outlay category.
15   A similar survey conducted in Australia by Withers, Throsby and Johnston (1994) using similar methodology found that 64 per cent of respondents felt that society received positive benefits from expenditure on education and 72 per cent from unemployment benefit outlays.
16   In the context of the Mexican government prioritizing external accountability of its fiscal policy, these survey results have important implications because the government is aiming to introduce fiscal reform to increase revenue from taxation. If the government is to obtain credibility for such a fiscal measure society must perceive that its taxes are being ploughed back to them as benefits. To some extent the low positive response rate obtained in the survey could be an indicator of the low level of credibility, and thus accountability, of the government.
17   The economist politicians in the Mexican government are a new breed of policy-makers who have studied in academic institutions in the United States. Since the government of Carlos Salinas de Gotari, nine out of nineteen ministers and the president were economists; five had earned their last degree in the United States. Furthermore the three main economic departments (budget and planning, treasury and finance) were all headed by economists who had done graduate studies at Yale and MIT (Poder Ejecutivo Federal 1989, cited in Dussel Peters 2000: 50).
18   The bailout of the banks was done initially without congressional approval. Due to the intensity of

the political debate, which held up the budget for nine months, the Zedillo government could not formally transform the costs of the banking sector rescue into public debt but an agreement was reached whereby the annual costs would be paid for by the government *in each year's budget*. The bonds issued by the FOBAPROA fund will be replaced by new ones that are tradable on the open market. The banks will hold the bonds, and the Mexican government will continue to provide the promissory guarantee (Mcquerry 1999).

19 These requirements result in an indirect payment for government services as does the need to buy pencils, uniforms, shoes and equipment to attend public schools. Lack of childcare restricts poor women's employment opportunities, which are consequently restricted to working at home or taking the children with them while they sell on the street or at the market. Furthermore other services such as obtaining water also absorb their precious time. Women who have to line up from 5 a.m. to obtain a coupon that will give them the right to a 'free' drum of drinking water do not have the time to queue again for a consultation number for a Pap smear. Under these circumstances few poor women use government services and they attempt to survive at the margin.

20 It is frequently assumed that poverty alleviation programmes including those related to gender equity have a positive impact. Obviously an injection of 20 thousand million pesos into the most marginalized zones of Mexico will have a positive impact. However the real issue is to question the basic assumptions and the theories behind these projects (Boltvinik 2004, Poder Ejecutivo Federal 1997: 29, Cervantes 2004).

References

Alvarez, Alejandro (2004) 'Mexico: Relocating the State within a New Global Regime', in Marjorie Griffin Cohen and Stephen Clarkson (eds) *Governing under Stress: Middle Powers and the Challenge of Globalisation*, London: Zed Books and Nova Scotia: Fernwood.

Alvarez, Sonia (1998) *Advocating Feminism: The Latin American Feminist NGO 'Boom'*. Available online, www.antenna.nl/~waterman/alvarez2.html.

Bakker, Isabella (2002) *Fiscal Policy, Accountability and Voice: The Example of Gender-Responsive Budget Initiatives*, New York: Human Development Report Office, UNDP.

Boltvinik, J. (2004) 'El oportunidades urbano evaluado', *La Jornada*, Viernes, 25 June.

Borges-Sugiyama, Natasha (2002) *Gendered Budget Work in the Americas: Selected Country Experiences*, Austin: University of Texas.

Budlender, Debbie (2002) 'Gender Budgets: What's in it for NGOs?', *Gender and Development*, 10: 82–7.

Casar, M. and Hérnandez, F. (2000) *Qué es el Presupuesto Federal*, Mexico: CIDE.

Cervantes, J. (2004) 'Asistencialismo, sello del foxismo: Boltvinik', *Diario del Sureste*, 14 October.

Commonwealth Secretariat (1999) *Gender Budget Initiative*, London: Commonwealth Secretariat.

Cooper, Jennifer and Guzmán-Gallangos, F. (2003) *Un Análisis Presupuestario con un Enfoque de Género*, Mexico City: Universidad Nacional Autonoma de Mexico.

Davis, G.; Wanna, J.; Warhurst, J. and Weller, P. (1993) *Public Policy in Australia*, 2nd edn, NSW, Australia: Allen & Unwin.

Dussel Peters, E. (2000) *Polarizing Mexico: The Impact of Liberalization Strategy*, London: Lynne Rienner.

Elson, Diane (2004) 'Engendering Government Budgets in the Context of Globalisation(s)', *International Feminist Journal of Politics*, 6, 4: 623–42.

Elson, Diane and Catagay, Nilufer (2000) 'The Social Content of Macroeconomic Policies', *World Development*, 28, 7: 1347–64.

Escobar Latapí, Agustín and Rocha, Mercedes González de la (2002) *Evaluación Cualitativa del Programa de Desarrollo Humano Oportunidades Seguimiento de impacto 2001–2002 Comunidades de 2,500 a 50,000 habitantes*, Mexico: Secretaria de Desarrollo Social.

Espinoza Damián, Gisela (2004) 'Presupuestos sensibles al género', in C. Rozo Bernal and M. Saleme Aguilar (eds) *Tecnologia y Finanzas en un Marco de Política Económica Sistémica*, México: Universidad Autónoma Metropolitana Xochimilco.

Espinosa Damián, Gisela; Paz Paredes, Lorena and Rodríguez, V. (1999) *Salud Sexual y Reproductiva en México: Los Programas, Los Procesos, Los Recursos Financieros*, Mexico City, Mexico: UAM Xochimilco.

Estévez, Dolia (2002) 'Rotundo fracaso del consenso de Washington', *El Financiero*, 22 July. Available online, www.clas.berkeley.edu:7001/Events/fall2002/09-26-02-journalists/estevez2.html.

Franco-Barrios, Adrian (2003) Building a Transparent and Honest Government in Mexico: Institutional Reforms and Anticorruption Policy, Paper presented at the CRC/CARR/Aston Business School joint workshop Risk Regulation, Accountability and Development, University of Manchester, Manchester, June.

Freyermuth, D. D. y G. (2004) *Muerte Materna y Presupuesto Público*, Mexico: Fundar.

Fundar (2000) *El ABC de Egresos de la Federación: Retos y Espacios de Acción México*, Mexico: Fundar.

Gill, Stephen (1998) 'New Constitutionalism, Democratisation and Global Political Economy', *Pacific Review*, 10, 1: 23–40.

Goetz, A.M. and Jenkins, R. (2002) Voice, Accountability and Human Development: The Emergence of a New Agenda, Background Paper for the HDR, Occasional Paper 2002/4, New York: Human Development Report Office, UNDP.

Gordon, D. and Spicker, P. (eds) (1998) *The International Glossary on Poverty*, London and New York: Zed Books, p 38.

Guerrero, J.P. and López, M. (2000) *Manual Sobre la Clasificación Funcional del Gasto Público*, Mexico: CIDE.

Himmelweit, Susan (2002) 'Making Visible the Hidden Economy: The Case for Gender Impact Analysis of Economic Policy', *Feminist Economics*, 8, 1: 49–70.

Hofbauer, Helena (2002) 'Mexico: Collaborating with a Range of Actors', in Debbie Budlender and Guy Hewitt (eds) *Gender Budgets Make More Cents: Country Studies and Good Practice*, London: Commonwealth Secretariat, pp. 84–97.

Instituto Nacional de las Mujeres (2003) *Manual para el Desarrollo de Indicadores de Evaluación con Perspectiva de Género*, Mexico City: Inmujeres.

—— (2004) *Resultados de la Evaluacion de la Incorporacion de la Perspectiva de Genero en las Reglas de Operacion de Programas con Subsidio Federal*, Mexico City: Inmujeres.

Mcquerry, Elizabeth (1999) 'The Banking Sector Rescue in Mexico', *Economic Review* (Atlanta, GA), 84, 3, July: 14–29.

Mejía Madrid, Fabrizio (2004) 'México violento, el miedo considerado como una de las bellas artes', *Proceso*, 1469, 26 December: 7.

Miraftab, Faranak (2004) *Invited and Invented Spaces of Participation: Neoliberal Citizenship and Feminists' Expanded Notion of Politics*. Available online, http://web.cortland.edu/wagadu/issue1/Miraftab.html>.

Organisation for Economic Co-operation and Development (OECD) (2001) *Best Practices for Budget Transparency*, Paris: Organisation for Economic Co-operation and Development.

Onis, Ziya and Senses, Fikret (2005) 'Rethinking the Emerging post-Washington Consensus', *Development and Change*, 36, 2: 263–90.

Otero, Gerardo (ed.) (2004) *Mexico in Transition; Neoliberal Globalism, the State and Civil Society*, London: Zed Books.

Pérez Silva, Ciro and Garduño, Roberto (2002) 'Destinó el gobierno en 2001 más de la mitad de su presupuesto a gasto corriente y deuda', *La Jornada*, 24 June. Available online, www.jornada.unam.mx/2002/06/24/006n1pol.php?origen=index.html.

Poder Ejecutivo Federal (1997) *Programa de Educación, Salud y Alimentación*, Mexico: Poder Ejecutivo Federal.

Presidencia de la República (2001) *Primer Informe de Gobierno México*, Mexico: Presidencia de la República.

Ramirez Cuevas, Jesús (2005) 'Provida al desnudo' , Suplemento Masiore, *La Jornada*, *Domingo*, 6 March: 7.

Rogozinsky, Jaques (1994) 'La privatizacion de empresas paraestatales: la experiencia de México', in J. Carreño and J. Ganas (eds) *Resumen de una Visión de la Modernización de México*, México: Fondo de Cultura Económica.

Rubin, M.M. and Bartle, J.R. (2005) 'Integrating Gender into Government Budgets: A New Perspective', *Public Administration Review*, 65, 3: 259–73.

Sawer, Marian (2003) *The Ethical State? Social Liberalism in Australia*, Melbourne: Melbourne University Press.

Sharp, Rhonda (2003) *Budgeting for Equity: Gender-Budget Initiatives within a Framework of Performance-Oriented Budgeting*, New York: United Nations Development Fund for Women (UNIFEM).

—— (2005) 'Engendering Budgets, Budgetary Reform and Sustainable Human Development' in *Transforming the Mainstream: New Goals and Strategies. Proceedings of the 9th International Interdisciplinary Congress on Women*, Ewha Women's University, Seoul, Korea, 22 June 2005, Seoul: Korean Women's Development Institute.

Sharp, Rhonda and Broomhill, Ray (2002) 'Budgeting for Equality: The Australian Experience', *Feminist Economics*, 8, 1: 25–47.

Transparency (2002) *Transparency International: Corruption Perceptions Index 2002*. Available online, www.transparency.org/cpi/2002/cpi2002.en.html.

Withers, G.; Throsby, D. and Johnston, K. (1994) *Public Expenditure in Australia*, Economic Planning and Advisory Commission Paper No 3, Canberra: Australian Government Publishing Service.

World Bank (2004) *World Development Report 2004: Making Services Work for Poor People*, Washington, DC: World Bank.

12 Transnational class and gender networking between the north and the south

Overcoming diversity or reproducing dependencies?[1]

Edmé Domínguez Reyes

The consolidation of our network Red de Mujeres Sindicalistas (RMSM) has been possible, in a large part, thanks to the solidarity of Canadian and other trade unions. The fact that we all are trade union members has been the strongest point in our relationship.

(Mexican leader of RMSM)

Introduction

Women's organizing, both at the local and global level, through transnational networking, has been a significant force in the resistance to global restructuring. For many of these movements in the periphery countries the issue is not the rejection of economic globalization as such but the reform and control of such a process by civil society. For female workers this involves the creation of international norms and mechanisms that can survey and guarantee worker and human rights.

Transnational organizing is particularly vital for workers connected to economic globalization and most of them in particular regions happen to be women. The gendered organization of labour also may affect the way this organizing is taking place, the issues involved in transnational networking, and the leadership styles. Although the entanglement of the identities of class and gender is often complicated, it also opens new possibilities for the creation of alternative labour organizations that reject the authoritarianism and patriarchal hierarchies that have traditionally plagued trade union organization. Transnational organizing opens new windows of opportunity with respect to new resources, new ideas and new ways of framing demands. However, transnational organizing also entails risks and raises obstacles that have to do with contextual, cultural, political, social and ideological differences between the people of different countries as well as their asymmetric access to resources. In other words, the transnational solidarity of labour networks, although positive in themselves, can become extremely complicated when put into practice.

This chapter explains how these transnational labour networks, specifically American and Canadian organizations supporting women workers in Mexico, can function. Some of the issues this chapter will try to deal with are:

Is transnational organizing among countries differently located in the global system, a valid strategy for strengthening local worker organizations in their fight against transnational capital?

How is gender implicated in these efforts of resistance?

Do transnational networks and their actions advance some notion of a global citizenship, particularly global regulations to protect individual and collective rights?

Global restructuring, resistance and global citizenship from a gendered perspective

NAFTA's designers did not anticipate that the process of regional integration would also provoke regionally based civil society resistance and organization. Resistance to regional and global neoliberal restructuring is directly linked to the way that one analyzes this process and to the national context of the movements in question. According to Suzanne Bergeron, in the current accounts of globalization there is a certain ambiguity regarding the power of global capital in relation to the state. While some authors suggest that global capital neutralizes the power of the nation-state, others contend that the state still has some power to manage national economies and protect weak sectors of the population. Debates about constraints on the national state in an era of globalization are important, especially with respect to political strategy and resistance (Bergeron 2001: 988–9). It is equally important, however, to take into account the position of each state within the international political economy. The strength of global capital or of the state depends on whether the state belongs to the so-called 'core economies', or to economies that are peripheral or semi-peripheral to the core (Ikeda 2004: 269). The strategies of resistance would thus differ: a state in the core economy may be as strong as transnational capital, making it necessary to combine a so-called 'national management' with a 'global imperative' approach. In contrast a state in the periphery with little power would perhaps require a strategy aimed at controlling transnational capital. In most cases a hybrid strategy that combines the struggle against the state with that against global capital will need to be articulated. But the optimal combination of action focusing on capital or the state will depend on the place of the state within the global order.

In the case of NAFTA, there are three states belonging to different zonal positions in the global system (ibid.: 264). The United States belongs to the upper core while Canada and Mexico would be part of the upper semi-periphery and upper periphery respectively (ibid.: 267). In this context Mexican and Canadian groups have been able to join forces in common efforts of resistance. The choice of joint strategies in this resistance will not be unproblematic, but the obstacles confronting coordination will not be as difficult to overcome as in the case of alliances between Mexican and American groups. This is in part due to their belonging to such different zonal positions in the global system.

Similar pre-conditions given by similarities of position in the world system and common concerns regarding transnational capital are important in the choice of joint strategies, but a number of other factors need to be taken into account. In the case of Mexico and Canada their different anti-NAFTA movements' general aims (the Canadian movement being anti-free trade and the Mexican movement works more for some sort of socially responsible regional integration) and industrialization experiences and levels (regarding their exposure to outsourcing for example) do challenge coordination of efforts. Among the central questions posed by coordination are the issues regarding 'ethical codes of conduct' for transnational corporations or the struggle for international rights regulation. Also to be asked is how and if the efforts should aim to make the state enforce already existing laws or to create new laws and regulations that can protect vulnerable actors such as workers and women. Another important issue has been how to empower civil society in the confrontation against transnational capital interests.

As we have seen, top-down integration schemes can also create the preconditions for regionally based social organization. That has been the case for feminist and women's transnational activities in the Americas. New efforts of resistance have emerged around the issues of global restructuring at the macro and micro level, although not all of them count on nor require transnational support and solidarity. At the local level this gendered resistance has often taken the form of community organizing, civic participation, demonstrations to demand services or protest budget cuts, survival strategies, strikes, trade union organizing, pressures on political parties, and so on. At the transnational level, this resistance has acquired a continental shape focusing on gender issues linked to free trade schemes in the Americas. Thus, women's organizations appeal to the shared responsibility of the state, transnational and international actors to defend and improve women's rights associated with a multiplicity of identities: as mothers, as workers, as consumers, as heads of households, as part of the political community. In this sense we could say that such demands and actions are part of a process of building some kind of 'global citizenship' or at least a 'regional' one.

Historically, the struggle for rights linked to citizenship has had two movements – from top to bottom and from the bottom to the top. Citizenship building from below has broadened the culture of rights so as to be recognized and protected. This affects both the type of rights and the spaces of the struggle. The local becomes global and vice versa (Vargas 1999). Every day we see examples of local movements, including peasant or indigenous movements 'going global' by taking their message and struggles to international forums and by the organization of 'global social forums' that include all kinds of movements with heterogeneous agendas. These global forums share the dual goals of the democratization of global decision-making and the demand of the recognition of human rights at the local, national and global space. This situation, however, raises several problems as to how to democratize this new global civil society to ensure that all groups have a say in the creation of new normative transnational systems and how to make these systems accountable to the demands of these groups. But even the creation of such systems is still an issue of debate among these groups.

According to Richard Falk, 'citizenship is tied to democracy and global citizenship should in some way be tied to global democracy, at least to a process of democratization that extends some notion of rights, representation and accountability to the operation of international institutions' (Falk 1994: 128). In this sense 'transnational militancy regarding the environment, human rights, women's rights, indigenous rights' associated with the rise of regional political consciousness would contribute to create a 'new global civil society' (ibid.: 138).

The workers' and the women's movements have shared for at least two centuries global aspirations for the recognition of their rights. Globalization or economic restructuring has updated the need to 'act globally' (Gita Sen quoted in Bergeron 2001: 995). In the case of the women's movement there is a growing literature presenting the experiences and possibilities of this kind of strategy that covers regional forums and world conferences on different issues, diverse thematic networks and even the transformation of powerful international organizations such as the UN, the World Bank, the International Monetary Fund or the World Trade Organization (Alvarez 1999, Marchand and Runyan 2000).

By trying to understand their choice of strategies in relation to their contexts (regional, national and local) and potential allies, we can examine how the different groups opposing globalization act. We can also assess the potentialities of these actions to influence the state, global capital and their own social orders to challenge existing power hierarchies. Concerted resistance can take the form of organized networks, exemplifying Falk's last image of global citizenship, with concrete agendas joining forces around a single issue or alliances with more long-term objectives and platforms. And in the case of women, resistance may involve going beyond the so-called 'practical demands' into the strategic ones transforming women's sense of individual and collective identity by questioning their roles and places within the household, the workplace and the community (Bergeron 2001: 999).

The issue of strategies regarding transnational alliances has been studied by several authors (Smith *et al.* 1997, Willets 1999). Keck and Sikkink develop the notion of *transnational advocacy networks*, TANs. These non-traditional international actors succeed in mobilizing information strategically to help create new issues and categories in order to persuade, pressure and gain leverage over much more powerful international actors. There is a double aim in this action: to influence policy outcomes and to transform the terms and nature of the debate. These network actors frame issues to reach broader audiences and to fit with favourable institutional values, and at the 'right moment,' they bring new ideas, norms and discourses into policy debates and serve as sources of information and testimony. They promote norm implementation by pressuring state actors, for example, but also pressure other kinds of actors like transnational companies or international organizations to adopt new policies, and they monitor compliance with international standards. Keck and Sikkink enlist a typology of tactics around information, symbols, leverage and accountability (1998: 16) by which these networks try to affect the practice of national sovereignty by blurring the boundaries between a state's relations with its own civil society and the recourse both citizens and states have to the international system to influence state behaviour (in a 'boomerang pattern'). Frequently these new transnational actors may go beyond the aim of policy changes to advocate fundamental changes in the 'institutional and principled basis of international interactions' (ibid.: 2).

TANs also can be considered as an instrument in the process of building a global citizenship: they help to create issues and set agendas, and they try to exercise influence on the discourses and behaviour of states, international organizations and on institutional procedures. Various grassroots movements within NAFTA concerned with many different issues provide examples of TANs. They can be considered two-way streets (rather than as networks) where partners enrich each other by their mutual experience, cross-fertilizing issues in order to be more effective, thereby connecting the issues of labour, indigenous people, women, refugees, the environment, and human rights.

However, transnational networking and cross-border mobilizing involve many challenges because there are inherent risks of dependency or asymmetry. Local NGOs and movements are typically dependent for funds on upper core to upper semi-periphery countries or international NGOs. Financing also involves conditions, imposed priorities, or imposed strategies, which the 'periphery' partners (be they NGOs or movements) may resent. This is especially true in the NAFTA case where asymmetries can obstruct transnational activism or make it more difficult and less effective, even taking solidarity as a compensatory factor (Cooper 2000).

Another problem affecting the collaboration between core and periphery or semi-periphery organizations is the difference of cultures and experiences that make the choice of tactics and strategies difficult. These differences are even noticeable among the groups in periphery countries. Such groups (whether NGOs, trade unions or networks involving both) show an enormous heterogeneity regarding goals, strategies and type of 'feminism,' if any. Moreover, international activism complicates heterogeneity by creating new kinds of hierarchies, with international activists at the top working from above and grassroots organizations or movements working from below, as Sonia Alvarez has exemplified in the case of the 'NGOization' of the women's movement in Latin America (Alvarez 1999: 182). On the other hand, as feminist (and other) NGOs become administrators of self-help, social service and training programmes, their critical advocacy potential becomes compromised (ibid.: 183).

Thus, in order to analyze and appreciate the potential of the new efforts of resistance of women workers taking place in periphery countries, we have to analyze the position of the countries involved within the global system, the position of these groups within their own countries, their potential conflicts with other sectors, groups and classes, the different interests, experiences and asymmetries among the movements and groups involved, their short-, middle- and long-term aims, and, consequentially, the potentialities or contradictions of the transnational advocacy networks they can build.

In the case of women workers' transnational networking, we also have to look at the effect of this networking on class and gender contradictions and to explore the potential of these struggles to advance the construction of a 'new global civil society' beyond the class and territorial origins of the liberal citizenship concept.

Transborder-tri-national organizing within NAFTA

Not surprisingly, an important part of transborder organizing between Mexico and the US has focused on maquiladora production due to the character of a typical export-free-zone process. In the maquiladoras, female labour has traditionally predominated although relegated to the less skilled and lower-paying production sectors.[2]

Although international labour and environmental activism existed long before NAFTA, particularly in the US–Mexico border area, where maquiladora production became the focus of this activism, NAFTA 'framed' this activism, giving different organizations a stronger motivation for organizing across borders.[3] American trade unions (particularly the AFL-CIO) pressed for an agreement on labour cooperation that together with that on environmental issues gave grassroots organizations an institutional framework towards which they could direct their demands. Such demands are presented to NAO (National Administrative Office), an authority created by the NAFTA to survey the labour parallel agreements. However, NAO's rulings are only recommendations to the respective state responsible of enforcing existing norms against employers and this has naturally proved quite ineffective.

The building of NAFTA opened the possibility of contacts among organizations between Canada and Mexico.[4] Women's groups in Canada had already started organizing seriously in 1984 around the first free trade agreement with the US and were very important actors in the Pro-Canada Network (Action Canada Network) during the massive national debate and election on free trade in 1988. In fact contacts between Mexico and Canada were already on their way since 1989 with visits from women representatives from the above mentioned organizations to Mexico who met with trade unionists, teacher and other women's groups.[5] At the beginning of the 1990s, these contacts multiplied in the form of invitations, training courses, conferences and sharing in a systematic way experiences and differences regarding economic restructuring and organizing (Gabriel and Macdonald 1994 in Domínguez 2002).

Transnational contacts in the area have flourished and many labour conflicts in Mexico have had the support of activists from both Canada and the US in the border area (Carr 2002, Bandy 2004, Williams 2002). However, 'outsourcing' – favouring cheap labour countries, like Mexico and Central America – initially resulted in protectionist positions from some parts of the American labour movement. These positions have nevertheless evolved in a more progressive way and as Ronaldo Munck depicts it, 'the international agenda of the trade unions has undergone significant renewal in recent years' (Munck 2002: 146).

The 'New Global agenda' produced by the 'Global Labor Summit' in 1997 called for alliances with NGOs – a position traditionally rejected by international trade unions – and for more attention to gender and a progressive approach to development issues. This agenda was also supportive of global networks for trade unions and even for integration shop steward organizations (Ibid). Following these lines the AFL-CIO moved into a certain internationalism, trying to support immigrants, supporting their appeals for amnesty (Staudt and Coronado 2002: 124), opening offices in Mexico and joining the border active Coalition Pro-Justice in the Maquiladoras (CJM) (see below). Similarly, the Canadian Auto Workers Union

(CAW) became active in transborder activism and as we shall see played a key role in organizing female trade unionists.

Case studies on transborder organizing[6]

Female workers historically have been neglected by worker organizations, especially by trade unions. Traditional trade unions are well known for their hierarchical and patriarchal structures from which female workers feel particularly alienated. If one adds to this the context of a Mexican strongly male dominated society with a long history of corporative and state controlled unions, we can see the kind of obstacles Mexican female workers have had to confront. Moreover, to organize workers along the Mexican–US border has always been rather difficult as the alternative to state-dominated unions have been a kind of 'white trade unions' organized by or in collusion with company managers, what Quintero calls 'subordinate unions' (Quintero Ramirez 2002). Such unions are not only oblivious to the rights of workers, but they also are particularly negligent of the situation of female workers. This is the context for the emergence of alternative organizations that advise and organize the workers to claim these rights through community grassroot work and transnational contacts. The following analyzes the organization and actions of an umbrella organization, a coalition called the Coalition Pro-Justice in the Maquiladoras (CJM) and two of its member organizations, Comité Fronterizo de Obreras (CFO) and Red de Mujeres Sindicalistas (RMSM). As will be shown, the CJM has developed its own profile that can be differentiated from those of the other two groups.

Coalition pro-justice in the Maquiladoras[7]

The CJM is a network that appeared in 1989 in the eastern part of the border between Mexico and the US and that, in 2004, officially housed some 180 organizations.[8] Initially CJM included about 40 groups, mostly American religious organizations, but also including environmental and some worker groups from the southern states of the US.[9] Among these organizations was the American Friends Committee that helped other worker groups, like the CFO (see below) to organize. Within Mexico the CJM also included several NGOs working with maquiladora workers. The creation of this network coincided with the beginnings of NAFTA and a time when American trade unions were becoming extremely suspicious of the implications of the treaty.

In 1991 the network decided to organize itself as a 'coalition', sharing principles, tactics and strategies. At the beginning, the concerns of these groups had to do mostly with health and environmental problems. Thus the most successful campaigns of CJM in this period were the condemnation of pollution and dangers that plants such as Stephan Chemical and Química Flour represented. The production of documentaries to illustrate these risks became an important tactic. For example there was the documentary produced in 1992 'Stephan Chemical: Poisoning of a Mexican community' and the documentation of health risks for women workers employed by maquiladoras using dangerous toxics, which was dramatically documented in the Discovery Channel's in 1995 production, *Toxic Border*. With the inclusion of Mexico in NAFTA, the CJM's focus started to change to labour issues, but labour security and health as well as sexual harassment continues to be an ongoing part of the CJM's organizational focus. Also, from the beginning, CJM has attempted to influence corporations investing in Mexico through their shareholders, and by encouraging corporate responsibility. Religious orders and others have been encouraged to invest their money in responsible corporations and to try to attend and influence shareholder meetings. It has had some success in changing Mexican worker conditions through these tactics (Staudt and Coronado 2002: 122–3).

The CJM started to participate in labour conflicts for the first time in 1993. This was a conflict involving the firm Kemet. Their most important involvement, however, was in the Sony conflict in Nuevo Laredo in 1994 in which the workers tried to get an independent and representative union. In this conflict we see for the first time the coordination of several of the CJM's NGOs, including American Friends Service Committee, the International Labor Right Education, and the Asociación Nacional de Abogados Democráticos (Mexican National Association of Democratic Lawyers). The case was presented to the National Administrative Office, NAO, which made some recommendations to the Mexican government. Although these were not successful, (they rarely are) the company finally agreed to respect the workers' basic rights to organize. In other cases where the CJM got involved, like with disputes with Ford Motor Company, Zenith, Alcoa and Custom Trim, the results were not as successful and sometimes led to the closing of plants.[10] Since 1994, the CJM has documented and supported diverse cases of workers demanding their rights from the enterprises employing them. By 2002, there had been 23 different cases of support of Mexican workers involved in diverse conflicts, with variable results.[11]

The CJM had to pay attention to womens' rights from the beginning because over 60 per cent of the workers in the maquiladoras were women.[12] According to its general director Martha Ojeda, most activities including several workshops and courses were specially focused on a gender perspective. Moreover, within the CJM's board in 1992 15 were women.[13] The president of the CJM, who has held the job since 2001, is a woman, Rosario Ortiz from Red de Mujeres Sindicalistas de México (Network of Union Women in Mexico) (RMSM), as is the executive director, who has held the position since 1996. Both have a background as workers and, in the case of the president, as a trade unionist and feminist.

However, as in many popular organizations (with the exception of feminist organizations), in the CJM women's rights are contemplated mostly as part of general demands and are not given priority unless the strategy requires it and even then other identities, as a worker, as a wife or as a mother, are often emphasized. For example, in the campaign that led to the Discovery Channel's documentary, *Toxic Border*, the focus was on the effects of chemical contamination that resulted in birth defects in the children of female maquiladoras workers who had come in contact with chemicals while pregnant. Thus the emphasis of the campaign was on environmental damage on women workers' health as mothers.

Another example was the campaign organized by Human Rights Watch (HRW) in 1998 to denounce compulsory pregnancy testing in the maquiladoras. The CJM (as well as member local organizations like the CFO described below) was involved in gathering the information on which the campaign was based. This was a typical case of a transnational advocacy network strategy that involved lobbying at different levels within both Mexico and the US and resulted in recommendations to stop these compulsory pregnancy tests. Although ineffective in the case of the Mexican government, the campaign did affect the conduct of several corporations (Domínguez 2002: 227–8). Part of the success may have had to do with the focusing on human rights and not so much on women's rights. Thus, as in *Toxic Border,* the emphasis was again on the women workers' rights as potential mothers, their right not to be discriminated against because of pregnancy, not on their right to privacy. Also the fact that such a well known transnational organization such as HRW had the lead may have contributed to this success.

The CJM has also sponsored several courses, workshops and general training that focus on women workers. For example, in 2003, it organized two workshops: one designed to teach women skills related to collective bargaining and workers' rights, and another that focused on harassment and sexual discrimination. The latter was organized by the RSMS, Rosario Ortiz' organization, in Ciudad Juárez. In 2004, the CJM co-sponsored a 'Workshop on Gender and the Global Economy' in Mexico City together with public services workers unions, Reabock Workers, and Colectivo Feminista de Tijuana, Servicio, Desarrollo y Paz, SEDEPAC and others (CJM 2004). Although the emphasis within these courses was on women as workers, other less traditional foci such as leadership and gender equality have been encouraged.

The CJM's general activities on women's rights is complemented by some of the grassroots CJM's member organizations. One of them is the recently created (March 2004) Colectiva Feminista Binacional (Bi-National Feminist Collective), a NGO that organizes activists around women worker issues in the region of Tijuana, Mexico and California, USA. Most of these activists are Mexican or of Mexican origin and some of them previously belonged to another organization that was a member of the CJM from the beginning, Factor X.[14] The latter organization had worked since 1993 in the defence of labour-gender related rights among maquiladora workers but it was dissolved in 2004. According to Carmen Valadez, one of the founders of both Factor X and Colectiva Feminista Binacional, Factor X disappeared because of organizational and financial problems. Theirs was a typical case of dependence on international financing that affected their work in rather negative ways. It was not only a question of priorities being decided by the financing agencies, but also of the need to constantly search for new financial sources. This took a significant part of their time and energy that otherwise would have gone to their projects.

> We want to break away from this dynamic and instead focus on what we really want to do, what we think is important for the defence of women labour rights at the maquila, in order to train them, to support the women working at the

community level, to create spaces where we can be creative, to speak of the issues we are interested in … sometimes we start our meetings speaking about how we feel, what personal problems we have, something we had not done before because we were forced to accomplish what the financial agencies were expecting of us … [15]

Factor X joined with other women-focused organizations like SEDEPAC in an informal network of female workers in the maquiladoras. These groups have organized a number of workshops on labour health, reproductive health and sexual rights. They try to link the safety risks in the maquiladoras to the control the plants want to have on women's sexual life and reproductive rights and to convince all worker organizations to introduce a woman's perspectives in their struggles. In 2002/3 they created a national school for labour and gender rights promoters that had participants from diverse organizations from several northern states in Mexico. They have also contributed to different regional and national campaigns against gender violence, and some focused specifically on the case of women murders in Ciudad Juarez.[16] All these activities have benefited from transnational contacts.

The groups like SEDEPAC and other womens' and feminist groups within the CJM, in contrast to their umbrella organization, do not restrict the struggle to the role of women as workers or mothers but broaden their perspective to encompass women's other identities, such as their roles as community leaders and activists. Their vision tends to grasp the whole reality and not only labour or health aspects and they try to link their personal development to the realization of their projects and activities illustrating the connection between the private and the public. Generally they reject forming a dependent relationship with transnational allies and try to maintain certain independence in their activities. Apart from this gender perspective the CJM during the last ten years has gone from an American coordinated NGO that was distrustful of trade unions to a process of 'Mexicanization' and trade union orientation. This process began in 1997 when for the first time 50 per cent of its board came from Mexican organizations. This trajectory toward Mexicanization advanced further after a historic meeting with several independent Mexican organizations in Ciudad Juarez, Chihuahua, Mexico in 1999 when a new kind of collaboration between the Mexican groups and the CJM began.[17] Another key development in this collaboration and the CJM's transformation was the election of Rosario Ortiz, the main coordinator of the RMSM, to the presidency of the CJM. Rosario Ortiz combined key traits that would affect the renewal of the CJM, particularly a long experience of trade union organizing within the telephone industry, and an equally long feminist activism, first, with MAS (Mujeres en Acción Sindical) and then with RMSM. Thus, the CJM not only enriched its Mexican affiliation but also its trade union contacts and gender perspective. Perhaps, not surprisingly, the discourses also began to change, from a human rights-solidarity tone to a more labour rights-class centred emphasis.[18]

The Comité fronterizo de Obreras (Border Committee of Women Workers) (CFO)

The CFO, a labour organizing NGO, started its activities in the 1980s as an initiative from a member of the American Friends Service Committee (AFSC) within their programme on Peace and Justice. Within this programme, different projects aimed at improving the situation of workers are deployed in diverse countries with the intent that they would eventually be taken over by local organizations. Designed initially as a research project, it led to the formation of a Mexican NGO that would deal with the problems affecting women workers in the maquiladoras. Developing their contacts transnationally, they joined forces with American trade unions, like the United Steelworkers of America, the United Auto Workers, the United Electrical Workers, and several Canadian trade unions. According to CFO's main coordinator, Julia Quiñonez, the strategic alliances with diverse organizations abroad are very important for them, 'but it is equally important for the CFO to be respected, that is to say, that international allies cannot impose their programmes or agendas'.[19]

The CFO chose to work at the educational level, advising workers on their rights and possibilities for action against employers through door-to-door visits at the workers' houses. This tactic is generally favoured by alternative organizations and more suited to reach female workers than is work-place activism. Although not claiming to have an explicitly feminist agenda, the CFO, according to Quiñonez, started as a women's movement.[20] The organization claims to enhance the 'participation of women workers in the process of renewing and reforming male-dominated unions to become more alert and responsive to the concerns of women workers'. However, as in the case of the CJM, the CFO's aims are not particularly centred on women's issues but on the usual demands of maquiladora workers regarding salaries, benefits and profit-sharing as well as the protection of health, life and welfare (CFO 1999).

The CFO, like the CJM, works both locally and globally. At the local level, within the neighbourhoods, it informs women on their rights and encourages them to organize and gather information on abuses to determine how to confront managers. It also provides workshops on labour, environmental and women's rights in order to form 'discreet, well organized, well advised, self developed movements of women workers' (Ibid). At the global level, it uses its transnational contacts, particularly within the NAFTA area, as in the case of the HRW campaign, to stop pregnancy testing in the maquiladoras. This alliance, which is a typical case of a transnational advocacy network, was regarded by the CFO as rather successful.[21]

Like the CJM, the CFO is also in a process of 'Mexicanization' and 'trade-unionization'. According to Quiñonez, the CFO has started to focus on advising workers as to how to reform the existing trade unions or how to create new independent ones.[22] The process of strengthening links with Mexican organizations is also under way: a pact has been established with the Unión Nacional de Trabajadores (UNT), one of the biggest coalition of trade unions in Mexico and with other national trade unions.[23] Also, since the new millennium, the CFO's board has been composed only by Mexicans.[24] However, relations with other border organizations, like the CJM, have sometimes been conflictual.

The CFO joined the CJM quite early after the latter's creation and was active in CJM's campaigns. But according to the CFO leadership, the CJM started to favour rather radical and confrontational tactics in contrast to the preferences of local organizations like the CFO, who favoured more moderate activities (such as courses and workshops).[25] These differences between both organizations became clear during the 'Duro' conflict in Rio Bravo. In this case, a majority of the workers tried to organize an independent union to replace the official one that already existed within the enterprise. As in previous cases, the Mexican labour authorities tried to stop the registration of this new union thus provoking the reaction of the CJM as well as the Canadian organized Maquila Solidarity Network, which supported the protesting workers. According to Martha Ojeda from CJM, Duro was an example of a broad and successful coordination of efforts of NGOs and trade unions that involved tactics such as lobbying the American Congress and presidency and even with the Mexican presidency, initiating an information campaign of 25 American and Canadian cities, establishing contacts with consumer groups, providing information to shareholders, coordinating actions with Mexican lawyers, and putting pressure on Mexican authorities.[26] In other words it was a vivid example of a transnational network that focused on information and lobbyism. But according to the CFO the CJM's aggressive tactics led to violent confrontation between the new and the old trade union activists. Moreover the all-too-evident engagement from American activists (acting on behalf of the CJM) was used as a propaganda weapon that nourished traditional anti-American feelings against the new trade union. At the height of the conflict representatives of the company contacted the CFO and asked them to intervene in order to neutralize the CJM's influence. The CFO rejected the offer as they did not want the conflict to grow deeper.[27] Even within the CJM, afterwards, there were critical voices of the involvement and imposing style of some of the American organizations.[28] The conflict did not have a positive outcome in the sense that the new union failed to achieve representation of the workers and the enterprise closed.

As we can see, this may be a case of counterproductive transnational support. Different views and perspectives on tactics among and within the different organizations involved contributed to a negative outcome. Moreover, as a consequence of this experience and other factors, key member organizations of the CJM like the Maquiladora Solidarity Network and the AFL-CIO as well as the CFO chose to have a discrete profile and decided to participate no longer in the CJM's events, even if officially they continued to be considered members.[29]

The CFO for its part 'became very selective as to their links with foreign groups' and even designed certain criteria on how to mould their relations with those groups. Such relations are 'to be reciprocal and egalitarian but also respectful of processes and times'.[30] This conflict reflects both the asymmetries and the difference in cultural contexts, in mentalities, principles and goals that result in disagreements regarding tactics and strategies between organizations from different countries but even among national groups. Obviously this challenges the effectiveness of transnational networking and alliance making. The information shared is interpreted in different ways and thus the framing of the issues is difficult if not often unsuccessful. The problem may also be related to the nature of the organizations involved: trade unions have been depicted as part of the old social movements while NGOs represent in part the so-called 'new social movements' that 'stress their autonomy from party politics and prioritize civil society over the state' (Munck 1999: 9).[31] But perhaps the collaboration among the same kind of social movements may be less problematic?

Transnational collaboration at the trade union level: the case of the RMSM (Red De Mujeres Sindicalistas de México) (Network of Union Women of Mexico)

A different example of a transnational regional network is the result of a long-term and well established form of solidarity. This is the case of the RMSM and its long-term cooperation with the Canadian Auto Workers Union (CAW). In a similar way to the CFO-AFSC case, this involves the influence of an external organization in order to develop feasible strategies of resistance through new organizations. However, in this case (and in contrast to the CJM and CFO examples) the CAW-RMSM network focused on the transmission of strategic capabilities for female trade union members organizing from a *feminist* workers' perspective. And these strategic capabilities in the case of Mexico are particularly relevant because they focus on changing the deep patriarchal structures that are present in all kinds of unions, even in the independent and worker-committed ones.[32] As already noted, most unions in Mexico fall into the corporatist model although some independent unions survived, and it was among the latter that the resistance movement against NAFTA found a base. It is among these independent unions that a limited organizing of female workers started to take place in the mid-1990s.[33]

The Canadian–Mexican trade union cooperation began as a result of the contacts made at the second national conference of women workers organized in Oaxtepec in October 1995 with representatives of the Canadian Labour Congress (CLC) and the Canadian Auto Workers Union. These contacts led to a long-term exchange and collaboration that resulted in several leadership and consciousness raising courses. The result was the creation of the Red Mexicana de Mujeres Sindicalistas de Mexico (Mexican Network of Union Women) (RMSM) in March 1997 with 52 members and a coordinating committee drawn from eight participating unions.[34] The unions represented in this network are among the most important in Mexico, including those within the UNT (Union Nacional de Trabajadores) and telephone and electricity workers' unions. This cooperation also provided the opportunity for 70 women from 14 different unions to find new ways of working within their unions, to learn how to establish international contacts by themselves (avoiding NGO mediation) and to discuss such issues as codes of conduct, sexual harassment and proportional representation of women in union executives (Cooper 2000: 7).

In contrast to the case of other NGOs born with American support, the Canadian collaboration developed 'according to the demands of the Mexican side' (CAW 1998). It was based on the feminist workers' perspective building on the triple identities as worker, woman and unionist. For example trainers were worker facilitators instead of academic experts. Moreover, this was a long-term alliance, a 'commitment of the CAW union members to a longer term relationship with the Mexican unionists, rather than one-time project funding' (ibid.):

> the shared identity of being trade-unionists gave us strong links with both the Canadian Labour Congress and with the CAW. The projects the RMSM presented to the CAW coincided with their aims and ways of working. This has been extremely important to consolidate the relationship and make it rather symmetric.[35]

However becoming a formalized network and getting officially registered as an association gave the RMSM the status of an NGO and this was problematic, given RMSM's criticisms of NGOs whom they considered 'coopted' by the political system. Moreover, according to RMSM's members, NGOs' dependence on international financing made them sacrifice their goals and links with grassroot movements.[36] There was also the question of political differences regarding strategies and tactics of feminist NGOs working with labour issues. These differences had already led to a rupture between many of the RMSM organizers and MAS, Mujeres en Acción Sindical (Women in Trade Union Actions) shortly after the meeting that started the collaboration process with the Canadian unionists in 1995.[37] In this context it was difficult for the RMSM to accept CAW financial support. Such financing was finally accepted because it came from another union and would be used as 'seed money' on the understanding that it had to raise the rest itself in order to consolidate its work (Cooper 2000: 14).

The alliance CAW-RMSM did achieve what Keck and Sikkink call a 'boomerang pattern' (Keck and Sikkink 1998: 12–13). Through its foreign network associates, this Mexican women's-cum-feminist organization has been able to legitimize and thus strengthen their demands in relation to their own 'patriarchal' union leaderships. They have organized campaigns on labour–human rights, against labour violence and sexual harassment and cooperated with the Mexico City government in order to create special centres for women workers suffering from workplace related problems.[38] According to their coordinators, the RMSM has created spaces of its own in nearly all the trade unions belonging to the network and has been able to extend its work and organizational contacts to other southern states within the country, especially Oaxaca and Chiapas. In other words, the seeds planted by foreign cooperation have enabled the RMSM to consolidate as an independent organization and to establish a long-term-solidarity relationship aimed at structural changes of gender relations within the workplace and within trade union's structures.

Nevertheless the impact of the RMSM in the trade union environment at large in Mexico is still limited and its range of influence varies very much from trade union to trade union. On the other hand most trade unions have accepted the legitimacy of equality programmes and other female workers' demands within their general aims – something to which the RMSM has contributed. The RMSM has been associated with CJM since 1997 and it has played an important role in the CJM's progress towards 'trade unionism' and 'Mexicanization'. As already noted, RMSM's leader Rosario Ortiz became President of the CJM by 2002 and this also contributed to a certain feminist orientation within the CJM. The link with RMSM also permitted the CJM to extend its work in the South of Mexico following the maquiladoras' trail in search for even cheaper and more docile labour.[39] By joining the CJM the RMSM acquired the border, maquiladora perspective that reinforced the RMSM's globalist dimension.

Reflecting on the problems involved in transnational networking, Rosario Ortiz points to the significance of differences in political cultures. The American political culture has privileged lobby work by labour organizations both within the public sphere and at the enterprise level. Mexican labour activists rule out such lobby work as ineffective because the Mexican political culture has traditionally been authoritarian: corporativism has predominated and legislative representatives have never been responsive to public demands. This creates important differences as to choice of tactics and strategies but also creates enormous disappointments when the tactics applied elsewhere do not work as expected. The case of DURO was, according to this leader, an illustrative example. Another is the case of Custom Trim where workers from this company in Matamoros and Valle Hermoso testified about the health consequences from the use of dangerous chemicals and other risky production activities. These testimonies were documented in a report from the NAO in a complaint put together by 25 different organizations including the CJM. However, this action failed to make the Mexican government comply with the recommendations to satisfy the demands of the workers.[40]

According to Ortiz, divergences are not only North–South but exist even among the northern parts of the CJM. The AFL-CIO had important differences with the CAW and the Canadian Labour Congress as to the way to visualize solidarity. While the AFL-CIO linked solidarity to their members' interests, for the Canadian organizations solidarity was conceived as a long-term project not necessarily linked to their own concrete needs. There were, however, according to this leader, differences between the AFL-CIO central leaders and some of its member organizations with which the RMSM has had good relations and experiences.[41]

But even within the South cooperation may be problematic. For example, the RMSM contributed to the gender platform of the Hemispheric Social Alliance[42] but the RMSM's aim to create a Latin American network of women unionists proved to be more difficult. According to Ortiz, they had contacts with women within the Brazilian Central Unica dos Trabalhadores (Workers Unified Trade Union) (CUT) as well as unionists in Argentina and Uruguay but coordination of efforts did not solidify. Even cooperation within Central America was regarded as difficult because it entailed cooperating with NGOs and because of the codes of conduct for enterprises issue. Such codes of conduct, according to Ortiz, are tactics based 'on a moral discourse in which the capital–labour relationship is addressed

in a superficial, 'light' way'. Moreover, such tactics cannot become long-term strategies if they are not translated into 'class positions'.

> We in the CJM, speak of democratizing the relationship capital–labour. The
> problem is how to implement that. A tactic cannot become a strategy because
> at a certain moment this tactic will lead you into a confrontation in the rela-
> tionship capital–labour. The problem is how do you build within this sector
> [maquiladoras] workers a new vision regarding trade unions – because even if
> I myself struggle against the corporative trade unions I still believe in a new
> kind of trade union.[43]

Thus the RMSM-CAW illustrates the case of long-term solidarity established on
the basis of trade union links and based on a commonality of goals and principles as
well as on a reciprocal and symmetric cooperation. The tools the RMSM obtained
from this collaboration permitted it to become a new actor within the struggle of
women workers' rights in Mexico, striving to change structural oppressive conditions in the trade unions where they are active. However, even this organization's
experience of transnational networking shows asymmetry problems as well as fric-
tions in the collaboration with NGOs – not the least regarding tactics and strategies
and general views on aims. For example, there are clear differences regarding trade
union organizing and eventually establishing international legislation regarding
enterprises against codes of conduct.[44]

Concluding remarks

From the experiences presented here, we can conclude that transnational organizing has become an important part of the resistance efforts that workers linked to
export industries – but also to other kinds of industries – have developed in their
struggle against global capital and the restructuring of labour relations. Alliance-
building among groups in NAFTA countries has helped to create and inspire new
local organizations, that, in the case of Mexico, have definitely given new resources
to female workers and have contributed to organizing in relation to their needs
both as workers and as women. Of course, this has varied from organization to
organization. In the border areas, the two organizations discussed in this chapter,
the CJM and the CFO, have focused on more traditional identities associated with
female workers presenting them as mothers affected by the lack of safety, for
example, in campaigns around environmental problems provoked by maquiladora
production. However, even other rights' violations associated with female sexuality, such as sexual harassment and salary discrimination, have been campaign
issues. Several of these alternative labour organizations have female leaders and
the trade unionization process within CFO and CJM seems to point towards new
forms of trade union organizing that is more strongly oriented to the grassroots and
more responsive to female workers' demands and interests. In the case of the CJM,
we are seeing more prominence given to feminist member organizations whose
actions of resistance are also crossing the public–private divide and trying to

challenge patriarchal structures in society. This is even more the case with RMSM where feminist trade unionism is setting new standards in some of the key trade unions in Mexico. Thus, transnational organizing is opening new alternatives for female workers in Mexico, but it is also giving organizations in all three countries new ideas and weapons of resistance.

There remain, however, serious problems that hinder this transnational collaboration. This is particularly true of the NAFTA countries where the position of each country has influenced the kind of collaboration established within these networks. An upper periphery country like Mexico seems to have fewer problems of collaboration with a semi-periphery country like Canada at the level of organizations than with a core country such as the United States (with the exception of organizations like the CFO). National asymmetries are reflected in transnational organizing, given the unequal distribution of resources among the participants. Differences in background experience, regional context (not only relating to national divides but also within the same country as in Mexico), political culture, and political and ideological positions may provoke serious problems in forming a consensus around local tactics. Institutional frames are also important – especially the relationship to state structures, which are so radically different among the NAFTA countries. These problems seem to be aggravated by the crisis facing the maquiladora border production in Mexico where corporations are always looking for cheaper and more flexible labour.

The opinions and other facts presented here also confirm that a 'hybrid approach' in organizing plus a recognition of the 'zonal membership' of the countries involved is always useful when strategizing to take into account the local, the regional and the global. All levels of political and economic life are intrinsically interrelated affecting each other continually.

Ultimately in question is the notion of global norms of regulation regarding labour. Can workers' rights be part of such a notion of global citizenship? It is difficult to give a definite answer to these questions but the opinions of the RMSM and RMALC's leaders regarding norms of conduct as against international legal regulations seem to confirm that the debate is part of their concerns.

Finally, the lessons of these experiences are mixed. We can observe a difficult process of transnational resistance that is only beginning. This resistance has to transcend multiple divides but shares a belief in the need to achieve a fairer social order beyond borders and beyond gender oppressions.

Notes

1   This paper is part of a research project on women and NAFTA by Edmé Domínguez and Cirila Quintero, 'Transnational Networking around Free Trade Issues Seen by the South: The Experience of Mexican Organized Women Workers'. It was funded by SIDA-SAREC, the Swedish International Development Agency, during 2004–06.

2   'Maquiladoras', foreign owned 'off-shore assembly plants' that appeared during the 1960s along the Mexico–US border can nowadays be found everywhere in Mexico. Women represented about 100 per cent of labour in this sector in the 1970s but diminished to 55 per cent in 2000 (Quintero 2002). Since the mid-1980s male recruitment has increased in several sectors and regions of

maquiladora production. Males are preferred to women as technical workers marking certain trends of de-feminization (De la O Martinez 2004: 85).

3 During the NAFTA negotiation, several sectors, particularly trade unions, contacted each other in order to have input into this process (Carr 2002, Macdonald 1999, Staudt and Coronado 2002).

4 With the help of Canadian organizations RMALC (Red Mexicana Frente Al Libre Comercio) was created.

5 Information from Marjorie Griffin Cohen (2004) who was at the time co-chair of the Pro-Canada Network and a Vice-President of NAC.

6 The following sections are based on interview material gathered during 2002 and 2004/5.

7 Part of the material used in this section regarding the CJM comes from Domínguez and Quintero (2005).

8 Consulted, online < www.haleokal.com/cjm > (accessed May 18, 2004), and interview with CJM's director, Martha Ojeda, July 30, 2002.

9 Interview with CJM's director, Martha Ojeda, November 2004.

10 Various interviews and CJM's year reports.

11 Interview with CJM's director, Martha Ojeda, July 30, 2002.

12 By 2002, according to INEGI's figures, female workers accounted for 54 per cent of maquiladora labour force. See also De la O Martinez 2004: 73.

13 Interview with CJM's director, Martha Ojeda, July 30, 2002.

14 Interview with Carmen Valadez, *Colectiva Feminista Binacional,* Rio Bravo, November 2004.

15 Ibid.

16 About 400 murders of women have taken place in Ciudad Juarez (Northern border), Chihuahua since 1993 and in spite of national and international protests very little has been done to find the murderers or to take care of the families of victims.

17 Interview with Juan Manuel Sandoval, representative of RMALC, a member organization of CJM, December 2004.

18 Ibid.

19 Interview with Julia Quiñonez, E-mail (November 2001).

20 Ibid. According to Quiñonez, the CFO is very inclusive and is accepting men in the organization given the fact that the proportion of women in the maquiladoras is diminishing.

21 For a complete account of this campaign see Domínguez 2002; and online, available www.hrw.org/reports98/women2/ > (accessed November 25, 2001).

22 Interview with Julia Quiñonez, Piedras Negras, Aug. 2002. Also interviews with CFO activists, fall 2004.

23 The UNT is a coalition formed by reformed trade unions many of them belonging to the recently privatized sectors of the economy. Although not completely antagonistic to the official corporatists unions they became an alternative to them.

24 Interview with CFO's activist, Atanasio Martinez, Reynosa, Tam, Mexico, July 2002.

25 Interviews with several CFO's activists in Reynosa, Mexico, July 2002.

26 Interview with CJM's director, Martha Ojeda, November 2004.

27 Interview with Quiñonez July 2002, and with Atanasio Martinez, July 2002. In contrast to this case one can find success stories of transnational solidarity like the Kukdong case in Atlixco Puebla (Brandy 2004).

28 Interview with one member of the CJM board, 2002.

29 Interviews with CFO in Piedras Negras (2002) and AFL-CIO activists in Mexico City (2004).

30 Interview with Quiñonez Ramirez, November 2001.

31 These new movements have contributed to a questioning of the line between the private and the public and to redefining the very notion of power, exposing the limits of state politics.

32 An example of such unionism is the FAT, an umbrella organization of independent, autonomous trade unions and other kind of cooperative organizations from the peasant and popular urban sectors.

33 Although the FAT womens' groups started to organize in 1997 and were allowed a space, their presence and importance has been continually toned down by several FAT leaders. Interviews with Matilde Arteaga, 1998, 2001 and 2002.

34 See Cooper 2000 and Domínguez 2002. See also CAW 1998. Afterwards these courses were adapted to Brazilian conditions.
35 Interview with Rosario Ortiz in Mexico City, August 2002.
36 Ibid.
37 According to Ortiz, this rupture started to take place previously and had to do with political and strategic differences regarding long-term goals and their view on the Chiapas uprising.
38 Ibid
39 Through RSMS's contacts CJM has been able to extend its activities to Oaxaca and Chiapas (Interview with Rosario Ortiz, 2002). Maquiladoras have since the 1980s and 1990s moved to non-border regions in Mexico, recruiting vulnerable new groups such as young male, homosexual, or indigenous people, as workers (De la O Martinez 2004).
40 See Red de Solidaridad de la Maquila Network (2001) pp. 1, 8.
41 Interview with Rosario Ortiz in Mexico City, August 2002.
42 The Hemispheric Social Alliance (HAS) is the umbrella organization organized by hundreds of grassroots organizations opposing the building of a free trade scheme for the whole continent, the FTAA (online, available www.asc-hsa.org/rubrique.php3?id_rubrique=52>). HAS has a women's committee (online, available www.asc-hsa.org/article.php3?id_article=246>) that has an elaborated gender platform. See: Alternativas para las Americas (Hemispheric Social Alliance), Gender chapter (2001) online, available www.asc-hsa.org/article.php3?id_article=211>
43 Interview with Rosario Ortiz, August 2002.
44 For example, while RMSM-CAW is for trade union organizing, many NGOs are sceptical about trade unions in general and as we have already noted, while RMSM-CAW is for international legislation, many NGOs prefer instead the establishment and respect of codes of conduct within each enterprise.

References

Alvarez, Sonia E. (1999) 'Advocating Feminism: The Latin American Feminist NGO Boom,' *International Feminist Journal of Politics* 1, 2: 181–209.
Bandy, Joe (2004) 'So what is to be done? Maquiladora Justice Movements, Transnational Solidarity, and Dynamics of Resistance' in Kathryn Kopinak (ed.) *The Social Costs of Industrial Growth on Northern Mexico*, San Diego, California: La Jolla, Center for US–Mexican Studies, University of San Diego, pp. 309–42.
Bergeron, Suzanne (2001) 'Political Economy Discourses of Globalization and Feminist Politics', *Signs*, 26, 4: 983–1006.
CAW (Canadian Autoworkers Union) (1998) 'La Mitad del Cielo, La Red de Mujeres Sindicalistas de México: A Project Case Study', Ontario, Canada: CAW, Social Justice Fund.
Carr, Barry (2002) 'Labour Internationalism and the North American Free Trade Agreement', in James Goodman (ed.) *Protest and Globalization, Prospects for Transnational Solidarity*, Australia: Pluto Press, pp. 203–15.
CJM (Coalición Pro Justicia en las Maquiladoras) (2004) Year Report, 15 Aniversario y Directiva y Asamblea, Rio Bravo, November, 11–14.
CFO (Comité Fronterizo de Obreras) (1999), CFO Annual letter, 10 December, Piedras Negras Coahuila, Mexico.
Cooper, Jennifer (2000) Union Women Activists, Cross Border Education and Solidarity between Canada and Mexico, Paper presented at the International Studies Association Annual Meeting, Los Angeles.

De la O Martinez, María Eugenia (2004) 'Women in the Maquiladora Industry: Toward Understanding Gender and Regional Dynamics in Mexico', in Kopinak Kathryn (ed.) *The Social Costs of Industrial Growth on Northern Mexico*, La Jolla, California: Center for US–Mexican Studies, UCSD.

Domínguez, Edmé (2002) 'Continental Transnational Activism and Women Workers' Networks within NAFTA', *International Feminist Journal of Politics*, 4, 2: 216–39.

Domínguez, Edmé and Quintero, Cirila (2005) Gender and Class networking between the North and the South: The Case of the CJM, Paper presented at the conference: *Gendering Citizenship and Globalization*, University of Huelva, May 2005.

Falk, Richard (1994) 'The Making of Global Citizenship', in Bart van Steenbergen (ed.) *The Condition of Citizenship*, London: Sage Publications.

Gabriel, C. and Madconald, L. (1994) 'NAFTA, women and organizing in Canada and Mexico: forging a feminist internationality', *Millenium*, 23, 3: 535–62.

Hemispheric Social Alliance (2001) *Alternativas para las Americas (Hemispheric Social Alliance)*: Gender chapter. Available online, www.asc-hsa.org/article.php3?id_article=211.

Human Rights Watch (1998) 'A Job or Your Rights: Continued Sex Discrimination in Mexico's Maquiladoras Sector', *Human Rights Watch* 10, (1B), December. Available online, www.hrw.org/reports98/women2/.

Ikeda, Satoshi (2004) 'Zonal Structure and the Trajectories of Canada, Mexico, Australia, and Norway under Neo-liberal Globalization', in Marjorie Griffin Cohen and Stephen Clarkson (eds) *Governing under Siege: Middle Powers and the Challenge of Globalization*, London: Zed Books and Nova Scotia: Fernwood Publishing, pp. 263–90.

Keck, M. and Sikkink, K. (1998) *Activists beyond Borders*, Ithaca and London: Cornell University Press.

Macdonald, Laura (1999) 'Trade with a Female Face: Women and the New International Trade Agenda', in Annie Taylor and Caroline Thomas (eds) *Global Trade and Global Social Issues*, New York: Routledge, pp. 53–71.

Marchand, Marianne and Runyan, Anne Sisson (2000) 'Feminist Sightings of Global Restructuring: Conceptualizations and Reconceptualizations', in Marianne Marchand and Anne Sisson Runyan (eds) *Gender and Global Restructuring: Sightings, Sites and Resistances*, London and New York: Routledge, pp. 1–22.

Munck, Ronaldo (1999) 'Labour Dilemmas and Labour Futures', in Ronaldo Munck and Peter Waterman (eds) *Labour Worldwide in the Era of Globalization: Alternative Union Models in the New World Order*, London: Macmillan Press, pp. 3–23.

—— (2002) 'Labour, Globalization and Transnational Action', in James Goodman (ed.) *Protest and Globalization, Prospects for Transnational Solidarity*, Australia: Pluto Press, pp. 143–53.

Quintero Ramirez, Cirila (2002) 'The North American Free Trade Agreement and Women: The Canadian and Mexican Experiences', *International Feminist Journal of Politics* 4, 2: 240–59.

Red de Solidaridad de la Maquila Network (2001) *El Boletin de la Red de Solidaridad de la Maquila*, 6, 2, Junio, Toronto, Ontario.

Sen, Gita (1997) 'Globalization, gender and enquiry: a gender perspective', *Development*, 40, 2: 21–6.

Smith, J., Chatfield, C. and Pagnucco, R. (eds) (1997) *Transnational Social Movements and Global Politics: Solidarity beyond the State*, Syracuse, NY: Syracuse University Press.

Staudt, Kathleen and Coronado, Irasema (2002) *Fronteras No Mas (Towards Social Justice at the US–Mexico Border)*, Hampshire: Palgrave Macmillan.

Vargas, Virginia (1999) 'Entre la exclusión y la ciudadanía global', ALAI, América Latina en movimiento. Available online, http://alainet.org/active/show_text.php.

Willets, Peter (1999) 'Transnational Actors and International Organizations', in John Baylis and Steve Smith (eds) *Global Politics: The Globalizations of World Politics*, Oxford: Oxford University Press, pp. 287–310.

Williams, Heather (2002) 'Lessons from the Labor Front: The Coalition for Justice in the Maquiladoras,' in David Brooks and Jonathan Fox (eds) *Cross Border Dialogues: The US Social Movement Networking*, San Diego, California: La Jolla, Center for US–Mexican Studies, University of San Diego, pp. 87–111.

Index

(movimiento de las mujeres) 212, 233;
National Action Committee on the Status
of Women 168, 171, 189, 195; National
Foundation for Australian Women 200;
Native Title Amendment Bill 199; Royal
Commission on the Status of Women
168; What Women Want programme
200; Women for Wik 199
women's organizations 173, 223, 225;
Muslim women 199; nonprofit
community 152; non-governmental

205; transnational networking 223;
voluntary sector 162; unionists
237
World Bank 3, 15, 20, 22, 112, 117, 212,
217, 226; structural adjustment and
stabilization programmes 6, 15, 112,
136, 194, 212, 218n1, 218n2
World Trade Organization (WTO) 1, 3,
15, 22, 152, 226; Doha round 1;
General Agreement on Tariffs and
Trade (GATT) 152

For Product Safety Concerns and Information please contact our EU
representative GPSR@taylorandfrancis.com
Taylor & Francis Verlag GmbH, Kaufingerstraße 24, 80331 München, Germany

www.ingramcontent.com/pod-product-compliance
Ingram Content Group UK Ltd.
Pitfield, Milton Keynes, MK11 3LW, UK
UKHW021617240425
457818UK00018B/602